Also in the Variorum Collected Studies Series:

MARIE-THÉRÈSE D'ALVERNY
La connaissance de l'Islam en Occident médiéval

CYRILLE VOGEL
En rémission des péchés
Recherches sur les systèmes pénitentiels dans l'Eglise latine, (IIe-XIIIe siècles)

VICTOR SAXER
Pères saints et culte chrétien dans l'Eglise des premieres siècles

BERNARD MCGINN
Apocalypticism in the Western Tradition

RICHARD E. SULLIVAN
Christian Missionary Activity in Early Medieval Europe

GILLES VEINSTEIN
Etat et société dans l'Empire Otoman, XVIe-XVIIIe siècles

CHARLES W. JONES
Bede, the Schools and the *Computus*

HANS E. MAYER
Kings and Lords in the Latin Kingdom of Jerusalem

SEBASTIAN BROCK
Studies in Syriac Christianity: History, Literature, Theology

SEBASTIAN BROCK
Syriac Perspectives on Late Antiquity

LESLIE S. B. MACCOULL
Coptic Perspectives on Late Antiquity

JOSEPH MÉLÈZE-MODRZEJEWSKI
Statut personnel et liens de famille dans les droits de l'Antiquité

W.H.C. FREND
Archaeology and History in the Study of Early Christianity

HAN J.W. DRIJVERS
East of Antioch
Studies in Early Syriac Christianity

Studies in Armenian
Literature and Christianity

Robert W. Thomson

Studies in Armenian
Literature and Christianity

VARIORUM
1994

This edition copyright © 1994 by Robert W. Thomson.

Published by VARIORUM
  Ashgate Publishing Limited
  Gower House, Croft Road,
  Aldershot, Hampshire GU11 3HR
  Great Britain

Ashgate Publishing Company
Old Post Road,
Brookfield, Vermont 05036
USA

ISBN 0-86078-411-8

British Library CIP Data
  Thomson, Robert W.
  Studies in Armenian Literature and Christianity
  (Variorum Collected Studies Series: CS 451)
  I. Thomson, Robert W. II. Series
  891

US Library of Congress CIP Data
  Thomson, Robert W., 1934-
  Studies in Armenian Literature and Christianity / R.W. Thomson.
  1st ed. p. cm. -- (Collected Studies Series: 451)
  Includes index.
  ISBN 0-86078-411-8 (alk. paper)
  1. Armenian literature--to 1800--History and criticism.
  2. Christian literature, Early--Armenian authors.
  3. Christian literature, Armenian. 4. Armenia--Church history.
  I. Title. II. Series: Collected Studies: CS451.
  PK8515. T49   1994   94-4742
  891'.99209--dc20   CIP

The paper used in this publication meets the minimum requirements of the American National Standard for Information Sciences – Permanence of Paper for Printed Library Materials, ANSI Z39.48-1984. ∞ ™

Printed by Galliard (Printers) Ltd
  Great Yarmouth, Norfolk, Great Britain

COLLECTED STUDIES SERIES CS451

CONTENTS

Preface   ix–xi

Acknowledgements   xii

I   The origins of Caucasian civilization:
the Christian component   25–43
Transcaucasia: Nationalism and Social Change,
ed. Ronald Grigor Suny. Ann Arbor: University of
Michigan Press, 1983

II   The Armenian image in classical texts   9–25
The Armenian Image in History and Literature,
ed. Richard G. Hovannisian (*UCLA Studies in
Near Eastern Culture and Society 3*). Los Angeles,
Calif.: University of California Press, 1981

III   Mission, conversion, and Christianization:
the Armenian example   28–45
Harvard Ukrainian Studies 12/13. Cambridge, Mass.:
Ukranian Research Institute, 1988/89

IV   The formation of the Armenian literary tradition   135–150
*East of Byzantium: Syria and Armenia in the Formative
Period,* ed. Nina Garsoïan, Thomas Mathews, and
Robert W. Thomson. Washington, D.C.: Dumbarton
Oaks Research Library and Collection, 1980

V   Jerusalem and Armenia   77–91
Papers of the 1983 Oxford Patristic Conference,
ed. E. A. Livingstone (*Studia Patristica 18*). Kalamazoo,
Mich.: Cistercian Publications, 1986

VI   A medieval Armenian view of the physical world:
the cosmology of Vardan Arewelc^{c}i in his
Chronicle   191–208
Revue des Études Arméniennes 23. Paris: Association
de la Revue des Études Arméniennes, 1992

VII	The Maccabees in early Armenian historiography *Journal of Theological Studies 26*. Oxford: Oxford University Press, 1975	329–341
VIII	Number symbolism and patristic exegesis in some early Armenian writers *Handes Amsorya 90*. Vienna: Mechitaristen-Kongregation, 1976	117–138
IX	Architectural symbolism in classical Armenian literature *Journal of Theological Studies 30*. Oxford University Press, 1979	102–114
X	Muhammad and the origin of Islam in Armenian literary tradition *Armenian Studies in Memoriam Haïg Bérberian*, ed. Dickran Kouymjian. Lisbon: Calouste Gulbenkian Foundation, 1986	829–858
XI	'Let now the astrologers stand up': the Armenian Christian reaction to astrology and divination *Dumbarton Oaks Papers 46*. Washington, D.C.: Dumbarton Oaks Research Library and Collection, 1992	305–312
XII	The fathers in early Armenian literature *Studia Patristica 12*. Berlin: Akademie Verlag GmbH, 1975	457–470
XIII	The transformation of Athanasius in Armenian theology *Le Muséon 78*. Leuven: Association Le Muséon, 1965	47–69
XIV	The Armenian version of Ps. Dionysius Aeropagita *Acta Jutlandica 57*. Aarhus: Aarhus University Press, 1982	115–123
XV	The Armenian version of David's *Definitions of Philosophy* *David Anhaght, the 'Invincible' Philosopher*, ed. Avedis K. Sanjian (*UCLA Studies in Near Eastern Culture and Society 7*). Los Angeles, Calif.: University of California Press, 1987	37–46
XVI	The Armenian version of the Georgian *Chronicles* *Journal of the Society for Armenian Studies 5*. New York: Society for Armenian Studies, 1990/91	81–90

XVII	Some philosophical terms in the *Teaching* of Gregory *Revue des Études Arméniennes n.s. 1. Paris: Association de la Revue des Études Arméniennes, 1964*	41–46
XVIII	Gregory of Narek's *Commentary on the Song of Songs* *Journal of Theological Studies 34. Oxford: Oxford University Press, 1983*	453–496
XIX	Vardan's *Historical Compilation* and its sources *Le Muséon 100. Louvain-la-Neuve: Association Le Muséon, 1987*	343–352
	Index	1–10

This volume contains xii + 322 pages

PUBLISHER'S NOTE

The articles in this volume, as in all others in the Collected Studies Series, have not been given a new, continuous pagination. In order to avoid confusion, and to facilitate their use where these same studies have been referred to elsewhere, the original pagination has been maintained wherever possible.

Each article has been given a Roman number in order of appearance, as listed in the Contents. This number is repeated on each page and quoted in the index entries.

PREFACE

The articles gathered in the following collection were not originally composed with a common theme in mind. Some began as lectures for particular occasions; others were intended to give preliminary results of research, which later was published in book form; still others were written as introductory studies for topics which held my attention at the time, but which were in fact not pursued much farther. Yet these various pieces do have a common thread in that they were intended to make some contribution to an understanding of Armenian ideas as expressed by Armenian writers.

In other words, these articles touch on related aspects of my work over many years. How did the Armenians develop an original literature, influenced by the written traditions of late classical antiquity as well as the early Christian cultures in Syriac and Greek, and drawing on their own ancient oral traditions? How did they view themselves in their ambiguous position between Byzantium and Iran? How did they express those views in their historical writing? And how did the early formulations affect later Armenian explanations of historical events? It is tempting to project back into the past the rationale of today's explanations. And it is certainly true that my early work in patristic texts (Greek, Syriac and Armenian) did not have the same focus as my later research in Armenian literature. But over the years I became more and more interested in two related questions: the formulation of a 'received tradition', and the impact of that tradition, taken out of its original context, on writers of later ages.

Since in the Caucasus there is no such thing as 'ancient' history, today's problems are often expressed in terms taken from old writers, and those old writers are pressed into service for modern causes. When writing long ago on 'The Transformation of Athanasius in Armenian Theology', where I studied the way in which the champion of orthodoxy against Arianism became a champion of Armenian orthodoxy against Chalcedonian error, it did not then strike me that such uses and abuses of history would still be prevalent. The adaptation of older models for later events has since remained one of my particular interests.

I have never attempted to write a 'History of Armenia', but rather have tried to elucidate what writers of 'Histories of Armenia' said about themselves and their people. My first foray into Armenian literature (at the prompting of Gérard Garitte) was a translation with commentary of the neglected 'Teaching of Saint Gregory', an exposition of the Christian faith incorporated into the standard account of Armenia's conversion by the enigmatic 'Agathangelos'. Only gradually did I realise that whole areas of Armenian writing were quite unknown outside the smallest circle of scholars and that such English renderings were of value not only to students struggling with the early stages of the language. By attracting the attention of a much broader group of scholars to such documents I found that Armenian evidence for more general questions was welcomed; and conversely, by setting these texts in a wider context the individuality and idiosyncracy of Armenian traditions could be more readily identified and appreciated. Thus began a series of studies of Armenian authors, in which I used translations as a means to approach problems of dating, authenticity, use of sources, and motivation.

The images of Armenian individuality developed by the classic Armenian historical writers continued to influence Armenians long after those authors were dead. The critic who seeks to establish the sources of a given historian, to investigate his aims, and to place the work in its historical and literary contexts, will thus find that such an undertaking is no 'academic exercise'. These works are living entities, interpreted in diverse ways at different times. They cannot be divorced from a long Armenian experience. Indeed, one of the ways in which 'Armenian-ness' can be defined is through a study of the meaning of these classic historians for Armenian readers through the ages.

The formation of the 'received tradition' is perhaps easier to grasp in the realm of historical writing than in other literary areas, for the simple reason that the histories have been more intensively studied and many of them have been critically edited. The study of other fields of Armenian literary activity has not proceeded at an equal pace. My work on the Armenian version of Pseudo-Dionysius was prompted by curiosity as to the reception of these obscure texts in medieval Armenia, for numerous commentaries had been written on that corpus of philosophical theology. But before the commentaries could be explored, it was clearly necessary to produce a text. This took several years to accomplish; unfortunately, the commentators still await attention.

Biblical exegesis is another area which has been surprisingly neglected. My review of Gregory of Narek's *Commentary on the Song of Songs* marked a return to questions I first addressed in the *Teaching of Saint Gregory*. But again it was prompted by a more general interest in what Armenians made of old themes, how they adapted earlier works, native or foreign, to their own purposes, what was new and creative in a particular literary work, and how an original composition might start a new trend or have an unpredictable impact on later generations.

It remains for me to thank Variorum for suggesting this collection of articles, and the many friends and colleagues with whom at one time or another I have discussed the themes adumbrated in this volume. I am sure that today I would approach some of the topics differently. But taken in their original form they not only constitute a record of my scholarly interests, they show the development of my own thinking. If as such they enter the 'received tradition' of Armenian scholarship, the coming generation will soon realise the preconceptions which lie behind them. But at least I can vouch for the dating and the authenticity.

ROBERT W. THOMSON

Oxford 1993

ACKNOWLEDGEMENTS

Grateful acknowledgement is made to the following copyright holders for kindly permitting the reproduction of the studies included in this volume: The University of Michigan (for study I); The Regents of the University of California (II, XV); The President and Fellows of Harvard College (III); The Trustees for Harvard University (IV, XI); Peeters Publishers (V); Association de la Revue des Études Arméniennes (VI, XVII); Oxford University Press (VII, IX, XVIII); Mechitaristen-Kongregation, Vienna (VIII); Fundação Calouste Gulbenkian, Lisbon (X); Akademie Verlag GmbH, Berlin (XII); Association 'Le Muséon' (XIII, XIX); Aarhus University Press, Denmark (XIV); Society for Armenian Studies (XVI).

I

THE ORIGINS OF CAUCASIAN CIVILIZATION: THE CHRISTIAN COMPONENT

The Caucasus has been home for members of the human race since the early Stone Age, yet it is only in comparatively recent times—in the last 1500 years or so—that the two most significant peoples of the area, the Armenians and the Georgians, have acquired truly individual cultures expressed in their own native languages. I shall not be concerned here with the origins of these peoples, with the thorny question of the mingling of newcomers and indigenous inhabitants, or with the development of social and material culture in the pre-Christian era. This paper will deal with Christian Armenia and Georgia, for it was only with their conversion that the Armenians and Georgians developed their own scripts and native literatures. Not that they were illiterate and ignorant until then. Indeed, they had played a role in the Greco-Roman world, and in the Old Persian Empire and the civilizations of the Near East that had preceded it. But with the development of their own literature and art in a Christian context the Armenians and Georgians set themselves apart from these other civilizations to a certain extent and moulded more truly national cultures out of the heritage they owed to Greece, Rome, and Iran. However, despite many common elements in that heritage, Armenia and Georgia did not find unity or even mutual sympathy in their Christianity.

The Armenian and Georgian scripts were invented within ecclesiastical circles for the express purpose of promoting and strengthening Christianity in those countries. This took place in the early fifth century, two or three generations after the first introduction of Christianity. So the written sources in Armenian and Georgian do not reflect a contemporary view of the conversion of the royal families and the spread of the church, but rather the official view of later ages unfamiliar with the precise historical situation of Armenia and Georgia at the earlier time, of their active pagan culture, and of their ambiguous position between the major powers of Rome and Iran. This is particularly true of the Armenian tradition concerning the origins of Christianity there. For not only did Armenian historians ignore the division of their country into Roman and Iranian spheres

I

of influence, they attempted to fuse the originally separate traditions of missionary activity from Syrian and from Greek territory. As time went on they pushed the origins of the Armenian church further back in time. Caught up in the rivalries of Eastern Christendom the Armenians came to claim an apostolic origin for their church. There is, of course, nothing peculiar to the Armenians in this regard. The very nature of episcopal succession encouraged churches to trace their bishops back in an unbroken line to one of the original apostles, who were provided with elaborate itineraries showing the places where they had established churches on their missionary travels. But the fact that such claims played an important role in ecclesiastical politics does not make them any the more historical.

A further factor which influenced the tendentious version of the conversion of their country offered by Armenian historians was that by the time the account was put in writing the Armenian monarchy was no more. The Arsacid line came to an end in 427/8. In later generations the church, in the person of the patriarch, more and more took the place of a national leader transcending the interminable feuding of the noble families—or at least, that is the picture that the Armenian historians, all of whom came from church circles, attempted to present. It is therefore difficult to assess the actual role of the Armenian kings in the conversion, from the shadowy figure of Trdat (Tiridates) converted by St. Gregory the Illuminator in the early fourth century, to Vram-Shapuh who encouraged the monk Mashtots and the patriarch Sahak nearly a hundred years later to invent a script and lay the foundations of a national literature. And the division of Armenia in 386/7 between Theodosius I and the shah Shapuh III, after which time the patriarchs and the surviving royal line resided in Eastern Armenia, made it difficult for later historians to appreciate the position of earlier kings and patriarchs vis-a-vis the Roman emperors. For the first Armenian patriarchate was established at Ashtishat in Taron, west of Lake Van. There was a close connection with the Greek church of Cappadocia, formalized in the requirement that each newly elected Armenian patriarch be actually consecrated in Caesarea. Thus the Armenian church was drawn into the theological and ecclesiastical quarrels of Greek Christendom and into the political problems caused by Arianizing emperors.

But despite the misleading accounts of some later writers, it is possible to indicate some of the factors that were of continuing importance in the Christian culture of Armenia. That the first missionaries there came from Syria may be deduced from the Christian Armenian vocabulary. For such basic words as "priest," "monk," "sabbath," "hymn," "congregation," "preaching," "fasting" were taken from Syriac. On the other hand, those terms which refer to a more organized church with an established hierarchy, "bishop," "catholicos," "patriarch," were taken from Greek. The Greek connection has left its imprint in the specific activities recorded in the Life of Gregory the Illuminator, who was the first bishop consecrated for the Armenian church—an event plausibly dated to 314 or so. But the Syrian connection is much more tenuous. There are, however, two interesting pointers. The Armenian historian Faustos says that James of Nisibis (an important bishop of the early fourth century who attended the Council of Nicaea in 325) had been active in S. Armenia and indeed had been searching for Noah's ark in the mountains of Korduk, the biblical Ararat. (The idea that the ark landed on modern Mt. Ararat, known to the Armenians as Masis, is not an Armenian tradition and does not seem to predate the Crusades.) The second pointer is that Koriun, the biographer of Mashtots, who invented the Armenian script, says that a Syrian bishop Daniel had already tried to adapt a Semitic alphabet for Armenian (circa 400) but that it was not adequate. One can only imagine that the purpose of such an invention was for Syrian missionary activity and that it was not a mere pastime. But the Armenian attempt to adapt the story of the conversion of the Edessan king Abgar by the missionary Addai or Thaddaeus to the Armenian situation is pure invention.

Even more than Armenia, Georgia was divided into two fairly distinct areas that were not in fact united until the twelfth century of the Christian era. Western Georgia looked to the Black Sea. And as in past ages Greek merchants had settled along the coast from Trebizond to the Crimea, so in Christian times there were churches established along the eastern shore of the Euxine. These long-established contacts, and the greater ease and rapidity of sea travel, meant that Western Georgia had closer ties with Constantinople and the church of the Byzantine Empire than did landlocked Armenia. On the other hand, central Georgia—Iberia as opposed to Colchis—looked more directly towards Armenia and Iran. It was in the Armenian Georgian borderland that Armenian missionaries were active in the fourth century; indeed, the Armenian historian Faustos claims that Gregory the Illuminator's grandson, the young bishop Grigoris, was killed there. However, Christianity did take a firmer hold in Iberia on the conversion of King Mihran around the middle of the fourth century. The earliest version of that conversion (for as with the Armenian conversion story in Agathangelos, later ages added many layers of even more legendary accretion) is found in the *Church History* of the Latin monk Rufinus (d. 410). The story was told to him by an Iberian from the royal family, Bacurius, who had served in the Roman army as a *dux* on the Palestine frontier. It runs as follows.

In Iberia a captive Christian girl gained public notice by the efficacy of her prayers in curing a child; the queen too was cured of a desperate malady. One day, when the king was out hunting, there was a sudden eclipse and the king became lost. In his anxiety he vowed that if Christ, the god of the slave-girl who had cured his wife, would lead him out of the darkness he would worship him. The darkness passed, the king returned

I

home, summoned the girl, and proclaimed himself a Christian. All were converted and the king had a church built. But it proved impossible to set one of the columns in place. After the workers had gone home, the girl spent that night in prayer. And when the king returned the following day, he and everyone were astonished to see the refractory pillar hovering in space a foot above its appropriate socket. All the other colums were now easily set up, and the faith of the Georgians confirmed by these miracles. At the girl's urging, an embassy was sent to the Emperor Constantine to seek priests for the newly converted land.

This story mentions no names, either for the slave girl or for the king, but the miracle of the pillar is remembered in the name of the cathedral at Mtskheta: *Svėti tskhoveli*, the living pillar. Bacurius, who told this story to Rufinus, is known: He was a Roman client and served in the Roman army before returning to Georgia in the early fifth century. He is mentioned by Koriun at the time of Mashtots' first journey to Georgia. The king who was converted is generally recognized to be Mihran, whose dates are unclear but who probably died in 361. The reference to Constantine is most improbable; by a common confusion his son Constantius is more likely meant. As for the slave girl, later tradition is unanimous in calling her Nino. She may have been a captive from the Armeno-Georgian frontier where there were frequent quarrels and raids, but her origins are totally unknown. The attempt by later Armenian writers to claim that Nino was one of the group of nuns that included Rhipsime and who figure so prominently in the story of St. Gregory the Illuminator is pure fabrication. However, another building at Mtskheta has retained a memory of a further story associated with Nino which is found in both Armenian and Georgian sources. During the reign of Mihran the Georgians used to worship an image of Aramazd (Ahura-Mazda) on the hill across the Aragvi. After his conversion Mihran had the image pulled down and a cross set up in its place. The later church on the site retained the name: Juari.

Naturally the Georgian tradition assumes that all of Georgia was converted at the same time as King Mihran, just as the Armenians supposed the same with King Trdat. And later Georgian writers tell of the visit of the apostles Simon Zelotes and Andrew to Georgia, just as the Armenians claimed Thaddaeus and Bartholomew as apostolic founders. But all these simplifications and tendentious claims are to be rejected. The conversion of Caucasia was a slow process. By the third century there were unorganized groups of Christians at various places where Greek and Syrian merchants and missionaries passed. When the king was converted, as in Iberia, Armenia, and later on in Lazica, a formally organized church came into being. But there was long resistance on both the social and political levels as the *History* of Faustos and the *Biography of Mashtots* by Koriun make abundantly clear.

The influence of Syria—or more properly speaking, of Syriac Christianity which covered Syria, Mesopotamia, and Northwest Iran—and the influence of Greek-speaking Christianity were both vital for the development of Armenian and Georgian literature. Although these literatures both have their origins in church interests and have several common features, it is noteworthy that there are significant differences between them. For reasons which will be clear from what follows, it is more appropriate to begin with Armenia.

The actual invention of the Armenian script by Mashtots took place in North Syria. It is therefore quite natural that the first texts translated into the new script included many Syriac ones. Indeed, the first rendering of the Gospels was made from Syriac, and later revised on the Greek. Mashtots and the patriarch Sahak, according to the former's biographer, founded schools where youths were taught the script and Syriac or Greek (or both) and then dispatched abroad to the main centers of Christian learning: Edessa, the cities of Asia Minor, and most especially Constantinople. To this list were later added Alexandria, Athens, and other cities more famous for the pagan learning of late antiquity than the purity of their Christian doctrine. The basic texts in liturgy, theology, church history, biblical commentary, canon law, etc., were then rendered into Armenian. By the end of their lives these translators had begun to compose original works in Armenian. Now it would be wrong to suppose that only with the invention of a script had Armenians become interested in learning and scholarship. For hundreds of years previously there had been Armenians interested in Greek culture. King Artavazd in the first century B.C., for example, had an international reputation as a writer. Armenians had studied at the great schools of the Eastern Mediterranean. Libanius in Antioch had correspondence with numerous former Armenian students and their sons who came to study with him in their turn. During the fourth century the clerics of the Armenian church had used Syriac or Greek. So the importance of Mashtots' invention was not so much that the leading circles of Armenian society suddenly became educated—they had been such all along—but that their learning was transposed into the Armenian idiom and adapted to the Armenian situation. This explains the amazing rapidity of the development of a native Armenian literature. And it also helps explain why the early historical works by Armenian authors are so indebted to foreign models for their imagery in describing events that occurred in their own land.

By the sixth century Armenian scholarly interests had expanded beyond strictly ecclesiastical texts to the world of secular learning as known in the schools and universities of the Eastern Mediterranean. Although some of the elaborate grand tours attributed to Armenian scholars have been exaggerated by the wishful thinking of their pious biographers, there is no doubt that the great cities of the Greco-Roman world offered many attractions to Armenian students. There followed another spate of translations, this time of philosophical, grammatical, rhetorical, scientific, and other technical works, with particular emphasis on the texts used in the University of Constantinople. Commentaries on Aristotelian logic and Neo-Platonism were rendered into Armenian and new ones composed by Armenians. The works of Philo had a significant influence in their Armenian version; mathematics and astronomy were now studied in Armenian. However, the prime interest of Armenian writers and scholars remained linked to ecclesiastical concerns. There were very few authors who were not monks, priests, or bishops. The private education given to the children of the nobility was not an academic but a social one; schools in the proper sense were church or monastery schools.

One other foreign center was of importance for the developing Armenian individuality—the holy places of Palestine and the city of Jerusalem. After the time of Constantine, Christians from many lands came flocking to visit the shrines of the Holy Land, to meet the internationally famous monks and ascetics who had settled there, and to admire the grand churches built at the most important sites. (According to a late and tendentious document, many of these churches were built not by Constantine but by King Trdat and Gregory the Illuminator!) Armenians and Georgians were among these visitors and they have left tangible evidence of their settlements in the form of mosaic pavements with inscriptions in their respective languages. Many of the pilgrims stayed in Palestine as monks, Armenians and Georgians at first living in Greek monasteries and worshiping in their own tongues. As confessional differences came to separate the Armenians from the Greeks and Georgians, they built their own monasteries and churches. But the great importance of Jerusalem for the Christian Caucasus was in the field of liturgical usage and the ordering of the Christian year. The earliest ritual traditions of Armenia and Georgia owe much to those of Palestine before the rites of Constantinople came to dominate Eastern Christendom. As we shall see, later Georgian scholarship was enriched by numerous translations made from Christian texts in Arabic by Georgian monks in Palestine. But for the Armenians, their religious differences with the Greek church—and hence with the Georgians, who remained in communion with the Greeks—made Jerusalem less a place of common learning than a center of pilgrimage. To these confessional differences and the split between the churches we must now turn.

The conversion of Armenia to Christiantiy entailed many consequences of a social and political nature. But not least troublesome was the fact that Armenia now became involved in the theological quarrels of Christendom, quarrels which themselves often had social and political overtones. For example, in the fourth century the pro-Arian policies of some Roman emperors caused conflict between church and state in Armenia: The kings were anxious to cultivate good relations with the Christian emperors of Constantinople, the patriarchs were anxious to preserve the true faith against the Arian heresy.

But after the invention of an Armenian script with the consequent development of a native Armenian theological tradition, and later the abolition of the Armenian monarchy with the consequent increase in the church's position as the leading national force, then the Armenian attitude to the international theological controversies of the time became a truly significant issue. In the reign of Justinian (527–565) the split between the Greek and Armenian churches became irrevocable, despite various later attempts at reunion. It is therefore appropriate here to trace the development of the Armenian tradition and the history of the Armenian reactions to the Christological controversies that split the Christian world.

The theological problem centers in the question: How are we to interpret the Christian declaration that Jesus Christ is both truly man and Son of God? In Alexandria the tradition was to stress the divinity and unity of Christ; in Antioch and Cilicia the tradition was to place emphasis on the humanity as well as divinity of Jesus—to over-simplify a very complicated question. At the beginning of the fifth century the two main protagonists were Cyril, Archbishop of Alexandria, and Theodore, Bishop of Mopsuestia in Cilicia. Although the theologians of Asia Minor and Constantinople did not on the whole support the extremists in either group, Cyril had won the day at the Third Ecumenical Council, held in Ephesus in 431. The Armenians were brought into the conflict because the works of Theodore were circulating in Armenia (having been brought earlier from Edessa) after Theodore's condemnation at Ephesus. Acacius, Bishop of Melitene, on the southwest border of Armenia with Asia Minor, protested, sending two letters to Mashtots and Sahak to inform them of the dangerous heretical tendencies implicit in Theodore's teachings. In their reply the Armenians agreed in condemning the heretical ideas concerning the person of Christ attributed to Theodore, but denied that any such heretics existed in Armenia.

The decisive step in this controversy was taken by a pupil of Mashtots, Eznik, in his mature years the author of a unique philosophical work on the problem of the origin of evil. In the 430's Eznik had gone to Syria to study Syriac in Edessa; from there he moved on to Constantinople, joining other Armenian students who were already there studying Greek. The theological controversies surrounding the works of Theodore induced Eznik to request an authoritative statement from the Patriarch of Constantinople Proclus. So Proclus sent a letter—his so-called *Tome*—to the Armenian clergy and nobility, explaining in detail the teaching of the Council of Ephesus. The lasting significance of this letter lies in the fact that it came to serve as a basis for the Armenian theological position: The Council of Ephesus became the touchstone of orthodoxy. So when in later times the definitions of Ephesus were revised, such revisions were rejected by the Armenians as innovation.

It was only another twenty years later that the Fourth Ecumenical

I

Council was summoned in Chalcedon by the Emperor Marcian. For the decisions of Ephesus had not brought peace and concord. No Armenian representative was present at Chalcedon; Armenian sources stress that the Armenians were at that time preoccupied with a revolt for religous freedom against the Iranian Shah. But in fact no Armenian representative had attended any ecumenical council save that of Nicaea in 325, when the Armenian See was closely connected with that of Caesarea. There is no evidence that Armenian bishops from beyond the Roman-Iranian border were invited to the later councils; but whether invitations were sent and ignored, or whether invitations were not sent out as a matter of policy, is unknown.

But neither did the Council of Chalcedon solve the problems to the liking of all. It was resolved that Christ, being truly God and truly man, is one person in two natures. The extremists of the Antiochene school, the followers of Theodore and Nestorius, who in speaking of two natures were accused of separating God and man in Christ, were condemned. Their teaching was to become the standard doctrine of the Syrian Church in Iran. But within the Empire, major opposition to the Chalcedonian formula came from the followers of the late Cyril of Alexandria who spoke of "one nature of the divine Logos incarnate." This phrase is found in Cyril, who was misled by forgeries to suppose that it was Athanasian, and it became the rallying-cry of the opposition. In Egypt, Syria, and elsewhere, the religious opposition went hand in hand with national or local feelings and separatist tendencies. But it would be rash to suppose that economic or social considerations were the prime cause of the divisions in Christendom. They did not cause them, though they did reinforce them.

Several compromises were tried at different times. But all failed to heal the breach. Gradually the monophysites (partisans of the "one nature [*physis*]") developed their own theological traditions, organized themselves into separate churches and ordained their own separate clergy. This process was a long one and only concerns us here insofar as Armenia was affected.

The Council of Chalcedon did not have any immediate repercussions in Armenia. When the Armenian Church was asked at the beginning of the sixth century to take a dogmatic stand, the Catholicos declared that the Armenians, Georgians, Albanians (Ałuank'), and Greeks were all in agreement. But one has to bear in mind that the *Henotikon* of Zeno (Emperor 474–491) was in force at that time within the Empire. The *Henotikon*, published in 482, was an edict recognizing the first three ecumenical councils but passing over the issue of "one" or "two" natures. The Armenians seem to have been happy with the compromise, as Zeno is referred to as the "blessed Emperor" in Armenian sources. However, the Armenian clergy were persuaded by a Syrian delegation to reject explicitly the offending Council of Chalcedon, but without anathematizing the Greek Church as such.

But in fact the apparent unanimity of the Greek and Armenian churches had no deep foundations. Zeno's policy of compromise was rejected in 518, when under Emperor Justin, the Greek Empire and Church made their peace with Rome and stood firmly behind the definitions of Chalcedon. However, not until 555 were the Armenians prompted to repudiate the Greek return to Chalcedonian orthodoxy. In that year the Catholicos Nerses II and the Armenian bishops received a delegation of Syrians belonging to the monophysite church in Iran, who claimed that they were being persecuted by the majority group (the so-called Nestorians who held to the teaching of the school of Antioch and formed the officially recognized church in Iran) and needed to find foreign bishops to consecrate their candidate to episcopal rank. The Armenians obliged. But from the correspondence which surrounds this episode it is clear that not only was the Council of Chalcedon rejected again, the Greek Church was anathematized for its heresy. And only on occasion, and under pressure, did any significant group of Armenians later ever change their mind and accept communion with the Greeks.

On the other hand, in Georgia a specifically national tradition in literature and theology was slower in forming, and its ultimate development was on different lines from the tradition in Armenia. Although Armenian writers claim that Mashtots invented a script for the Georgians and the Caucasian Albanians as well as for themselves, there is no corroborating evidence. Certainly the script was invented in the fifth century in ecclesiastical circles (despite certain chauvinistic claims that it has a much more glorious antiquity); the first texts translated into Georgian were liturgical and biblical, and it was Armenian texts that served as models. The earliest dated surviving document in the Georgian language is the inscription of the Church of Bolnisi Sion (483); other inscriptions in Palestine have also been attributed to the same century. However, the volume of material translated in the early centuries of literacy in Georgia is not at all comparable with what was achieved in Armenia. Nor was there a sudden efflorescence of original compositions. The earliest narrative work is the *Martyrdom of Saint Shusanik*. (She was the daughter of the Armenian general Vardan Mamikonean, killed on the battlefield in the revolt against Iran in 451 and immortalized in the *Histories* of Ełishe and Łazar.) Shushanik had married Varsken, *vitaxa* (governor of a border province) of Gogarene on the Armeno-Georgian border. But he apostatized, married the Shah's daughter, and so maltreated Shushanik that she died. Although the martyrdom purports to have been written by Shushanik's father confessor, there are reasons for supposing that the text as we have it was not composed until after the separation of the Armenian and Georgian churches. Shushanik is revered in both churches and her story is known in both languages. But Georgian scholars insist on the primacy of the Georgian version, which they regard as the first mature production of

Georgian literature. Be that as it may, hagiography did remain the principal sphere of interest for Georgian writers for several centuries. Interesting and valuable as many of these texts are, they do not cover so wide a spectrum as the products of early Armenian literature. Of wider historical interest are accounts of the conversion of Georgia, the story of the legendary invasion of Alexander into the Caucasus, and lists of Georgian kings which may go back to the seventh century. But before discussing Christian Georgian literature after that time—when, in fuller maturity, it shows interests different from those of Armenians—we should turn to the Georgian reaction to the quarrels of Eastern Christendom that caused irrevocable schisms lasting to the present.

At the Council of Dvin in 505 there had been unanimity among Georgians, Armenians, and Albanians in rejecting Chalcedon, though not the Greek Church. The Georgian Peter, who became Bishop of Mayuma near Gaza in the second half of the fifth century, had been even more violently anti-Chalcedonian. (Curiously enough, the much later Georgian *Life* of Peter reflects the later position of the Georgian Church and makes of him a pious Chalcedonian.) But most Georgian monks who went to Palestine remained loyal Chalcedonians, joining in Greek monasteries. In the sixth century several Syrian monks went to Georgia, where they played an important role in developing local monastic communities on the Egyptian and Syrian models. These were the so-called Thirteen Syrian Fathers, whose *Lives* have survived in various recensions, the oldest fragments of which go back to the sixth or seventh century. These monks were refugees from monophysite Syria, and they had a significant effect on the Georgian attitude to Chalcedon.

At the Second Council of Dvin in 555, when the Greek Church was specifically anathematized, there were no Georgians present. Nor is there any reason to suppose that the Georgians ever rejected their unity with the Greek Church. Their attitude in 505 had corresponded with the official Byzantine position. Justinian's wars in Lazica only helped increase Byzantine influence, both military and religious. Hence the Georgians rejected Armenian overtures in 572, when monophysite Armenians at home were resisting the enforced union of refugee Armenians in Constantinople following an attempted revolt against Iranian control. (This rebellion of 572, led by another Vardan Mamikonean, is not to be confused with that of 451.)

The final split between Armenians and Georgians came in 608 during the patriarchate of Kyrion. Kyrion had lived since his youth in Greek territory and then in Armenia. The Armenian Catholicos had made him Bishop in Ayrarat in 594 and in 598/9 had consecrated him Catholicos of Georgia when that see fell vacant. Despite his friendship with the anti-Chalcedonian Armenian Catholicos Moses, once he was Catholicos of Georgia, Kyrion showed himself more and more sympathetic to the Greek

Church. He refused to participate in the synod called in 607 to elect a new Armenian Catholicos (Abraham), and the following year he was denounced by an Armenian council in Dvin. In the encyclical letter promulgated on this occasion, Abraham extended to the Georgians the interdictions previously laid against the Greeks: No Armenian was to communicate with them, to eat with them, to pray with them, or to marry them. The schism thus formulated was never rescinded. The Georgians had never committed themselves to the monophysite position of the Armenians, and from now on they remained in communion with the Byzantine Church. This had concomitant political overtones, but it also meant that Greeks and Georgians could live and work in the same monasteries—with a profound effect on later Georgian literature and scholarship. Armenians too continued to frequent the University of Constantinople and other centers of Greek learning; and there were important groups of Chalcedonian Armenians even in Armenia proper. However, there could never be an open, unsuspicious relationship between Armenians and Greeks.

A further point in this regard needs emphasis: the difference in rites and practice. For Christians were divided not only by credal statements and theological interpretations of dogma; differences of ritual practice were (and remain) of equal if not greater significance in the perpetuation of antagonisms. A declaration by the Armenian Catholicos Moses II (574–604, mentioned above) is of particular interest and relevance. When summoned by the Emperor Maurice to attend a synod in Constantinople where the union of the churches might be effected, he exclaimed: "I shall not cross the river Azat, or eat fermented bread, or drink warm water." The river Azat then marked the frontier between Byzantine and Iranian spheres of influence, but Moses is playing on its meaning "free." The references to fermented (leavened) bread and warm water are to differences between Greeks and Armenians in the celebration of the liturgy; for the latter use unleavened bread and wine unmixed with water (warmed in the Greek rite). These differences were as significant and irreconcilable as any point of doctrine.

But if Armenia and Georgia were going their own ways in the world of religion, they were forced into the same strait-jacket of political subjection to the Muslim Caliphate. The position of the Caucasus was of course different from that of Mesopotamia, Syria, Egypt, and all the Mediterranean lands that so rapidly fell to the new invaders. For the Caucasus was not overrun or assimilated into the Muslim cultural and religious world. The Muslim authorities demanded subjection, taxes, and military contingents—in many respects perpetuating the earlier relationship between the Caucasus and Sasanian Iran. Armenia, Georgia, and Albania were grouped together as the province of *Arminiya*, with the city of Dvin as its administrative capital. Garrisons were posted in various strategic centers, and several towns became Muslim enclaves in the midst of a native Christian population. But despite some periods of harsh oppression, especially under the Abbasids, the Armenians and Georgians were generally left to pursue their traditional ways; scholarship and the arts certainly did not come to a sudden halt.

Armenians were divided on the issue of resistance to the Muslims. Theodore Rshtuni, whose lands south of Lake Van were in closest contact with them, came to terms with Mu'awiyya in 653/4. But this alliance was not welcome to all Armenians. The historian Sebeos calls it an alliance with Antichrist, and the later John Catholicos says that Theodore and the other nobles who signed it "signed an oath with death and swore allegiance to hell." However, all Byzantine efforts to regain control of the Caucasus were in the end unsuccessful. Yet the hold of the Caliphs was tempered by their increasing inability to control their own far-flung empire. For the Muslim world of the eighth and ninth centuries was not a solid unity; it was too vast and disparate. Not long after the establishment of the Abbasid Caliphate (750) local rulers from Spain to Central Asia were claiming independence. This fragmentation in some ways worked to the advantage of the Armenians (except when abortive rebellions brought bloody reprisals). For in the ninth century the leading nobles made direct submission to the Caliph, bypassing the authority of the local Muslim governors who tended to treat the provinces as their own petty kingdoms. The power and prestige gained by a few predominant families thus led to their emergence as ruling houses once Muslim domination had been overthrown.

It is not necessary for us to follow the rise and fall of individual families at this period, but one important difference between the fortunes of Armenia and Georgia must be stressed. In Armenia the leading role came to be played by the Bagratuni family, whose homelands were in the northwest, on the Chorukh River close to the Georgian frontier. Although they gained control of Northern and much of Western Armenia at the expense of the Mamikonean family (who had played the leading role in Sasanian times), they did not extend their sway over Southeastern Armenia. Here the Artsruni family, in closer contact with the Muslim authorities and particularly with the influential emirs of Azerbaijan, gained independent standing and a royal title. So the Armenian Bagratunis failed to unite the country. Furthermore, their hold over their own lands was fragmented. Following the tradition that sons divided the inheritance, no sooner had a powerful prince extended his control than on his death the principality might be divided or fought over. The Bagratunis were recognized as princes and then kings by Constantinople and Baghdad, but their kingdom was not like that of Tigran the Great or even that of the Armenian Arsacids in the Sasanian period. It was weak and partial, perpetually splintered into smaller holdings.

On the other hand, the fortunes of the Georgian branch of the Bagratuni family show a continuous expansion and strengthening of their hand. At the beginning of the eleventh century Western Georgia (Abasgia) and Central Georgia (Iberia) were united under the rule of Bagrat III (1008–1014), though the eastern region, Kakheti, remained independent until 1104. Tiflis itself was not captured from the Muslims until 1122. Nonetheless, Bagrat was ruler of a formidable kingdom, which under his successors became the predominant power in the Caucasus, and indeed in the whole area between a declining Byzantium and a waning Caliphate.

But it is not necessary here to rehearse the well-known tale of Armenia's dismemberment by the encroaching Byzantine Empire and then the fatal collapse of Byzantine defenses before the Seljuk Turks in the eleventh century, or to elaborate on the expansion of Georgia in the following century. Since our purpose is to show how the Armenian and Georgian paths diverged despite the close proximity of the two countries, it will be more helpful to turn to the beginnings of the Armenian diaspora and to the divergent literary and scholarly interests of the two peoples.

Although the modern image of Armenians as urban dwellers, merchants and professional men, does not correspond at all with the patterns of Armenian society before the Seljuk invasions, even by that time the diaspora of Armenians was no new thing. From the sixth century, notably under the Emperor Maurice, groups of Armenians were often deported wholesale to man the frontiers. Similarly the Sasanian shahs brought Armenian communities to their borders in Central Asia. The removal of the Armenians from the kingdoms of Ani, Kars, Vaspurakan, and elsewhere to be settled in Cappadocia as the Byzantine Empire expanded in the tenth and eleventh centuries was but a continuation of a long-standing policy. (As was also the removal of the population of Julfa to New Julfa near Isfahan by Shah Abbas at the beginning of the seventeenth century.)

But some Armenians left their country willingly, either to seek their fortunes in foreign lands (and many Armenians rose to prominent rank in the Byzantine administration), or to flee persecution and the ravages of Arab or Turk. Furthermore, many Armenians had come willingly to settle in lands won back from the Muslims by the Byzantine armies in the tenth century. It was from these colonies, plus refugees fleeing from the Turks, that Cilician Armenia was peopled.

But the Georgians, living beyond the Byzantine-Iranian sphere of military operations, were never subjected to such treatment. And since they were to the north of the main routes that led from Central Asia through Iran to Asia Minor along the Araxes valley and across the Armenian Plateau, they were far less touched by the Turkish invasions. Certainly some Georgians, especially from Western Georgia, played a role in the Byzantine world. But the Georgian diaspora was rather one of individuals, notably monks and scholars, who were significant for their influence on life and culture back home.

We have already noted the Georgian monastic settlements in Palestine as early as the fifth century. In the centuries that followed, Georgian monks lived and worked not only in Palestine, but also on Mt. Sinai, Mt. Athos, the Black Mountain near Antioch, and elsewhere. In the Palestinian monasteries they made translations not only from Greek but also from Arabic, which by the end of the eighth century had largely superceded Syriac as the spoken tongue of Christians in Muslim countries. The most curious non-Christian text translated from Arabic into Georgian is the *Balavariani*, an adaptation of the Arabic *Bilavhar and Budasaf*. From the Georgian a Greek version was made, probably by Euthymius (on whom more below), and hence the Christian world came to revere the Buddha as a Christian saint. After the eighth century the influence of Armenian texts, which had been strong in the earliest period of Georgian literature, weakened as the Armenians and Georgians became increasingly hostile to each other. But the most significant development came during the late tenth century, when Georgians began turning to Greek models in centers of Greek learning. The renewed impetus given to philosophical studies during the eleventh century in Byzantium rubbed off on these Georgian scholars abroad, and had a distinct influence not only on Georgian ecclesiastical literature but also on the secular writers and poets. We ought to mention the most prominent writers of this Graecophile movement.

Among the nobles at the court of David Curopalates of Taikʻ (who was murdered in the year 1000) was one called John (known as John the Athonite), who in middle life abandoned his family in order to become a monk. He went to the great ascetic center of Mt. Olympus in Bithynia. While he was there his youngest son Euthymius was taken to Constantinople as a hostage, and John managed to secure his release. Euthymius then joined his father on Mt. Olympus, where he received his education. Since this was in Greek, he began to forget his Georgian, and according to his pious biographer the Virgin Mary herself had to appear and loose his tongue, so that he became as proficient in Georgian as he was in Greek. For his father had set him to work at an early age making translations.

But the most significant part of his work was done after John and Euthymius had moved to Mt. Athos, sometime after 965. Mt. Athos had long been a refuge for hermits living either alone or in small lauras. By the mid-tenth century the monks had formed a loose organization, but their life was changed by the arrival of Athanasius, orginally a noble from Trebizond and a friend of the emperor. The emperor (Nicephorus Phocas) gave him funds to build a vast monastery, and a chrysobull giving it valuable possessions and independence from all authority save that of the emperor. Thus began organized monasticism in the Lavra, founded in 961 on the model of the Studion in Constantinople. When John arrived on Mt. Athos, he was eager to establish a monastery for Georgian monks. He exchanged properties in his personal possession for monasteries in Greek lands, including a laura on Mt. Athos. This now became the great monastery of Iviron ("of the Iberians," as the Greeks called the Georgians), and it was here that Euthymius did most of his work.

The significance of Euthymius' translations was that in the field of the Bible text, liturgical matters, dogmatic, hagiographical and ascetic literature, not only was new material made available but the earlier Georgian texts were superceded by strict copies of Greek ones. It is true that the Armenians at about the same time were taking a renewed interest in translating Greek literature: Gregory Magistros in the field of secular literature, his son Gregory Vkayaser in the field of hagiography. But the Armenians were eager to preserve their own traditions, whereas with the Georgians a fresh start was made and the old largely forgotten. In less accessible places, notably Svaneti and Mt. Sinai some ancient manuscripts have survived that predate this Graecophile tendency and which have preserved the earlier Georgian versions of biblical and liturgical texts.

Euthymius' work was carried on by George, who himself became Abbot of Iviron about 1046 and wrote a life of his predecessor (d. 1028). George *Mtatsmindeli* ("of the holy mountain") was born in Trialeti and spent his younger years in monasteries in Georgia and on the Black Mountain before going to Mt. Athos.

But the most important of these Georgian translators was Ephrem *Mtsire* ("the less"), who received a Greek education at the capital of the Byzantine empire and spent his adult life in one of the monasteries on the Black Mountain. (This area between Antioch and the Mediterranean is no longer a monastic refuge, and is not so well known as Athos or Sinai. But in medieval times it was of great significance. For here Greeks, Georgians, Armenians, Syrians, and, after the arrival of the Crusaders, Latins all had monasteries. Consequently there was a great ferment of scholarly activity, as learned clerics translated texts not found in their own libraries. Armenian sources, for example, mention journeys made by scholars to this area, who went from monastery to monastery searching for the works of Syrian or Greek authors that had not yet been rendered into Armenian. The Black Mountain was therefore a much more cosmopolitan center than Mt. Athos, though it did not rival the latter's ascetic and spritiual fame.)

Ephrem carried the work begun by Euthymius and George much further, bringing to the art of translation a rigorous method and scrupulous accuracy. Also important are the extensive scholia that he added to his translation of various tests, notably the Neo-Platonic works of Dionysius the Areopagite and the patristic writings of Gregory of Nazianzen.

The work of Euthymius, George, and Ephrem is particularly significant from the point of view of Georgian theological literature. But of wider impact was the philosophical work of John Petritsi that influenced secular literature and spread Neo-Platonic ideas in medieval Georgia. Like many Georgians of his time John received his schooling in Constantinople; here his teachers were the famous philosophers Michael Psellus and John Italos. With this background John Petritsi spent the next thirty years of his life (from after 1067 to after 1100) in the monastery of Petritsos—whence his name. This monastery, in Bulgaria, was a purely Georgian foundation. In the early twelfth century John returned to Georgia to the monastery and academy of Gelati, near Kutaisi. This complex had been founded by David II the Restorer (1089—1125), Kutaisi being still the capital of the united kingdom. John headed this academy, and the philosophical tradition that he founded in Georgia was to have profound influence on Georgian culture.

Like his predecessors, John Petritsi made a number of translations of Greek theological works. But his real interests lay in the realm of philosophy, although here his actual translations number only four: two logical works of Aristotle, and one work each of the Neo-Platonists Proclus and Nemesius. His original works include a commentary on Proclus and on his own teacher Michael Psellus. But John's work cannot be judged merely by the number of his writings or by their style. For like the Armenian translators of the "Hellenophile" school of the sixth and seventh centuries, John's renderings were slavishly literal and too difficult to comprehend for them to set a new trend in Georgian literature. However, the scholastic tradition that he tried to establish did not predominate for long; it was soon swamped by the influence of secular Persian literature. Nonetheless, in the greatest achievement of medieval Georgian writing, the *Man in the Panther's Skin*, the blending of Persian motifs with Neo-Platonic philosophical ideas has created a truly unique epic, and one that is purely Georgian.

That Persian influence in literature should now wax and Greek should wane in the twelfth century is not too surprising. The Turks who came to Asia Minor and the Caucasus were familiar with Iranian culture and literary traditions. Throughout Armenia and Southern Georgia there were large colonies of Muslims (as in Ani, Dvin, Gandze, Tiflis), and it is hardly surprising that their literary motifs, often derived from Persia, should have exerted a strong appeal in both Armenia and Georgia—witness the development in Armenian ecclesiastical circles of mystical poetry in the guise of love poetry based on Persian themes. On the other hand, Byzantine power had been dealt a mortal blow by the Seljuks. Direct Greek contacts in Armenia came to an end by the late eleventh century, though Georgia kept in touch with Constantinople by sea. But more importantly, the Byzantine influence, culturally speaking, was primarily religious. Byzantium had little to offer to the leisured classes of the prosperous Georgian kingdom, and the masterpieces of Persian literature—but not the more sober works of theology and history in Arabic—found a ready welcome. They were translated, adapted, and on those patterns original Georgian compositions created.

It is perhaps curious that despite their even closer contacts with Iran the Armenians never developed a style of literature that incorporated Persian belles-lettres with their own heritage from the Hellenistic and Christian worlds. History, theology, philosophy, grammar predominate in Armenian writing. There was an interest in wisdom literature, such as the legend of Ahikar; there was a good deal of lyric poetry, primarily religious in nature; there were compilations of law, both ecclesiastical and secular; and there was a certain interest in medicine and technical subjects. Orally stirring tales circulated describing the exploits of heroes who defended Armenia from foreign invaders. The extraordinary diversity of dialect in which versions of the *Sasna-dzrer* (less accurately known as *David of Sasun*) have been recorded testifies to the widespread popularity of this folk epic, though literary references to it are rare indeed. But medieval Armenia did not produce works comparable with the *Amiran-Darejaniani*, the *Vis-Raminiani*, or most notably the *Vepkhis-Tqaosani*, even though in the first centuries of literacy the breadth and sophistication of Armenian writing far exceeded that of the Georgians. So in the earlier period the latter do not have their Eznik, their Elishe or their Moses Khorenatsi. Of course, comparisons of this kind are always misleading, invidious, and suspect of chauvinism. But this paper will have served its purpose if it has traced in summary fashion a few of the distinctive differences between Armenia and Georgia in the period when their churches and literatures grew to maturity. Although heirs to many common traditions from Iran, the Graeco-Roman world and from early Christianity, Armenia and Georgia went their separate ways, divided by temperament and historical circumstance. But to the bemused observer a certain continuity may be discernible in their mutual rivalry. The debate in scholarly journals of the 1970's over the primacy of Armenia or Georgia in the field of ancient church architecture is remarkably parallel to the debate among the hagiographers 1500 years ago over the Armenian or Georgian version of the *Life* of St. Shushanik.

BIBLIOGRAPHICAL NOTE

A general survey of the political history of Armenia and Georgia in the period covered by this paper may be found in C. Toumanoff, "Armenia and Georgia," Chap. 14 of the *Cambridge Medieval History*, Vol. IV, *The Byzantine Empire*, Pt. 1 (Cambridge, 1966), pp. 593-637. There is an excellent bibliography of both original and secondary literature, Ibid., pp. 983-1009. More detailed points have been taken up by the same author in his *Studies in Christian Caucasian History* (Washington, D.C., 1963). For Armenian and Georgian literature a useful summary is included in G. Deeters, G.R. Solta, and V. Inglisian, *Armenisch und kaukasische Sprachen*, Handbuch der Orientalistik, 1e Abteilung, 7te Band (Leiden, 1963). There is nothing in a western language comparable for Armenian to M. Tarchnišvili, *Geschichte der kirklichen georgischen Literatur*, Studi e Testi 185 (Vatican City, 1955), which is based on the first volume of the massive *K̇ rt ̇uli literaturis istoria* by K. Kekelidze. The standard survey for Armenian remains M. Abełean, *Hayots' hin grakanut'yan Patmut'yun*, 2 vols. (Erevan, 1944-1946), which has been reprinted several times and translated into Russian.

The conversion of Armenia to Christianity is the theme of the *History* attributed to Agathangelos. For the text, with translation and commentary, see R.W. Thomson, *Agathangelos, History of the Armenians* (Albany, N.Y., 1976). The problem of the relationship of the numerous versions of this story in Armenian, Greek, Arabic, and Syriac has attracted much attention. For a recent discussion see M. van Esbroeck, "Le resumé syriaque de l'Agathange," *Analecta Bollandiana*, 95 (1977), pp. 291-358. For Georgia see P. Peeters, "Les débuts du christianisme en Géorgie d'après les sources hagiographiques," *Analecta Bollandiana*, 50 (1932), pp. 5-58.

The invention by Mashtots of scripts for Armenian, Georgian, and the language of the Caucasian Albanians (Aluank') is described by Koriun. There are some variations in the accounts of Mashtots' work in the *Histories* by Lazar P'arpets'i and Movses Khorenats'i. An important collection of essays on this topic was published as volume 7 of the *Banber Matenadarani* (Erevan, 1964). See also P. Peeters, "Pour l'histoire des origines de l'alphabet arménien," *Revue des études arméniennes*, 9 (1929), pp. 203-37. But there is no confirmation from the Georgian side that Mashtots was active outside Armenia. For the earliest Georgian writing see M. Tarchnišvili, "Les recentes découvertes épigraphiques et littéraires en géorgien," *Le Muséon*, 63 (1950), pp. 249-60.

For information about texts translated into Armenian from Greek and Syriac see N. Akinean, "Hay Matenagrut'ean Oskedarĕ," *Handes Amsorya*, 46 (1932), cols. 105-28; G. Zarp'analean, *Matenadaran Haykakan Targmanut'eants' Nakhneats'* (Venice, 1889). For more technical subjects (logic, grammar, etc.) which were usually translated in a very literal fashion known as the "Hellenistic school," see N. Adontz, *Denys de Thrace et les commentateurs arméniens* (Louvain, 1970) – a translation from the original Russian; H.A. Manandean, *Yunaban dprots ĕ ew nra zargats'man shrjannere* (Vienna, 1928); A.N. Muradyan, *Hunaban dprots ĕ ev nra dere hayereni k'erakanakan terminabanut'yan steltsman gortsum* (Erevan, 1971).

For Armenians in the Holy Land see in general A.K. Sanjian, *The Armenian Communities in Syria under Ottoman Dominion* (Cambridge, Mass., 1965). Sanjian has also edited the tendentious list of Armenian monasteries, "Anastas Vardapet's List of Armenian Monasteries in Seventh-Century Jerusalem: A Critical Examination," *Le Muséon*, 82 (1969), pp. 265-92.

The Georgian monastic presence in Palestine was even more important for the development of Georgian literature because Georgians had not rejected the Council of Chalcedon (451) and broken relations with the Greek Church. For these theological problems – which loomed large in the politics and literature of both Armenia and Georgia – see: N. Akinean, *Kiwrion kat'olikos Vrats'* (Vienna, 1910); A. Alek'sidze, *Epist'olet ̇a Tsigni* (Tbilisi, 1968); G. Garitte, *La Narratio de Rebus Armeniae*, CSCO Subsidia 4 (Louvain, 1952) (which has an important commentary – the remark of the Catholicos Moses II, cited in the text above, is taken from this text); K. Sarkissian, *The Council of Chalcedon and the Armenian Church* (London, 1965); M. Tallon, *Livre des lettres, 1er groupe*, Mélanges de l'Université Saint Joseph, 32 (1955), fasc. 1.

Early Georgian literature is rich in hagiographical texts. Some have been translated by D.M. Lang, *Lives and Legends of the Georgian Saints*, 2nd ed. (London, 1976). See also P. Peeters, "Sainte Sousanik, martyre en Arméno-Géorgie," *Analecta Bollandiana*, 53 (1935), pp. 5-48, 245-307, and his important translation of the lives of four Georgian saints of the ninth to eleventh centuries, "Histoires monastiques géorgiennes," *Analecta Bollandiana*, 36-37 (1917–1919, pub. 1922). For Georgian historical writing see C. Toumanoff, "Medieval Georgian Historical Literature (VIIth – XVth Centuries)," *Traditio*, 1 (1943), pp. 139-82, and *idem*, "The Oldest Manuscript of the Georgian Annals: The Queen Anne Codex (QA), 1479–1495," *Traditio*, 5 (1947), pp. 340-44.

For Armenia in the period of Muslim dominion see the recent revision of J. Laurent, *L'Arménie entre Byzance et l'Islam*, by M. Canard (Lisbon, 1980). For Armenians in the Byzantine Empire see P. Charanis, *The Armenians in the Byzantine Empire* (Lisbon, 1963). For Georgians on Mount Athos see Peeters, "Histoires monastiques," cited above; and for the Black Mountain see W.Z. Djobadze, *Materials for the Study of Georgian Monasteries in the Western Environs of Antioch on the Orontes*, CSCO Subsidia 48 (Louvain, 1976).

For the Georgian reworking of the Buddha legend see D.M. Lang, *The Balavariani –Barlaam and Josaphat* (London, 1966). The "Man in the Panther-Skin" has been translated into many languages. The standard English rendering is M.S. Wardrop, *The Man in the Panther's Skin* (London, 1912). For a more recent translation see R.H. Stevenson, *The Lord of the Panther-skin* (Albany, N.Y., 1977). For a discussion of the secular literature not covered by Tarchnisvili and Toumanoff, see R.P. Blake, "Georgian Secular Literature, Epic, Romantic and Lyric (1100–1800)," *Harvard Studies and Notes in Philology and Literature*, 15 (1933), pp. 25-48.

For the Armenian epic popularly known as "David of Sasun," see the excellent French rendering by F. Feydit, *David de Sassoun, epopee en vers* (Paris, 1964).

II

The Armenian Image in Classical Texts

My task in this essay is to attempt to elucidate the image of the Armenians as found in classical texts, the literature of ancient Greece and Rome. But it will be interesting to tackle the texts in early Armenian as well, to see if there is any correlation between the way in which Armenians were seen and the way in which they looked back on themselves and their past.

Several difficulties immediately present themselves. In the first place, Armenia was not often at the center of the stage for the writers of classical antiquity. Not that they ignore Armenia; but the references to Armenians and things Armenian are somewhat haphazard, scattered over a long period of time, and give only a patchy view of Armenian life. Second, Armenian literature does not begin until the fifth century A.D. There is therefore no contemporary Armenian source with which to compare, say, Xenophon or Plutarch. And then Armenian literature is imbued with a Christian outlook—which is different from the outlook not only of the Greeks and Romans, but of the earlier Armenians themselves.

Equally significant is the fact that Armenian historians interpret the past in different ways for their own purposes. But it does not mean that they do not share certain characteristics, or, to put it another way, that there are not certain characteristics common to the class that they represent.

So I begin by considering the main features that Greek and Roman authors associate with Armenia. It will then be possible to amplify the picture by comparing their comments with the more copious material in the works of early Armenian writers.

Additional Note: For the development of the Armenian 'self image' see item IV below.

II

The first significant references to the Armenians occur in Herodotus (III 93); he says that they formed the thirteenth satrapy of the Old Persian empire. The Alarodians, who were included in the eighteenth satrapy, were another of the peoples occupying what we now call Armenia. They represented the earlier inhabitants; for the Armenians were regarded not as indigenous to the region but as settlers. They came from Phrygia, says Herodotus, when he describes the Armenian contingent in Xerxes' army at the time of the invasion of Greece in 480 B.C. (VII 73). At a later date Strabo gives a long account of the Armenian people, stressing that they derive from Thessaly. Their ancestor Armenus accompanied Jason on his quest for the Golden Fleece and remained in the East. Strabo adds (XI 14.12): "They also say that the clothing of the Armenians is Thessalian, for example, the long tunics which in tragedies are called Thessalian . . . since the Thessalians in particular wore long robes, probably because they of all the Greeks lived in the most northerly and coldest region. . . . And they say that their style of horsemanship is Thessalian."

The natural geographic features of Armenia, the mountain ridges interspersed with plains and valleys, meant that the country was inhabited by many diverse tribes. Strabo notes that as the tribes range the mountains they are given to brigandage (*Geography* XI 12.4). Without stressing overmuch the lawless side of Armenian life, we must admit that the restlessness of the small units and the rivalry of families or clans remained a permanent feature of Armenian society. Hence, also, the slowness with which the Armenian language became the common tongue; according to Strabo, only after the time of Artaxias (Artashes) in the early second century B.C. did the inhabitants of Armenia speak the same language (ibid. 14.5).

But by the time of Tigran the Great, when the Romans first had direct dealings with Armenia, the monarchy had imposed some cohesion and unity on the country. Tigran, of course, was not a typical king, in that he had briefly brought under his sway many non-Armenian areas to the south and west. But to Plutarch Tigran was the image of a barbarian potentate, whose subjects lived in a state of oppression quite incompatible with the rights of free Roman citizens. It is worth quoting the first contacts between Tigran and the messenger for the Roman general Lucullus (Plutarch, *Lucullus,* 21):

> Now the sway of the Armenian was intolerably grievous to the Greeks. Above all else, the spirit of the king himself had become pompous and haughty in the midst of his great prosperity. All the things which most men covet and admire, he not only had in his possession, but actually thought that they existed for his sake. For though he had started on his career with small and insignificant expectations, he had subdued many nations. . . . Many were the kings who waited upon him, and four, whom he always had about him like attendants or body-guards, would run on foot by their master's side when he rode out, clad in short blouses, and when he sat transacting business, would stand by with their arms crossed. This attitude was thought to be the plainest confession of servitude, as if they had sold their freedom and offered their persons to their master disposed for suffering rather than for service.
>
> Appius, however, was not frightened or astonished at all by this pomp and show, but as soon as he obtained an audience, told the king plainly that he was come to take back Mithridates, as an ornament due to the triumph of Lucullus, or else to declare war against Tigranes. Although Tigranes made every effort to listen to this speech with a cheerful countenance and a forced smile, he could not hide from the bystanders his discomfiture at the bold words of the young man. It must have been five and twenty years since he had listened to a free speech. . . . He was vexed with Lucullus for addressing him in his letter with the title of King only, and not King of Kings. . . .

And when Lucullus does invade Armenia: "Since the first messenger who told Tigranes that Lucullus was coming had his head cut off for his pains, no one else would tell him anything" (§ 25).

But there was more than a touch of Greek culture in Armenia. Plutarch claims that the Carthaginian Hannibal showed King Artaxias the advantages of the site for his capital Artaxata and drew a plan for it (*Lucullus,* 31). Whatever the truth of that story, Tigran's later capital Tigranocerta had a Greek colony and a theater. Tigran's

II

son Artavazd was famous as an author of tragedies, orations, and histories (in Greek, of course, not Armenian), some of which were extant in Plutarch's day (Plutarch, *Crassus*, 33). And when king Tiridates returned from his reception in Rome, Nero gave him money and artisans to rebuild Artaxata (Dio Cassius, *Epitome* to Book LXIII).

Even so, Armenian life did not revolve around the city in the Greco-Roman sense. Although the Armenian kings built numerous capitals along the Araxes River, their importance was economic, but not political or social. A side comment in Tacitus is revealing (*Annals* XII.45): "Nothing is so completely unknown to barbarians as the appliances and refinements of siege operations—a branch of warfare perfectly familiar to ourselves."

The economic wealth of Armenia was known to the earliest Greek writers. Herodotus (V 49) informs us that the Armenians were "rich in flocks." The general richness of Armenia in agriculture and husbandry is emphasized by Xenophon, whose *Anabasis* gives us the most elaborate firsthand account of the country in antiquity. We cannot repeat here details of all the provisions served by the Armenians to the Greek mercenaries: the various meats, vegetables, fruits, wines, beer (only the olive does not grow properly here, notes Strabo [*Geography* XI 13.7]). But since eating and drinking remained important aspects of Armenian social life—at least among the nobility—it is worth noting even at the early date of Xenophon the emphasis that the Armenians put on hospitality (*Anabasis* IV 5.30-33):

> On the next day Xenophon took the village chief and set out to visit Cheirisophus; whenever he passed a village, he would turn aside to visit the troops quartered there, and everywhere he found them faring sumptuously and in fine spirits; there was no place from which the men would let them go until they had served them a luncheon, and no place where they did not serve on the same table lamb, kid, pork, veal and poultry, together with many loaves of bread, some of wheat and some of barley. And whenever a man wanted out of good fellowship to drink another's health, he would draw him to the bowl, and then one had to stoop over and drink from it, sucking like an ox. To the village

Armenian Image in Classical Texts

> chief they offered the privilege of taking whatever he wanted. He declined for the most part to accept anything, but whenever he caught sight of one of his kinsmen, he would always take the man to his side. Again, when they reached Cheirisophus, they found his troops also feasting in their quarters, crowned with wreaths of hay and served by Armenian boys in their strange, foreign dress.

Eight centuries later another foreigner comments on the laws of hospitality, this time laws that had been broken at the murder of the Armenian King Pap (Ammianus Marcellinus XXV 22): "By such treachery was credulity basely deceived, and at a banquet, which ought to be respected even on the Euxine Sea, before the eyes of the god of hospitality a stranger's blood was shed [note the play on Euxine; *euxinos* = hospitality]."

The wealth of Armenia in natural products and her mines for metals and precious stones are noted by many writers. As a sign of this wealth, says Strabo (XI 14.9), not only could the Armenians pay tribute in gold, silver, and horses, they could also put tens of thousands of fully armed cavalry into the field (cf. Plutarch, *Crassus*, 19). And the fame of the Armenians as soldiers was to endure for many centuries. Procopius in the time of Justinian, for example, describes how the Byzantine palace guard was selected from among Armenians (*Secret History* XXIV 15.17). Another consequence of the richness of Armenia was that Antony's troops suffered from dysentery in 36 B.C. because of the excess of everything that they found to eat (Plutarch, *Antony*, 50).

The physical size of Armenia, too, was a matter of comment. Justin in the third century A.D. for example, abbreviating the history of the earlier Pompeius Trogus, notes (XLII 2):

> But since we here make a transition to Armenia, we must go a little further back into its origin; for it is not right that so great a kingdom should be passed in silence, since its territory, next to that of Parthia, is of greater extent than any other kingdom. Armenia, from Cappadocia to the Caspian Sea, stretches over a space of eleven hundred [Roman] miles, and is seven hundred miles in breadth.

II

14

Of the more personal qualities ascribed to the Armenians we have already noted their pride—vainglory to the Romans—and their hospitality. Of course, our classical authors are often using the supposed qualities of Armenians as a foil for the qualities they wish to emphasize in their own heroes or villains. So the Armenian is a barbarian slave in contrast with the free Roman gentleman, whereas Armenian hospitality is contrasted with a specific case of Roman treachery. In this regard it is very interesting to read Dio Cassius' account of Tiridates' visit to Rome in 66 A.D. in order to receive the crown of Armenia from Nero. For one has the distinct impression that the Armenian is used here as a foil more to pour scorn on Nero than to praise Tiridates. Having described the investiture in some detail, Dio then adds (Epitome to Book LXIII): "Such, then, was this occasion; and of course they had a costly banquet. Afterwards Nero publicly sang to the lyre, and also drove a chariot, clad in the costume of the Greens and wearing a charioteer's helmet. This made Tiridates disgusted with him; but he praised Corbulo [the general], in whom he found only this one fault, that he would put up with such a master." And a little later Dio has another story: "Tiridates one day viewed an exhibition of the pancratium [a kind of combined boxing and wrestling match], at which one of the contestants after falling to the ground was struck by his opponent. When the king saw this, he exclaimed: The fight is unfair. It is not fair that a man who has fallen should be struck."

Tacitus, however, is not so complimentary about Tiridates (*Annals* XV 31): "Accustomed as he was to foreign pride, he lacked all knowledge of ourselves who prize the essentials of sovereignty and ignore its vanities."

On the other hand, the Armenian spirit could be admired. Dio Cassius, for example, speaks of the Armenians taken captive and brought with King Artavazd to Egypt by Antony in 34 B.C. (XLIX 40):

> Then he left his legions in Armenia and went once more to Egypt, taking the great mass of booty and the Armenian [king] with his wife and children. Sending them with the

captives ahead of him into Alexandria in a kind of triumphal procession, he himself drove into the city upon a chariot, and he not only presented to Cleopatra all the other spoils but brought her the Armenian and his family in golden bonds. She was seated in the midst of the populace upon a platform plated with silver and upon a gilded chair. The barbarians, however, addressed no supplications to her, nor made obeisance to her, though much coercion was brought to bear upon them and many hopes were held out to them to win their compliance, but they merely addressed her by name; this gave them a reputation for high spirit, but they were subjected to much ill-treatment on account of it.

The point of gold or silver bonds is brought out also by Ammianus Marcellinus. Describing the arrest of King Arshak by treachery, he says (XXVII 12.3): "After his eyes had been gouged out, he was bound in silver chains, which among that people is regarded as a consolation, though an empty one, for the punishment of men of rank." Much earlier, in Herodotus III 130, we read of Darius giving a Greek as a present a pair of golden foot chains.

References to the religion of the Armenians are few. Tiridates is described by Dio Cassius as a devotee of Mithra, and by Suetonius (*Life of Nero* XXX 6) as a magus, that is, a Zoroastrian priest, which is appropriate in view of his Parthian origin. But again Suetonius's comments tell us more about Roman attitudes than about the real nature of the religion of the magi: "He had brought magi with him, had initiated Nero into their banquets; yet the man giving him a kingdom was unable to acquire from him the magic art. Therefore let us be convinced by this that magic is detestable, vain and idle; and though it has what I might call shadows of truth, their power comes from the art of the poisoner, not of the magi."

The idea of the Armenian religion being related to that of the Persians brings us back to the supposed ancestor of the Armenians, Armenos (*var.* Armenios). For at the end of the last book of his *Republic* Plato introduces a model of the structure of the universe in the form of a vision attributed to Er, son of Armenios, a native of Pamphylia. The tenth-century lexicon called *Suida* explains the name Er as a Hebrew one, no doubt influenced by its appearance in Luke 3.28 as the name of one of the ancestors of Jesus Christ. But the earlier Christian writer and philosopher Clement of Alexandria identified Er with Zoroaster (*Stromata* V 157). Whatever the origin of the name, Plato clearly meant his readers to ascribe an Eastern origin of great antiquity to the myth.

The only serious observer of Armenian religion was Strabo, who draws attention to the special respect paid by Armenians to Anahit (XI 14.16):

> Now the sacred rites of the Persians, one and all, are held in honour by both the Medes and the Armenians; but those of Anaitis are held in exceptional honour by the Armenians, who have built temples in her honour in different places, and especially in Acilisene. Here they dedicate to her service male and female slaves. This, indeed, is not a remarkable thing; but the most illustrious men of the tribe actually consecrate to her their daughters while maidens; and it is the custom for these first to be prostituted in the temple of the goddess for a long time and after this to be given in marriage; and no one disdains to live in wedlock with such a woman. Something of this kind is told also by Herodotus in his account of the Lydian women.

The honor paid Anahit is, of course, well known from the later Armenian Christian sources. And this same shrine of hers, according to Agathangelos, was the site of the initial confrontation between King Trdat and Saint Gregory the Illuminator. When the shrine was later destroyed, there was—again according to Agathangelos—an armed conflict between the demons and the forces of piety (§ 786):

> After this he [Gregory] came to the neighboring province of Ekeleats [the Greek Acilisene]. Here the demons appeared in the places of worship of the most important shrines of the Armenian kings, in the temple of Anahit in the town of Erez. The demons gathered together and gave battle in the form of an army carrying shields; with a tremendous shout they made the mountains echo. They were put to flight, but as they fled the high walls collapsed and were flattened. Those who had arrived, saint Gregory, the king and the pious army, broke into pieces the golden image

of the female deity Anahit, and they completely destroyed and pillaged the place, seizing the gold and silver.

This brings us to the question of Christianity in Armenia. The earliest reference to the Armenians being Christian appears in Tertullian (who died c. 220). In his treatise *Adversus Judaeos* 7, he lists various peoples who have accepted the Christian religion: "Parthi, Medi, Elamitae, et qui inhabitant Mesopotamiam, Armeniam, Phrygiam, Cappadociam, et incolentes Pontum et Asiam et Pamphylam. . . ." This list is, in fact, a verbatim quotation from Acts 2.9 ff., where in the place of Armenia the Greek text has Judaea. The geographical order, however, does not favor Judaea; in the Greek the form of Judaea is an adjective and not a noun; and this list names the countries whose languages the Jews were surprised to hear the apostles speaking—whereas it would not be surprising if they spoke their own native tongue. For these reasons some ancient writers proposed the names of other countries. Tertullian and Augustine have Armenia, Jerome has Syria, John Chrysostom proposes India, and Eusebius omits it. So Tertullian's evidence is to be rejected.

The next foreign author to refer to Christians in Armenia is Eusebius. In his *Ecclesiastical History* (VI 46.2) he mentions a certain Meruzanes (in Armenian, Mehruzhan) as bishop in Armenia to whom Dionysius, bishop of Alexandria from 247 to 264, wrote a letter. The problem here is what to understand by Armenia, since the term could be used of Lesser Armenia, west of the Euphrates, where there were Christian communities in the third century. This Mehruzhan is certainly unknown to Armenian tradition. And, curiously enough, the Armenian translator of Eusebius here uses the non-Armenian form *Armenia* (not *Hayastan*), strongly implying that he thought of it as a Roman province and not as standing for the whole of his native country.

Later in his *History*, when discussing Maximin's persecutions in the East in 312-313, Eusebius says (IX 8.2): "The tyrant had the further trouble of war against the Armenians, men who from ancient times had been friends and allies of the Romans; but as they were Christians and exceedingly earnest in their piety towards the Deity, this hater of God, by attempting to compel them to sacrifice to idols and demons, made of them foes instead of friends, and enemies instead of allies."

Whether or not we are to interpret this persecution as the occasion for the martyrdom at Ejmiatsin of Rhipsimé, Gaiané, and their companions, as Paul Peeters would have us believe,[1] we have at any rate now reached the point where the foreign sources and Armenian traditions begin to converge. (To say that they "correspond" would be going too far.) So it is time to take stock and to compare the comments on Armenians found in the classical texts we have been discussing with the local Armenian traditions.

With regard to the origin of the Armenians, there is no suggestion in Armenian sources that they derive from Phrygia or from Thessaly. Rather, Armenia was settled by the eponymous ancestor Hayk from Mesopotamia. Two points in the tradition are worth noting. According to both Moses Khorenatsi (I 10) and the *Primary History* there were some settlers in Armenia before the arrival of Hayk and his family. So the Armenians were not the earliest inhabitants of the land. And then the Armenian traditions are integrated into the Christian traditions based on the genealogies of Noah's descendants as found in the scriptures. Hence the various references to the descendants of Hayk as the race of Japheth or of Torgom or of Ashkenaz. Here the influence of Eusebius's *Chronicle* played a very important role. We may also note in passing that the Armenian writers of the classical period pay no particular attention to the descent of Noah's ark on the mountains of Ararat (not the modern Mt. Ararat, of course, but the mountains of southern Armenia around Lake Van). Although Faustos (III 10) claims that Jacob, bishop of Nisibis, went searching for the ark in the province of Korduk', there is never any suggestion that the Armenians had any special preeminence because of Noah's landing there.[2]

---

[1] *Analecta Bollandiana*, 60 (1942), 106.
[2] This is in contrast to the claim in Scarron's ridiculous play *Don Japhet d'Armenie* (1653), Act II, sc. 5:

II

Armenian Image in Classical Texts

As for Armenia being within the Iranian cultural orbit, that is the subject of a separate communication.[3] So I pass over it with simply a reminder that according to Moses Khorenatsi (I 9) the only written record of early Armenian traditions was kept in Parthian archives. This archive, like those of Armenian documents at Edessa or Ani, is fictitious. But the point is that the Armenian historian does not look to the West; rather, he assumes that it is in the Iranian sphere that Armenian culture has its origins.

Armenian writers do not describe the geography of their native land in detail. They frequently refer to Armenia as being "in the Northern regions." Again, this is relative to Iran rather than to Greece or Rome. The only geographer of the classical period, the anonymous author of the *Ashkharhatsoyts*, was interested in the political divisions of Armenia, not the natural features. Nor do the shorter documents that give routes and distances between places have anything to say about the physical features of the land, its natural products, and so forth. So there is nothing to compare with Strabo or Pliny. We do find, however, numerous passages describing individual sites; for example, the beauty of the area around Lake Van where Moses claims that Semiramis built a summer palace, or the description of Aghtamar in the Continuator to Thomas Artsruni. These are idealized images, though based on personal knowledge of the sites. As an idealized image of the province of Ayrarat we might quote a few lines from the reflections of King Arshak III on leaving for exile in the West, as found in the pages of Łazar P'arpetsi—who himself had been forced to leave the country for some time (I 8):

> With all these thoughts in his mind, King Arshak departed, abandoning the fortunate and patrimonial inheritance of his ancestors, the magnificent, famous and illustrious province

---

Car je suis don Japhet, de Noé petit-fils:
D'Arménie est mon nom, par un ordre préfix,
Qu'avant sa mort laissa ce fameux patriarche,
Parce qu'en Arménie un mont reçut son arche.

[3] Nina G. Garsoïan, "The Locus of the Death of Kings: Iranian Armenia—The Inverted Image," pp. 27-64, below.

II

of Ayrarat, which produces all varieties of plants and crops, which is stocked to overflowing with all resources necessary for the livelihood, pleasure and recreation of men. Its plains are extensive and abundant with game; its encircling mountains are beautifully situated and rich in pasture, and abound with cloven-footed animals and ruminants, and many others in addition. From their summits flow streams watering the plains that need no irrigation. These provide for the numberless multitudes in the capital, women, men and their families, an abundance of bread and wine, vegetables of sweet savour and the taste of honey, and various types of olive. To those who turn their gaze for the first time to the flanks and level tops of the hills, the colours appear not to be flowers but garments, scattered so copiously, richly and luxuriantly. The overflowing abundance of the grass satisfies the numberless herds of domesticated donkeys and the ferocious herds of wild animals which thrive and fatten and show their whole bodies well covered with fat. The strong and sweet odour of the flowers which surrounds the valiant hunters, archers and herders who live in the open, gives health, strengthens the senses of the mind, and brings renewal. There are found every sort of root and plant useful for the needs of medicine; they are prepared according to the knowledgeable skill of the most expert physicians— ointments efficacious in dispelling maladies and potions which restore health to those who have long suffered from pain....

The plains not only reveal and offer what is advantageous for men's needs, but even more they indicate to diligent workers the profits that are hidden under the earth, that they may gain treasure for themselves and the pleasures of this world; they serve for the majesty of kings and the increase of revenue—gold and copper and iron and precious stones. These skillful hands receive and fashion grandiose ornaments for kings; they fit them into tiaras and crowns and garments embroidered in gold. With irrigation the plains provide natural sweetness for those eating the varieties of victuals. Likewise not in vain does the delectable plain of Ayrarat nourish in itself stems of [sugar] cane; from it are also born [silk] worms for purple decoration, offering profit and delight for those who appreciate luxury. Furthermore, the courses of the rivers teem with many species of fish, great and small, of varied flavor and appearance, which fill those who labor and diligently toil with joy and gratitude for their prosperity and sated stomachs.

The land also nourishes through its canals an abundance of birds for the delight and vigor of the nobility addicted to the hunt: flocks of partridges and pheasants that murmur sweetly, that love the craggy places, lurk among the rocks and hide in holes; or the race of wild birds, fat of flesh and sweet to the taste, that dwell among the reeds and hide among the bushes and thickets; and the large and powerful aquatic birds that seek out weeds and feed on moss—the swan, duck and goose, and many other numberless coveys of birds. With encircling nets, snares and traps, groups of princes and nobles' sons come out to hunt; some chase after the onagers and wild goats with encouraging shouts to the archers; others gallop after herds of stags and birds, demonstrating their prowess with the bow; others again with swords, like men in single combat, overthrow herds of massive boars and kill them. Many of the youngest noble children with their tutors and servants hunt various kinds of birds with falcons and bring them back to increase the delight of the feast. Thus, when each one has had his fill of the chase, joyfully they return.

They are awaited according to daily custom by the children of the fishermen who fathom the waters; running to meet the nobles, they bring and offer to their lords fish they have caught, the young of various wild birds and eggs from the islands in the river. The nobles willingly accept a portion from them, and from their own catch give liberal presents in return. So, they return to each one's mansion loaded with every blessing, and on those who remained occupied at home they bestow choice offerings, being especially liberal to strangers. One can see at everyone's repast heaped up upon each other the multitude of game with their heads set out in order; they give festive joy to those who eat the fish and meat. But even more than by the sweetness of these delicacies, by spiritual food—psalms and prophet's canticles—they bless Christ the liberal donor who fills us with all his blessings.

You will note that it is primarily life on the land which interests Łazar. Like most early Armenian writers he reflects the social life of the class to which he belonged—or at least of the patrons for whom he was writing. So the comments in Moses Khorenatsi on townspeople in Vałarshak's organization of the country are unusual (II 8):

> He appointed judges at court and judges in the cities and towns. He ordered that the townspeople be more highly esteemed and honored than the peasants, and that the peasants

should respect the townspeople like princes. But the townspeople were not to vaunt themselves too much over the peasants but to live on brotherly terms for the sake of harmony and life without rancor—which are the causes of prosperity and peace. [I refrain from commenting on the fact that this information supposedly came from the Parthian archives.]

The picture of Tigran the Great as the image of an Armenian king as found in Plutarch is not reflected in Armenian tradition—naturally enough. For Moses, Tigran was not a despotic autocrat, but a king who was just and impartial. His main claim to fame was his prowess at war (I 24):

He of all our kings was the most powerful and intelligent and the most valiant. . . . He extended the borders of our territory and established them at their extreme limits in antiquity. . . . Who among true men and those who appreciate deeds of valor and prudence would not be stirred by his memory and aspire to become such a man? He was supreme among men and by showing his valor he glorified our nation. . . . He was just and equal in every judgment, and he weighed all the circumstances of each case impartially. He did not envy the noble nor did he despise the humble, but over all alike he spread the mantle of his care.[4]

It is interesting to compare this idealized image of a remote figure with the more contemporary—if equally idealized—image of the monarch in John Catholicos. For he borrows verbatim from Moses to describe the elevation of Ashot to royal status:[5] "Of great wisdom and gentleness of speech, he did not emulate the rich in banqueting yet neither did he despise the poor; but over all he spread the mantle of his care. In the scales he weighed first himself and then the conduct of everyone else. In short, he never withheld anything humankind might need." On the other hand, the Continuator to Thomas Artsruni describes *his* patron's

---

[4] The image of Tigran as modest is reflected in English Renaissance drama, e.g., Beaumont and Fletcher's *A King and No King*.

[5] Tiflis, 1912, p. 174.

claim to royal status in different terms. For him the Bagratid Smbat (son of Ashot just mentioned) had abdicated his responsibilities (IV 3): He did not pursue the way of peace, he did not send tribute to the Caliph in accordance with Christ's command to give to Caesar what was Caesar's, and he had brought much harm on the holy church and God's people. Whereas, says Thomas, Gagik was worthy of the crown because he was an orthodox and faithful Christian.

One could pursue further the matter of idealized portraits to consider the ideal noble—valiant, hospitable, and generous, but proud of his honor—or the ideal religious figure whose asceticism is a source of general inspiration, but space does not permit. I therefore conclude with a few more general comments on what Armenian writers say about the Armenians as a whole. How, if at all, did they conceive of Armenians as different from other people, even if only in a negative fashion by way of contrast with non-Armenians?

Since classical Armenian literature is the product of Christian writers, we might begin by asking how Armenians viewed their church in relation to other Christian churches. That raises a host of problems, but one or two points are perhaps relevant here. In the first place, the Armenians were not missionary minded. Only in the first century of organized Christianity in Armenia, in Faustos or Koriun, do we read of proselytising beyond the borders of Armenia. But once the Armenian church had formulated its own theological position and developed its individual ritual, these traditions were regarded as specifically Armenian and not for export.

In Ełishē we already find the emphasis that to abandon the covenant, which is a covenant of Armenians, is to be both a traitor and an apostate. Ełishē was strongly influenced by the Maccabees, whose concept of religion included the whole traditional Jewish way of life. Again and again, the same phrases used by the Jewish heroes in those books are echoed in Ełishē: it is for their ancestral customs that the Armenians are fighting. So it is significant that although Ełishē was indebted to Christian hagiographical texts for much of his imagery, his *explicit* models are not the early Christian martyrs who died for their faith alone regardless of ethnic background, but the generals and leaders of ancient Israel.

Although the Armenians were Christian, that was not the most important factor for writers likeEłishē; rather, their religion was only the framework within which something more important was happening. The Armenians were not the defenders of Christendom at large holding back the heathen on the eastern border. They were defending their ancestral way of life and their individual traditions. It is therefore not at all surprising that in later generations those ecumenically minded Armenians who endeavored to bridge the gap between the Christian churches in the East met with no lasting success. Most Armenians were not willing to lose their Armenianness as part of a larger church. And those who for one reason or another accepted communion with the Greeks were regarded as traitors to their country. Although the Greeks were Christian that did not matter. The Zoroastrian Persians were "impious and irreligious" forEłishē as were the Muslims for Thomas Artsruni. But they were not regarded in any worse light than the Byzantines. Hence the famous comment of the Catholicos Moses II; when summoned by the emperor Maurice to attend a synod in Constantinople where the union of the churches might be effected, he exclaimed (*Narratio*, § 102): "I shall not cross the river Azat or eat fermented bread or drink warm water." The river Azat then marked the frontier between Eastern Armenia and Byzantine territory, but Moses is playing on its meaning "free." The references to fermented bread and warm water are to differences between Greeks and Armenians in the celebration of the liturgy, differences that are as significant and irreconcilable as differences in the theology of the Christian faith itself.

Armenians were also kept separate from non-Armenians by their language. Sēbeos's comment on Smbat Bagratuni is relevant here. About A.D. 600 Smbat found a colony of Armenians in eastern Iran who had forgotten their native tongue. So he had a priest sent to them to teach them

Armenian again as well as to minister to their spiritual needs (chap. 14).

As for the view that Armenians had of their own language, there do not seem to be many comments in the sources. One reads of the horribly cacophonous tongues of the inhabitants of the Caucasus, so I presume that by contrast Armenian is to be considered euphonious. But I am not aware of any claims that Armenian was the language spoken in Paradise by Adam. The eighth-century scholar Stephen of Siunik' has a few lines on Armenian as compared to other languages which are worth quoting: "All the variations and different properties of words and expressions of different people derive from an original and uncultivated language. The Greek language is delicate; Latin is severe; the language of the Huns is arrogant; Syriac is diffident; Persian is luxurious; the language of the Alans is pleasing; that of the Goths humorous; Egyptian is hard; Indian tremulous. But Armenian is delightful and capable of containing all the virtues of the others.[6]

It is difficult to point to anything in the early sources that gives a picture of Armenians as a whole in a more positive manner. There are examples of brave Armenians and of cowardly ones; of sincere, hospitable Armenians, and of treacherous ones; of Armenians given to things of the spirit, and of others addicted to the pleasures of the flesh. But there is no simple definition of an Armenian per se. Rather, an Armenian is one who is born into a group that speaks a distinct language (or at least did so at one time), and who holds to certain individual traditions including a Christian faith that is exclusive rather than inclusive. Over the centuries military, economic, and social circumstances varied enormously. So the "typical" or "ideal" Armenian kind of life underwent tremendous variations. But there did remain some internal sense of solidarity that tends to elude the penetration of an external observer.

[6] Quoted in C. F. Neumann, *Mémoire sur la vie et les ouvrages de David* (Paris, 1829), pp. 27-28; the passage is repeated in Vardan's *Hawak'umn Patmut'ean* (Venice, 1862), § 5.

III

Mission, Conversion, and Christianization: The Armenian Example

Armenia as a country, and the Armenians as a people, have on various occasions attracted attention in the world at large. But foreign interest in Armenia has been sporadic at best; and outsiders have rarely commented on the internal history of that land, reserving their ink for such events as involved their own countries. Any investigation of Armenian history is thus heavily dependent on local sources. With regard to the present theme—the conversion of Armenia to Christianity—this drawback poses a special difficulty. For not only do the first documents written in Armenian postdate the conversion of the Armenian court by a century or more; all Armenian literature was produced by Christians, most of them clerics in the Armenian church.[1] Not surprisingly they present a generally self-serving interpretation of the establishment of Christianity in their country, and they bring an anachronistic view to their historical enterprise.

The development of Armenian literature may thus be seen as a stage in the Christianization of that people—not necessarily as the final stage, but as the point when the self-awareness of Armenians as a distinct branch of Christendom took root. So in this paper I endeavor, first: to trace the origins of Christianity in Armenia—the "Mission"; second, to describe the

---

[1] Although there are echoes of pre-Christian epic tales and songs in the later written literature, such pagan themes and their singers (*gusan*) were discouraged by the Christian clergy. For a general view of Armenian literature, see V. Inglisian, "Die armenische Literatur," in *Armenisch und Kaukasische Sprachen*, Handbuch der Orientalistik, I 7, ed. B. Spuler (Leiden and Cologne, 1963). The most noteworthy remnants of epic tales and songs are preserved in the works of P'awstos Buzand, *Patmut'iwn Hayoc'* (St. Petersburg, 1883), reprinted with introduction by Nina G. Garsoian (Delmar, N.Y.), 1984; and Movsēs Xorenac'i, *Patmut'iwn Hayoc'* (hereafter Movsēs) (Tiflis, 1913), reprinted with an introduction by R. W. Thomson (Delmar, N.Y., 1981), translation and commentary in R. W. Thomson, *Moses Khorenats'i: History of the Armenians*, Harvard Armenian Texts and Studies, 4 (Cambridge, Mass., 1978). The system of transliteration used here for Armenian is that of the *Revue des études arméniennes*.

Reprinted from *Harvard Ukrainian Studies*, 12/13 (1988/1989), pp. 28-45. Copyright © 1990 by the President and Fellows of Harvard College. Reprinted by permision.

establishment of a regular ecclesiastical structure and the extension of the Christian faith over the country (these do not necessarily coincide)—the "Conversion"; third, to assess the role of the church[2] as an increasingly dominant force in Armenian society—the "Christianization"; and finally, to point to the growth of a specifically "Armenian" attitude which prevented the reunion of this branch of Christendom with the neighboring churches after the schisms of the sixth and seventh centuries. So although the comparable events that took place in Kievan Rus' in the tenth century will not receive direct attention, I trust that the discussion of these themes in the Armenian context will provide worthwhile analogies for a better understanding of the general question of Christianization.

Armenians were no more immune than other peoples from the desire to claim an apostolic origin for their local church. The spread of the various traditions that described the supposed missionary travels of Jesus' own disciples is not our concern here.[3] Suffice it to say that already in the late fifth century a tradition that Thaddaeus, one of the seventy, had preached in Armenia and had been martyred there was known to some Armenian writers.[4] And by the eighth century it was thought that the apostle Bartholomew had reached Armenia.[5] In any event, there was never any suggestion that these early missionaries had founded viable Christian communities. So if Saint Gregory the Illuminator was considered to have taken over the chair of Thaddaeus,[6] that cathedra had been unoccupied for two and a half centuries. Our historical investigation must begin in the third century, when the first hints are made in contemporary sources that there were Christians in Armenia.

The earliest reference to Christians in Armenia seems to be in Tertullian.[7] However, he is adapting the passage in Acts 2.9–10, which gives a list of people who heard the apostles preaching in their own tongues. It is

---

[2] By "church" I mean here hierarchy and formal organization, not the community of the faithful.
[3] For a general view, see F. Dvornik, *The Idea of Apostolicity in Byzantium and the Legend of the Apostle Andrew*, Dumbarton Oaks Studies, IV (Cambridge, Mass., 1958).
[4] P'awstos, III, 1; Movsēs, II, 33–34. The story of Addai/Thaddaeus is based on an adaptation of the Syriac *Teaching of the Apostle Addai*: Labubna, *T'ult' Abgaru* (Venice, 1868). See further M. van Esbroeck, "Le roi Sanatrouk et l'apôtre Thaddée," *Revue des études arméniennes* 9 (1972): 241–83.
[5] Movsēs, II, 34. See further M. van Esbroeck, "Chronique arménienne," *Analecta Bollandiana* 80 (1962): 423–45 (esp. pp. 425–29, S. Barthélemy).
[6] The connection between Thaddaeus and Gregory was made even clearer by the tradition that the latter was conceived over the tomb of Thaddaeus. See the Karshuni version of Agathangelos, par. 8 (ed. M. van Esbroeck, "Un nouveau témoin du Livre d'Agathange," *Revue des études arméniennes* 8 [1971]: 13–167), and Movsēs, II, 74.
[7] *Adversus Judaeos*, VII, 4.

thus not hard evidence. In the middle of the century a letter was sent by Dionysius, bishop of Alexandria, to the Armenians "whose bishop was Meruzanes." The document does not survive, so it is unclear who the "Armenians" were. The term was applied to Armenians living outside the historical boundaries of Greater Armenia, in Cappadocia and Pontus— "Armenia Minor." So a bishop with an Armenian name in such a community does not imply that there was yet a regular church in Armenia Magna. (This "Meruzanes" is otherwise unattested.)[8] Eusebius refers to the Armenians as Christians at the time of Maximin's persecution (312–313). But again it is not clear which Armenians are intended, since Maximin's persecution extended over Asia Minor, and this passage in Eusebius's *Ecclesiastical History* was written well after the conversion of the Armenian court.[9]

If we disregard the story of Thaddaeus/Addai, which was adapted by Armenians from the Syriac account of the conversion of Edessa and dated the foundation of the Armenian church to the time of Jesus' disciples, Armenian tradition is unanimous in regarding Gregory the Illuminator as the founder of that church. The accounts of the life and works of Gregory are numerous and indicate a continuous reworking of tradition. The earliest Armenian written version (which could not predate the creation of the Armenian script in the early fifth century) is lost, though renderings in Greek and Arabic survive. The standard Armenian version is attributed to a certain "Agat'angelos." The complications of this story and its involved textual history are not immediately relevant.[10] The main points are straightforward.

---

[8] Eusebius, *Ecclesiastical History*, VI, 46.2. The only Armenians with the name Mehrujan or Merujan attested in literary sources were members of the Arcruni family, whose territory was in the area east and south of Lake Van. The name is of Iranian origin; see H. Hübschmann, *Armenische Grammatik* (Leipzig, 1897), pp. 52–53.

[9] Eusebius, *Ecclesiastical History*, IX, 8.2. In the *Demonstratio Evangelica*, I, 6.20d, Eusebius again refers to the Armenians as being Christians "in our day." This work was written after 314, but before the Council of Nicaea.

[10] The Armenian text, *Agat'angelay Patmut'iwn Hayoc'*, was published in Tiflis in 1909. For the direct Greek translation see G. Lafontaine, *La version grecque ancienne du livre arménien d'Agathange*, Publications de l'Institut orientaliste de Louvain, 7 (Louvain, 1973). The Arabic and subsidiary Greek versions were published by G. Garitte, *Documents pour l'étude du livre d'Agathange*, Studi e Testi, 127 (Vatican City, 1946). The main versions are compared in the introduction to R. W. Thomson, *Agathangelos: History of the Armenians* (Albany, 1976). For more recent discoveries and general discussion, see G. Winkler, "Our Present Knowledge of the History of Agat'angelos and its Oriental Versions,' *Revue des études arméniennes* 14 (1980): 125–41.

(1) Gregory had been raised as a Christian in Caesarea in Cappadocia. He returned to Armenia with the king, Trdat, while the latter was still a pagan, and was imprisoned.

(2) The immediate occasion for the miraculous conversion of the Armenian king Trdat was the martyrdom of nuns, supposedly refugees from Roman persecution. Torments fell on Trdat as punishment, and he was cured by Gregory.

(3) Gregory was sent to Caesarea for consecration as bishop. On his return the pagan shrines were overthrown and churches established on their sites.

(4) The site of the main church was at Ejmiacin where the nuns had been martyred, near the royal court.

(5) Gregory established a regular system of bishoprics and handed over the patriarchate to his son.

Some of these points are confirmed by evidence from other sources, other aspects are not so confirmed. In what follows I shall base my point of departure on Armenian texts and endeavour to show how different writers give different clues to a complicated process.

(1) The basic role of Gregory and his descendants as leaders of the fledgling Armenian church is corroborated elsewhere. In fact, the social position of Gregory's noble family, the Pahlavids, gave him standing; and conversely, his descendants used their position in the church to gain further prominence and social power.[11]

(2) The connection with Caesarea continued for several generations of patriarchs, who had to return to that city for consecration by the metropolitan.[12]

(3) That the conversion of Trdat was preceded by martyrdoms is not implausible in light of Maximin's persecution, as just noted. If the number of years ascribed to Gregory's imprisonment by Agat'angelos is correct, and the return of Trdat to Armenia occurred in 298 after Shah Narses ceded much of Armenia to Galerius, then the date of Trdat's conversion and Gregory's consecration could plausibly be 314.[13] The conversion to Christianity of an Armenian king before the edict of Milan in 311 and Maximin's

---

[11] For the holdings in land of the patriarchal family, see H. Gelzer, "Die Anfänge der armenischen Kirche," *Berichte der königlichen sächsischen Gesellschaft der Wissenschaften* 47 (1895): 107–174, esp. pp. 148–50.
[12] P'awstos, III, 12, 16, 17; IV, 4.
[13] See Thomson, *Agathangelos*, p. lxvi, and P. Ananian, "La data e le circostanze della consecrazione di S. Gregorio Illuminatore," *Le Muséon* 84 (1961): 43–73, 319–60.

defeat by Galerius in 313 seems most unlikely, especially in view of the difficulties it would entail with the Sasanian shahs.

(4) The main difficulty in the story related by "Agat'angelos" is the ascription of the principal church to the site of Ejmiacin. Other sources indicate that the first church in Armenia was on the site of the former temple at Aštišat, west of Lake Van. It was only after the division of Armenia into Roman and Iranian spheres in 387 that the prelates of eastern Armenia established their seat near the capital of Vałaršapat within sight of Mount Ararat.

(5) The succession of patriarchs from the family of Gregory into the fifth century—with appointments from outside only when the relative due to succeed was quite unworthy[14] —is unanimously confirmed by all sources. So well established was the practice that the return of the patriarchate to that family was as cherished a theme in later Armenian apocalypses as the return of the monarchy to the Arsacid family.[15]

Other than later claims of an apostolic origin for the Armenian church, there are no written accounts of the origin of Christianity in Armenia that offer a divergent view from that of Agat'angelos—or more exactly, the variations within the general tradition expounded by the many versions of "Agat'angelos." However, there do exist some indications that missionary activity in that country had not been restricted to envoys from Cappadocia, the numerous assistants whom Gregory the Illuminator is said to have brought back with him after his consecration as bishop in Caesarea.[16]

In the Epic Histories known as the *Buzandaran* of P'awstos there is a story describing the search by the famous bishop of Nisibis, Jacob, for Noah's ark in southern Armenia and Jacob's involvement in local affairs there.[17] Whatever the historicity of this search, and the authenticity of the fragment of wood given him by an angel, the fact remains that such interference in local affairs by the notable fourth-century bishop from Syria was easily believable in the fifth century when the text was put into writing. Furthermore, in the *Life* of Maštoc', inventor of the Armenian script, which was written in the mid-fifth century, there is an elaborate description of the

---

[14] As noted by P'awstos, III, 13.
[15] See, for example, the Vision of Sahak in Łazar Parp'ec'i, *Patmut'iwn Hayoc'* (hereafter Łazar) (Tiflis, 1904), reprinted with an introduction by D. Kouymjian (Delmar, N.Y., 1985), ch. 17 (which refers to events due to occur 350 years after the vision, i.e., in the mid-eighth century); or Arak'el of Bitlis in the fifteenth century predicting the future liberation of Constantinople, Jerusalem, and Armenia. For this see A. K. Sanjian, "Two Contemporary Armenian Elegies on the Fall of Constantinople, 1453," *Viator* 1 (1970): 223–61.
[16] Agathangelos, § 806.
[17] P'awstos, III, 10.

attempt of another Syrian bishop, Daniel, to adapt a Semitic alphabet for the Armenian language.[18] This was superseded by Maštoc''s own invention. The actual impact of Syrian missionary activity in southern Armenia during the fourth century is hard to assess in the absence of any written record. However, the use of Syriac loanwords in the fifth-century texts for fundamental Christian expressions strongly hints at the influence of Syrian Christianity.[19]

Indeed, it would be rather surprising if the numerous colonies of Jews attested in Armenia from the first century B.C. had never been visited by a Christian missionary. The great number of Aramaic loanwords in Armenian for commercial expressions points to the importance of connections with Syria.[20] But it is significant that contacts between the foreign colonies (*gałut'* —an Aramaic word) and the mainstream of Armenian political and social life were not close. The cities in Armenia played a commercial but not a political role.[21] The Christian church in Armenia developed within the social fabric of that country—with interesting variations from the way it developed in the Greco-Roman world. Therefore, any Christians among the foreign communities (if any did in fact ever exist) left no trace in the later Armenian record. For that record was set down in writing by persons unsympathetic to city culture, who ignored aspects of life that did not directly affect their own social milieu.

For the same reason it is difficult to trace the expansion of Christianity within the country and the establishment of a regular hierarchy. According to the received version of Agat'angelos, Saint Gregory baptized more than four million Armenians in a week, following which churches were built in every village, preaching was undertaken in every area so that "in the twinkling of an eye" the "oafish" peasants became acquainted with the prophets and the gospel, and more than four hundred bishops were ordained by Gregory himself for every region.[22]

---

[18] Koriwn, *Vark' Maštoc'i* (Erevan, 1941), reprinted with an introduction by K. H. Maksoudian (Delmar, N.Y., 1985), § 6.
[19] See Hübschmann, *Grammatik*, pp. 281–321: "Die syrischen Lehnwörter im Armenischen." There are also certain calques, such as the use of *pahem* (I keep) in the sense "I fast"; cf. Syriac *nṭr*.
[20] See H. A. Manandian, *The Trade and Cities of Armenia in Relation to Ancient World Trade*, trans. Nina G. Garsoian (Lisbon, 1965), ch. 3, esp. p. 65.
[21] See N. G. Garsoian, "The Early-Mediaeval Armenian City: An Alien Element?," Ancient Studies in Memory of Elias Bickerman, *The Journal of the Ancient Near Eastern Society* 16–17 (1984–85): 67–83.
[22] Agat'angelos, § 835, 840, 856.

III

This optimistic assessment of Gregory's activity is not very helpful. The Epic Histories of P'awstos make it clear that the first bishopric was established in western Armenia at the site of a former pagan temple, not at the royal capital.[23] It is also clear from the nomenclature of the bishops given by the early texts that their sees were not the transitory commercial centers known as cities and built in various places by succeeding monarchs, but rather the estates of the great noble families. When bishops are identified by see, it is not a town but a province that is named, and many provinces are identified by the name of the family that controlled them.[24] In the Greco-Roman world Christianity spread from city to city; and the more important the city the more important the wider role played by its bishop. In Armenia Christianity spread through the social and political structure indigenous to that country.

Thus at the beginning of the fourth century it was the noble family of the Pahlavunik' and the direct descendants of Gregory who played the leading role. Despite the conversion of the king and the emphasis placed by "Agat'angelos" on the cooperation of Gregory and Trdat in the rapid conversion of the whole country, the ecclesiastical authority and the royal authority might (and did) clash, just as the political interests of the great noble families and of the monarchy were frequently at variance before the abolition of the Arsacid line in 428.

The patriarchs in the line of Gregory were descended from an ancient noble family of Parthian Iranian origin. Just as in the secular arena the great offices of state were hereditary in certain families, so the Pahlavids regarded their ecclesiastical role as one due them by right. The lands belonging to the patriarch were his in the same way as family estates belonged to the magnates of the realm, and they were passed on by inheritance. The patriarchs thus had a secure base—and not just the moral support of the clergy—from which to oppose the royal will, should that be necessary. For their part the Armenian kings had to resort to exile, or even murder, in order to overcome ecclesiastical opposition to what they might consider political concerns. The actions of the patriarchs thus receive much attention by Armenian historians who describe this formative period. For in

---

[23] P'awstos, III, 14; cf. Agat'angelos, § 814–815, and below, fn. 26.
[24] See the Armenian conciliar lists conveniently gathered in the appendices to N. Adontz, *Armenia in the Period of Justinian*, trans. with partial revisions by Nina G. Garsoian (Lisbon, 1970), pp. 94*–101*.

many regards there was little distinction between the patriarchs and other magnates.²⁵

But our sources leave us quite in the dark concerning the actual spread of Christianity in a geographical sense. P'awstos describes how in the mid-fourth century the Patriarch Nersēs was able to summon a council of "all the bishops of Armenia,"²⁶ and even earlier "all the bishops" had been summoned by the king on those occasions when it was necessary to elect a successor to Gregory's sons as patriarch. But how rapidly and in what order the noble families created bishops on their lands is not explained.

The account of Gregory's idol-smashing journeys given by Agat'angelos describes the destruction of local pagan cults, the building of churches on those sites once the demons had fled, and the fate of the pagan clergy—conversion or death.²⁷ Although the information about the cult sites and the deities there worshipped is precious for our knowledge of pre-Christian religion in Armenia,²⁸ the later writers give no hint that these sites formed bases for missionary activity directed at local communities, or that they became the sees of bishops. (There is one exception—the last temple destroyed by Gregory, at Aštišat, where on his way back from consecration in Caesarea he established the first church. This did become the patriarchal see until that was moved to northeastern Armenia after the division of 387.) Since the later Armenian sources concentrate on the leading personalities and the conflicts between them, only by indirect hints can we assess the spread of Christianity beyond the uppermost social circles. P'awstos and Agat'angelos wax rhetorical in their descriptions of teaching and missionary activity throughout the countryside. But the eradication of former pagan beliefs and the acceptance of Christian attitudes took many generations, and was by no means a uniform process.

Nor was opposition limited to recalcitrant peasants. The conversion of the king was an act of state and the establishment of an official and organized clergy was also an act of state. So those great princes who opposed the pro-Roman policies of the kings and espoused closer relations with Iran, to whose social ethos Armenians were far closer, quite naturally rejected Christianity and promoted the Zoroastrian cult of fire. It was not until the

---

²⁵ For Armenia in this formative period see the studies of N. G. Garsoian, gathered in her *Armenia between Byzantium and the Sasanians*, Variorum Reprints (London, 1985).
²⁶ P'awstos, IV, 4. The council was held at Aštišat, "the mother of all the churches" and the traditional place where synods had been convened by the predecessors (*naxneac'*) of Nersēs.
²⁷ Agathangelos, § 777–815.
²⁸ Movsēs (II, 12) used the information in Agat'angelos as a basis for his (unhistorical) explanations of the origin of pagan cults in Armenia; see also A. Carrière, *Les huit sanctuaires de l'Arménie payenne* (Paris, 1899).

end of the fourth century that the major revolts were finally crushed.[29] After the abolition of the monarchy, the Sasanian shahs tried on various occasions to impose their own orthodoxy on that sector of Armenia within their orbit.[30] But their success was never permanent.

The church, then, was from the beginning a vital social and political force in the upper echelons of society. The role of the patriarchs and bishops in affairs of state is attested in the historians of the early period. But our sources are not much interested in the details of the spread of Christian practice among those less newsworthy. They say little or nothing about how or in what places Christianity was spread among the populace in an organized fashion. Although P'awstos gives elaborate details of various kinds of hospices set up by the patriarch Nersēs I and indicates that they continued to be run from the patriarchal palace, he does not show that there was any general plan of Christian expansion behind these philanthropic institutions.[31] We have to look elsewhere for the main source of local preaching—to the activities of holy men and ascetics in deserted places.

In the Epic Histories we read about the miracles worked by some of these ascetics and the miraculous visions they enjoyed.[32] The more famous of them attracted disciples. Although later historians describe the organization of such groups in anachronistic terms (based on their experience of organized monastic communities), the impact both of anchorites and of their wandering counterparts was considerable. Their most famous representative was Maštoc'.

Maštoc', who was born in western Armenia in the mid-fourth century and had received a good Greek education, abandoned a promising secular career at court for the religious life of a hermit. In due course he attracted disciples, and like others before him led these pupils in missionary activity in remoter parts of the country. It is significant that his biographer Koriwn[33] gives Maštoc' no official standing, save only as a respected friend of the patriarch, and later of the king. Maštoc' was a free agent, without a base in an organized monastery or attachment to a bishopric. It is also significant that Łazar, writing at the end of the fifth century, speaks of the

---

[29] These conflicts form the substance of the Epic Histories (the *Buzandaran*) of P'awstos.
[30] The *Histories* of Ełišē and Łazar describe the resistance of the Armenians in the fifth century. For Łazar, see above, fn. 15. The critical text of Ełišē, *Vasn Vardanay ew Hayoc' Paterazmin*, was published in Erevan in 1957; translation and commentary by R. W. Thomson, *Elishe: History of Vardan and the Armenian War*, Harvard Armenian Texts and Studies, 5 (Cambridge, Mass., 1982).
[31] P'awstos, IV, 4; VI, 5.
[32] P'awstos, V, 25–28; VI, 2–16.
[33] For Koriwn, see above, fn. 18.

use of Syriac in eastern Armenia; and that the role of Maštoc' as interpreter is brought out by the later Movsēs Xorenac'i.[34]

In other words, up to the end of the fourth century oral preaching was naturally conducted in the vernacular. But any scriptural readings or liturgical ceremonies—anything based on a written text—had to be conducted in Greek or Syriac. Since the use of Syriac was associated with the Iranian sector of divided Armenia, and Greek with the area under Roman domination, there were political problems involved with the official encouragement of these foreign languages. And on a more basic level, the vast majority of Armenians would find the Christian message rather meaningless if presented in a tongue not their own.

It is difficult to assess what role political considerations played in the development of a native script, though the interest of the king is stressed in all accounts of that invention. Quite naturally, the Armenian historians, themselves Christians if not clerics in the Armenian church, emphasize the desire of Maštoc' to bring the gospel to the people in their own language. An adaptation of a script used for an (unnamed) Semitic language was first tried but found to be unsatisfactory.[35] Around 400 A.D. a totally new script was successfully invented, based on the principles of the Greek alphabet.[36]

As soon as the script had been invented, the bilingual background of Christian activity in Armenia became even more obvious. For Maštoc', with the encouragement of patriarch and king, set groups of his disciples to learning either Greek or Syriac (or both). He sent them to the centers of Syriac and Greek theological learning—Edessa, Melitene, and eventually Constantinople. Very rapidly a corpus of texts became available in Armenian. First biblical, liturgical, and theological works were translated from Greek and Syriac. Then the first translators began to compose original works in their own language—Koriwn being a prime example of a translator who turned to authorship himself. The process of translation was not halted once a native literature had developed, but continued (at varying levels of intensity) through the Middle Ages. An ever-widening circle of scholarly endeavour was made available in Armenian and adapted to the Armenian situation. These texts then formed the basis for original

---

[34] Łazar, ch. 10; Movsēs, III, 47.
[35] See above, fn. 18.
[36] There is a large body of secondary literature on this invention. See in particular P. Peeters, "Pour l'histoire des origines de l'alphabet arménien," *Revue des études arméniennes* 9 (1929): 203–237. Volume 7 of *Banber Matenadarani* (Erevan, 1964) was devoted to studies of Mesrop Maštoc' on the occasion of the 1600th anniversary of his birth. Further Armenian bibliography is given by Maksoudian in his introduction (pp. xxix–xxxi) to the 1985 reprint of Koriwn; see above, fn. 18.

III

Armenian work and the elaboration of Armenian traditions.[37]

The invention of the script and its promulgation by Maštoc' and his disciples had a further implication. The written use of a common language provided for the first time a direct tie between Armenians on both sides of the Roman-Iranian border. Koriwn describes a journey undertaken by Maštoc' as far as Constantinople in order to obtain imperial permission for him (a subject of Iranian Armenia) to work amongst Armenians in Roman territory. Movsēs Xorenac'i hints at the political difficulties this straddling of the border entailed.[38] It was one thing for bishops in Roman territory to give appropriate obedience to Roman ecclesiastical authorities, and for bishops in Iranian territory to give their allegiance to their patriarch and sovereign, but quite another for such political loyalties to be confused. The use of a common written language no doubt encouraged the growth of a sense of common Armenian identity, but it complicated the unstable balance of Armenians poised between two jealous imperial powers. And the fact that different traditions, liturgical and theological, had developed in the Greek-speaking and Syriac-speaking worlds meant that a common Armenian tradition would take time to develop.[39]

Our understanding of this period in Armenian history is complicated by the fact that the Armenian sources were written in Iranian Armenia and more or less ignore the different circumstances over the border to the west. The patriarchs resided in Vałaršapat (modern Ejmiacin) and their patronage of scholarship extended only over the territory subject to the shah. The forging of Armenian identity in that, larger, part of the ancestral homeland owed much to the struggle of the church against attempts to impose Zoroastrian orthodoxy. Involvement in the theological quarrels of the Roman Empire was a secondary consideration. The final stage in the Christianization of Armenia was essential for the future self-consciousness of Armenians, but in that process a substantial minority in Roman territory was left out.

---

[37] For a brief survey of the early stages in the development of Armenian literature, see R. W. Thomson, "The Formation of the Armenian Literary Tradition," *East of Byzantium: Syria and Armenia in the Formative Period*, ed. Nina G. Garsoian, Thomas F. Mathews, and Robert W. Thomson (Washington, D.C., 1982), pp. 135–50; and A. Terian, "The Hellenizing School," ibid., pp. 175–86.

[38] Koriwn, ch. 21; Movsēs, III, 57.

[39] For the development of Armenian liturgical traditions see the introduction to G. Winkler, *Das armenische Initiationsrituale*, Orientalia Christiana Analecta, 217 (Rome, 1982), and the extensive bibliography on pp. 15–44.

III

MISSION, CONVERSION, AND CHRISTIANIZATION

The emergence of a distinctly Armenian Christian tradition was conditioned by a variety of pressures. The struggle with Sasanian Iran was significant for the development of later ideology—as we shall see in a moment. Pressure from the Roman empire to the west prompted reaction of a different kind. Although it would be simplistic to think of the tension as theological to the west and social/political to the east, the problems facing the Armenians were not identical in both cases. So it may be convenient first to trace the deepening involvement of the Armenian church in the theological quarrels that rent Christendom after Constantine had summoned the first ecumenical council, and then to turn to the emergence of a distinctly "national" outlook.

Aristakēs, second son of Gregory the Illuminator (who succeeded his father as bishop of Greater Armenia), attended the council held at Nicaea in 325.[40] He and his successors gave their firm support to the anti-Arian stand there upheld. This staunch defense of Nicene orthodoxy brought the patriarch Nersēs I into conflict with the court when royal policy favored the Arianizing outlook of later Roman emperors, notably Valens.[41] But there was never any important pro-Arian faction in Armenia at large. It was only after the division of Armenia in 387 that Armenian sources refer to serious theological controversy within the country. By that time the Armenian patriarchs were resident in Iranian Armenia and had also broken formal ties with Caesarea. The last bishop to be consecrated there was Nersēs. His son Sahak was patriarch at the time of Maštoc' and played a major role in the development of a written Armenian tradition. But he was not consecrated in Greek territory, and after him the Armenians continued to anoint their own ecclesiastical leaders quite independently.[42] In the matter of *appointment*, however, they were not entirely independent, since the Sasanian court played a major role in the governance of its sector of Armenia.

The invention of the Armenian script paved the way for the circulation of books, both those officially recognized and those of more dubious origin. Koriwn, describing the work of the first translators, notes that the "false" books of Theodore of Mopsuestia were brought to Armenia.[43] He does not say by whom, though in the early fifth century Theodore had many supporters in Syria and Cilicia on the southern border of Armenia. However,

---

[40] Agat'angelos, § 884; P'awstos, III, 10; Movsēs, II, 89–91.
[41] For the Arian question, see N. G. Garsoian, "Politique ou Orthodoxie?," *Revue des études arméniennes* 4 (1967): 297–320 (reprinted in her *Armenia between Byzantium and the Sasanians*).
[42] See G. Garitte, *La Narratio de Rebus Armeniae*, CSCO Subsidia, 4 (Louvain, 1952), § 31, and his commentary on pp. 99–100.
[43] Koriwn, ch. 23.

III

Theodore's teaching on the Incarnation was condemned at the Council of Ephesus in 431. Immediately thereafter Acacius, bishop of Melitene, where Maštoc' had sent disciples to study, warned the Armenians of the danger of Theodore's heretical views. The correspondence culminated in a letter from Proclus, patriarch of Constantinople, which was accepted as an authoritative statement of the faith.[44] In the lifetime of Maštoc', then, his efforts to bring together Armenians on both sides of the border catapulted him into the conflict of opposing theologies; in that debate the Armenians sided with Constantinople. But equally as important as the position reached is the fact that this first foray into doctrinal debate gave the Armenian church a base from which its officials were reluctant to budge in future controversies. Positions incompatible with Proclus's interpretation of the teaching of Ephesus came to be regarded as innovations. This is of some relevance in the debate over Chalcedon that eventually divided Armenia from the imperial church.

Although representatives from Iranian Armenia were not present at Chalcedon in 451, and there are no direct contemporary Armenian references to its decisions, there do exist hints of the reverberations caused in Armenia by the controversy that that council had addressed.[45] However, no formal theological declarations were made concerning the natures and person of Christ until early in the following century, during the period when the *Henotikon* of Zeno was in effect. The accord of the Armenian church with the imperial orthodoxy of that time emerges very clearly from the correspondence concerning the first council of Dvin, held in that administrative capital of Iranian Armenia in 505. A delegation of Syrians opposed to the church in Persia (which favored Nestorianism) appeared, requesting confirmation of their orthodoxy. It is not known why a council of Armenian, Georgian, and Caucasian Albanian bishops and nobles was sitting; however, they approved the creed of the Syrians, among whom figured the Monophysite enthusiast Simeon of Beit-Arsham. The council agreed in condemning the false teaching of Nestorius and that of others like him at Chalcedon, and noted that the Syrian declaration of faith was in agreement with that of Greeks, Armenians, Georgians, and Albanians.[46]

---

[44] For this correspondence (preserved in the *Book of Letters* [*Girk' T'lt'oc'*], Tiflis, 1901), see M. Tallon, "Livre des Lettres. 1er Groupe," *Mélanges de l'Université Saint Joseph* 32, fasc. 1 (1955).

[45] See K. Sarkissian, *The Council of Chalcedon and the Armenian Church*, 2nd ed. (New York, 1975), pp. 151ff.

[46] For the correspondence, see the *Book of Letters*, pp. 41–51.

However, the abrogation of the *Henotikon* in 518 (which seems to have had no immediate echo in Armenia) meant that the Greek church reaffirmed the formulation of Chalcedon. That council—as opposed to persons attending—was explicitly denounced for the first time in Armenia at Dvin in 555. Again a delegation of Syrians opposed to the Nestorians in Iran had come to Armenia, this time requesting episcopal consecration for one of their number. It was this formal condemnation of Chalcedon as teaching erroneous doctrine opposed to that of Nicaea that led to the irrevocable split.[47] The break with the Georgians at the beginning of the seventh century,[48] and the efforts of the imperial government to effect a reunion over the next hundred years, merely confirmed the isolationist tendencies of the Armenians. Their separation was reinforced by differences of ritual as well as of doctrine. Resistance was expressed in aphoristic terms by the patriarch Movsēs, who refused to meet the emperor Maurice, saying: "I shall not cross the Azat [into Roman territory]; I shall not eat *phournitarion* [leavened communion bread]; nor shall I drink hot water [mixed with the communion wine]."[49]

The closing of Armenian ranks against the Greek church was never total and unanimous. Many individuals adhered to the Chalcedonian creed, all scholars continued to admire Greek culture and learning, and visits to Constantinople were frequently made for political and scholarly reasons. Nonetheless, there gradually developed a clearer sense of individuality and separateness. The new ideology received its classic expression in the work of Ełišē, to whose interpretation of the Armenian position we must now turn.

Agat'angelos had made it clear that Gregory the Illuminator was the first to establish an organized church and hierarchy in Armenia, though other Armenian writers did not hesitate to push back the origins of their church to the apostle Thaddaeus. The antiquity of Christianity in Armenia is a theme particularly stressed in the work of Ełišē, *The History of Vardan and the Armenian War*—although he does not mention Thaddaeus. His *History* is an account of the Armenian rebellion of 450–451 against Sasanian Iran, led by Vardan Mamikonean.[50] The rebellion was unsuccessful as a military venture, and Vardan was killed in the dramatic confrontation on the field of

---

[47] *Book of Letters*, pp. 52–77. See also R. W. Thomson, "An Armenian List of Heresies," *Journal of Theological Studies*, n.s. 16 (1965): 358–67, esp. pp. 359–60.

[48] See the correspondence in the *Book of Letters* and in the second book of the historian Uxtanēs; translation in Z. Arzoumanian, *Ukhtanes of Sebastia: History of Armenia* (Fort Lauderdale, 1985).

[49] See the *Narratio*, § 102, and the commentary of Garitte, pp. 242–44.

[50] For the Armenian text and recent translation, see above, fn. 30.

III

Avarayr. Ełišē goes on to describe the fortitude of the prisoners in Iranian jails, the martyrdom of some, and the promise of eventual release for the survivors. Armenian resistance did prevent the shah from succeeding in imposing Zoroastrianism on this province of his empire; in fact, a generation later a good measure of political independence was granted when Vahan Mamikonean, a nephew of Vardan's, was appointed governor.

The importance of Ełišē's work is not so much his record of events. For it is an elaborately constructed book with much rhetorical speech-making, and the account of the same war in Łazar, who was a contemporary and friend of Vahan's, was composed closer to the time. Rather the great significance of Ełišē lies in his interpretation of the struggle, which is seen in absolute terms of truth versus falsehood, loyalty versus perfidy. Two basic themes emerge: the Armenians as a people fighting for their ancestral traditions, alone against all odds, in which struggle death is a greater victory than submission; and the concept of a covenant, accepted by the church, the army, and the common people, a covenant which is synonymous with the identity of the Armenians as a people and which involves both religious and political loyalty. Those who reject or abandon the covenant are both traitors to their people and apostates with regard to the faith. These two loyalties are inseparable, so the role of the Armenian church as the keeper of the faith and the guardian of the nation's integrity is crucial.

Ełišē's formulation of covenant and ancestral tradition was a keystone for later Armenian self-identification. Fifteen hundred years later his themes still have relevance, even if interpretations have shifted in emphasis over the centuries. The literary origins of the dual theme are clear: it is to the Maccabees that Ełišē looks for a model.[51] He sees in their struggle the model of the Christian Armenians fighting against the Sasanians (as the Jews fought the Seleucids) for their ancestral way of life. Certainly the Armenians were not the only people to find inspiration in the story of the Maccabees and to see close parallels between events of that time and the present tribulations of their people. The question here is: How accurately does this image portray the actual state of Armenia in the fifth century? Ełišē offers us the vision of Armenia as a Christian nation. Was it more than an ideal to which succeeding generations should aspire?

Ełišē refers to the Roman Empire as a Christian nation, whose emperor refused to help the Armenians—fellow-Christians—in their hour of need. The actual policy of the emperor Marcian with regard to Armenia and

---

[51] See the introduction to Thomson, *Elishe*; and in general R. W. Thomson, "The Maccabees in Early Armenian Historiography," *Journal of Theological Studies*, n.s. 26 (1975): 329–41.

III

MISSION, CONVERSION, AND CHRISTIANIZATION

Sasanian Iran is not our concern here. The significant point is that Ełišē ignores the Armenians living in Roman territory. He views his compatriots as a homogeneous entity poised between two great powers. This was a distortion of the political reality, for there were several Armenian princely houses on the western side of the frontier. They had the status of *civitates foederatae* under the *comes Armeniae*, with duties towards their sovereign, yet with internal autonomy and freedom from taxation. Not until the time of Justinian were these princedoms suppressed.[52] A much more accurate picture of the situation at the time of the revolt in 451 is given by Łazar, who names the Armenian princes in Roman territory to whom the rebels turned for help. But it was Ełišē's version of events, not Łazar's, that became accepted and authoritative. In later centuries, Armenians forgot their compatriots whose destiny had been linked to the Roman Empire, they simplified the complex tug-of-war of loyalties, and magnified the fate of a large part of the country into a paradigm for the whole.

To regard Christianity in Armenia as an ancestral way of life was also anachronistic for the time of Vardan. A central theme in the histories of both Ełišē and Łazar is the split between the supporters of Vardan and the supporters of the officially appointed governor, Vasak, prince of Siunik', who remained loyal to the shah. He and the leaders of many princely houses accepted Zoroastrianism, which was not a new or strange religion. Indeed it was Iranian traditions—admittedly more those of the Parthian than of the Sasanian era, but Iranian nonetheless—that were ancestral in Armenia.[53] The innovators were the Christians, who saw in this newly planted religion a focus for Armenian aspirations. In the long run their expectations were fulfilled. Christian Armenia survived the destruction of Zoroastrian Iran; and the Armenian church provided national leadership for many centuries. Never were all Armenians loyal members of that church. But Christianity did become an ancestral way of life, even if it had not been so as early as the fifth century.

There is another aspect of "ancestral" which should also be noted. When Ełišē has Vardan and the church leaders urge their followers to heroism, he quite naturally speaks in biblical terms, contrasting salvation through faith in Christ with eternal destruction through rejection of that faith. When death in battle looms before one, it is the Cross which gives

---

[52] See C. Toumanoff, *Studies in Christian Caucasian History* (Washington, D.C., 1963), pp. 133, 152; and Adontz, *Armenia*, trans. N. G. Garsoian, chs. 5–6.
[53] See Nina G. Garsoian, "Prolegomena to a Study of the Iranian Elements in Arsacid Armenia," *Handes Amsorya* 90 (1976): cols. 177–234 (reprinted in her *Armenia between Byzantium and the Sasanians*).

III

hope and the moral courage to face the enemy. However, Ełišē does not equate ancestral customs with the Christian church in the wider sense. That is, the Armenians are not fighting to preserve Christendom as a whole, but to free their fellows from the imposition of a foreign faith. In passing, it is worth noting that Armenian authors all speak of the secular loyalty owed the shah. Taxes and military service are due their sovereign, just as other Armenians serve the Roman Caesar. But Armenians do not bow their heads to fire and false deities.

If the faith extolled by Ełišē is an Armenian faith, then Armenian ancestral tradition is an exclusive rather than an inclusive one. To be sure, individual Persians may so admire the heroism of Armenian martyrs that they confess Christ themselves.[54] But Armenians do not *seek* converts for Christ. In this regard, there was a shift from earlier attitudes. In the Epic Histories the activity of Gregory the Illuminator's grandson Grigoris among the neighboring Georgians and Ałuank' (the Caucasian "Albanians") is given much attention. Grigoris is said to have met his death among the Massagetae near the Caspian Sea.[55] Towards the end of the century Maštoc' and his disciples were much occupied with preaching among the same peoples; in facts, Koriwn and later Armenian writers attribute the invention of native scripts for Georgian and Albanian to Maštoc'—a claim not supported by outside sources.

After the solid rooting of Christianity in Armenia this interest in proselytizing waned. Only in Caucasian Albania did Armenian influence have any lasting effect. Although in later years the relationships between the two peoples was often strained, the continuing use of Armenian for written texts marks the abiding impact of Armenian influence.[56] Elsewhere in the Caucasus the Armenians were resisted. And by the time that Armenian colonies were established outside the homeland (notably in the reign of Maurice and later), the concept of a "national" church had taken firm hold. The effort of Smbat Bagratuni in the early seventh century to revive a sense of Armenian identity in a colony established in Vrkan is marked by his sending a priest to teach both religion and language.[57] Religion, language, and sense of cultural identity were already interlocking.

There is no neat conclusion to be drawn from a long and complex process of Christianization. So by way of ending we may simply note the interlock-

---

[54] E.g., the *mogpet* who was in charge of the Armenian captives; see Ełišē, p. 152.
[55] P'awstos, III, 6.
[56] E.g., the *History of the Caucasian Albanians* by Movsēs Dasxuranc'i.
[57] Sebēos, *Patmut'iwn*, ed. G. V. Abgaryan (Erevan, 1979), pp. 96–97.

ing of several trends, which were not coordinated at the time, but which in retrospect were seen as a coherent whole by the formulators of the Armenian past.

By the beginning of the fourth century unknown and unorganized missionaries had reached the borders of Armenia from the Greek-speaking west and the Syriac-speaking south. The conversion of the Arsacid king Trdat (Tiridates, probably in 314) was an act of state; Trdat's personal motivation remains obscure. This act of state brought into being an official hierarchy which was run on traditional Armenian lines—the right of a prominent family to a certain office, and the succession of holders of that office from father to son (or closest relative). Opposition to Christian policy was strong among other noble families, and had political as well as social motivation.

It was not so much the officially established hierarchy as the unorganized activity of wandering holy men that effected the extension of Christianity among the populace at large. The most significant stage in this process was the development of a script for the native tongue by one of those independent missionaries, Maštoc'. In his endeavors he received support from the patriarch and king; this support meant that his disciples were able to travel to the centers of Christian learning in both Syriac- and Greek-speaking lands. With the development of a written Armenian literature came the formulation of Armenian liturgical traditions, heavily influenced by the first involvement of Armenians in the theological disputes of the time. They looked back to the first three ecumenical councils as providing correct interpretation of the faith, and came to regard Chalcedon with suspicion as leaning to the Nestorian viewpoint.

More important than doctrine was the gradual development of an individualistic attitude to their church as a common link between Armenians under different political administrations. The Armenian polity was always fragmented, the great noble families surviving by playing off one major power against another. But cultural unity, expressed through language and common traditions, was guarded by the sole group that cut across the political and social spectrum. In their later explanations of how the church authorities had attained such importance, it is not surprising that Armenian historians often evince an anachronistic attitude or compress a long, complicated process into a generation or two. Nonetheless, the Armenians, an ancient people with a long-established culture, gained with Christianization a more definite common bond and a sense of individuality.

IV

THE FORMATION OF
THE ARMENIAN LITERARY TRADITION

THIS paper attempts to assess the literary influences that shaped the development of Armenian writing down to the ninth century.[1] The main concern is with what Armenians say about themselves, and more especially with how they say it—that is, with the literary images that Armenian authors used to express their own experience.[2]

Written texts give us only part of the composite picture that Armenians built up of themselves and their place in the world around them. But the importance of written texts is enhanced by the fact that the more significant literary works not only inform us about the ideologies of their authors, their interests, and their concerns for the problems of the moment. These texts live on, become part of the historical record, and are reinterpreted in succeeding generations. So the formation of a tradition, in literary terms, is a complex procedure. Although one may point to a beginning at a specific moment—for the sake of argument, let us say the invention of the script, though in fact literary ideas and traditions in Armenia go back much earlier—so then although there may be a beginning there is no end, for traditions are being reworked all the time. And old ideas or images which have dropped out of common use, or even common knowledge, may surface again, as in the Armenian renaissance beginning in the eighteenth century, when the heroes of ancient Armenia reemerge as national symbols.

But tradition may also have a life of its own. In literary terms this is nicely illustrated by the Armenian interpretation of St. Athanasius of Alexandria. Many of his works were translated into Armenian, some in the fifth century, some a little later. But these accurate renderings of the Greek did not have a very wide circulation and only a few manuscripts containing the early translations survive. On the other hand, quotations from Athanasius abounded in florilegia, dogmatic treatises, official letters, and other such documents which quoted the great fathers of the church as authorities for certain theological positions. But, as is well known, such collections of quotations are likely to be tendentious, and curious changes sometimes creep in. Thus in some texts Athanasius is portrayed as the champion of the anti-Chalcedonian view espoused by the Gregorian Armenians.[3] There is nothing peculiarly Armenian about such distortions. But the purpose of the illustration is to suggest that different views of the same person or event may well coexist, and hence that it may be difficult to speak of *the* Armenian literary tradition. The historical texts reflect the fragmented state of Armenian society, even though by a natural tendency toward simplification many Armenian

Reprinted from *East of Byzantium: Syria and Armenia in the Formative Period*, ed. Nina G. Garsoïan, Thomas F. Mathews and Robert W. Thomson, Washington, D.C., 1982, pp. 135-150. Copyright © Trustees for Harvard University. Reprinted by permission.

IV

136

historians did gloss over the divisions within their country,⁴ and many of their simplifications have lived on.

My general purpose in what follows is twofold. First, to indicate in general terms those literary models that were used by Armenian writers. And second, to elaborate in greater detail on how Armenian writers adapted their models and literary themes to the Armenian situation and formulated their response to problems of their own time. I begin by plunging into two texts in order to indicate the kind of adaptations that might be made. I shall then go back to the origins of Armenian literature and attempt to build up a more general picture of Armenian writing, its themes, and its interests.

We have in Armenian two accounts of the revolt against Iran that culminated in defeat for the Armenians on the battlefield at Avarayr in 451. The shorter account, that in the historian Łazar, was written within fifty years of the event—though the text of Łazar as we now have it has been subjected to later embellishment.⁵ The longer account is by Ełišē, the date of whose work is a matter of fierce dispute.⁶ But here it is only important to note that Ełišē has introduced into his narrative—or rather, has so framed his narrative to include—concerns of a more general religious and patriotic nature. Some interesting contrasts emerge when we compare the two accounts of the harangues to the Armenian troops before the final battle.

Łazar claims that both the Armenian general Vardan and the priest Łewond addressed the troops. The priest Łewond spoke of the glorious fate of previous Christian martyrs, especially St. Gregory the Illuminator, and urged the soldiers to hasten to share in the inheritance of the saints in the heavenly Jerusalem. (The reference to Gregory is particularly relevant to Łazar, for the patron of his *History* is Vahan Mamikonean, uncle of the martyred Vardan, descended from a marriage tie between the family of Gregory and that of the Mamikoneans.) The general Vardan then repeated the same exhortation to martyrdom, again reminding the Armenians of St. Gregory. Each of these speeches is summarized by Łazar in one paragraph.⁷

But Ełišē's account is very different. Some time before the battle he has Vardan give a four-page exhortation. Vardan urges the soldiers to accept a holy death, but on no account to mingle cowardice with valor. This contrast of earthly cowardice and heavenly valor or virtue is an important theme that runs through the whole of Ełišē from beginning to end, based not only on biblical themes but also on passages taken from the Armenian version of Philo.⁸ Vardan then reminds his troops of the cause for which they are fighting: their ancestral and divinely bestowed religion. This is repeated later, always in terms taken directly from the Armenian version of Maccabees. Particularly significant is the fact that the term religion used by Ełišē (awrenkᶜ) is a literal rendering of the Greek nomoi. It carries in Armenian the connotation of a whole way of life and does not refer to specifically religious practices separate from traditional mores.⁹ Vardan does not refer to the Armenian example of Gregory or even explicitly mention earlier Christian martyrs.

Following this speech, says Ełišē, Vardan continued to encourage his soldiers, not neglecting the argument of liberal pay; and then Ełišē gives a brief summary of the wars of the Maccabees which, he claims, Vardan had read out to the whole army. That summary is important, not merely because of the specific comparison between the situation of the Armenians and that of the Jews facing Antiochus, but for bringing out other themes vital to Ełišē's *History*: not only martyrdom for traditional laws, but also the themes of the holy covenant to which not all Armenians (or Jews) had been faithful, the temples and impure rites of the foreign and heathen Persians (or Greeks), and the contrast between those who held firm to the end and those who slackened. All these themes had been woven into Ełišē's *History* from the very beginning and reappear in the later section that describes the fate of prisoners in Iran following the defeat at Avarayr.[10]

Closer to the time of the battle, according to Ełišē, the priest Łewond gave another address to the Armenian troops, which runs to eight pages in the Armenian text.[11] Łewond begins with an injunction to remember our forefathers who lived before the birth of Christ. In elaborate fashion he recalls the great models of virtue in the Old Testament: Noah, Abraham, Moses, Pinehas, who removed profanation by slaughter, David, who scattered the forces of foreign invaders, the generals of ancient Israel who purified their land from heathen idolatry. What is particularly interesting about this speech is not the absence of Christian parallels or references to St. Gregory, nor even the recollection of Old Testament heroes, but the close parallel in structure with the speech of Mattathias to his sons before his death as given in I Macc. 2.

So the contrast between Łazar and Ełišē in their approach to the same events is striking. Łazar is concerned primarily with the overt glory of the Mamikonean family to which his patron belonged, and the specifically Armenian hero Gregory. Ełišē is more subtle. His hero is the same Vardan, but the cause for which he fights is a combination of heavenly virtue and Armenian ancestral traditions. Although Łazar twice uses the term "ancestral" in his *History* with reference to Armenian customs and religion, he does not make this the overriding theme. Neither historian wishes to recall that in fact Christianity was not the ancient, ancestral religion of Armenia but marked a new turn in Armenian culture that had not won complete acceptance even by the time of the revolt led by Vardan.[12] But only Ełišē sees such a direct parallel between the Armenians and the Maccabees that not only is his whole work suffused with verbal reminiscences of the Armenian version of those books, but its basic structure depends on themes taken from them. It is not the Christian martyrs from the times of Roman or Sasanian persecution who are explicitly cited as examples—though the influence of both Greek and Syriac hagiography is profound in Ełišē[13]—but the heroes of Israel who made no distinction between religion and patriotism.

There is another Armenian writer who sees an even closer link between Armenia and ancient Israel—Movsēs Xorenacʻi. Like the generality of Armenian historians he is concerned with the glory of his patrons—in this case the Bagratuni family, whose ancestry he traces back to one of the leading Jews taken captive by Nebuchadnezzar.[14] But of more direct concern for the present theme is Movsēs' general approach to Armenian history. For despite his specific glorification of the Bagratids, Movsēs is unique among Armenian historians of the period before 900 in trying to place Armenia on the stage of world history. That is, Movsēs not only traces the development of the Armenian nation from its origins in the days of the giants and sets out the descent of the earliest Armenian rulers from Japheth, he places the story of Armenia in its historical perspective vis-à-vis the great empires of the past.[15] At the very end of the first book of his *History* Movsēs gives himself away—or at least admits to a susceptibility to wishful thinking: referring to the Armenian Zarmayr who led a small Ethiopian army to assist Priam in the Trojan war, Movsēs notes that Zarmayr was killed at Ilium: "By Achilles I would like to think and not by any other hero."

Now although Movsēs refers to Homer by name in this paragraph, he is not in fact quoting from the Iliad but from the description of the Trojan war in the *Chronicle* of Eusebius. And it is on the basic framework of the *Chronicle* that Movsēs bases his whole first book, appropriately entitled "Genealogy of Armenia." The debt of Movsēs to the *Chronicle* and to Eusebius' *Church History* (which was also available in Armenian translation, this one from Syriac rather than directly from the Greek) has been examined elsewhere.[16] But Movsēs also had another model in mind. He frequently refers to antiquarians or antiquarian lore, and opens the third book by stating: "there is no study of the antiquity of our land." The term in Armenian is "hnaχawsut‛iwn," a calque on the Greek ἀρχαιολογία. Moses seems to be the first to use this particular word and its cognate hnaχaws for "antiquarian," though the first chapter of the Armenian version of Dionysius Thrax's *Ars Grammatica* renders ἱστορία by "hnagēt patmut‛iwn."[17] Now ἀρχαιολογία is a term used frequently by Greek writers for a title to histories, the most famous being Josephus' Ἰουδαϊκὴ ἀρχαιολογία. Movsēs' debt to Josephus therefore deserves further comment.

It is ironic that Movsēs quotes Josephus by name five times but on each occasion either the information is not in Josephus or Movsēs has used a different source. It is, for example, a common thing for Movsēs to use Eusebius' *Chronicle* and *Church History* as direct sources; and if Eusebius mentions an earlier writer on whom he was relying, Movsēs claims that he used that source directly himself. So, in describing the worms that grew inside Herod because of his presumption against Christ, Movsēs adds "as Josephus narrates." But Movsēs' description is taken from Eusebius, where Josephus is indeed quoted as the source.[18] Perversely, Movsēs' *direct* use of Josephus is unacknowledged. In his second book, Movsēs elaborates on the account in Josephus' *Jewish Wars* of the wars between Rome and Parthia in order to boost the role of the Armenian kings Tigran and Artawazd. The involvement of Tigran in Palestine then gives Movsēs an opportunity to explain the origin of the numerous Jewish colonies in Armenia known to him from the Armenian history P‛awstos Buzand.[19]

But more important than the rewriting of history to the greater glory of Tigran or of the Bagratids was Movsēs' basic attitude to his country and its historical role. The passage (I 3) is famous, but it merits repetition. Movsēs is commending his patron for commissioning this *History of the Armenian People* and contrasting his interest with the neglect of earlier Armenian princes:

> I do not wish to leave the unscholarly habits of our first ancestors without a word of censure, but to insert here at the very beginning of our work the reason for reprehending them. If in truth those kings are worthy of praise who in written accounts fixed and ordered their annals and wise acts and inscribed each one's valour in narratives and histories, then like them the compilers of books or

IV

THE ARMENIAN LITERARY TRADITION

archives who were occupied with similar efforts are worthy of our eulogies. Through these, I say, when we read their accounts we become informed about the course of the world, and we learn about the state of civilization when we peruse such wise discourses and narratives—those of the Chaldaeans, Assyrians, Egyptians and Hellenes. It is indeed to the wisdom of these men, who undertook such studies, that we aspire.

So then it is clear to us all that our kings and other forefathers were negligent towards scholarship and unconcerned with the life of reason. For although we are a small country and very restricted in numbers, weak in power, and often subject to another's rule, yet many manly deeds have been performed in our land worthy of being recorded in writing; nonetheless, not one of these undertook to have them written down.

The first paragraph is based on Eusebius, who at the beginning of his *Chronicle* refers to the same peoples who have written histories in the same order. The second paragraph is more interesting. "We are a small country, very restricted in numbers"—there are verbal parallels here with the Armenian text of the opening of Josephus' *Jewish Wars*: "They disparage the actions of the Jews. But I fail to see how the conquerors of a small people deserved to be accounted great." Movsēs "reprehends" the unscholarly habits of our ancestors as Josephus "reprehends" the Greeks. Both make a great "effort" to present a "faithful" but "brief" account of their respective nations' histories, not injecting anything "inappropriate" but expounding only the "truth."

To enter into a more detailed discussion of Josephus' influence on Movsēs would take us away from the main theme.[20] But it should be fairly clear that by the time of Ełišē and Movsēs, Armenian historians were capable of sophisticated interpretations of events and could adapt foreign sources to the Armenian situation with considerable finesse. Let us now go back to the beginning and see how Armenian literary interests and skills developed.

It would be misleading to begin with the invention of the Armenian script by Maštocʿ around A.D. 400.[21] That invention was of profound significance for the transposition of Armenian learning into the Armenian idiom. But one must not suppose that there had been no Armenian learning or scholarship before the time of Maštocʿ. Five hundred years earlier the enthusiasm of King Tigran for Greek culture was widely noted by classical writers; and Plutarch extols the tragedies, orations, and histories of Tigran's son, King Artawazd—though alas nothing has survived.[22] Of more direct relevance to Christian Armenia was the fact that in the fourth century numerous Armenians studied under Libanius in Antioch; his correspondence with Armenian pupils spans two generations.[23] And individuals from Armenia might make a name for themselves in the Greco-Roman world. Prohaeresius, for example, came from Persian Armenia.[24] As a Christian sophist working in Athens, he included among his pupils Basil of Caesarea and Gregory Nazianzenus. Of course we have to beware of claiming such international figures imbued with Hellenistic learning as being consciously

Armenian. It may be that, as in the Byzantium of later centuries, one's ethnic origin was of less importance than one's cultural orientation.

It was therefore perfectly natural for a young Armenian of good family to receive an education in Greek literature, as did Maštocᶜ, the later inventor of the Armenian alphabet. His biographer Koriwn gives us scant details of his early life, concentrating his energies on Maštocᶜ's Christian virtues as monk and missionary. But Koriwn does expressly state: "In the years of his youth he was educated in Greek literature (varžeal hellenakan dprutᶜeamb)" before becoming attached to the royal divan at the Arsacid court. So when Maštocᶜ finally was able to fashion a script for Armenian in the city of Samosata, we are not surprised to read that he was aided by a certain scribe named Rufinus, who is described as being versed in Greek literature (hellenakan dprutᶜean).[25] However, Maštocᶜ's purpose in inventing an Armenian script was not to make the literature of antiquity available to his fellow countrymen who had not had the benefit of a classical education; his efforts were entirely directed to providing Christian texts needed for missionary work and for the strengthening of the church in Armenia. According to Koriwn, Maštocᶜ's first translation, made with two of his pupils, was the book of Proverbs.[26] This they took back to Armenia from Samosata as an example of what could be accomplished with the new script. And Koriwn then compares Maštocᶜ's triumphal return home with the descent of Moses from Mount Sinai bearing in his arms the divine law. The joy of the Armenians in having the words of God in Armenian (hayabarbaṙ, hayerēnaχaws) was indeed no less than that of the Israelites on seeing the tablets inscribed in Hebrew. This and other elaborate comparisons in Koriwn's biography are illustrations of the influence of Greek rhetorical practice—here sunkrisis—on the earliest compositions in Armenian. We shall return later to the formal Armenian texts on rhetoric.

The next task of Maštocᶜ and the Armenian patriarch Sahak was to organize groups of young pupils who were set to learning the new script. Many of these young men were then sent abroad with instructions to render into Armenian the most important Christian texts in Syriac and Greek. So rather than the centers of pagan learning, it was now the turn of Edessa, Melitene, and most notably Constantinople, to see an influx of Armenian students, though we should not ignore the continuation of traditional pagan study. Zacharias Rhetor, for example, who studied in Beirut with Severus, notes the presence of an Armenian among the law students who were renowned in magic.[27]

Although we could draw up a long catalogue of works translated into Armenian in the fifth century,[28] the Armenian writers of that period themselves rarely mention titles. Koriwn refers to "many inspired books of the fathers of the church," to Sahak's translation of the "collection of ecclesiastical writings"—generally interpreted as the bible—to commentaries on scripture and to the canons of Nicaea and Ephesus which were brought back from Constantinople by Eznik, Łewond, and Koriwn himself.[29] And, according to Koriwn, Maštocᶜ later composed many homilies based on scripture with special emphasis on the hope of the resurrection, in order to arouse the ignorant and those occupied with worldy affairs to the good news. There has been some debate as to whether any surviving Armenian homilies are to be identified with Maštocᶜ's own compositions. The answer is probably no.[30] But from our point of view the significant thing is that Armenians earlier set to translating now were composing original works in Armenian. This helps explain the amazing rapidity with which Armenian literature developed.

The next stage in our discussion will be to examine the adaptation to specifically Armenian situations of Greek and Syriac texts that were studied and translated by the succeeding generations of Armenians.

Adaptation can be deliberate (whether acknowledged or not) or unconscious. By the latter I mean the use of literary topoi that were "in the air," so to speak. Just as Maštocʿ's homilies were reportedly drawn from the scriptures, so later works might reflect the Armenian versions of John Chrysostom, Gregory Nazianzenus, Eusebius, or even the Alexander Romance, without any deliberate attempt to deceive or mislead. Some specific examples should clarify the distinction between deliberate adaptations and the use of topoi.

In the *History* of Agatʿangełos which describes the conversion of Armenia and the work of St. Gregory the Illuminator, we read that Gregory's son Aristakēs attended the council of Nicaea. (And his name does indeed appear in the list of signatories.)[31] He also supposedly brought back to Armenia the Nicene canons—to which St. Gregory made additions, thereby rendering his own see of Armenia still more glorious. However, this passage is based on Koriwn's description of the return of Eznik and Łewond from Constantinople.[32] In fact, this whole section of Agatʿangełos is borrowed, often verbatim, from Koriwn; for Agatʿangełos credits Gregory with the missionary endeavors undertaken by Maštocʿ, and even ascribes to Gregory the same homilies concerning the hope of the resurrection. This is what I would call a deliberate, fraudulent, but unacknowledged adaptation.

On the other hand, in the first part of his *History*, Agatʿangełos describes the torments inflicted on Gregory and the martyred nuns in terms very reminiscent of common hagiographical themes. As with the anti-Christian edicts ascribed to Trdat before his conversion, Agatʿangełos is merely following standard literary practice, fleshing out his narrative with picturesque details taken from the hagiographical stockpot.[33] However, if one looks at the *History* as a whole, then a more meaningful parallel does come to mind.

The text of Agatʿangełos as we have it in Armenian is not the product of the circle around Maštocʿ. But here we are not concerned with the dating, with the subsequent additions to the story, or with the variants in other languages. It is the general format that is of relevance. Roughly speaking, the material falls into the following stages:

1. The scene is set for the arrival of a missionary from abroad.
2. The king is converted because of the miraculous cure effected by the missionary.
3. The missionary preaches a very long sermon expounding the Christian faith.
4. The king encourages the building of churches and the establishment of a regular ecclesiastical hierarchy.
5. The proper succession within that hierarchy is arranged before the death of the original missionary.

It is no coincidence that the general structure of Agatʿangełos' *History* follows the pattern of the Syriac *Teaching of Addai*. Although for Agatʿangełos Gregory is the prime mover in the conversion of Armenia and he makes no effort to push the story back to apostolic times, the story of the conversion of Edessa had been known in Armenian from the fifth century, and was presumably familiar from Greek and Syriac sources even earlier.[34] Addai, in fact, was later adopted as the first missionary in Armenia, and Abgar came to join the roster of Armenian monarchs.[35] But for our immediate purpose, the *History* of Agatʿangełos gives us examples of three kinds of adaptation:

1. Of general format
2. Of literary themes or topoi
3. Of deliberate falsification

I am not suggesting that there is anything peculiarly Armenian about this kind of borrowing and adaptation. But our theme is how such devices were used in an Armenian context.

If, then, we turn our attention to those basic works in which Armenian authors expressed their views of Armenia and the Armenians as an individual people and country, we should not be surprised to find that many of the concepts used or even the framework do not have their origin in Armenia itself. Thus Koriwn begins his biography of the master with the following words: "When was the divinely-bestowed script completed for the race of Aškenaz and the land of Armenia?" Note the order of the Armenian: "zAzkʿanazean azgin ew Hayastan ašχarhin zAstuacapargew groyn. . . ." With the very first word Armenia is placed within the framework of the biblical exposition of the origin of mankind.[36]

This introductory phrase of Koriwn was later adapted by Agatʿangełos, with one interesting change. In the *Prologue* to his *History*, like Koriwn, he explains what his subject will be: the bringing of the divinely bestowed gospel (again Astuacapargew) to the race of Torgom and the land of Armenia (zTʿorgomay azgis, zHayastan ašχarhis). Toward the end of the book, when the king had been converted, then "the grace of the gospel flowed forth for the Armenians of the house of Tʿorgom," a phrase repeated again.[37] And even earlier than Agatʿangełos, the phrase "house of Torgom" appears in the canons of the council of Šahapivan held in 444.[38] Except for Koriwn, Armenian writers generally consider that Torgom rather than Aškenaz provides the link between Japheth and the Armenians, following the Greek tradition already established by the time of Hippolytus.[39] But sometimes one reads of "our Aškenaz,"[40] and Movsēs Xorenacʿi uses the reference in Jeremiah 51:27 to "the kingdoms of Ararat and the army of Aškenaz" to prove the existence of an Armenian kingdom at that time.[41]

The *geographical* distribution of the various races that descended from Noah receives some attention in Armenian writers, but only after the period with which we are here concerned. However, from the beginning Armenians regarded themselves as living "in the Northern regions," a phrase found first in Koriwn and emphasized several times by Agatʿangełos. Ełišē refers to the "benighted regions of the North which

King Trdat illuminated by his faith in Christ." Movsēs Xorenacʿi speaks of Armenia as being in the North by way of contrast with Babylon and Assyria, and he notes that Armenia is "superior to all other nations of the North."[42]

But in general early Armenian writers paid little attention to geography. They take for granted the threefold division of the world into Europe, Libya, and Asia known to the classical geographers, Armenia being in Asia.[43] This division, however, does not correspond to the division of the human race into three branches as descendants of Sem, Ham, and Japheth. For according to this second division the Japhetic nations occupied lands in both Asia and Europe.[44] But Armenian writers do tend to correlate the two divisions without indicating that there may be discrepancies.[45]

In their accounts of the settlement of these Northern regions by their ancestors, Armenian sources indicate that there were already a few scattered human settlements even before the arrival of the Armenian eponymous ancestor Hayk. These sources, the so-called *Primary History*[46] and Movsēs Xorenacʿi, integrate the story of Hayk's coming to Armenia into the account of the tyranny of Bel the Titan as known from Eusebius' *Chronicle*. The tale of Hayk's successors and their expansion over the land had supposedly been preserved by a certain Syrian, Mār Abas, who took it from an old inscription. Elaborating on this, Movsēs Xorenacʿi claims that the earliest source for Armenian history had been written in "Chaldaean" and had been deposited in the Parthian archives at Nineveh. Alexander the Great had had a Greek version made, from which Mār Abas extracted what was relevant.

The idea that traditional legends may be authenticated by discoveries in archives is a very old theme.[47] In a Christian context the correspondence between Jesus and King Abgar preserved in the archives of Edessa immediately springs to mind—and in fact is relevant to our theme, since Movsēs claims that Abgar was an Armenian monarch and that the Edessan archives also contained other documents relevant for Armenian history. But the content of Mār Abas' find at Nineveh is an amalgam of information from Eusebius' *Chronicle* and remembered Armenian tradition, which Movsēs has reworked to the greater glory of his patrons, the Bagratids. We would have been saved much ink and paper if more attention had been paid to Movsēs' clever use of a literary device than to the assumed integrity of the historian.

But of more relevance to our immediate theme is the fact that Armenian geographical interests are restricted to political geography. There is only one major work of geography in early Armenian literature, the *Ašχarhacʿoycʿ*, which probably dates from the seventh century.[48] But its unknown author is not interested in the physical geography of Armenia; although he has a few comments on the fauna of various regions and describes the rivers and mountains, his prime concern is with the borders of the different provinces. Of course the classical geographers were also concerned with borders and frontiers. But the detailed divisions and subdivisions of the *Ašχarhacʿoycʿ* do remind one of the careful listings of noble families, the *Gahnamaks*, which recorded the order of precedence so vital for the harmonious regulation of the naχarar system.[49]

The Armenians hardly ignored the natural beauties of their land. But it is noteworthy that the numerous rhetorical descriptions of Armenia's scenery are couched in terms of the ideal outdoor life of the noble and his pleasure in the hunt.[50] Again, these are features basic to the naxarar structure of Armenian society. The Armenian idealized landscapes are a far cry from the groves of Statius or Ovid, for they do not reflect the stylized longings of city culture. On the other hand, images from nature do play a large role in Armenian literature; but these are primarily themes with a Christian content which have their closest parallels in the Cappadocian fathers. The sea and voyaging, for example, are very common themes; but they are taken from biblical and patristic sources rather than from a common Armenian experience. And images of birds and trees, of the wonders of the seasons—especially of spring—are literary topoi paralleled in Gregory Nazianzenus and other fathers well known in Armenian.[51]

In this regard it is particularly interesting to note the influence of such works as Basil of Caesarea's *Hexaemeron* in a context neither literary nor theological. As noted above, the prime interest of Maštocʿ's circle of pupils was on providing Armenia with ecclesiastical texts. To that effect, they studied abroad and became proficient in Syriac and Greek. This pattern of foreign study was not new in Maštocʿ's own time, and for many hundreds of years it remained a standard feature of Armenian scholarly life. So it is not surprising that within a few generations of the invention of the script Armenian versions of secular Greek texts began to appear, notably of the texts used in Constantinople and elsewhere for rhetoric, grammar, logic, followed by Armenian adaptations of mathematical and astronomical studies. The peculiar thing about many of these works is not their content but their style.[52] But of interest here is the fact that one of the works on science attributed to the seventh-century Armenian mathematician Anania of Širak is but a rewriting of the Armenian version of Basil's *Hexaemeron*, a version which itself is very aberrant from the original.[53]

Now Anania is interesting for another reason. He has left a short autobiographical statement in which he describes his travels in search of teachers of mathematics. After visiting Theodosiopolis and Constantinople, he eventually found a suitably learned instructor in Trebizond. This man was named Tychikos; he had been born in Trebizond, had served in the Roman army in Armenia during the reign of Tiberius (578-82), and there he had learned Armenian. Wounded in a Persian attack on Antioch (c. 606/7), he visited Jerusalem and then spent three years in Alexandria. From there he went to Rome for a year and finished his studies in Constantinople. Finally he returned to his hometown, where Anania met him. Anania ends his own autobiographical sketch with pejorative comments about his fellow countrymen's ignorance; he pours scorn on those pupils of his who studied with him for only a short time before setting up on their own: "They taught what they did not know; hypocrites, they pretended to possess knowledge and demanded to be addressed as 'teacher.' "[54] Similar sentiments may be found in the *Letter* of the historian Łazar (though its authenticity is suspect), in which he defends himself against his calumniators by emphasizing his own learning gained in Greek lands by studying the great Fathers of the church, whereas his enemies were pupils of Arius, Apollinarius, Nestorius, and Eutyches—an unlikely combination of teachers! They were ignorant and lazy, says Łazar, and to them applies the proverb: "At a pig's wedding the baths are sewers."[55]

But more important for our theme than such examples of scholars' pique is the itinerary of studies that Anania ascribes to Tychikos. It is picked up, for example, by Movsēs Xorenacʻi. He claims to have been sent to study rhetoric in Alexandria; he then went to Rome, being blown to Italy while making for Greece. From Rome he went on to Athens and Constantinople. Unfortunately, the death of his master Maštocʻ cut short his merry time at the capital—for Movsēs was a young man and very fond of dancing—and he had to return home.[56] And at the end of his *History*, writing as an old man with an old man's jaundiced view of the world, not only does Movsēs say, "Students are lazy to study and eager to teach; they are theologians before their examinations," he adds, "Even the teachers are ignorant and presumptuous, lovers of gold and envious." The description of his journey is based on literary sources, for Movsēs was writing about 300 years after the events he describes; and his account of Alexandria owes much to Pseudo-Callisthenes. Another journey from the eighth century also seems to be based on the grand tour of Tychikos. In this case the traveler is Stephen of Siwnikʻ, among whose important translations is the work of Pseudo-Dionysius the Areopagite. There are several versions of his travels in later sources. The first, Movsēs Dasχurancʻi, says that Stephen went to Rome to study and brought back books of the faith. It is not immediately clear whether Old or New Rome is meant, though Movsēs then adds a garbled version of the Iliad and Aeneid and notes that 1000 years after the founding of Rome Constantine transferred the kingdom to Byzantium. But later versions have Stephen staying in Constantinople and Athens. From there he went to Rome, then returned home "having traveled thousands of miles on the bosom of the vast ocean."[57] It is difficult to take these later elaborations as gospel truth; but the important thing is that there was a recognized pattern of scholarly travel which included Athens and Rome as well as the known Armenian colony in Constantinople. Although this had a basis in fact, it was elaborated in literary texts as a topos.

The emergence of Athens and Rome in Armenian texts as great centers of learning naturally leads to the question of Armenian knowledge of classical antiquity and its literature, Constantinople and Alexandria being important to Armenians as Christian cities. The Armenian interest in Aristotelian logic and Neoplatonism would naturally make Athens a necessary stop on the grand tour. But Rome and the Trojan war were more remote to Armenian concerns, despite the reference noted above in Movsēs Xorenacʻi. What then did Armenians know of classical literature that would influence their own literary concerns and interests?

There are clear borrowings in Eznik, for example, one of the earliest Armenian writers, from Achilles Tatius. This Achilles is not the Alexandrian novelist but the author of a commentary on the *Phainomena* of Aratus. Eznik quotes from him when describing the immobility of the earth in the middle of the celestial sphere, and in offering an example of apparent versus real motion: for an ant crawling from west to east on the rim of a wheel that is itself turning from east to west, because of the more rapid motion of the wheel seems to be moving in a westerly direction. Although Eznik is untypical in using Greek texts in the original, he is typical in using a late antique source of the second or third century A.D., rather than going back to the earlier authors.[58] More widely known, because available in Armenian, was the *Progymnasmata* of the Alexandrian rhetorician Theon;[59] on this, and on the *Progymnasmata* of Aphthonius, was based an Armenian guide to rhetoric later ascribed to Movsēs Xorenacʿi.[60] But these translations, like those of the *Scholia* to Gregory Nazianzenus by Nonnus,[61] were not the product of the first translators but of the Hellenizing school—if indeed one should use the term "school" of texts that share certain linguistic peculiarities as their basic common feature.

It was through such works of rhetoric, through scholia, through works on grammar (for the *Ars Grammatica* of Dionysius Thrax was translated and adapted for the Armenian language),[62] and through the Armenian version of the *Alexander Romance*[63] that Armenians learned of the world of antiquity. There was no rendering of Euripides, Thucydides, Hesiod, or Callimachus—to take some names at random. Of Homer, however, it is more difficult to be sure. The only extant translation was made in the eighteenth century. But there are numerous references in manuscripts to Homer the poet and to a philosopher Homer.[64] In a sixteenth-century manuscript in Paris there is a vocabulary of Homeric words;[65] and in a manuscript of 1776 dealing with grammar there are miniatures of Maštocʿ, the translators, the eighth-century Stephen of Siwnikʿ, the seventeenth-century Simeon of Julfa, and Homer.[66] Among the books of Stephen of Siwnikʿ there was supposedly an account of the destruction of Ilium and the building of Rome, of which Movsēs Dasχurancʿi gives a summary.[67] But his tale is such an extraordinary imbroglio that one must doubt whether the historian was really familar with either the Iliad or the Aeneid.

Since the world of classical antiquity was not meaningful for Armenians, it is interesting to note how some of the Greek technical texts were adapted for an Armenian audience. For example, the rendering of the *Definitions of Philosophy* attributed to David the Invincible Philosopher omits most references to Alcibiades, who would be unknown, and to gymnastics, which was not a typically Armenian sport. It changes Hector to Tigran, and turns Greek mythological creatures into Armenian ones such as the višap. On occasion nymphs are metamorphosed into angels and demons; other such liberties are taken.[68] But original Armenian literature in its formative stage was definitely the product of a Christian culture in which reminiscences of classical pagan antiquity were used only for decorative effect.

From the point of view of literary *tradition* the significant works are those that set a trend and are later perceived as authoritative. Thus Eznik's treatise on God and the nature of evil[69] will not in the long run be as significant—despite its intrinsic value both as historical evidence and as an example of philosophical reasoning—as the *History* of Ełišē. For Eznik did not set a pattern, either in form or matter. The emphasis that textbooks of classical Armenian put on Eznik as a stylist is somewhat misplaced,[70] in that his style is most untypical and his work was more or less unknown to Armenians after his own time. On the other hand, Ełišē has lived on through the centuries to the present day, and his *History* has shaped the outlook of succeeding generations of Armenians to questions of patriotism and national identity.

Our symposium is concerned with Armenia and Syria up to the ninth century. In Armenia some fields of literary endeavor did not mature until well after that time: biblical commentaries, for example, or most forms of poetry. Nonetheless, the ninth century does mark an important stage in the development of Armenian literature, and most especially historical writing. For after the ninth century scholars made conscious efforts to put the past in order—that is, to sort out the previous histories, to place them in a chronological progression, and to fill in details about their authors. It is after the ninth century that the major figures I have had occasion to mention are grouped together to form a body of disciples of a common master, Maštoc͑. It would take us beyond our present purpose to study in detail this process of physical assimilation, whereby Ełišē, Movsēs Xorenac͑i, David the Invincible Philosopher, and others, become contemporaries of Koriwn and Eznik and share their journeys to Constantinople and elsewhere.[71] Thanks to this impulse to group the formative writers around the master, not as pupils many times removed or pupils by a common heritage, but as direct associates, we are able to celebrate this year the fifteen hundredth anniversary of David the Invincible Philosopher.

But if one looks at the historical productions and other literary works of Armenia in what we have called the "formative period," does any general picture emerge? Are there any common characteristics that are peculiarly Armenian? Let us, then, review the main themes of the preceding discussion.

Whether or not the literary interests of Armenians at Tigran's court in the first century B.C. had any lasting impact that carried over into Christian times is hard to say. For example, Euripides had been popular, as Plutarch indicates. But there was no theater in Christian Armenia, and those Armenian homilies which attack theatrical productions seem to reflect the continuation of Christian literary themes rather than dangers to Armenian morals.[72] (In parentheses I may add that many conclusions about social life in Armenia based solely on literal readings of such homilies rest on a precarious footing; just as in Ełišē, for example, one cannot draw conclusions about fifth-century Armenian arms and armor from Pauline imagery.) However, the not inconsiderable number of Armenians who studied and traveled abroad would have been personally familiar with the Greek theater, and would have kept alive in Armenia proper an appreciation of the merits of a classical education.

In Christian Armenia horizons were broadened by the influence of Syriac. Before the invention of the Armenian script, according to P͑awstos Buzand, only those with some acquaintance of Greek or Syriac were able to grasp the full significance of the Christian message. For only those with knowledge of either tongue could resist the appeal of Armenian pagan mythology with its lively oral traditions.[73] P͑awstos had his axe to grind. But the influence of Syrian Christian literature in fourth-century Armenia was a new and significant development. After the invention of the script a vast mass of Syriac literature was rendered into Armenian, both original Syriac works like the homilies of Afrahat or the hymns of Ephrem, and translations into Syriac such as Eusebius' *Ecclesiastical History*. However, the influence of Syrian themes on Armenian writing has not been studied in depth.[74] The fairly obvious impact of hagiographical imagery, for example, that of the Syrian Martyrs on the *History* of Ełišē, is well known.[75] But the more significant influence of Syriac works on Armenian theological writing in its various forms has hardly been broached, save for the study of liturgical texts. For up to now the study of Armenian theology has mostly been restricted to the more formal works, those dealing with Christological problems where the influence was more palpably Greek.

In view of the long-standing involvement of Armenia in the Greco-Roman world it is natural that Greek literature provided the most influential models in the development of a native historiography, and that Constantinople was regarded (in Łazar's words) as the fountain of science whose streams spread out in all directions.[76] Nonetheless, for complex reasons that would take another paper to expound, the Armenians never identified themselves wholly with Greek culture. Nor did they find solidarity in their Christian culture with their neighbors the Syrians or the Georgians. Armenian literature reflects this sense of separateness, for although nearly all writers were ecclesiastics, they were very conscious of belonging to a society that was foreign to the city culture of the Hellenistic world and of sharing ancient traditions that derived from the Iranian world. In their effort to articulate this sense of Armenian individuality, early writers found many parallels with the situation of the Jews in Seleucid times. The imagery adapted byEłišē from the books of Maccabees to the Sasanian period was adapted again by Tʿovma Arcruni[77] to the Armenian situation under Muslim domination, and remains vivid to the present day as a reflection of Armenian experience. So the formative period of Armenian literature that we have been considering is of profound significance. For it has shaped the expression of a national ethos that is as alive today as it was in the days of Maštocʿ.

---

1. The 9th century is an appropriate terminus, for by then the most influential Armenian histories had been written and it is only *after* the 9th century that these major works are quoted and adapted and that legends about their rather obscure authors begin to emerge.

2. For a convenient summary of Armenian literature, see V. Inglisian, "Die armenische Literatur," *HO*, 1, 7 (1963), 156-250. The present paper attempts to generalize and to expand on some of the topics of a literary nature treated in the introductions to English translations of three classics of early Armenian historiography: R. W. Thomson, *Agathangelos: History of the Armenians* (Albany, 1976); R. W. Thomson, Moses Khorenatsʿi, *History of the Armenians* (Cambridge, Mass., 1978); R. W. Thomson, *Ełishē: History of Vardan and the Armenian War* (in press).

3. On this, see R. W. Thomson, "The Transformation of Athanasius in Armenian Theology," *Le Muséon*, 78 (1965), 47-69.

4. See, for example, N. G. Garsoïan, "Politique ou orthodoxie? L'Arménie au quatrième siècle," *REArm*, n.s. 4 (1967), 297-320.

5. Łazar Pʿarpecʿi, *Patmutʿiwn Hayocʿ*, ed. G. Tēr-Mkrtčʿean and S. Malxasean (Tiflis, 1904) is the only critical edition. But for fragments that predate the recension known from the manuscripts, see C. Sanspeur, "Le fragment de l'histoire de Lazare de Pʿarpi, retrouvé dans le Ms. 1 de Jérusalem," *REArm*, n.s. 10 (1973-74), 83-109; and C. J. F. Dowsett, "The Newly Discovered Fragment of Lazar of Pʿarp's History," *Le Muséon*, 89 (1976), 97-122.

6. Ełišē, *Vasn Vardanay ew Hayocʿ Paterazmin*, ed. E. Tēr-Minasean (Erevan, 1957). On the date, see Inglisian, "Armenische Literatur," 168-69.

7. Łazar, 70-71.

8. Ełišē, 100-104. For the parallels in Philo, see the introduction to Thomson, *Ełishē* (in press).

9. See R. W. Thomson, "The Maccabees in Early Armenian Historiography," *JThS*, n.s. 26 (1975), 329-41.

10. Ełišē, 105.

11. Ełišē, 106-13.

12. Fourth-century opposition to Christianity is described in detail by Pʿawstos Buzand. The biography of Maštocʿ (inventor of the Armenian script) by his pupil Koriwn makes it clear that in the first part of the 5th century Christianity had only a tenuous hold in many parts of the country. Both Łazar and Ełišē draw attention to the large number of Armenians who opposed Vardan's rebellion, submitting to the shah in both political and religious matters.

13. Most notable are the verbal parallels with the Armenian version of Syrian martyrdoms in 4th-century Iran. The Armenian text is attributed to Abraham Xostovanoł, mentioned in both Łazar and Ełišē as a survivor of imprisonment in Iran following the battle of Avarayr in 451. *Abrahamu Xostovanołi Vkaykʿ Arewelicʿ*, ed. G. Tēr-Mkrtčʿean (Ējmiacin, 1921).

14. Movsēs Xorenacʿi, *Patmutʿiwn Hayocʿ*, ed. M. Abełean and S. Yarutʿiwnean (Tiflis, 1913), I 22.

15. On Movsēs' attitude to historical writing and his use

IV

THE ARMENIAN LITERARY TRADITION

of earlier sources, see the introduction to Thomson, *Moses Khorenats'i*.

16. See the previous note.
17. See N. Adontz, *Denys de Thrace et les commentateurs arméniens* (Louvain, 1970), 1 (lines 14-15).
18. Movsēs Xorenac'i, II 26.
19. For Movsēs on the Jewish colonies, see Thomson, *Moses Khorenats'i*, 28-29.
20. See further Thomson, *ibid.*, 25-31, and esp. 56-58.
21. The invention of the script is described by Koriwn, Łazar, and Movsēs with some variations on the details. An important collection of essays on this topic was published as vol. 7 of the *Banber Matenadarani* (Erevan, 1964).
22. Plutarch, *Life of Crassus*, § 33.
23. See P. Petit, *Les Etudiants de Libanius* (Paris, 1957).
24. Eunapius, *Vitae Sophistarum*, ed. I. Giangrande (Rome 1956), X 1, 8.
25. Koriwn, *Patmut'iwn Varuc' ew Mahuan srboyn Mesropay Vardapeti* (Tiflis, 1913), 9, 15. Cf. the description in Agat'angełos, § 863, of King Trdat as "versed in Greek secular literature [yunakan ašxarhakan dprut'eann]."
26. Koriwn, 15, indicates that this was used as a text in instructing young scribes.
27. Zacharias Rhetor, *Vita Severi*, ed. M. A. Kugener, PO, II, 1 (1907), 57.
28. But it is not always possible to date translations from Greek or Syriac precisely. For a general guide to translations into Armenian, see G. Zarp'analean, *Matenadaran Haykakan T'argmanuteanc' Nayneac'* (Venice, 1889) and Inglisian, "Armenische Literatur."
29. Koriwn, 26, 31.
30. On the attribution of these homilies, see R. W. Thomson, *The Teaching of Saint Gregory* (Cambridge, Mass., 1970), 37. Agat'angełos, § 886, ascribes the same homilies to Gregory the Illuminator.
31. H. Gelzer, H. Hilgenfeld, and O. Cuntz, *Patrum Nicaenorum Nomina* (Leipzig, 1898), 72, 198.
32. Agat'angełos, § 885, and the note thereto in Thomson, *Agathangelos, ad loc.*
33. See the details in the introduction to Thomson, *Agathangelos*.
34. The Armenian rendering of the Syriac text is not a strict translation but an adaptation: *Labubneay T'ułt' Abgaru* (Venice, 1868). The basic story would be known in Armenian from the translation of Eusebius' *Ecclesiastical History*, itself made from the Syriac translation: *Eusebiosi Kesarac'woy Patmut'iwn Ekełec'woy* (Venice, 1877).
35. The further elaborations were in force by the time that the *History* of Movsēs Xorenac'i was written. Addai's death in Armenia is described in the *Martyrdom of Thaddaeus and Sandukht: Vkayabanut'iwn ew giwt nšxarac' s. T'adēi Ałak'eloy ew Sandxtoy kusi* (Venice, 1853). On this text, see N. Akinean and P. Tēr-Połosean, "Matenagrakan hetazōtut'iwnner, T'adēi ew Sandxtoy Vkayabanut'iwnə," *Handes Amsorya*, 83 (1969), 399-426; 84 (1970), 1-34, 129-48.
36. I.e., among the descendants of Noah via Japheth; see Gen. 10:3.
37. Agat'angełos, § 776, 796.
38. *Kanonagirk' Hayoc'*, I, ed. V. Hakobyan (Erevan, 1964), 426, 429.
39. Hippolytus, *Chronik*, ed. A. Bauer and R. Helm, GCS, XLVI (Berlin, 1955), 12.
40. E.g., Vardan, *Hawak'umn Patmut'ean* (Venice, 1862), 14.
41. Movsēs Xorenac'i, I 22. Movsēs Dasxuranc'i, *Patmut'iwn Ałwanic' Ašxarhi*, ed. J. Emin (Moscow, 1860), I 14, refers to Armenia as "the land of Torgom and the descendants of Aškenaz."

42. Koriwn, 24; Agat'angełos, §175; Ełišē, 72; Movsēs Xorenac'i I 10, 17; III 68.
43. E.G., Movsēs II 2.
44. Hippolytus, *Chronik*, 10.
45. E.G., Stephen of Tarōn, *Patmut'iwn tiezerakan*, ed. S. Malxaseanc' (St. Petersburg, 1885), I 4; A. Soukry, *Géographie de Moïse de Corène* (Venice, 1881), 14.
46. This is published as a preface to the *History* of Sebēos: *Patmut'iwn Sebēosi*, ed. G. V. Abgaryan (Erevan, 1979), 47-55. English translation in Thomson, *Moses Khorenats'i*, 357-68.
47. See W. Speyer, *Bücherfunde in der Glaubenswerbung der Antike*, Hypomnemata, XXIV (Göttingen, 1970).
48. This exists in two recensions. The longer has been edited by Soukry; see note 45 above. The short recension may be found in Movsēs Xorenac'i, *Matenagrut'iwnk'* (Venice, 1865), 585-616, and in Anania Širakac'i, *Matenagrut'yunə*, ed. A. G. Abrahamyan (Erevan, 1944), 336-54.
49. For the *Gahnamaks*, see N. Adontz, *Armenia in the Period of Justinian*, translated with partial revisions, a bibliographical note and appendices by N. G. Garsoïan (Lisbon, 1970), 188-234.
50. E.g., the soliloquy of Aršak III on leaving his homeland as given in Łazar, 8-12.
51. Such parallels with nature are a notable feature of the *Teaching of Saint Gregory*, for which, see note 30 above.
52. See Y. Manandean, *Yunaban Dproc'ə ew nra Zargac'man Šrjannerə* (Vienna, 1928), and A. N. Muradean, *Hunaban Dproc'ə ew nra Derə Hayereni K'erakanakan Terminabanut'yan Stełcman Gorcum* (Erevan, 1971).
53. See G. V. Abgaryan, "Širakac'un veragrvac 'Yałags Ampoc' ew Nšanac'' Ašxatut'ean masin," *Patma-banasirakan Handes*, 52, pt. 1 (1971), 77-94. For the Armenian text of the *Hexaemeron*, see *Čark' vasn vec'ōreay arač'ut'ean* (Venice, 1830).
54. The text of Anania's autobiography may be found in Abrahamyan, *Anania Širakac'i*, 206-9 (cf. note 48 above). See also H. Berbérian, "Autobiographie d'Anania Širakac'i," *REArm*, n.s. 1 (1964), 189-94; and P. Lemerle, "Note sur les données historiques de l'Autobiographie d'Anania de Shirak," *ibid.*, 195-202.
55. Łazar, 193.
56. Movsēs Xorenac'i, III 62, 68.
57. For the various accounts of Stephen's travels, see S. Gero, *Byzantine Iconoclasm during the Reign of Leo III*, CSCO, Subsidia, 41 (Louvain, 1973), 143-49.
58. For Eznik's sources, see L. Mariès, "Le De Deo d'Eznik de Kołb," *REArm* 4 (1924), 1-212.
59. Theon, *Progymnasmata*, ed. H. Manandean (Erevan, 1938).
60. This text is known as the *Girk' Pitoyic'* (lit. "Book of χρεῖαι"). Text in Movsēs Xorenac'i, *Matenagrut'iwnk'* (Venice, 1865), 341-579. On this, see A. Baumgartner, "Über das Buch 'die Chrie,'" *ZDMG*, 40 (1886), 457-515; and R. Sgarbi, "Contributo allo studio delle fonti dell'opera *yałags Pitoyits'* attribuita a Mosè Corenese," *Rendiconti*, Istituto Lombardo, Accademia di Scienze e Lettere, Classe di Lettere e Scienze morali e storiche, CII (1969), 78-84.
61. A. Manandian, "Die Scholien zu fünf Reden des Gregor von Nazianz," *Zeitschrift für armenische Philologie*, 1 (1903), 220-300.
62. See note 17 above.
63. *Patmut'iwn Alek'sandri Makedonac'woy* (Venice, 1842). On this Armenian version and its medieval revision, see N. Akinean, "Die hanschriftliche Überlieferung des armenischen Übersetzung des Alexanderromans von Pseudo-Kallisthenes," *Byzantion*, 13 (1938), 201-6.
64. The philosopher Homer is credited with a treatise on

the *Three Powers (zawrut'iwnk'*) *of Heaven;* see, e.g., Vienna, Arm. 649, fols. 188ª-190ª.
65. Bibliothèque nationale, Arm. no. 260, fols. 32ᵛ-147ʳ.
66. Matenadaran, no. 5996.
67. Movsēs Dasxuranc'i, III 18.
68. Armenian text in Dawit' Anyałt', *Sahmank' Imastasirut'ean,* ed. S. S. Arewšatyan (Erevan, 1960); Greek text in A. Busse, *Davidis Prolegomena et in Porphyrii Isagogen Commentarium* (Berlin, 1904), 1-79.
69. Eznik de Kołb, *De Deo,* ed. L. Mariès and C. Mercier, PO, XXVIII, 3, 4 (1959). Cf. note 58 above.
70. E.g., A. Meillet, *Altarmenisches Elementarbuch* (Heidelberg, 1913), 2.
71. See, e.g., Stephen of Tarōn, I 1; the Preface to David's Elegy on the Cross, in his *Matenagrut'iwnk'* (Venice, 1932), 5; Samuel of Ani (long recension of the *Chronicle*) in M. F. Brosset, *Collection d'historiens arméniens,* II (St. Petersburg, 1876), 385; Vardan, *Hawak'umn,* 54-55; Kirakos Ganjakec'i, *Patmut'iwn Hayoc',* ed. K. S. Melik'-Ōhanjanean (Erevan, 1961), 28, 36.

72. See Homily no. 17 in the *Čark'* attributed to John Mandakuni (Venice, 1860) 131-37, and the passing reference in Homily no. 9 (*ibid.,* 85).
73. P'awstos Buzandac'i, *Patmut'iwn Hayoc'* (Venice, 1933), III 13.
74. The recent work of R. Murray, *Symbols of Church and Kingdom* (Cambridge, Mass., 1975), shows that many themes from early Syrian Christianity were known in Armenia through translations. But the history of the Armenian use of those themes and their adaptation to the Armenian situation remains to be written.
75. This was first indicated by B. Kiwlēsērean, *Ełišē, k'nnakan usumnasirut'iwn* (Vienna, 1909). Cf. note 13 above.
76. Łazar, *Patmut'iwn,* 4.
77. A study of the literary sources of the 10th-century * historian Thomas by the present author is in progress.

*This appeared as *Thomas Artsruni: History of the House of the Artsrunik'*, Translation and Commentary by Robert W. Thomson. Wayne State University Press, Detroit, 1985.

V

JERUSALEM AND ARMENIA

Prince Vard Rshtuni the Patrician had a guilty conscience. During the wars between Iran and Byzantium at the beginning of the seventh century he had betrayed a Roman army, leading 30,000 men into an ambush prepared by the Persians. For he had promised to lead the Roman army over the river Gayl, the Lykos, and to guard the bridge; but once the Romans were on the other side he pulled down the bridge, leaving them to their fate. When he returned to his own palace in the province of Rshtunik' on the southern shore of Lake Van, Vard had a fateful dream. He was in the midst of a sea of blood; a heavy iron weight was suspended from his feet; and he was near to drowning. On waking up he confessed his crime to the bishop of Rshtunik', Gregory. The latter advised him that he still had time to save himself. A local hermit, Simeon, was summoned, and he told Vard to build churches with his many treasures throughout his province. They were to be dedicated to Saint Stephen, who had first shed his own blood in return for the saving blood of Christ. Vard numbered his castles and villages: they totalled 1,000 inhabited places. He began to build churches, while Simeon travelled to Jerusalem in order to procure a relic of St. Stephen with which the churches could be blessed. For three years Simeon performed ascetic practices at the martyrium of the protomartyr. Then Stephen appeared in a vision to the sacristan, directing him to give Simeon a part of his holy relics. When the churches built in Armenia by Vard had been blessed with this relic, Vard saw again the vision of the sea of blood. But this time he saw as well 1,000 priests gripping his hands; the hermit Simeon cut the iron weight from his feet; and like the flight of an eagle they brought him to the fountain beside his palace. With the water from the fountain they washed away the blood from his body, dressed him in white garments, and put a crown of glory on his head. On waking from this dream, Vard distributed his treasures to the poor, and donned a hair-shirt under his clothing for the rest of his life.

This edifying tale comes from a curious work, first printed in 1921 in an incomplete version, and edited fully in 1971. Wrongly identified by its first author as the lost *History* of the ninth century Shapuh Bagratuni, it is a collection of exploits of Artsruni princes in southern Armenia to which have been prefixed three separate sections dealing with the emperors Maurice and Heraclius, and with Muhammad and the rise of Islam.[1]

The story of Vard's dream is not the only reference in Armenian to hermits going to Jerusalem in search of relics. During the reign of Heraclius, we are informed by Moses Daskhurantsi, a certain hermit Mkhitar travelled to the holy city with two companions. After a year he obtained relics of St. Stephen and St. George. On his way back to Armenia he also acquired a relic of St. Andrew from the saint's shrine in the Taurus. Encouraged by this success, more monks went to Jerusalem, though they were distressed to see that all there were tainted by adherence to the Council of Chalcedon.[2] Moses Daskhurantsi then quotes a brief description of the major holy sites, which is probably the work of one of those pilgrims, the hermit Yovsep.[3] Following that, Moses quotes a different source, the monk Anastas, for a short list of monasteries in Jerusalem built by Armenians and Caucasian Albanians, the Ałuank'. A much longer list attributed to Anastas is found in late manuscripts. A clearly tendentious work, it not only gives the names of seventy monasteries, most of them built by different Armenian noble families, but also claims that king Trdat and Saint Gregory the Illuminator collaborated with the emperor Constantine in founding the famous churches of Jerusalem.[4]

The Armenian presence *in* Jerusalem is not my theme. I shall be primarily concerned with the influence of Jerusalem back in Armenia and various ramifications in fantasy as well as fact. None the less, it is worth noting that there is more reliable evidence for Armenian pilgrimage than the sources just quoted. Some of the various mosaic pavements with Armenian inscriptions at Jerusalem can be dated to the sixth and seventh centuries;[5] while Cyril of Scythopolis refers to Armenians in the holy land in the late fifth century.[6] Armenian pilgrims on their way to Saint Catherine's monastery on Jebel Musa scratched their names in the wadis of the Sinai peninsula;[7] and a seventh century author has left a long description of the monastery on Mount Tabor.[8] The importance of the Armenian pilgrim traffic in Jerusalem comes out clearly from an exchange of letters between Modestos, bishop of Jerusalem, and Komitas, Catholicos of Armenia from 615 to 628, which are quoted by the historian Sebēos of the late seventh century.[9] Modestos wrote to the Armenian patriarch following the recapture of Jerusalem after the Persian attack of 614. Referring to the Armenian pilgrims who had previously come to the holy city, Modestos tells Komitas about the restoration of the holy places, and requests his prayers and more tangible help for the holy shrines. In his reply Komitas rejoices at the peace re-established in the holy city, and describes in rhetorical terms the joy that Armenian pilgrims experienced from their journeys to Jerusalem and Mount Sinai. But there is no reference to a cash contribution.

The recovery of the True Cross by Heraclius is described in sober terms by Sebēos after this exchange of letters.[10] But later Armenian tradition elaborated the role of the Armenians. The text wrongly identified as the *History* of Shapuh Bagratuni, which provided the tale of Vard Rshtuni quoted earlier, contains details of the negotiations of the emperor's envoy to the Persians.[11] Supposedly, the Greek noble posed as a merchant and became well known in the Persian capital. But when invited to dinner by a local dignitary he refused to eat meat, since he was in mourning for the loss of the Cross. His Persian friend showed him the room in the shah's palace where the Cross was kept. The envoy then sent word to Heraclius, who came to Persia, defeated the shah, and recovered the Cross from the treasury. In this expedition Heraclius was assisted by Armenian troops sent by the princess of Siunik'—'a beautiful woman and very wise, who pleased the emperor Heraclius.'

On his return from Persia, Heraclius wished to thank the Armenian princess for her support and the thousand troops who possessed four hundred suits of armour made of beaten gold.[12] She only desired a fragment of the Cross, but the emperor did not dare take a sword to cut off a piece. However, through the prayers of twelve Armenian bishops and a multitude of priests, two fragments miraculously broke away. The princess, rejoicing, went back towards Siunik'. But when she reached Hatsiwn, west of the river Araxes which marked the border of Siunik', the relics refused to proceed farther—just as the relics of John the Baptist and Athenogenes had indicated the site of the first church in Armenia to Saint Gregory the Illuminator by refusing to budge.[13] The princess constructed a monastery to house the fragments of the True Cross. However, this Cross at Hatsiwn does not play a major role in Armenian tradition. More important was the relic of the Cross kept near Van, on Mount Varag in the land of the Artsruni princes. The most famous of these princes, Gagik, was the first Artsruni to gain royal status. He was responsible for the palace and royal church dedicated to the Holy Cross on the island of Ałt'amar in Lake Van. And more interesting for our immediate purpose, his other church building on the mainland was carried out in deliberate imitation of certain sites in Jerusalem.

The Cross of Varag brings us back to Vard the Patrician; for it was in his days, according to Pseudo-Shapuh, that the Holy Cross was revealed on the mountain of Varag.[14] But the origin of this relic of the Cross takes us back even earlier. That the True Cross had been discovered in Jerusalem by Helen, mother of Constantine, was known in Armenia. Lazar, for example, writing about the year 500, gives a brief account.[15] But in the Armenian rewriting of the story of Addai and the conversion of Abgar of Edessa, the discovery of the Cross by Patronice, wife of the emperor Claudius, figures prominently.[16] Naturally later writers combine details of the two accounts.[17] More interestingly, however, an Armenian connection is introduced in a text ascribed to the mysterious historian Moses Khorenatsi. Earlier Agathangelos had described the conversion of king Trdat to Christianity, linking the conversion to the martyrdom of Rhipsimē and her companions; these were pious nuns who fled from Diocletian in Rome to Armenia. The text ascribed to Moses Khorenatsi, but certainly not by the author of the famous *History* and of later date, explains that Agathangelos was unable to include all the details of Rhipsimē's earlier career, so he fills in some gaps.[18] Since she was of royal descent, Rhipsimē had inherited from her ancestor Patronice a fragment of the Cross which the empress had found in Jerusalem. This she wore suspended from her neck. On their flight from Rome to Armenia, Rhipsimē and her companions had time to visit all the sites in Jerusalem as well as Edessa. The nuns then wandered on through many regions of Armenia, and two accompanying priests remained at Varag, where the saints had left the relic. After the martyrdom of Rhipsimē the relic was forgotten until the days of Vard.

This Cross of Varag figures prominently in the *History of the Artsruni House* by Thomas Artsruni.[19] But before discussing such later texts we should return to the earlier period to see how Jerusalem was regarded not just as a source of holy objects but as a source of authoritative teaching.

In this regard it is most surprising that contemporary sources entirely disregard Jerusalem when discussing the origins of the texts translated into Armenian after the invention of the Armenian script. Describing that momentous invention by Mashtots, the latter's pupil Koriun gives some details about the journeys he and others made to Edessa, Melitene or Constantinople in search of Greek and Syriac texts. He talks in rather vague terms about the bible, the church fathers, and the canons of Nicaea and Ephesus. But there is no reference to any liturgical texts, which were for the fledgling church at least as important as homilies by John Chrysostom.[20] The importance of the ritual of Jerusalem, in particular the lectionary, for Armenia has been carefully documented in recent decades.[21] But one would never guess that Jerusalem had any significance for the development of fifth century Armenian practice by reading the classic historians' descriptions of Mashtots' work.[22]

The later tenth century Moses Daskhurantsi, whose interest in pilgrims to Jerusalem we have already noted, does claim that Mashtots visited the holy city and brought back a relic of the True Cross. But his version of Mashtots' activity is full of unsubstantiated details designed to cast lustre on the region of the Aluank'; little credence can be given to this tale or to the claim that Mashtots' disciples also supposedly visited Jerusalem in search of a spiritual leader after Mashtots' death.[23]

Nor in colophons — for like the Syrians, Armenian scribes were fond of adding circumstantial details to manuscripts — do we find many references to Jerusalem as a centre for the translation or copying of texts.[24] However, Nersēs Akinean once wrote of a 'Jerusalem school,' and since then (i.e. 1932) writers have enlarged this into a fifth century scriptorium.[25] Now by the term 'school (*dprots*)' Akinean was referring to certain stylistic traits that he associated with texts of a liturgical or hagiographical type. There is one colophon in a manuscript dated to 1403 that contains the Armenian version of Athanasius' *Life of Antony* which refers to Jerusalem. It says: 'This book was translated in the holy city of Jerusalem in the year 450 of the coming of our Lord Jesus Christ, in the year when the blessed Mashtots died.'[26] There are problems with this. Mashtots died in 439 or 440. Therefore Akinean proposed emending Mashtots to Hesychius — which is a little more plausible in Armenian than in English. The dating from the year of the coming of the Lord is unusual in Armenian, but by no means unprecedented.[27]

Akinean's only other evidence for an actual scriptorium in Jerusalem is an undated medieval text containing a medley of information on religious and philosophical matters, such as the names of the seventy-two apostles, or the names of the wives of the twelve. One section deals with the translation of various rituals. It claims that the ritual of the benediction of the water (i.e., on Epiphany) was composed by Basil of Caesarea in Jerusalem. The Armenian patriarch Sahak (the supporter of Mashtots) had sent a certain Khosrov the translator (*t'argmanich'*) to Jerusalem, where he came across the text of Basil's and brought it back to Armenia.[28] Now a Khosrovik 'the translator' is a known figure of Armenian literature. Interested in liturgical matters, he attacked the Greek celebration of Christmas on December 25th instead of

January 6th, and in general opposed the Chalcedonians. He lived in the eighth century, not the fifth.

The only plausible evidence for a fifth century Armenian scriptorium in Jerusalem is thus the fifteenth century colophon claiming that the *Life of Antony* was translated in the holy city. Not until the ninth century does another colophon indicate that another text — in this case the *Autobiography* of Pseudo-Dionysius the Areopagite — was translated in Jerusalem.[30] Nor do colophons refer to early copying of manuscripts there by Armenians. Of course, thousands of manuscripts have been destroyed; and only fragments survive from the early centuries. But the lack of references in all other sources to copying of manuscripts at Jerusalem tends to confirm that this was not a significant activity.

However, Jerusalem as a centre of authoritative teaching does emerge once the Armenians found themselvs in conflict with Greeks and Georgians over questions of faith and ritual. Cyril of Scythopolis notes in his *Life of Saint Sabas* that theological differences caused problems at the beginning of the sixth century.

> Ch. 32: 'In the year 501 Saint Sabas moved the Armenians from the small chapel to the large church (which had just been built) so that they could celebrate the canonical office in their own tongue. He recommended that they say separately in Armenian the readings from the gospels and the rest of the office, but that they join the others who spoke Greek at the moment of the communion. However, when some of the Armenians began to sing the *Trisagion* with the addition "who was crucified for us" that had been invented by Peter the Fuller, then the holy old man, rightly indignant, ordered them to sing this hymn in Greek according to the ancient tradition of the Catholic church and not according to the innovation of Peter, who shared the errors of Eutyches.... Thus Saint Sabas rejected the additions and held to ecclesiastical tradition.'

We are not here interested in the break between Armenians and Chalcedonians per se,[31] but the role played by bishops of Jerusalem is certainly relevant. The best known of those bishops was certainly Cyril (350-386). His *Catecheses* were among the texts translated in the fifth century. (That the five Mystagogical treatises were included is unlikely, though some of these were known indirectly.)[32] The influence of the *Catecheses* is discernible in the composition known as the *Teaching of Saint Gregory*, which takes the form of a long sermon — supposedly lasting sixty-six days — preached to king Trdat before his baptism.[33] But Cyril of Jerusalem is not quoted by Armenian authors very often. In his *Letter* of self-justification the historian Lazar mentions him in passing with other famous fathers of the church.[34] The sixth century Catholicos John II (557-574) refers to him as a castigator of heretics who confirmed the readings established by the apostles.[35] The later Stephen of Siunik' is more explicit in attributing those readings to James the brother of the Lord; Cyril merely professed them (*dawaneats*).[36]

Cyril's role as a hammer of heretics is picked up in a late document of the eleventh century, which links his name more closely with Armenia. This fictitious *Life of Cyril* claims that the Armenian patriarch Nersēs the Great (who was poisoned by King

Pap in 373), had been recalled from exile by the emperor Theodosius in order to chair the council of Constantinople in 381. As co-chairmen of that council the Armenian patriarch was joined by Cyril of Jerusalem, the two Gregories of Nyssa and Nazianzen, and Meletius of Antioch.[37]

We must reject the cooperation of Nersēs and Cyril in the struggle against Arians and other heretics. None the less, later bishops of Jerusalem did concern themselves with the Christians in Armenia, worried that they were not adhering to the straight path of orthodoxy. The *Book of Letters*, a thirteenth century compilation of official documents including letters exchanged between Armenians, Syrians, Greeks, and Georgians, contains a letter sent by Macarius of Jerusalem to Armenia. It poses certain problems.

In the *Book of Letters*, where it is not in its chronological place, and in separate copies found in later manuscripts, the letter is entitled: 'Of the blessed Macarius of the holy city of Jerusalem, canonical letter to the Armenians concerning the regulation of the rites of the Catholic church.'[38] It deals primarily with baptism and baptismal unction. In the text of the letter Macarius indicates that he is replying to a query from Armenia, and addresses the 'archbishop (*episkoposapet*) Vrt'anēs.' The title is common for a chief bishop or patriarch; and both P'awstos Buzand and Moses Khorenatsi refer to an *episkoposapet* Vrt'anēs—he was the son of Gregory the Illuminator, who followed his brother as third prelate of Armenia, circa 333.[39] If that identification is correct, Macarius would be the first bishop of that name, bishop of Jerusalem from 313 to 334. The same text is preserved in the *Kanonagirk'*, the official compilation of canon-law begun in the eighth century by the Catholicos John of Odzun.[40] There is one reference to this letter in a homily attributed to Anania. Some critics have identified that Anania with Anania of Shirak of the seventh century; others with Anania of Halbat of the eleventh century.[41] It is not quoted again until the thirteenth century, in the catena known as the *Root of Faith*.[42] Doubtful that the ritual described by Macarius dated to the early fourth century, Nersēs Akinean proposed that the second Macarius of Jerusalem, bishop 565-574, must be the author. Vrt'anēs would then be the bishop of the province of Siunik' circa 562-584. Now this Vrt'anēs is known from other sources, for Siunik' had withdrawn from Armenian jurisdiction in the second half of the sixth century—though the rift was later healed—and Vrt'anēs refused to join the Armenian anti-Chalcedonian party after the attempted reunion of the Armenian and Byzantine churches in 572.[43]

That the letter was written by Macarius II to Vrt'anēs of Siunik' was accepted by the editor of the *Kanonagirk'*, the late Vazken Hakobyan. But one big stumbling block remains. Describing the rite of communion, Macarius enjoins the Armenians 'to put warm bread on the altar, according to the tradition of the apostles,' and to ensure that 'the cup is unadulterated (*anapak*), without any admixture, because we are not saved by anything corruptible but by the incorruptible (*anapakan*) body and blood of the pure and immaculate lamb.' It was not the tradition of Jerusalem to leave the wine unmixed with water. One is immediately reminded of the famous remark of the Armenian Catholicos Moses II (574-604), who was staunchly opposed to the Greek church and refused to accept attempted reunion in 591, declaring: 'I shall not drink hot water.'⁴⁴ I am not competent to pass judgment on the authenticity of the baptismal ritual. But if the letter supports the Armenian tradition of unmixed wine at communion, one wonders if it is not a tendentious forgery rather than a lost Greek text which has been tampered with. In that case its ascription to the first Macarius and the identification of Vrt'anēs with the son of Gregory the Illuminator would be perfectly appropriate.

The hardening hostility of the Armenians to the Greek church in the second half of the sixth century elicited another letter from Jerusalem. Like that of Macarius, it is known only in Armenian. John IV, bishop of Jerusalem after Macarius II (574-94), wrote to Abas, Catholicos of the Caucasian Albanians, the Ałuank' (552-96), urging them not to join the Armenians in rejecting the council of Chalcedon.⁴⁵ John had heard from an Ałuan monk in Jerusalem about the Armenian decision taken at the council of Dvin in 555—which marked the final, irrevocable stage in the separation of the Armenian church from Byzantium. He exhorts Abas to expel the Armenian heretics from monasteries in Albania, stating that the Armenians had been deceived by the Syrians—which shows some familarity with the proceedings at Dvin.⁴⁶ He also mentions the Armenian corruption of the *Trisagion* hymn, to which Sabas had objected earlier.

This letter is interesting for its information about Armenians and Albanians in Jerusalem. Unlike the letter attributed to Macarius, it does not seem to have been doctored in a pro-Armenian fashion. And it fits into the historical situation known from other sources. For Abas was also being courted by the Armenians. The Catholicos John II wrote to him some time before 572, urging him to hold fast to the three councils and to reject the wicked doctrines of Chalcedon.⁴⁷ The collapse of the Armenian revolt against Iran in 572 brought John and various Armenian nobles to Constantinople. John died there two years later, apparently having been inveigled into accepting what he earlier rejected. But Abas of Albania received other letters from the Armenians after 572, according to the pro-Chalcedonian *Narratio de Rebus Armeniae* of the early eighth century.⁴⁸ So the letter from Jerusalem fits with the continuing effort of the anti-Chalcedonian Armenians to gain support in Caucasia. Yet it is curious that these doctrinal differences are ignored by Sebēos in the seventh century when he refers to Armenian pilgrims in Jerusalem. And he even claims that Zacharias, patriarch of Jerusalem 609-31, supported the Armenian position against Chalcedon at a convocation held at the Iranian court following the capture of Jerusalem by the Persians.⁴⁹

But by far the most frequent references to Jerusalem as the source of orthodoxy come in the correspondence exchanged between Armenian and Georgian bishops at the beginning of the seventh century. The correspondence is preserved in the *Book of Letters*, and the constant references to Jerusalem underscore the common links of Armenians, Albanians, and Georgians in the holy city and in the monasteries of Palestine. In a general document concerning the councils of the Dyophysites written in 606, bishop Moses of Tsurtavi quotes Isaiah 2.3: 'Out of Sion shall go forth the law, and the word of the Lord from Jerusalem.' It was that true faith of Jerusalem which Saint Gregory (the Illuminator) taught us.⁵⁰ On the Georgian side Kiwrion wrote to the Armenian Catholicos Abraham: 'Our fathers and your fathers held the faith of Jerusalem,' and we shall cleave to it as to the sole rule of the Roman emperor.[51] In response Abraham echoes the claim that 'our fathers and yours held the faith of Jerusalem,' to which we (the Armenians) shall cling, and we urge you (the Georgians) not to abandon it for alien teaching.[52] None the less, Armenians and Georgians went their separate ways.[53] The only later reference to Jerusalem as the source of right teaching in the *Book of Letters* comes in a letter of Stephen of Siunik' in the early eighth century. The text has attracted attention as containing the first datable reference to the martyrdom of the apostle Bartholomew in Armenia. But Stephen was primarily concerned with rebutting the celebration of the Annunciation and the Nativity on the 25th of March and December respectively. We reject that, says Stephen, because our faith has its origin in Jerusalem, where the apostles established correct rituals.[54]

But we cannot leave the Georgians without noting another connection with Jerusalem. As we noticed earlier, Armenian sources are not informative about the role of the holy city as a source of texts translated into Armenian. However, a colophon dated to 329 of the Armenian era (which began on 20th April, 880) states that the *Autobiography* of Dionysius the Areopagite was rendered into Armenian in Jerusalem by a certain John the doctor (*Yovhannēs bzhishk*), otherwise unknown.[55] The corpus of writings attributed to this elusive Dionysius had been translated in Constantinople at the beginning of the previous century.[56] But the Armenian version of his *Life* was made from a Georgian text. Not many translations were made from Georgian, though Armenians did adapt the Georgian *Chronicles*.[57] More significant is the fact that this translation was made in Jerusalem, where Armenians and Georgians could still meet. The surge of Georgian scholarly activity in the next two centuries that is associated with Iviron on Mount Athos naturally had no effect on the anti-Chalcedonian Armenians.

Jerusalem in its Christian aspect does not appear in Armenian written sources as often as one might expect. So a rare reference to the holy sites as models for Armenian churches is particularly noteworthy. I refer not to the heavenly Jerusalem or Sion on high which are prefigured in the design and decor of a church building. The image of the church as a symbol of the celestial city is common in Armenian. But the many passages which liken the dome to heaven; which see a parallel between the threefold division of sanctuary, nave and narthex with the three decks of Noah's ark; or the various interpretations of the columns, walls, stones or windows of the physical structure—none of these have direct reference to Jerusalem.[58] However, the historian Thomas Artsruni has some pertinent comments on the constructions of his patron prince Gagik.

We have already mentioned the Cross of Varag which was revealed in the days of prince Vard and whose legendary origin is connected with Patronice. Thomas Artsruni describes how Gagik embellished the reliquary containing this Cross.[59] He also gives details of the building activity of Gagik and his brother Gurgēn in southern Armenia at the very beginning of the tenth century. He describes their churches, fortresses and palaces[60]—though the most famous of those descriptions, that of the church and royal palace on Ałt'amar in Lake Van, is by a later continuator, not Thomas; and curiously, it does not mention that the church was dedicated to the Holy Cross.[61]

Before attaining royal status in 908 Gagik had been responsible for a complex of churches at Van. There, beneath the famous rock, he constructed a church dedicated to the holy Sion in the city of Jerusalem.[62] To the right he built a church dedicated to the crucifixion of the Lord at Golgotha, and above it a church dedicated to the 'upper room of the mystical celebration of the transmission of the new covenant.' To the left of the main structure he built a church in commemoration of the resurrection of Christ, above which he added a church dedicated to the ascension and commemorating the second coming. The impression given by Thomas is that there was a single complex with five chapels, rather than five free-standing churches at different levels on the flank of the rock; but the text is not entirely clear. Thomas then goes on to describe Gagik's improvements to his father's constructions on the rock of Van: he added banqueting halls with verandahs, a staircase from the cistern below to the summit of the rock, and a water-tunnel from nearby Mount Varag.

I am not aware of any other text which links Armenian churches to a complex of holy sites in Jerusalem. It is, however, not irrelevant that the frescoes in Gagik's church on Ałt'amar reflect early Palestinian traditions. Nicole Thierry has shown that the depiction of Ascension and Pentecost, which are not in their normal place in the biblical cycle, is explicable by Palestinian iconography; the connection with the Second Coming is also brought out by one of the flasks of Monza on which themes of the Ascension, Pentecost, and Second Coming are combined.[63] This tradition elucidates a passage in Thomas's description of Gagik's churches at Van, which at first I had thought to be a garbled corruption. Describing the church dedicated to the Ascension, Thomas says: 'He built a church dedicated to the ascension to heaven and the sharing of the Father's throne, and in commemoration of the second coming, when he will come in the Father's glory with the angels *to the apostles*, bringing them the *consoling* and encouraging gospel.' Thomas has combined the ideas of Pentecost and the second coming in a rather confused way; but his description of the church which also recalled the ascension, reflects the tradition attested in Gagik's frescoes.

There was another way in which Armenians saw a connection between their country and Jerusalem. Although we now approach the realm of fantasy rather than of historical reality or even symbolic interpretation, these imaginary connections served a serious purpose. They were part of a propaganda campaign waged by the spokesmen of rival noble families anxious to demonstrate the antiquity of their patrons' origins and their early Christian faith.

For Agathangelos, who describes the conversion of king Trdat at the beginning of the fourth century, Saint Gregory the Illuminator was the first missionary to bring the Christian gospel to Armenia. But already in the fifth century the story of Addai's preaching in Edessa had been adopted by the Armenians: the Armenian version of the *Doctrine of Addai* takes him farther to the East after establishing an organized hierarchy in Edessa.[64] But the Christian community he supposedly founded in Armenia was later obliterated. By the time of Moses Khorenatsi—whose date is a hotly debated question—the legends about his martyrdom and that of king Sanatruk's daughter after her father's apostasy had taken shape.[65] But no one before Moses had introduced into the story of the conversion of king Abgar of Edessa any Armenian characters. Moses, however, consistently claims a Jewish origin for his patrons, the Bagratids, though earlier tradition made them native Armenians.[66] The early Bagratids were persecuted for their faith, claims Moses, but some remained true to their Judaism.[67] One of these, called Tobias, had fled to Edessa for safety from persecution. It was in the house of Tobias that the Greek and Syriac accounts had said that the apostle Thaddaeus or Addai lodged when he came to Edessa to heal and convert King Abgar. Since Tobias was also converted, the first Armenian Christian was a Bagratid.[68]

A little earlier in his *History* Moses Korenatsi had introduced an Artsruni general named Khosran. The Artsrunis had not yet attained the powerful position they reached in the ninth century, a position later justified by Thomas. Moses says that this Khosran had supported Aretas in his war against Herod. Herod's army was destroyed 'with the help of the brave Armenians,' so by divine providence the death of John the Baptist was avenged.[69]

The Bagratid claim to priority as Christians was challenged by Thomas Artsruni. He claims explicitly that the general Khuran (for the name Khosran underwent various transformations) had been baptised by Thaddaeus himself in Edessa. He then adds some fanciful details about Khuran's service in Spain for the emperor Tiberius, who honoured him 'with the purple and a baton.' Having become the first Armenian field-marshal, Khuran went to settle in Jerusalem where queen Helen of Adiabene was living. Moses had already made Helen a Christian. But Thomas adds that it was Khuran Artsruni who took her gold to buy corn in Egypt during the famine that occurred in the days of the emperor Claudius. He is thus the first attested Armenian entrepreneur. Thereafter Khuran lived in Jerusalem, dying at a good old age; in the world to come he will be crowned by Christ with queen Helen among the saints.[70] An even earlier Artsruni presence in Jerusalem is claimed by Thomas, though he was not followed by later historians. When the Jews returned after the Babylonian exile, Artsruni toops escorted the sons of Israel back to Jerusalem and entrusted the leadership of the Jews to Zorobabel.[71]

These fanciful notions about Armenians in Jerusalem had no great impact on later Armenian tradition. Even the historically attested Armenian pilgrims do not figure very prominently in the sources. Despite their Christian orientation, the Armenian historians do not regard Jerusalem as particularly significant or its bishops as very important. Rather it is with the pre-Christian Jews that Armenian writers see parallels in the Armenian situation, and on the history of the old dispensation that they build their image of Armenian fortunes.

There is a small number of Armenian histories which became classics in the sense that they established a received picture of the Armenian past that was handed down over succeeding generations. The work of Agathangelos brought order to floating traditions about the conversion of Armenia. P'awstos Buzand set his own stamp on the history of the fourth century, emphasizing the role of the patriarch Nersēs in establishing both orthodox belief and the pre-eminent place of the church in political and social life. Ełishē interprets the fifth century revolt against the shah in terms of a struggle of the virtuous against the forces of impiety. While Moses Khorenatsi gave for the first time a picture of the development of the Armenians as a nation, and described the growth of Armenian cultural individuality down to the time of Mashtots and the beginning of a native Armenian literature. The authors of these *Histories* are all unknown — pious legends to the contrary — and the dates when they were written are debated. But that they are sophisticated literary works and that they established the received tradition down to modern times can hardly be doubted.

These histories emphasize the Christian orientation of Armenian culture. But especially in Ełishē and Moses Khorenatsi, who were more influential than the others, Christian Armenia is not viewed as part of a larger whole. In Agathangelos there is the idea of an expanding Christendom which has now embraced Armenia;[72] while P'awstos refers to Armenian missionary work in the remoter Caucasus.[73] But by the time of Ełishē Christendom as such is remote. Martyrdom is a central theme in his *History of Vardan and the Armenian War*. But the martyrs do not die for their faith and Saviour alone, as did Rhipsimē and her companions in Agathangelos. Rather, they die for their national traditions — *hayreni awrēnk'*. This key phrase in Ełishē is the theme of the Maccabees, who fought for their *patrioi nomoi*, of which *hayreni awrēnk'* is a direct translation.[74] The influence of the books of Maccabees in the early Armenian historians has been treated before, so we need not go over the ground again.[75] The importance of Ełishē is that he links the idea of Christian faith indissolubly with national tradition. *Awrēnk'* can mean 'religion' or 'way of life' — or rather, these two are the same. The Armenians are not Christians fighting the Mazdaean Persians in the vanguard of Christendom. They are striving to preserve an individuality as Armenians; and if *that* individuality cannot be preserved, death is certainly preferable to life with ignominy. This is a far cry from the suggestion in Łazar P'arpetsi that it is better to live abroad under a Christian regime than to stay in Armenia but be subservient to a Zoroastrian sovereign.[76]

An explicit parallel with the Maccabees is made by P'awstos, Ełishē, and Moses. But Moses Khorenatsi adds a further dimension to this comparison between the Armenian nation and that of the Jews. Tracing the origin of the Armenians back to Torgom, descendant of Japheth, Moses frequently refers to his role as 'antiquarian.'[77] He is doing for Armenia what another historian had done in the *Antiquities of the Jews*.[78] Indeed, he refers to Josephus quite frequently, and was indebted to his *Jewish Wars* for his picture of Armenia between Rome and Parthia.[79] Even more explicit is Moses' declaration of intent: 'Although we are a small country and very restricted in numbers, weak in power and often subject to another's rule, yet many manly deeds have been performed in our land worthy of being recorded in writing.' This recalls, with verbal parallels in the Armenian version of Josephus' *Wars*, the latter's preface: 'They disparage the actions of the Jews. But I fail to see how the conquerors of a small people deserved to be counted great.'[80]

It seems to me that the national mythology created by the early Armenian historians may account for the contrast between the real importance of Jerusalem as a centre of liturgical authority and a holy site of pilgrimage, and the lack of references to that importance in the texts. Christian Jerusalem was not very relevant to the historians as a source of Armenia's individuality. Nor were Syrian Christian influences acknowledged. Only Constantinople could not be passed over; but the Byzantine capital was regarded as the prime source of learning and scholarship, not as a source of formative tradition.[81] The Greek connections of St. Gregory the Illuminator, emphasized by Agathangelos, were entirely ignored by Ełishē. And although Moses Knorenatsi does mention Gregory, he says nothing of his consecration in Caesarea, but emphasizes the roles of Thaddaeus and Bartholomew in apostolic times as the founders of the Armenian church. The image created by these last two writers is of a small nation alone in the larger world, whose Christian faith is a national one. Patriotism is to adhere to ancestral traditions—though Christianity had not existed in Armenia from time immemorial—while apostasy is the rejection of those traditions. The model for a people whose faith and whose land were so intimately connected, and for whom political and religious allegiance were identical, was not that of an international Christian church.

Now although topical relevance is not a theme popular in some academic circles, I would suggest that this picture of the Armenian people has been persuasive until the present. And since Jerusalem is the theme of this paper, I would remind you of the scenes depicted in the newly refurbished Armenian section of the Holy Sepulchre. What strikes the eye is not a representation of some aspect of the Christian faith appropriate to that holy shrine, but a different picture, no less holy perhaps: Mount Ararat, the symbol of a land and an individual culture.

Notes

* 1. G. Tēr-Mkrtch'ean, *Patmut'iwn Shaphoy Bagratunwoy*, Ējmiatzin 1921; M.H. Darbinyan-Melik'yan, *Patmut'iwn Ananun Zrutzagri (kartzelseal Shapuh Bagratuni)* (Erevan, 1971). The second edition contains a facing Russian translation. For the story about Vard see pp. 97-107. For the intitial section dealing with Muhammad see R.W. Thomson, "Armenian Variations on the Bahira Legend," *Euchristerion, Essays presented to Omeljan Pritsak*, Harvard Ukrainian Studies, 3/4 (1979/1980) pp. 884-895; and *idem*, 'Muhammad and the Origin of Islam in Armenian literary tradition,' *Études arméniennes-In Memoriam Haig Berbérian* (forthcoming).

2. II.50. Armenian text in Movses Kałankatuatsi, *Patmut'iwn Ałuanits ashkharhi*, ed. V. Ařak'elyan, (Erevan, 1983) pp. 280-82; English version by C.J.F. Dowsett, *The History of the Caucasian Albanians by Movsēs Dasxurançi*, London Oriental Series, 8 (London, 1961).

3. Moses Daskhurantsi, II.51. Cf. E.W. Brooks, 'An Armenian Visitor to Jerusalem in the Seventh Century,' *English Historical Review*, 11 (1896) pp. 93-97.

4. Moses, II.52. For a recent edition of the text attributed to Anastas with English translation and references to earlier literature see A.K. Sanjian, 'Anastas Vardapet's List of Armenian Monasteries in Seventh Century Jerusalem,' *Le Muséon*, 82 (1969) pp. 265-92.

*For an English translation of the 'History' of Pseudo-Shapuh with Introduction see R.W. Thomson, 'The Anonymous Story-Teller [also known as 'Pseudo-Šapuh'], *Revue des études arméniennes* 21 [1988–1989], 171–232.

Jerusalem and Armenia 89

5. Recent discussions with references to earlier sources in B.N. Arakelian, 'Armenian Mosaic of the Early Middle Ages,' *Atti del Primo Simposio internazionale di Arta armena* (Venice 1978) pp. 1-9; H. Evans, 'Nonclassical Sources for the Armenian Mosaic near the Damascus Gate in Jerusalem,' *East of Byzantium: Syria and Armenia in the Formative Period*, ed. N.G. Garsoian, T.F. Mathews, R.W. Thomson (Washington, D.C.: Dumbarton Oaks, 1982) pp. 217-22.

6. Cyril of Scythopolis, *Life of Saint Sabas*, ch. 20. For a discussion of references to Armenians in Palestine at this time see K. Hintlian, *History of the Armenians in the Holy Land* (Jerusalem, 1976): and in general, J. Wilkinson, *Jerusalem Pilgrims before the Crusades* (London, 1977).

7. M.E. Stone, *The Armenian Inscriptions from the Sinai*, Harvard Armenian Texts and Studies, 6 (Cambridge, Massachusetts, 1982).

8. R.W. Thomson, 'A Seventh-Century Armenian Pilgrim on Mount Tabor,' *Journal of Theological Studies*, N.S. 18 (1967) pp. 27-33.

9. Sebēos, *Patmut'iwn;* ed. G.V. Abgaryan (Erevan, 1979) ch. 35-36. French translation in F. Macler, *Histoire d'Héraclius* (Paris, 1904).

10. Sebēos, ch. 40.

11. *Patmut'iwn Ananun Zrutzagri* (see note 1) pp. 53-61.

12. *Ibid.*, pp. 63-67 for the story of the Cross of Hatsiwn.

13. Agathangelos (Agat'angełos), #811. The critical Armenian text of his *Patmut'iwn Hayots*, ed. G. Tēr-Mkrtch'ean and St. Kanayeants (Tiflis, 1909) has been reprinted by Caravan Books, Delmar, N.Y. 1980. English translation in R.W. Thomson, *Agathangelos, History of the Armenians* (Albany, 1976).

14. *Patmut'iwn Ananun Zrutzagri*, p. 107.

15. Łazar P'arpetsi, *Patmut'iwn Hayots;* ed. G. Tēr-Mkrtch'ean and S. Malkhasean (Tiflis, 1904) p. 4. French translation in V. Langlois, *Collection des historiens arméniens*, II (Paris, 1869) pp. 253-368.

16. Labubna, *T'ułt' Abgari* (Venice, 1868) pp. 12-16.

17. E.g. Moses Khorenatsi, II. 87. The critical Armenian edition of his *Patmut'iwn Hayots;* ed. M. Abełean and S. Yarut'iwnean, Tiflis 1913, has been reprinted by Caravan Books, Delmar, N.Y. 1981. English translation in R.W. Thomson, *Moses Khorenats'i, History of the Armenians*, Harvard Armenian Texts and Studies, 4 (Cambridge, Massachusetts, 1978).

18. The text of the 'History of the Holy Rhipsimeants' is found in Moses Khorenatsi, *Matenagrut'iwnk'* (Venice, 1865) pp. 297-303.

19. T'ovmay vardapet Artzruni, *Patmut'iwn Tann Artzruneats;* ed. K'. Patkanean (St. Petersburg, 1887). French translation (of the edition of Constantinople 1852) in M. Brosset, *Collection des historiens arméniens*, I (St. Petersburg, 1874).

20. Koriun, *Vark' Mashtotsi;* ed. M. Abełean (Erevan, 1941). English translation in B. Norehad, *The Life of Mashtots* (New York, 1964).

21. For the lectionary see A. Renoux, *Le codex arménien Jérusalem 121*, Patrologia Orientalis, 35.1, 36.2 (Turnhout: Brepols, 1969, 1971).

22. I.e. Koriun, Łazar, Moses Khorenatsi.

23. Moses Daskhurantsi, I.27, 28.

24. For colophons up to 1250 see G. Yovsēp'ean, *Yishatakarank' Dzeragrats* (Antelias, Lebanon, 1951).

25. N. Akinean, *Dasakan Hayerene ew Viennakan Mkhit'arean Dprotse* (Vienna, 1932) pp. 69-73. For the 'scriptorium' see, for example, A.K. Sanjian, *The Armenian Communities in Syria under Ottoman Dominion* (Cambridge, Massachusetts, 1965) p. 4.

26. The colophon is printed in Akinean, *op. cit.*, p. 70; G. Zarphanalean, *Matenadaran Haykakan T'argmanut'eants Nakhneats (Dar 4-13)*, (Venice, 1889) p. 286; and Yovsēp'ean, *op. cit.*, col. 1019-1020.

27. For systems of dating in Armenian manuscripts see A.K. Sanjian, *Colophons of Armenian Manuscripts, 1301-1480*, Harvard Armenian Texts and Studies, 2 (Cambridge, Massachusetts, 1969) pp. 34-41: 'The Calendrical Systems used in the Colophons.'

28. The text was published by F.N. Finck, 'Kleinere mittelarmenische Texte,' *Zeitschrift für armenische Philologie*, 1 (1903), pp. 1-32, 97-117, 177-219, 301-52; 2 (1904) pp. 81-111. For the passage in question see pp. 218-19.

29. No Khosrov (as opposed to the diminutive form Khosrovik) was known as *t'argmanich'*. There were

several later Khosrovs, including the famous commentator on the Breviary and the Liturgy, Khosrov Andzevatsi of the tenth century.

30. See below at note 55.
31. For this see V. Inglisian, 'Chalkedon und die armenische Kirche,' *Das Konzil von Chalkedon*, II; ed. A. Grillmeier and H. Bacht (Würzburg 1959) pp. 361-416; and K. Sarkissian, *The Council of Chalcedon and the Armenian Church* (London, 1965, reprinted New York, 1975).
32. A. Renoux, 'Une version arménienne des Catéchèses mystagogiques de Cyrille de Jérusalem,' *Le Muséon*, 85 (1972) pp. 147-53. For the Armenian text of the 18 treatises delivered before baptism see *Koch'umn Entzayut'ean* (Venice, 1832).
33. This sermon forms the longest part of the *History* of Agathangelos (see note 13 above). For a recent study and English translation see R.W. Thomson, *The Teaching of Saint Gregory: An early Armenian Catechism*, Harvard Armenian Texts and Studies, 3 (Cambridge, Massachusetts, 1970).
34. Lazar, p. 192.
35. *Book of Letters (Girk' T'łt'ots)*, (Tiflis, 1901) p. 88.
36. *Ibid.*, p. 325.
37. E. Bihain, 'Une vie arménienne de saint Cyrille de Jérusalem.' *Le Muséon*, 76 (1963) pp. 319-48.
38. *Book of Letters*, pp. 407-12. For a critical edition based on other manuscripts see N. Akinean, *T'ułt' Makaray B. Erusałemi hayrapeti ař Vrt'anēs episkoposapet Siwneats yałags kargats ekełetswoy* (Vienna, 1930). English translation in F.C. Conybeare, *The Key of Truth* (Oxford, 1898) pp. 178-85.
39. P'awstos Buzand, *Buzandaran Patmut'iwnk'* (Venice, 1933) III, 3, etc.; Moses Khorenatsi, III.5.
40. *Kanonagirk' Hayots*, ed. V. Hakobyan, II (Erevan, 1971) pp. 216-229.
41. Anania of Shirak according to Conybeare, *op. cit.*, pp. 185-86; Anania of Hałbat according to Akinean, *op. cit.*, pp. 81-84.
42. For a resume of the contents of one recension of this catena see R.W. Thomson, 'The Shorter Recension of the *Root of Faith*,' *Revue des études arméniennes*, N.S. 5 (1968) pp. 249-60. Cf. also *idem*, 'Quotations from Athanasius in the *Root of Faith*,' *Armenian and Biblical Studies*, ed. M.E. Stone (Jerusalem, 1976) pp. 182-203.
43. See G. Garitte, *La Narratio de Rebus Armeniae*, Corpus Scriptorum Christianorum Orientalium, 132, Subsidia, 4 (Louvain, 1952) pp. 210-13.
44. *Ibid.*, pp. 243-44.
45. Armenian text in K. Tēr-Mkrtch'ean, 'Erusałemi Yovhannēs episkoposi t'ułte,' *Ararat*, 29 (1896) pp. 214-15, 252-56. Translation in A. Vardanian, 'Des Johannes von Jerusalem Brief an den albanischen Katholikos Abas,' *Oriens Christianus*, N.S. 2 (1912) pp. 64-79.
46. For the Syrian Julianists and the council of Dvin in 555 see R.W. Thomson, 'An Armenian List of Heresies,' *Journal of Theological Studies*, N.S. 16 (1965) pp. 358-67.
47. *Book of Letters*, pp. 81-84; and Moses Daskhurantsi, II.7.
48. Garitte, *op. cit.*, p. 206. For various accounts of John II's years in Constantinople see N.G. Garsoian, 'Le rôle de la hiérarchie chrétienne dans les rapports diplomatiques entre Byzance et les Sassanides,' *Revue des études arméniennes*, N.S. 10 (1973/74) p. 136, n. 73.
49. Sebēos, ch. 46.
50. *Book of Letters*, p. 123. The same quotation is used twice by Abraham in letters to the Georgian Kiwrion; *ibid.*, pp. 176, 183.
51. *Ibid.*, p. 167.
52. *Ibid.*, p. 176.
53. On these events see N. Akinean, *Kiwrion Kat'ołikos Vrats. Patmut'iwn hay-vrakan yaraberut' eamts eōt'nerord daru mēj* (Vienna, 1910).
54. *Book of Letters*, p. 325. For Bartholomew see M. van Esbroeck, 'Chronique arménienne,' *Analecta Bollandiana*, 80 (1962) pp. 425-29.
55. For the colophon see Yovsēp'ean, *op. cit.*, col. 81-82. For the translation see P. Peeters, 'La version ibéro-arménienne de l'autobiographie de Denys l'Aréopagite,' *Analecta Bollandiana*, 39 (1921) pp. 277-313. For the armenian text see N. Akinean, *Niwt'er hay vkayabanut'ean hamar* (Vienna, 1914) pp. 35-42.
56. R.W. Thomson, 'The Armenian Version of Ps. Dionysius Areopagita,' *Acta Jutlandica*, 56 (1982) pp. 115-24.

57. I. Abuladze, *K'art'lis Tskhovrebis dzveli somkhuri t'argmani*, (Tbilisi, 1953).
58. R.W. Thomson, 'Architectural Symbolism in Classical Armenian Literature,' *Journal of Theological Studies*, N.S. 30 (1979) pp. 102-14.
59. Thomas, III.29, pp. 254-55 of the Armenian text.
60. *Ibid.*, pp. 251-57.
61. Continuator to Thomas, pp. 293-99. But see p. 229 of Thomas.
62. Thomas, III.29, pp. 252-53.
63. N. Thierry, 'Survivance d'une iconographie palestinienne de la Pentecôte au Vaspourakan,' *Atti del primo Simposio internazionale di arte armena* (Venice, 1978) pp. 709-22. For a general study of Gagik's church on Aɫt'amar see S. Der Nersessian, *Aght'amar, Church of the Holy Cross*, Harvard Armenian Texts and Studies, 1 (Cambridge, Massachusetts, 1965).
64. Labubna, p.45.
65. Moses Khorenatsi, II.34. For Moses' date see the Introduction to R.W. Thomson, *Moses Khorenats'i*.
66. Moses, I.22, denies that the Bagratids descend from Hayk, opposing the genealogy in the *Primary History*. This latter is a short text found at the beginning of the *History* of Sebēos, but having no relationship to it. See p. 51 of Abgaryan's edition for the ancestors of Bagarat. English translation of the *Primary History* in R.W. Thomson, *Moses Khorenats'i*, Appendix, pp. 357-63.
67. Moses, II.9, 14.
68. Moses, II.33.
69. Moses, II.29.
70. Thomas, I.6, pp. 47-49 of the Armenian text; cf. Moses Khorenatsi, II.35.
71. Thomas, I.5, p. 40.
72. This is especially emphasized in the *Teaching*, ## 685-98. But cf. the historical section, ## 16, 249.
73. P'awstos Buzand, III.5-6.
74. See the discussion in R.W. Thomson, *Elishē, History of Vardan and the Armenian War*, Harvard Armenian Texts and Studies, 5 (Cambridge, Massachusetts, 1982) pp. 10-16.
75. R.W. Thomson, 'The Maccabees in early Armenian Historiography,' *Journal of Theological Studies*, N.S. 26 (1975) pp. 329-41.
76. The idea is central to Arshak's soliloquy on leaving his patrimonial Ayrarat, Łazar, I.6-8.
77. Moses, I.6, 19; II.75; III.1
78. This parallel was brought out earlier by C. Toumanoff, *Studies in Christian Caucasian History* (Washington, D.C., 1963) p. 332.
79. For a discussion of Moses' use of Josephus see R.W. Thomson, *Moses Khorenats'i*, pp. 25-28, 56-58.
80. Moses, I.3; Josephus, *Wars*, I.1.3.
81. Cf. Łazar, p. 4. Armenian scholars continued to visit Constantinople in search of new texts over succeeding generations, at least through the eleventh century.

VI

A MEDIEVAL ARMENIAN VIEW OF THE PHYSICAL WORLD: THE COSMOLOGY OF VARDAN AREWELC'I IN HIS CHRONICLE*

The first Armenian historians dealt with themes of immediate interest and importance to their contemporary audience, and with circumscribed periods of time. And since Armenian literature begins only in Christian Armenia, the prime concern of Koriwn, P'awstos, or Agat'angełos was naturally with the origin and development of Christianity in their own country. However, Armenians were familiar with a broad spectrum of scholarship — both Christian texts in Greek and Syriac, and the learning of late classical antiquity — so it is not surprising that succeeding authors soon placed Armenia on a larger stage. The first, and most influential, of these historians was the enigmatic Movsēs Xorenac'i. He adapted — with enduring success — the surviving oral traditions about early Armenian history to the framework of world history as codified by Eusebius of Caesarea in his *Chronicle*. After Movsēs it became quite common for an Armenian historian to give a brief resume of early biblical history, to trace the development of nations from Noah's three sons, and to emphasize the antiquity of the Armenians as descendants of Japheth through Torgom[1].

The story of mankind begins with Adam and Eve. According to the book of Genesis they were created on the sixth day. And since — as Movsēs Xorenac'i strongly averred — there is no history without chronology[2], perhaps it is not unreasonable to place the events of the previous five days within the purview of the historian. Armenian scholars had long been familiar with Christian interpretations of the story of creation (the "hexaemeral" literature), with earlier Greek scientific works dealing with the physical universe, and with Philo's interpretations of Genesis and Exodus. Such investigations might find a place in an historical work — for example, in the *Teaching of Saint Gregory*, the long sermon in the middle of Agat'angełos' account of the conversion of Armenia; or in the defense of Christian doctrine in letters

---

* A small token in affectionate remembrance of Sirarpie Der Nersessian, whose influence thirty years ago led me into a career I would never have anticipated.

[1] E.g. Yovhannēs Drasxanakertc'i; T'ovma Arcruni; Asołik.
[2] M.X., II 82.

Additional Note: For Vardan's *Chronicle* see further below item XIX.

reported by Ełišē and Łazar, documents which treat of the fundamental elements in nature, amongst other themes. But generally the speculations we might call "science and astronomy" were not included in specifically historical narratives. It was therefore a novelty when Vardan Arewelcʻi began his *Chronicle* — or, to be more accurate, his *Historical Compilation* [*Hawakʻumn Patmutʻean*] — not with Adam, but with God, and proceeded to describe the creation of the physical world as a prelude to the fall of Adam and Eve from grace and the subsequent sad story of human misfortune.

In his account of the creation of the world Vardan touches on many themes discussed in earlier writers. In what follows I shall try to trace his sources for that first section of his *Chronicle* — or to be more precise, to discuss his views in the light of earlier Armenian traditions. By "traditions" I mean generally accepted views which might be found in historical works, in homilies, and more general works of theology. I shall not here discuss, except in passing, Armenian renderings of Greek technical works. To such "popular" ideas there are parallels in the introduction to Vardan's brief *Geography*; and the same themes were addressed a generation later by Mxitʻar Ayrivanecʻi in his own *Chronicle*. But here I shall concentrate on Vardan's *Chronicle* and confine my comments to sources in published texts. [Since most of the vast mass of Armenian biblical commentaries remain unpublished, I must here omit any reference to Vardan's ideas as expressed in his commentary on Genesis][3].

Vardan begins by discussing the nature and essence of God. When Moses asked God on Mount Horeb: "What shall I say when they ask me his name?" he was told: "I am he who is — *Es em astuac or ēn*". [Into this passage in Exodus, 3.14, the Armenian introduces the word "God", which is not found in the Hebrew and Greek.] There are two parts to this. "He who is" refers to God's eternal uncreated being;

---

[3] For a general overview of Vardan and his works see the two volumes by Pʻ.Pʻ. Antʻapyan, *Vardan Arevelcʻi*, Erevan, 1987, 1989. Studies on the "technical" texts known or written in Armenia [such as B.E. Tʻumanyan, *Hay Astłagitutʻyan Patmutʻyun*, Erevan, 1964] are not relevant to this present enquiry.

Some of the themes discussed below were already raised in the commentary to my translation of the *Chronicle* [DOP, 1989]. Here I wish to expand on their earlier history in Armenian writers. A preliminary version of this article was read in October, 1990, in Bologna at the meeting of the *Association internationale des études arméniennes*. I am grateful to the audience for some comments, and especially to Peter Cowe for his presentation as Respondent.

whereas "God — *astuac*" refers to his creative activity. Vardan derives the Armenian word from the phrase *ast acel*, "to bring [into being] here". This is the standard etymology for "God" in Armenian, though it does not seem to be attested before the tenth century[4]. It is found in Xosrov Anjewacʻi's *Commentary on the Prayers of the Liturgy*, and is echoed in Nersēs Lambronacʻi's more elaborate *Commentary on the Liturgy*. It is closest to the Greek interpretation for *theos* derived from *tithēmi* (to place, put). The other Greek etymologies deriving *theos* from stems such as: *theō* (to run), *theaomai* (to see), *aithō* (to burn), seem to have no echo in Armenian[5]. The comment attributed to Gregory in the *History* of Agatʻangełos that the pagan gods are *hastuackʻ* [i.e. "fabricated"], not *astuackʻ*, is more of a pun than an etymology. It comes in the midst of numerous tortures, where Gregory taunts Trdat and derides idolatry [§ 71].

Vardan now turns to the fact that God is one. In mathematics the single is the origin of multiplicity and exists without it[6]. This argument would be familiar to all Armenians from the very popular introduction to philosophy by David the "Invincible" Philosopher, his *Definitions and Divisions of Philosophy*. Chapter 14 begins: "... It should also be known that there are two kinds of numbers — even numbers and odd numbers... The common origin for even and odd numbers is one". Anania of Širak attributes this idea to Plato. Likewise, argues Vardan, "He who is" is one and single. But he adds that understanding of the Trinity was not hidden from Moses, the author of the book of Genesis. For he had used the plural form of the verb several times when referring to God's activity — "Let us create... let us go down", etc.

Vardan returns to this theme when discussing the creation of Adam. But here he notes that God is three because he has beginning, middle, and end. This has a close parallel in a mistaken rendering of the Greek in the Armenian version of the pseudo-Aristotelian *De Mundo*. The Armenian states: "[God] is beginning and middle and end, holding all beings". But the Greek original says: "God holds the beginning and end and middle of all beings". The passage is based on Plato's *Laws*[7].

---

[4] It is first attested in XOSROV ANJEWACʻI, p. 16. Cf. NERSĒS LAMBRONACʻI, *Meknutʻiwn Xorhrdocʻ Pataragin*, p. 349.

[5] For the Greek sources see LAMPE, *Lexicon*, s.v. *Theos*.

[6] See for example, the Armenian version of DAVID's *Definitions and Divisions of Philosophy*, ch. 14. Anania attributes this idea to Plato, p. 239.

[7] Armenian version, p. 542 = 401b25.

There is a parallel in Anania of Širak, who attributes the idea to Philo[8]. But it does not appear in the earliest Armenian sources, such as the *Teaching of Saint Gregory*, where the Trinity is discussed at length. In his *Geography* Vardan elaborates on the Father as begetter, the Son as begotten, and the holy Spirit as emanating from the Father — three Persons and one Nature. But in the *Chronicle* he proceeds immediately to the created world, omitting further discussion of "essence", "nature", or "being", which figure prominently in more theologically oriented works.

God is without distinction, or number, or qualities, says Vardan, yet he is recognized as "good". He did not wish to possess the good solely [for himself], but he made good creatures in order for them to enjoy his own inexhaustible goodness[9]. Later Vardan stresses that God foresaw that this liberal benevolence would be abused and that sin would enter the world. But first he turns to the creative activity of God the "craftsman [*aruestawor*]"[10]. This term does not occur in the Armenian bible; but the Greek equivalent, *technitēs*, is very common in patristic literature. Later Vardan will return to the theme of *aruest*, "art of craft", an important concept in the *De Mundo*.

God did not fashion matter that already existed into something new. Vardan notes that the word "matter [*niwt*]" does not occur in Genesis, but he passes over the ambiguous statement in Wisdom 11.18 that God's all-powerful hand created this world from "formless matter" [*hastateac' zašxarhs yankerparan niwt'oy*]. The phrase had been echoed in the *Teaching*[11], and several later authors had discussed the question of creation *ex nihilo*[12]. Vardan explicitly states that God made the form of heaven and earth from nothing [*yoč'ēic' ĕnč'ac'oyc*]. This terminology derives from Eznik, who was the first to adapt technical Greek vocabulary to Armenian[13]. The Armenian version of Basil's *Hexaemeron*

---

[8] P. 240.
[9] Cf. his *Geography*, 1.16ff. The theme is too common to note the parallels in theological literature.
[10] See also GRIGORIS ARŠARUNI, Hom. 3, GRIGOR NAREKAC'I, 63.2.
[11] §272.
[12] See SARKAWAG, p. 306ff., for a discussion of form and matter.
[13] See L. MARIÈS, "Étude sur quelques noms et verbes d'existence chez Eznik", *REArm* 8 (1928).

unequivocally states: *ac i č'goyē i goy*[14]. However, it is worth pointing out that the Greek original merely says that God brought into being what did not exist. The Armenian version of this influential text has been much studied in recent years, and we now have a good critical edition of the text. But the Armenian was not translated from the original Greek, but rather from an earlier Syriac rendering [preserved in its entirety in only one manuscript]. The Syriac, which is generally expansive, here follows the Greek. So the alteration was introduced by the Armenian translator. The same idea of creation *ex nihilo* is elaborated in greater detail in the Fourth Homily of the *Yačaxapatum Čaṙk'*.

God began by creating four "principles — *skzbuns*", which Vardan also calls "elements — *tarerk'*". These are fire, air, water, and earth; which are also defined as "warm, light, cold, and heavy". The notion of these four basic building blocks goes back to Greek antiquity, and is echoed by all Armenian writers who deal with the physical world. Although Vardan takes the idea for granted and does not elaborate on it, we may briefly note some of the earlier Armenian discussion and interpretations.

In the first place, Vardan's term *skizbn* is not usual. In addition to *tarr*, which is ubiquitous, one finds most frequently the term *niwt'*; less common are *hiwt'* [used by Yovhannēs Mandakuni, for example], and *yelanak* [which is found in the *Yačaxapatum Čaṙk'*][15]. The original term for these four elements in Basil's *Hexaemeron* is the Greek word *stoicheia*, which was transliterated as *estokse* in the Syriac. But the Armenian translator has rendered it by *bnut'iwnk'*, "natures", a term used by Eznik[16]. However, that expression was not common in native Armenian writers. The four elements are very frequently listed as pairs in opposition to each other, and in the *De Mundo* the discussion of opposing qualities is greatly expanded[17].

Biblical justification for these elements could be found; but only in

---

[14] P. 40; Greek, II 2, 14B. My comments on the Syriac are based on a reading of Sinai, Syriac no. 9. For the fragment in the British Library, Add. 17143, see L.H. TER-PETROSYAN, "Barseł Kesarac'u 'Vec'oreayk'i' hayeren T'argmanut'yan Naxorinakē", *PBH* 102-103 [1983, 2-3], 264-278.

[15] *Niwt'*: *Yačaxapatum*, Hom. 4, p. 34; ELIŠĒ, p. 33; *Girk' T'łt'oc'*, p. 23; GREGORY OF NAREK, 65.2. *Hiwt'*: YOVHANNĒS MANDAKUNI, Hom. 26, p. 198. *Yełanak*: *Yačaxapatum*, Hom. 4, p. 33.

[16] E.g. §2.

[17] §5, Armenian text, p. 531.

the *Questions on Genesis* attributed toEłišē are scriptural parallels adduced for all four. Fire is linked to the angels; wind to God and thunder; water is justified by Judith 9.17 [creator of the waters]; and earth from Gen. 1[18].

Then the number four has significance in and of itself. We are not here concerned with the very many interpretations to be found in Armenian writers of four in a Christian context. Here our interest is rather in the specific parallels with the four elements. These include Eznik's image of the world as a chariot drawn by four horses, all in competition with each other. But they are controlled and made to drive a straight course by God the charioteer. In this passage [§ 3] Eznik was primarily concerned with the single nature of God; but he refers to the four horses as the hot and the cold, the dry and the wet. This idea is also found in the Armenian version of George of Pisidia's *Hexaemeron*. But it did not become popular in Armenian writers[19]. George also compared to the four elements the four columns which support the world — an important theme in Psalm 74, to be discussed later. [In the King James version, 75.3: "The earth and all the inhabitants thereof are dissolved: I bear up the pillars of it".]

Gregory of Narek compared the four elements to the four points of the cross. The theme of the cross is very prominent in Armenian, first being elaborated in the *Teaching of Saint Gregory*; and numerous theological interpretations are given to the directions in which the arms of the cross point. But only in Gregory of Narek have I found the elements adduced in this regard[20]. He prays that the splendour of the four-armed cross may influence the four elements of his being: *č'oric's niwt'oc' imoys goyut'ean k'aṙat'ewid nšoyl azdesc'ē*. Yovhannēs Ōjnec'i compares the four psalms at evening prayer, in accordance with his especial liturgical interests[21].

The creation of these four principles did not occur in time. For "in the beginning" there was neither time nor place. Measurable time came into being on Day Four, with the creation of the sun and moon[22]. Vardan will discuss the explanation of days one to four later; first he

---

[18] P. 29.

[19] EZNIK, # 3; GEORGE OF PISIDIA, 1.339.

[20] NAREK, 65.2. For the *Teaching* and other similar theological parallels see THOMSON, "Number Symbolism".

[21] *Opera*, p. 54. Nersēs Šnorhali draws a parallel between the four *tarerk'* in the nature of the body and the four degrees of affinity within which marriage is prohibited, *T'ułt'k'*, p. 63.

[22] See below for the explanation of "days" one to four.

turns to God's creation of heaven and earth. Vardan starts with the three concentric spheres, *kamark'*, which circle the earth: closest is that of air, then water, and farthest away is fire. There are biblical parallels to this. Isaiah, 40.22, had referred to heaven as a *kamar* [and a *xoran*]. And in Wisdom, 13.2, the idea that the circles of fire, wind, air, and water, and the stars are gods is attacked. But Vardan's three rings have their origin in secular texts such as the *De Mundo* [though this adds ether][23]. Eznik had attacked the idea, taking it as a misinterpretation of Paul's "third heaven[24]. In his *Geography* Vardan calls these rings *bolorakut'iwnk'*, "circles". But the concept rarely appears in Armenian texts. Išox combines the idea with the seven spheres which carry the seven planets; and it is those *seven* spheres which are found in most writers who deal with the physical universe[25].

The earth, surrounded by these three rings, is held in place by the upward blowing wind. Too heavy to fly up, the earth is prevented by this wind from falling down. There are parallels in the earliest Armenian writers. In the *Teaching* we read that the universe is suspended without wings as if in flight[26]. And Eznik notes that this is not contrary to scripture, for Job says that God set the earth on nothing: *i veray oč'nč'i*[27].

However, scripture is not consistent, for Psalm 74.4 refers to the columns which support the world, and Job [9.6] says: "God shakes from its foundations what is under heaven, and its pillars tremble". This theme is endorsed by the *Yačaxapatum Čaŕk'* and Gregory of Narek[28]. Basil in his *Hexaemeron* avoids taking these quotations too literally, preferring to think of the "power of God" as supporting the earth; he then adds with more enthusiasm the theory of the "scientists"

---

[23] Armenian text, p. 521.

[24] EZNIK, § 289; the refutation comes at § 378.

[25] IŠOX, p. 84. The seven spheres are discussed below. The terms *kamar* and *xoran* have numerous biblical parallels (Ps. 103.2; Job 38.38; Is. 40.22) and are used in the *Teaching* as similes for the visible heaven, e.g. § 259; cf. *xoranajew* in GRIGORIS ARŠARUNI, *Hom.* 3. GREGORY OF NAREK, 75.10, likens the *kamar* of heaven to the church. The Armenian version of BASIL's *Hexaemeron* (p. 23) changes the *kamara* of the Greek (rendered *kamar* in the Armenian version of Isaiah) to *konk' gmbet'ard*. *Gmbet'*, "dome", does not appear in the Armenian bible. But ELIŠĒ, *Questions*, p. 27, interprets *xoran* as a "tent, as it were in the form of a dome — *vran ibr t'e gmbet'ajew*". For *vran*, cf. EPHREM, p. 4. *Gndajew* appears in GEORGE OF PISIDIA, 1.86.

[26] § 355.

[27] § 285; Job 26.7.

[28] *Yačaxapatum*, no. 22 (p. 233); NAREK, 63.2.

that the earth is in the middle of the universe, equidistant from all extremities, since all weighty bodies gravitate to the centre[29]. George of Pisidia calls the column theory a "myth"; and Nersēs Šnorhali explicitly rejects it[30].

The very different conception found in Cosmas Indicopleustes that the universe is hexagonal, patterned on the tabernacle of the Old Testament[31], does not seem to appear to be reflected in any original Armenian author. In his *Geography*, Vardan describes the earth [not the universe] as a cube, *kibikon*. And there is an interesting allusion to this idea in the Armenian version of the *Physiologus*. Describing the bee, the text notes that it fashions a cell [of a honeycomb] "like this hexagonal world — *nman vec'ankiwni ašxarhis*"[32].

Vardan now turns to the angels. He states: "When heaven came into being, it was given life with the fiery angels, as their region[33] is fiery". It is not clear whether heaven is in the outermost circle or beyond it. Vardan merely says: "Heaven is the upper veil between the angels and God"[34]. An equally vague definition is found in Išox, who refers to heaven as a "ceiling [*jełun*]". That the angels are spirits of fire is a natural conclusion from Ps. 103.4: "Who maketh his angels spirits; his ministers a flaming fire". This is quoted in the *Teaching* and elaborated by Eznik[35]. [But Eznik has a problem, for the angels are incorporeal. So he claims that "corporeal" means "composed of four elements [*i č'oric' hiwt'ic'*]", like men and animals. But to be incorporeal is to be of a simple nature [*parz bnut'iwn*], like angels, demons, and the souls of men.]

As for the angels themselves Vardan divides them into ten ranks. The later Mxit'ar Ayrivaneci does the same, but when listing the ranks by name he gives the traditional nine ranks plus the twenty-four elders of the book of Revelation. Ten ranks is contrary to the universal earlier view that there are nine ranks of angels[36]. These nine divisions are basic

---

[29] *Hexaemeron*, I 9-10. Cf. ROBBINS, p. 43. It is noteworthy that at III 4 of the *Hexaemeron* the reference to the columns is omitted in the Armenian version, p. 75.
[30] GEORGE, 1.129ff.; NERSĒS, p. 22.
[31] For Cosmas see WOLSKA, *La topographie chrétienne*.
[32] No. 36 [no. 37 in Marr's earlier edition]. VARDAN, *Geography*, p. 5.
[33] Region: *gawaŕ*, as at Heb. 11.14.
[34] Veil: *varagoyr*. Cf. IŠOX, p. 76: Heaven is a "ceiling [*jełun*]", not a biblical term.
[35] *Teaching*, § 324, cf. 262; EZNIK, § 114.
[36] The nine divisions are elaborated in PSEUDO-DIONYSIUS, *Heavenly Hierarchy*; cf. ELIŠĒ, *Questions*, p. 11, and NERSĒS ŠNORHALI, p. 30. For parallels between the nine ranks of angels

to the arguments of Pseudo-Dionysius, and they are acknowledged in all native Armenian writers. Many of them draw parallels with the nine ranks of the church hierarchy; and Smbat in his *Lawcode* extends this parallelism to the nine ranks of courtiers in the imperial palace at Constantinople. Even Vardan repeats the ninefold division in his *Geography*. The reason for his opinion in the *Chronicle* is obscure.

The six days of creation Vardan describes as six revolutions of heaven. Since the markers of time did not yet exist, one cannot talk about the "first" or "second" day. This is an important point, emphasized in the Syrian commentators, of whom Ephrem was particularly well known in Armenia, but also discussed in Greek writers[37]. It is picked up by Anania of Širak, who points out that the day the world came into being is not called "first", but "day one". This he links to number theory, since one is the origin of multiplicity[38]. Some commentators wondered how the first three days could be so reckoned. The *Questions* of Ełišē, for example, fudges the issue by distinguishing light as such from the stars, and by supposing that light came upon the earth and then withdrew in three successive stages. This view has patristic origins[39]. Ephrem interprets the first three days as a type of the three days that Christ was in the tomb before the resurrection[40]. But this does not seem to have had echoes in Armenian.

Vardan now proceeds to describe the successive stages of creation on each of the six revolutions, but he omits any reference to the seventh day of God's rest. The parallel of seven days with the six ages of the world, to be followed by a seventh age of rest, free of corruption and evil, was well known in Armenian. It had formed a major theme in the *Teaching*, and is echoed by many writers[41]. [The similar theory that this world would last seven ages, and that the eighth would be that of eternal rest, is echoed only in Anania of Širak.] But in his *Chronicle* Vardan passes over such speculations.

The creative power of God Vardan calls "nature". He says: "Now

---

and the nine ranks of the church hierarchy see Uxtanēs, ch. 63, Movsēs Dasxuranc'i, II 48, and Thomson, "The Armenian Version of Ps. Dionysius Areopagita".

[37] Levene, p. 73. For Greek thoughts on this problem see Alexandre, p. 100-101.
[38] Anania, p. 239.
[39] *Questions*, p. 38; cf. p. 28-29. For patristic sources see Robbins, p. 49.
[40] Armenian text, p. 6.
[41] References in Thomson, "Number Symbolism", under "Six" and "Seven". To those references to early writers add Isox, p. 95-96, who refers to the seven layers of skin and the seven doors of the ears; and Nersēs Šnorhali, p. 23, 27, for the seven ages.

philosophers say that in the first revolution of heaven came into being nature, which is the art [*aruest*] of God, the creative power after God, perhaps the energy [*nergorcut'iwn*] of the four elements". Earlier Vardan had called God a craftsman [*aruestawor*]; but here the personification of nature is directly reminiscent of the *De Mundo*, well known in its Armenian version. The theme is elaborated by Išox, whose work is entitled "Book concerning Nature, in general and particular". For him it is nature which gives life and creates the world. And nature is equated with art, the wisdom of God[42]. Parallels here with the traditions attributed to Hermes Trismegistus have already been noted by Mahé in his study on the Hermetic literature[43].

At the end of his description of the six stages of creation Vardan returns to this theme: "Nature moves the sphere of heaven", and: "According to Aristotle the general spirit gives existence to everything". But the concept of a *hogi ĕndhanur* seems closer to the *Timaeus* of Plato than to the Pseudo-Aristotelian *De Mundo*.

On the second day — that is, for Vardan, the second revolution — the firmament was established. Genesis, I 7, explains that the firmament divided the waters. The idea of the waters above the earth and the waters below is elaborated by early Armenian writers, such as Eznik and the *Teaching*[44]. And the division is put to symbolic purpose by Grigoris Aršaruni, who uses it to contrast the spiritual and corporeal in various contexts[45]. Vardan is more prosaic: the waters were divided for two reasons — to lighten the weight of the earth, and to protect corporeal creatures from the fire of heaven. The second reason has patristic origins[46]. In a different context Vardan notes that mankind has already experienced the effects of the circle of fire, for the higher one goes the warmer it becomes. Describing the tower of Babel later in his *Chronicle*, he indicates that the higher the tower rose the hotter the air became, until men were burned and could build no further. Vardan's elaborate description of the building of the tower has its closest parallels with two foreign texts translated into Armenian before his

---

[42] *De Mundo*, p. 530; Išox, p. 82, 85, 95.
[43] Mahé, *Hermès*, II, p. 348ff.
[44] *Teaching*, §§ 413-414; Eznik, § 285; cf. Ephrem, p. 3-4.
[45] Grigoris, § 3.
[46] Robbins, p. 49. For the general exegesis of this question see also Alexandre, p. 108-111.

time: the *Chronicle* of the Syrian patriarch Michael, and the adaptation of the Georgian *Chronicles*[47].

In the third revolution came into being the plants and trees. Vardan elaborates on Gen. 1.11-12. He states that the origin of plants is the mould of the earth [*borbos hołoyn*], the origin of trees is moss [*mamuṙn*], and the most perfect specimen [*katarumn*] is the palm, for these are divided into male and female. The repute of the palm tree could be found in Basil's *Hexaemeron*; but the role of mould as generating plants does not seem to be found in Armenian before Išox[48]. Vardan's comments are repeated by Mxit'ar Ayrivanec'i[49].

On the fourth revolution came into being light. First Vardan notes that light is an offshoot [*xzac*] of the ether. This is not an idea of Basil's, who distinguishes light and the ether; it is closer to Ephrem's description of light as "an emanation without anything material [*sp'iṙ tarac aṙanc' tarer ĕnč'i*][50]. The light is contained in vessels, as described by Eznik, Ełišē, or Ephrem[51]. It is interesting that the Armenian version of Basil's *Hexaemeron* uses the same term, where the Greek distinguishes light from its underlying *sōma*[52]. This alteration does not occur in the Syriac intermediary, which has *gušmā*, rendering the Greek exactly.

The most important of the lights are the sun, moon, and the other seven stars, says Vardan. This is a strange remark, for the seven planets — which earlier authors describe as having each its own sphere to carry it[53] — include the sun and moon. It is possible that the text is corrupt, for five and seven are easily confused when written as Armenian letters. The Armenian term for "sphere" varies considerably. In the *Chronicle* Vardan does not describe them, but his *Geography* refers to the seven *gawti*, a term used by Anania of Širak; in the *De Mundo*, the term is *bolor*, and in Basil's *Hexaemeron*, *bolorak*. Ełišē in his *Homilies* refers to the seven *parunak*, which he likens to the seven gifts of the Spirit. In his *Geography* Vardan includes the sun and moon in the seven spheres, and

---

[47] THOMSON, "Vardan", p. 146-147.
[48] *Hexaemeron*, 47A; IŠOX, p. 90.
[49] MXIT'AR, p. 233.
[50] BASIL, 19A (p. 54); EPHREM, p. 5.
[51] *Aman* in EZNIK, §310, and ELIŠĒ, p. 166; *anawt'*, in EPHREM, p. 5.
[52] *Hexaemeron*, VI 3, 51E; p. 173 of the Armenian.
[53] *De Mundo*, p. 520, *bolor*; *Hexaemeron*, p. 72, *bolorak*; ANANIA, p. 325, *gawti*; ELIŠĒ, *Homilies*, p. 322, *parunak* [parallel to the seven gifts of the Spirit]. See also VARDAN's *Geography*, 1.45, *gawti*.

adds the names by which "the Persians call them". Likewise, the names of the planets are given in the *De Mundo* immediately following the discussion of ether. Išox gives them the Arabic names, and Anania gives the Greek, Arabic, and Armenian [54].

With these lights time could first be marked. Vardan does not elaborate on the question of time, save that earlier he had said: "Time did not exist from the beginning". Much more important in Armenian than the marking of time — the days and years of Gen. 1.14 — was the interpretation of "signs [*nšans*]" in the same verse. As Question 32 in the text on Genesis attributed to Ełišē asks: "What are we to understand by Moses saying about the stars that God made them to be for signs? Is what the astrologers say correct; and can the stars do this?". The answer given by Ełišē is a definite "No", given at some length. For astrology was a continuing preoccupation of Armenian writers.

The early Armenian historians who describe the Iranian ruling classes, such as P'awstos, Ełišē, or Movsēs Xorenac'i, all refer to the astrologers as a prominent and official group [55]. In Armenia the proponents of astrology did not form an organized class, but their ideas are regularly attacked. The first to deal with the question was Eznik, who refutes the idea that the stars could influence births and deaths. In the homilies known as the *Yačaxapatum Čaṙk'* it is emphasized that the stars do not indicate one's future fortunes or fate [*baxt ew cnunds*]. Ełišē in the *Questions* attacks astrology, as does John Mandakuni in his homilies; and the same opposition is found in the translated texts of Basil and Nemesius. [However, this did not prevent the Armenians from translating Paul of Alexandria's *Introduction to Astrology*!] [56]. It is therefore rather surprising when Nersēs Šnorhali skirts around the issue in a mild fashion. In the poem "On Heaven" he states: "Although without life or reason, yet by their movement [the stars] have some influence. They do not have influence in themselves, but by the Word of him who created heaven" [57]. Vardan himself has no interest in the subject in his *Chronicle*, apart from stating that astrology [*hmayut'iwn astełac*] derived from king Aloros — a passage taken from Michael the

---

[54] *De Mundo*, p. 520; Išox, p. 80ff.; Anania, p. 325.

[55] P'awstos, IV 54; Ełišē, *History*, p. 18; Movsēs Xorenac'i, *On Fables*, and II 70.

[56] Eznik, §§ 216ff.; *Yačaxapatum Čaṙk'*, p. 233; Ełišē, *Questions*, p. 33; *Hexaemeron*, VI 5; Nemesius, ch. 35ff. For Paul of Alexandria see the edition by Bart'ikyan in *B.M.*, 12 [1977].

[57] P. 24.

Syrian's *Chronicle*[58]. Earlier Armenian authors follow Greek tradition in deriving the more respectable astronomy from the Chaldaeans. As David the Invincible Philosopher explained: "Astronomy was invented by the Chaldaeans, since a cloudless and constantly clear sky enabled them easily to comprehend the movements of the heavenly bodies".

Vardan notes that the paths of the seven planets take them through the twelve signs of the zodiac. Some of these signs had been named by Eznik, and Anania lists them all[59]. With his customary enthusiasm for number symbolism, Grigoris Aršaruni links the twelve signs to other uses of twelve in the Old Testament[60]; but he offers no further details about the zodiac. In the *Homilies* attributed to Ełišē the twelve apostles are regarded as healers of men who, in place of God, had gone astray after the twelve stars[61].

As the sun moves through the zodiac, explains Vardan, it moves higher and lower, thus causing the passage of the four seasons. The alternation of the seasons is likened by George of Pisidia to a dance, a figure that is prominent in the *De Mundo*[62]. But there, it is all the stars in their circular orbit which revolve in a solemn choral dance. The movement of the sun higher and lower means that the length of daylight varies, from the shortest day of four hours to the longest of twenty. Only in Lower India does the length of sunlight never vary: there is it always light for 12 hours and dark for twelve[63]. These matters are elaborated by Išox.

The inhabited world is divided into seven climes according to the philosophers, says Vardan. Išox names these philosophers Aristotle and Hermes[64]. He and Vardan agree that comparable to the seven climes are another seven in the world below the equator — but this is uninhabitable because of its being cold and dark. The Long Recension of the *Ašxarhac'oyc'* while referring to the *antichthōn*, does not describe

---

[58] VARDAN, p. 7. The earliest texts follow Greek tradition in deriving astrology from the Chaldaeans. The whole question of early Armenian ideas on astrology forms the subject of a separate study by the present author, and is not taken up here.

[59] EZNIK, §§ 219ff.; ANANIA, p. 323.

[60] Cf. PHILO, *In Ex.*, II 112ff.

[61] See THOMSON, "Number Symbolism", s.v. "Twelve".

[62] GEORGE OF PISIDIA, I, 290. Cf. *De Mundo*, 391b18, *parakic'k'* in the Armenian text, p. 519.

[63] This is described in greater detail by Išox, p. 78. See also ANANIA, p. 323-325.

[64] P. 78.

it as uninhabitable; but the shorter recension omits reference to this lower half of the earth.

Vardan does not elaborate on the seven climes. But it was an important theme in Išox, for the differences between the climes explain differences between different peoples[65]. Those to the north, for example, are wilder and more passionate than those of the south, who because of their greater gentleness did not became eaters of meat. The best clime is that in the middle, Mesopotamia, where the inhabitants are not swarthy like the Indians, nor are they fair like the Sarmatians. Here they are wise and skilled and intelligent. Therefore it is more desirable then all lands of imperial kings; and for the same reason it has been the most often ravaged. One may suspect that Išox's origins may have influenced his views here. Later, Mxit'ar Ayrivanec'i makes nine divisions, or climes. Rather optimistically he adds that seven of these with 67 nations are Christian, while only two with four nations are not. He does not list these nations, and the total of 71 is rather odd. For the number 72 is the standard exegesis. It is first found in Armenian in the *Teaching*, but goes back to earlier interpretations of the number of languages that resulted from the scattering at the tower of Babel[66].

Vardan runs together the fifth and sixth days, which describe the creation of the animals in the seas, in the air, and on land. Beginning with the zoophytes and sponges, says Vardan, these living creatures culminate in man, the perfect being with rationality. As examples of the humblest aquatic creatures sponges appear in Basil and Nemesius[67]; but Armenian writers are usually vague in their enumeration of species[68]. There are 1,000 species, claims Vardan, whose leaders — or perhaps, the most significant of whom [*glxaworawk' iwreanc'*] — are Leviathan in the waters and Behemoth on dry land in the desert. Neither of these names of animals occurs in the Armenian bible (or in the Greek); the Armenian renders Leviathan by *višap* and Behemoth by *gazan*. The two Hebrew names were used by the Syrian Ephrem in his commentary on Genesis; but the Armenian version of that is abbreviated,

---

[65] P. 94.

[66] MXIT'AR, p. 233; *Teaching*, § 612 [but cf. § 686 for the seventy apostles]. This and other early sources in Armenian, such as the translations of Eusebius' *Chronicle* and that of Hippolytus, describe the many nations who descended from Noah's three sons, but do not link them to the climes.

[67] *Hexaemeron*, VII 2, 64B (Arm. p. 223); NEMESIUS, ch. 1 (Arm. p. 13), quoting Aristotle.

[68] E.g. *Yačaxapatum*, Hom. 4; GRIGOR ARŠARUNI, Hom. 3.

and Leviathan and Behemoth do not seem to appear in Armenian before the tenth century. Leviathan is mentioned by Gregory of Narek, while both occur together in a homily by Nersēs of Lambron[69]. Grigor Aršaruni uses the biblical terms: *višaps* in the water and *gazan* on earth[70].

The fifth and sixth days of Genesis 1 refer only to the various kinds of created animals. Vardan adds a reference to plants and metallic substances — gold, silver, precious stones, and (more obscurely) "the other things which nature works through sulphur and mercury, as learned men say". This last phrase is very close to the description of minerals in Išox[71]. The fourth homily in the *Yačaxapatum Čaŕk'* refers to various metals and precious stones useful for mankind; and Łazar in his *History* offers a description of how plants are used for medicine, and minerals for adornment[72]. But working with sulphur and mercury [*ccmbov, žipakaw*] does not occur in the early texts.

Finally, a new nature was wonderfully fashioned from heaven and earth — man, who combines physical and spiritual qualities. Vardan does not refer to the "image" of Gen. 1.26, but simply states that man is like the Trinity. That the three persons of the Trinity joined in creating man was standard exegesis of "let us make", and is found in the *Teaching* and later Armenian texts[73]. But Vardan combines this with the idea of man being created in the way a picture is painted. His terminology is quite extraordinary: "Like good portrait painters, since they begin from the feet, [God] wonderfully fashioned some new nature from heaven and earth and what is in between, six hands engaged in the forming of one picture". The Armenian bible renders the Greek *kat' eikona* [according to the image], by *i patker*, which could also mean "into a picture". But there seems to be no evidence in Armenian that painters began from the feet up[74]. Furthermore, Vardan refers to six hands. This description of the creation of man which involves Father,

---

[69] See the *NBHL* s.v. Leviathan is attested earlier in Gregory of Narek. The two names in the Syriac of Ephrem, p. 22-23, do not appear in the abbreviated Armenian rendering, p. 6-7.

[70] Hom. 3.

[71] P. 82-83.

[72] *Yačaxapatum*, p. 34; Łazar, p. 9-10.

[73] § 263.

[74] The late Greek "Painter's Manual" has no explicit instructions in this regard. One would begin with an outline, then paint the garments, then the face. Cf. A.N. Didron, *Manuel d'iconographie chrétienne*, Paris, 1845, and P. Hetherington, *The "Painter's Manual" of Dionysius of Fourna*, London, 1974.

Son, and Holy Ghost, each using both hands to paint a picture, is to my knowledge unique!

BIBLIOGRAPHY

Armenian Texts

AGAT'ANGEŁOS
    Patmut'iwn Hayoc', ed. G. Tēr-Mkrtč'ean and St. Kanayeanc', Tiflis, 1909 [reprinted Caravan Books, Delmar, N.Y., 1980].

ANANIA OF ŠIRAK
    Matenagrut'yunē, ed. A. Abrahamyan, Erevan, 1944.

Ašxarhac'oyc'
    Long Recension, ed. A. Soukry, Venice, 1881. Short Recension, in MOVSĒS XORENAC'I, *Matenagrut'iwnk'*, Venice, 1865.

BASIL OF CAESAREA
    Hexaemeron. Armenian text, ed. K. Muradyan, Erevan, 1984. Greek text, ed. S. Giet, Paris, 1968.

GRIGOR NAREKAC'I
    Matean Ołbergut'ean, Buenos Aires, 1948 [reprinted Caravan Books, 1981].

GRIGORIS ARŠARUNI
    Meknut'iwn Ēnt'erc'uacoc', Venice, 1964.

DAVID
    Sahmank' Imastasirut'ean, ed. S.S. Arevšatyan, Erevan, 1960. Armenian text reprinted with English translation and notes in B. KENDALL and R.W. THOMSON, *Definitions and Divisions of Philosophy*, Chico, Calif., 1983.

De Mundo
    Armenian text in DAWIT' ANYAŁT', *Matenagrut'iwnk'*, Venice, 1932. Greek text in Loeb Classical Library.

EŁIŠĒ
    History: Vasn Vardanay ew Hayoc' Paterazmin, ed. E. Ter-Minasean, Erevan, 1957.
    Homilies: Matenagrut'iwnk', Venice, 1859.
    Questions et réponses sur la Genèse, ed. N. Akinean and S. Kogean, Vienna, 1928.

EPHREM
    Commentary on Genesis. Armenian text, Venice, 1836. Syriac text, ed. R.M. Tonneau, CSCO 152, Louvain, 1955.

EZNIK
    De Deo, ed. L. Mariès and Ch. Mercier, P.O. XXVIII 3-4, Paris, 1959.

GEORGE OF PISIDIA
    Hexaemeron. Armenian text, Venice, 1900.

Girk' T'lt'oc'
    Tiflis, 1901.
Išox
    Girk' i veray Bnut'ean, ed. S. Vardanyan, Erevan, 1979.
Kanonagirk' Hayoc'
    Ed. V. Hakobyan, 2 vols., Erevan, 1964, 1971.
Łazar
    Patmut'iwn Hayoc', ed. G. Tēr-Mkrtč'ean and S. Malxasean, Tiflis, 1904 [reprinted Caravan Books, Delmar, N.Y., 1985].
M.X. = Movsēs Xorenac'i
    Patmut'iwn Hayoc', ed. M. Abełean and S. Yarut'iwnean, Tiflis, 1913 [reprinted Caravan Books, Delmar, N.Y., 1981].
Mxit'ar Ayrivanec'i
    Patmut'iwn, ed. K. Patkanov, *Trydi Vostochago Otdelenija Imperatorskago Russkago Archeologicheskago Obschestva*, XIV, St. Petersburg, 1869.
NBHL
    Nor Baŕgirk' Haygazean Lezui, 2 vols., Venice, 1836, 1837 [reprinted Erevan, 1979, 1981].
Nemesius
    Yałags bnut'ean mardoy, Venice, 1889.
Nersēs Lambronac'i
    Meknut'iwn Xorhrdoc' Pataragin, Venice, 1847.
Nersēs Šnorhali
    T'ułt'k', Venice, 1871.
    Yałags erkni ev zarduc' nora, Erevan, 1968.
Paul of Alexandria
    H. Bartikyan, "Aratos Solac'u ew Połos Ałek'sandrac'u astłabašxakan erkeri hin hayeren t'argmanut'yunē", *B.M.*, 12 (1977), 137-162.
Philo
    In Exodum. Loeb Classical Library.
Physiologus
    Text in N. Marr, *Sborniki Pritch Vardana*, vol. III. St. Petersburg, 1894.
Pseudo-Dionysius
    Heavenly Hierarchy. Armenian text, ed. R.W. Thomson, CSCO 488, Louvain, 1987.
Sarkawag
    Hovhannes Imastaseri Matenagrut'yunē, ed. A.G. Abrahamyan, Erevan, 1956.
Teaching of Saint Gregory
    Armenian text in Agat'angełos [see above], # 259-715. R.W. Thomson, *The Teaching of Saint Gregory: An Early Armenian Catechism*, Cambridge, Mass., 1970.
Vardan
    Chronicle: Hawak'umn Patmut'ean, ed. Ł. Ališan, Venice, 1862.
    Geography: Ašxarhac'oyc', ed. H. Pērpērean, Paris, 1960.
Xosrov Anjewac'i
    Meknut'iwn Aławt'ic' Pataragin, Venice, 1869.

Yačaxapatum Čaṙk'
    Venice, 1954.
YOVHANNĒS ŌJNEC'I
    Opera, Venice, 1834.

Secondary Literature

ALEXANDRE, M.
    Le commencement du livre Genèse I-V. La version grecque de la Septante et sa réception, Paris, 1988.
ANT'APYAN, P'. P'.
    Vardan Arevelc'i. Keank'n u Gorcuneut'yunē, 2 vols., Erevan, 1987, 1989.
LAMPE, G.W.H.
    A Patristic Greek Lexicon, Oxford, 1968.
LEVENE, A.
    The Early Syrian Fathers on Genesis, London, 1951.
MAHÉ, J.-P.
    Hermès en Haute-Égypte, Tome II, Québec, 1982.
ROBBINS, F.E.
    The Hexaemeral Literature, Chicago, 1912.
THOMSON, R.W.
    "The Armenian Version of Ps. Dionysius Areopagita", *Acta Jutlandica* 57 (1982), 115-123.
    "Number Symbolism and Patristic Exegesis in some Early Armenian Writers", *Handes Amsorya* 90 (1976), 117-138.
    "Vardan" = "The Historical Compilation of Vardan Arewelc'i", *Dumbarton Oaks Papers* 43 (1989), 125-226.
WOLSKA, W.
    La topographie chrétienne de Cosmas Indicopleustes, Paris, 1962.

VII

THE MACCABEES IN EARLY ARMENIAN HISTORIOGRAPHY

WHEN Mashtots' invented a script for Armenian (c. A.D. 400) and the development of a written literature in the vernacular began, the first Armenian writers were not working in a vacuum. Indeed, the amazing efflorescence of Armenian literature in the early fifth century is only explicable because it took place within a literate group. Armenian clerics and scholars were well versed in the Greek and Syriac literature of the fourth century; they were familiar with patristic texts, texts of late Judaism, and a good deal of the ancient classical tradition.[1] Therefore when an Armenian scholar wished to compose an original work—be it a short sermon, a biography, a study of some philosophical or religious problem, or a full-scale history—his mind was no *tabula rasa*. The topic would be specifically Armenian, something new and original, but the Armenian scholar was familiar with a long tradition of literary genres. If he had to preach a sermon he would think of John Chrysostom or Gregory Nazianzenus (known as 'the theologian' *tout court*). If he wanted to compose the life of some notable person, he would think of innumerable saints' lives.[2] If his interests were of a philosophical bent, he would have read, perhaps not much of Plato or Aristotle, but several texts of later antiquity including Philo.[3] And if our Armenian scholar was planning a history of his times he would be familiar with numerous histories by Greek, Jewish, and Christian

---

[1] The only general guide to Armenian literature available in a Western tongue is V. Inglisian, 'Die armenische Literatur', in *Handbuch der Orientalistik*, Iste Abt., 7ter Band (Leiden/Köln, 1963). For a general study of Greek Fathers studied in Armenia in the first three centuries of literacy see R. W. Thomson, 'The Fathers in Early Armenian Literature', forthcoming in *Studia Patristica*, xii. For the late Jewish texts see M. E. Stone, 'The Apocryphal Literature in the Armenian Tradition', *Israel Academy of Sciences and Humanities, Proceedings*, iv. 4 (Jerusalem, 1969), pp. 59–78. There is no general study of classical texts in Armenian, but for recent scholarship see R. W. Thomson, 'Armenian Studies in Western non-Armenian Journals', an annual bibliography in *Patmabanasirakan Handes*, Erevan (Armenian S.S.R.) 1969 to the present.

[2] See especially two recent works: M. Avdalbegyan, *Hay gełarvestakan Ardzaki Skzbnavorumě* (V dar) (Erevan, 1971) and K. S. Ter-Davtyan, *Pamyatniki armyanskoy Agiografii* (Erevan, 1973).

[3] For the Armenian Philo see H. Lewy, *The Pseudo-Philonic De Jona, Part I* (Studies and Documents, 7) (London, 1936), pp. 1–24.

authors.[1] It is not immediately relevant whether these works in Greek and Syriac were known in the original or from Armenian translations. The point is that our hypothetical Armenian historian already had some idea of what historiography was before he put reed to parchment. Not only did he have a concept of the purpose of writing histories, of the moral lessons to be taught, he also had some knowledge of the canons of literary composition. And even if he had not studied rhetoric in a formal way,[2] from his earlier education he would be familiar with a host of figures of speech, turns of phrase, useful similes and metaphors, and even whole stories that could be used to good effect in his own composition.

It is surprising that, despite the interest shown in Armenian texts by students of the Classics, of the Church Fathers, or of late Jewish texts, little attention has been paid to the reverse side of the coin—the influence of these texts on *original* Armenian compositions. Of all such texts the most interesting are perhaps the books of Maccabees. For the fortunes of the Maccabees struck a particularly responsive chord in the Armenian mind, and here we have not only interesting examples of literary influence, we also have the influence of ideology.

It is not relevant here for us to study the complicated question of the attitude of the church to Maccabees as canonical books of scripture. In the Armenian version of the pseudo-apostolic canons the Maccabees are classified as canonical, as they are in the Armenian version of the 55th canon of Laodicaea;[3] this latter corresponds to the 60th canon of the Greek, which is probably a later addition. The early Armenian sources, however, do not say whether all or only some of the four books are acceptable.[4] Be that as it may, the first three books were known to early Armenian writers in an Armenian version.

Most of the attention given by Armenian scholars to the Books of Maccabees has focused on two points: the nature of the text that

---

[1] By far the most influential works in this regard were the *Ecclesiastical History* and *Chronicle* of Eusebius of Caesarea. For the latter see J. Karst, *Die Chronik des Eusebius* (G.C.S. 20, Leipzig, 1911), pp. xxxiv–xxxvi.

[2] For rhetorical texts see N. Adontz, *Denys de Thrace et les Commentateurs arméniens* (translated from the Russian edition of St. Petersburg 1915, Louvain, 1970); Y. Manandean, *Yunaban Dprots'ě* (Vienna, 1928); A. N. Muradyan, *Hunaban Dprots'ě ev nra Derě Hayereni k'erakanakan Terminabanut'yan Steltsman Gortsum* (Erevan, 1971).

[3] For the Armenian version of these various canons see V. Hakobyan, *Kanonogirk' Hayots*, 2 vols. (Erevan, 1964, 1971), especially i, pp. 113, 241.

[4] For the Armenian canon see M. Ter-Movsesyan, *Istoriya Perevoda Biblii na armyanskii yazyk* (St. Petersburg, 1902), esp. ch. 6; cf. the comments of M. E. Stone, 'Armenian Canon Lists—the Council of Partaw (768 C.E.)', *Harvard Theological Review*, lxvi (1973), pp. 479–86.

MACCABEES IN ARMENIAN HISTORIOGRAPHY 331

served as the basis for the Armenian version, and the identity of the translator.[1] We are not here interested in the textual problem for we shall be concerned with the *Armenian* text as a given entity; its textual provenance is less important for this inquiry than its literary impact. But the second point is more relevant.

In 1900 Norayr Biwzandats'i published an interesting book: *Koriun Vardapet and his Translations*.[2] Noting a wide range of similarities in vocabulary between Faustos of Buzanda, Agathangelos, Koriun, the Books of Maccabees, and the Armenian version of the Euthalian prologues, he came to the conclusion that Koriun was responsible for the Armenian redaction of Faustos and Agathangelos—and for the translation from Greek of the other works. So far as regards Agathangelos, I have demolished this theory elsewhere.[3] N. Biwzandats'i could not see the wood for the trees. For his method depended on a careful reading of the two massive tomes of the *Nor Baṙgirk' Haykazean Lezui*[4] and on a collation of examples from the quotations therein. The illustrations in that dictionary are very valuable, but they are incomplete and to some extent arbitrary for more common terms. But what the evidence collected by N. Biwzandats'i does indicate is something important, if less epoch-making: the first translators, schooled by Sahak and Mashtots', had a common training; they studied the same works, and naturally their literary style would have a certain common denominator. All early Armenian writers use biblical imagery almost unconsciously; the same is true, to a lesser extent, for patristic and other texts with which they were all familiar. Faustos, Koriun, and the redactor of the *History* of Agathangelos had a common literary background which is reflected in their phraseology.

In what follows we shall be concerned with only six Armenian texts: Koriun's biography of Mashtots' (the inventor of the Armenian alphabet);[5] the *History of the Armenians* by 'Agathangelos';[6] the *History of the*

---

[1] See S. Kogean, *Makabayets'wots' B. Grk'in Hayerēn T'argmanut'iwnĕ* (Vienna, 1923); Tsovakan (pseudonym for Norayr Poḷarean), *Koriun ev Makabayets'wots' Hay Targmanichĕ, Sion* (Jerusalem), N.S. 9 (1935), pp. 181–7.

[2] N. Biwzandats'i, *Koriun Vardapet ev norin Targmanut'iunk'* (Tiflis, 1900).

[3] See R. W. Thomson, *The Teaching of Saint Gregory—An Early Armenian Catechism* (Harvard, 1970), pp. 36–8.

[4] Ed. by G. Awetik'ean, Kh. Siwrmēlean, M. Awgerean (Venice, 1836–7).

[5] Critical edition by M. Abelyan (Erevan, 1941). N. Akinean's edition with commentary (*Mechitar Festschrift*, Vienna, 1949 = *Handēs Amsorya*, vol. 63; reprinted as vol. 1, fasc. 1 of Texts and Studies in Early Literature, Vienna, 1952) takes many liberties with the order of the text.

[6] Critical edition by G. Tēr-Mkrtchean and St. Kanayeants' (Tiflis, 1909). There are Greek, Arabic, and Karshuni versions indicating that another recension once existed in Armenian. See G. Garitte, *Documents pour l'étude du livre d'Agathange* (Studi e Testi 127, Vatican, 1946); M. Van Esbroeck, 'Un

VII

332

Armenians by Faustos Buzandats'i;[1] the *History of the Armenians* by Lazar P'arpets'i;[2] *On Vardan and His Companions and the Armenian War* by Elishe;[3] the *History of the Armenians* by Moses Khorenats'i.[4] The dating of these works is still a controversial matter, but a precise dating is not necessary for our immediate purpose, which is merely an assessment of the literary impact of the books of Maccabees. The first recension of Koriun was probably composed soon after Mashtots' death in 440; the Armenian recension (as we have it) of Agathangelos was probably composed in the second half of the fifth century, being clearly indebted to Koriun;[5] Faustos' *History* was written before that of Lazar, the latter being composed c. A.D. 500; Elishē's work is a later elaboration of part of Lazar's *History*;[6] and Moses' *History* dates from the eighth century,[7] though its author claims to have been pupil of Mashtots'.

In Polarean's study of Koriun and the first three books of Maccabees (which he thinks Koriun translated),[8] he notes some fifty verbal parallels. But in most cases these are merely common words or short phrases, many of which would occur in any reasonably long piece of narrative prose. Sometimes, indeed, the parallels consist of only one part of compounds. So, for example, *gazanakeats'* ('living like a wild beast', 6 Macc. v. 27) is compared to *lernakeats'* ('living in the mountains', Koriun § 22), which is feeble evidence for literary dependence. But in at least three places, a passage in Koriun does show a real dependence on the Armenian text of Maccabees. Two of these are from the paragraph in Koriun describing Mashtots' activity in Siunik': (§ 14) Mashtots' cares for the inhabitants like a *dayeak* (tutor or nurse), which has parallels in 3 Macc. iii. 15 (v. 9 of Arm.) where Ptolemy Philopator

nouveau témoin du livre d'Agathange', *Revue des Études arméniennes*, N.S. 8 (1971), esp. pp. 13-18.

[1] No critical edition has been published; references are to the Venice edition of 1933.
[2] Critical edition by G. Tēr-Mkrtchean and St. Malkhasean (Tiflis, 1904).
[3] Critical edition by E. Tēr-Minasean (Erevan, 1957).
[4] Critical edition by M. Abelean and S. Yarut'iwnean (Tiflis, 1913).
[5] See G. Lafontaine, *La Version grecque ancienne du livre arménien d'Agathange* (Publications de l'Institut orientaliste de Louvain, 7, Louvain, 1973), p. 38 for the date; the borrowings from Koriun were first noted by A. von Gutschmid, *Kleine Schriften*, ed. F. Rühl (Leipzig, 1892), iii, pp. 371-9 [Gutschmid's original study, 'Agathangelos', was published in the *Zeitschrift der deutschen morgenländischen Gesellschaft*, xxxi (1877), pp. 1-60]; see further pp. 14-15 of the Appendix to the Tiflis 1909 edition of the Armenian.
[6] See N. Akinean, *Elishe*, three vols. (Vienna, 1932, 1936, 1960).
[7] There is a vast (and polemical) bibliography on Moses Khorenats'i, not immediately relevant here. For the dating see C. Toumanoff, 'On the date of the Pseudo-Moses of Chorene', *Handēs Amsorya*, lxxv (1961), cols. 467-76.
[8] See reference above, p. 331, n. 1.

boasts of his kind treatment to the people of Syria and Phoenicia; and at 3 Macc. vii. 5 (v. 3 of Arm.) Ptolemy upbraids his overzealous officials in Egypt for outdoing the Scythians in their cruelty to the Jews, while the term *vayreni* (cf. ἀγριωτέραν ὠμότητα) is also found applied to the inhabitants of Siunik‛ in Koriun. But the only parallel that reflects a *common* situation is that between the eremitic life of Mashtots‛ and his companions (§ 22 of K) and that of Judas Maccabaeus and his companions in the wilderness (2 Macc. v. 27), a passage also adapted from Koriun by Agathangelos.

As noted above, Koriun's biography of Mashtots‛ is one of the primary sources of the *History* of 'Agathangelos'. Whole sections of Koriun were incorporated into this curious farrago which purports to describe the conversion of Armenia, the missionary work of Mashtots‛ being put back to the time of Gregory. In Agathangelos, not surprisingly, the influence of hagiographical and biblical themes is all-pervasive. So far as the Books of Maccabees are concerned, Agathangelos never mentions them by name but he (that is, the redactor of the Armenian text as we now have it) was clearly familiar with the Armenian version, at least of the first two books.

Some of the reminiscences of the Books of Maccabees are single words or short phrases that have no especial significance in the story, while others are of greater import. In the former category we may note the parallels between Khosrov's arrogance and that of Antiochus (!) (§ 9; 2 Macc. ix. 4); between Khosrov's murder and Ptolemy's taking king Antiochus aside (§ 32; 2 Macc. iv. 46); between Khosrov's death and that of the fourth brother (§ 34; 2 Macc. vii. 14); between Trdat's advance against the king of the Goths and the advance of Judas against Bacchides (§ 45; 1 Macc. ix. 12); between the mourning of the Armenians on hearing Gregory's first sermon and that of the Jews over the defiled sanctuary (§ 243; 1 Macc. iv. 39); between the lament of the demons over the destruction of their pagan temple and that of the Jews over the attacks of the Gentiles (!) (§ 780; 1 Macc. v. 14); between the temple of Vahagn and that built by Alexander the Great in Persia (§ 809; 1 Macc. vi. 1–2); and between the title given to the god Vanatur (*hiwrĕnkal*, cf. Διὸς Ξενίου) and that of the temple of Zeus in Garizim (§ 836; 2 Macc. vi. 2).

Somewhat more significant are the description of the death of Rhipsimē, when she willingly offered her tongue to be pulled out like the third brother (§ 197; 2 Macc. vii. 10); the comparison between the massive unhewn stones brought by king Trdat from Mount Masis for the martyrs' tombs and the whole stones used by Judas to rebuild the altar of the defiled sanctuary (§ 767; 1 Macc. iv. 47); and the insistence in the second half of the *History* that the Armenians could not make offerings to the martyrs' tombs nor Gregory raise altars until there was a properly constituted priesthood in the country. This last depends on the passage in Maccabees where Judas and his priests, having prepared the stones to rebuild the sanctuary, had to wait for a prophet to show what should be done (§ 762; 1 Macc. iv. 46).

We should also note the description of the cult of Anahit, for this has sometimes been interpreted as serious evidence for pagan Armenian religion. In the Armenian Agathangelos § 49 Trdat bids Gregory to present to Anahit's statue at Erez offerings of crowns and thick branches of trees. The latter have been interpreted as the *barsmunk'* used in Zurvanite worship and mentioned by Eznik.[1] But the whole passage comes from 2 Macc. xiv. 4 where king Demetrius is greeted at Tripoli by a renegade high priest with a crown of gold and the thick branches used in the cult of the temple (explained in 2 Macc. x. 7 as the feast of tabernacles). As one might also suspect from Agathangelos' description of the temple of Vahagn or the god Vanatur, he had no real idea of pagan Armenian cults; he is simply drawing on his knowledge of biblical lore to give more substance to his hagiographical imagination.

Less easy to elucidate are the sources of Faustos of Buzanda. Leaving aside the theory that his *History* was originally composed in a different tongue (Greek or Syriac) and then rendered into Armenian,[2] let us consider the Armenian text as we have it. Clearly the Armenian writer, or redactor, was familiar with the Armenian version of Maccabees, especially the first two books. Norayr Biwzandats'i collected 126 examples of parallel phraseology,[3] though many of these are so commonplace

[1] See S. Wikander, *Feuerpriester in Kleinasien und Iran* (Lund, 1946), p. 93; and Eznik §§145, 156 (edition by L. Mariès and Ch. Mercier, *Patrologia Orientalis*, Tome xxviii, Fascicule 3, Paris, 1959).

[2] The editors of the 1933 edition assume the original was in Greek; P. Peeters was more inclined to postulate a Syriac original, 'L'Intervention politique de Constance II dans la Grande Arménie en 338', *Bulletin de l'Academie royale de Belgique, Classe des Lettres*, xvii (1931), p. 17 [reprinted in *Recherches d'histoire et de philologie orientales*, vol. i (= Subsidia Hagiographica 27, Brussels, 1951)]. However, the fact that the sixth-century Procopius (*Wars* i. 5. 10–40) was indebted to this 'Armenian History' (ἡ τῶν Ἀρμενίων ἱστορία or συγγραφή) does not prove that there was a Greek *original*. A Greek version of the Armenian Agathangelos, for example, had been made in the previous century. Nor is it necessary to posit a written translation of the whole of Faustos (*pace* H. Gelzer, 'Die Anfänge der armenischen Kirche', *Berichte der Königlich sächsischen Gesellschaft der Wissenschaften zu Leipzig, Phil.-Hist. Classe*, lxxiv [1895], p. 115). There were numerous bilingual Armenians in Constantinople able to provide a translation of any Armenian text that interested Procopius, even if he had not interviewed Armenians when accompanying Belisarius on his Persian campaign.

[3] See above, p. 331, n. 2.

MACCABEES IN ARMENIAN HISTORIOGRAPHY

as to prove nothing. However, there are several passages, notably battle descriptions, where the Armenian text of Maccabees has provided imagery. For example:

F.B. iii. 7: the invasion of the Massagetae and F.B. v. 1: Musheḷ reviews his army; cf. 2 Macc. xv. 21, the description of Nicanor's army facing Judas Maccabaeus.

F.B. v. 43: Manuel attacks the Persians; cf. 2 Macc. xi. 11, the Jews put Lysias to flight.

F.B. v. 20: the description of Mushel's bravery; cf. 1 Macc. iv. 35 and that of Judas' soldiers opposing Lysias.

F.B. iii. 21: the Armenians take mutual counsel before a Persian invasion; cf. 1 Macc. ii. 40, the friends of Mattathias take counsel before resisting.

F.B. iv. 16: Mari and his fellow martyrs are buried in a common pit; cf. 2 Macc. x. 37, the Maccabees kill several Greeks on taking Gazara.

F.B. iv. 50: Vahan is lured by Merujan into revolt against Arshak; cf. 1 Macc. i. 12, some Jews lure others into a covenant with the heathen.

F.B. iv. 55: the Persians set fire to the wooden buildings in Artashat; several parallels in Maccabees.

There are also several passages where Faustos and Maccabees express in similar ways the willingness of their heroes to die for their land and people. But more important is the correlation of land, people, and religion. So the theme of the Maccabees becomes a crucial one for the early Armenian historians who describe the struggles of their countrymen for freedom of worship against Sasanian Iran. The parallel of the Armenians killed in battle with the brothers of Judas and Mattathias Maccabee is first explicitly made by Faustos (iii. 11). Furthermore he claims that the patriarch Vrtʻanes instituted an annual commemoration in which the fallen Armenians would be remembered in the liturgy immediately after the Maccabees. The feast of the latter was celebrated on 26 Hrotitsʻ (= 1 Aug.), but there is no reference in the later *synaxaria* to these Armenian soldiers.

The same explicit comparison between Armenians dying in battle and the Maccabees is made by Eḷishē. In an exhortation he puts into the mouth of Vardan Mamikonian to the assembled Armenian troops who are anticipating a Persian invasion after Easter in 451, Eḷishē gives a résumé of the story of the Maccabees. He is elaborating on the brief speech found in Ḷazar, p. 70, where the latter merely speaks of the heavenly crowns prepared for those who suffer with their companions. But Eḷishē, p. 105, expresses himself as follows: 'Taking up the text of Maccabees, he (Vardan) read it out to them all, and in extensive terms explained to them the outcome of events, how they had fought for the God-given law against the king of Antioch. Although they met a martyr's death, yet the repute of their valour has survived to this very day, not only on earth, but immortally in heaven. Likewise the general recalled how the house of Mattathias, breaking its covenant, had accepted the king's commands, had built temples, offered impure sacrifices, and abandoned God and received the punishment of death from the holy covenanters. But Mattathias and his companions had in no way been remiss but were strengthened all the more and plunged into warfare for an extended time.'[1]

If the Maccabees, then, are seen by Armenian historians as examples to be emulated, because the stand they took for religious freedom against the Seleucids offered close parallels to the position of the Armenians versus Sasanian Iran, the very expression used in Armenian for Religion—*awrēnkʿ* (law)—also appears to come from the same source. This term *awrēnkʿ* is standard in Łazar for Christianity, most notably in the letters and speeches that he attributes to the Armenian defenders of religious independence. And following Łazar, Ełishē makes it his key expression: it is to the defence of their *awrēnkʿ* that the Armenians rally.

In Armenian, however, *awrēnkʿ* is not a term exclusively applied to Christianity. Faustos (v. 43) refers to the *awrēns Mazdezantsʿn* (Mazdaean religion), and Sebeos (p. 72)[2] has the Persian king Khosrov Anushirvan refer in an edict to both Persians and Christians remaining in their paternal (native) religion: *yiwr hayreni yawrēns*. Ełishē also frequently uses the term *awrēnkʿ* both for Christianity and for Zoroastrianism: e.g. *awrēnkʿ mogutʿean* (pp. 18, 144) or the *zradeshtakan awrēnkʿ* (p. 143). But for the Persian religion another expression, *den*, is widely found in later Armenian writers (not in Faustos, Koriun, Agathangelos, or Łazar). Sebeos, in the edict mentioned above, equates *awrēnkʿ* and *den*: 'whoever does not observe his *hayreni den*, but rejects his *hayreni awrēnkʿ*, let him die.' Similarly in Ełishē *awrēnkʿ* and *den* are used interchangeably of the Mazdaean religion, and one finds the compound expression *awrenkʿ deni mazdezn* (p. 24). The two references in Moses Khorenatsi (iii. 34) to *den* as the Christian religion are not evidence for its acceptance by Christians, for it is put into the mouth of a Persian addressing king Arshak.

The central role of the term law (*awrēnkʿ*) in Łazar and Ełishē does not reflect a common Christian practice. Although in the New Testament Christianity is often described as the 'new law' in contrast to the

---

[1] The example of the Maccabees as martyrs for the faith was not, of course, an original Armenian development. For their cult in the fourth century, see, for example, H. Delehaye, *Les Passions des Martyrs et les genres littéraires*, 2ᵉ édition (= Subsidia Hagiographica 13B, Bruxelles, 1966), pp. 134–5, 163–5.

[2] *Patmutʿiun Sebēosi Episkoposi i Herakln* (Tiflis, 1913); this was written in the second half of the seventh century.

old, the use of 'law' as a general term for Christianity is rare in later Greek and unknown in Syriac. Only five examples of νόμος in this sense are noted in Lampe's *Patristic Greek Lexicon*. Of these, two are in imperial documents of Constantine I quoted in Eusebius, *Church History*, x. 5. 19 and 7. 1, thus unknown to the old Armenian version which ends at x. 4. 14; two are from Constantine II and Pope Damasus quoted in Theodoret's *Church History*, equally unknown in Armenian; and one is from the *Acts of Peter and Paul*, § 60, where the Armenian has *awrēnkʻ*.[1]

Armenian writers who use the term *awrēnkʻ* for Christianity were therefore not following a tradition long established in Eastern Christianity. But it is no accident that this term plays such a prominent role in Łazar and Ełishē. Just as they held up the model of the Maccabees as champions for the true religion against pagan aggression, here too they adapt the very expression found so often in those books. For example:

1 Macc. iii. 21: ἡμεῖς δὲ πολεμοῦμεν περὶ τῶν ψυχῶν ἡμῶν καὶ τῶν νομίμων ἡμῶν (*vasn awrinatsʻ merotsʻ*)

2 Macc. vii. 37: σῶμα καὶ ψυχὴν προδίδωμι περὶ τῶν πατρίων νόμων (*i veray hartsʻn awrinatsʻ*)

2 Macc. xiii. 14: ἀγωνίσασθαι μεχρὶ θανάτου περὶ νόμων, ἱεροῦ, πόλεως, πατρίδος, πολιτείας (*i veray awrinatsʻn, kʻalakʻin ew tacharin, ashkharhin ew tērutʻean*)

3 Macc. i. 23 (v. 12 in the Armenian, which in Book iii is very divergent from the Greek): ὑπὲρ τοῦ πατρῴου νόμου τελευτᾶν (*mer̄anel i veray kargatsʻn nakhneatsʻ ew hayreni awrinatsʻn*—to die on behalf of their ancestors' institutions and their paternal *awrenkʻ*)

In the Armenian version of the first three books of Maccabees there are 93 references to *awrēnkʻ*, rendering νόμος, νόμοι, or νόμιμα. It would indeed have been difficult to avoid this term while adapting the heroic stand of the Maccabees to the Armenian situation.

The last Armenian writer to be discussed here is Moses Khorenatsʻi, who more than any other historian was responsible for the fashioning of the Armenian tradition about the Armenian past. He adapted for his own purposes many of the earlier writers already discussed, notably Agathangelos, Faustos, Koriun, and Łazar. Moses was aware of the Maccabees from Josephus (whose *History* and *Antiquities* he ransacked and assimilated to Armenian circumstances), but he was also familiar with the Armenian version of 1–2 Maccabees. The following are the more important of his direct borrowings:

1. xxiv: The battle array of Tigran I is modelled on that of Antiochus in 1 Macc. vi. 39; 2 Macc. v. 3.
2. ii: The description of the Roman empire comes from 1 Macc. viii. 3.

[1] *Ankanon Girkʻ*, iii (Venice, 1904), p. 18.

2. ix: The description of the profanities imposed on the Jews in Armenia by Arshak I comes from 1 Macc. i. 43 (Antiochus' persecutions).
2. xiii: Artashes' military prowess is modelled on that of Antiochus, 2 Macc. v. 21.
2. xlvii: The description of noble insignia is based on 1 Macc. xi. 58 and the Book of Esther.
2. lii: The physical description of Smbat (tutor of Artashes) is based on that of Eleazar the martyr, in 2 Macc. vi. 23.
3. xxxvii: The description of the battle of Dzirav is based on 1 Macc. vi. 39 and 2 Macc. v. 3.
3. lxviii: A rhetorical contrasting of Antiochus and Mattathias.

But if for the earlier Armenian historians the theme of the Maccabees was appropriate and edifying, in Moses we find for the first time a more direct link being forged between Jews and Armenians, that is, the theory of the Jewish origin of the Bagratunis who gained royal status in the ninth century A.D. (We shall pass over the ludicrous extremes to which the Georgian branch of that family pushed their putative ancestry.[1])

We know that in the first century B.C. Tigran, and probably Artavazd too, had brought many settlers to Armenia from Cappadocia, Cilicia, and Syria, including nomadic Arabs.[2] These foreigners played the leading role in commerce and trade, and many of the Armenian terms relating to trade are Aramaic loanwords (*galut'*—colony; *shukay*—market; *hashiw*—account; *khanut'*—shop).[3] The historian Faustos knows of Jewish colonists in many cities of fourth-century Armenia, and he attributes their arrival to the policies of Tigran the Great, though he confuses this with the time of the high priest Hyrcanus.[4]

However, there was no interest in these artisans and traders in the cities on the part of the landed gentry and nobility. There was a great interest in the Holy Land and its Christian and biblical associations.[5] But there was no interest in or sympathy for contemporary Judaism.

[1] For this see C. Toumanoff, *Studies in Christian Caucasian History* (Georgetown University Press, 1963), pp. 328–9.

[2] See Plutarch, *Life of Lucullus*, 21.

[3] For a general discussion of the economic life of Armenia in the time of Tigran the Great see H. A. Manandian, *The Trade and Cities of Armenia in Relation to Ancient World Trade* (trans. by N. E. Garsoian, Lisbon, 1965), esp. pp. 57–66.

[4] Faustos, iv. 55. The account of Jewish settlements in Armenia in Moses Khorenats'i, ii. 19 and iii. 35 is full of fanciful embellishments. Moses' adaptation of Josephus, most notably in making Parthian characters into Armenians (!), merits separate discussion. For these passages in Faustos and Moses see G. Sargsyan, 'Albyurneri ōgtagortsman elanakě Movses Khorenats'u mot', *Banber Matenadarani* (Erevan), iii (1956), pp. 31–6.

[5] Cf. R. W. Thomson, 'A Seventh-century Armenian Pilgrim on Mount Tabor', *J.T.S.*, N.S. xviii (1967), pp. 27–33.

MACCABEES IN ARMENIAN HISTORIOGRAPHY 339

The pre-Christian Jews, however, were another matter. And here some general Christian ideas played a part. As early as Origen, the theme of the Christian church as the True Israel becomes important.[1] And in fourth-century theologians, the more precise analogy of the kingdom of David being continued in the church finds expression. In Byzantine political theory the idea of the emperor representing the one God and offering leadership in spiritual as well as secular matters also led to the adoption of Old Testament parallels. Christians could not accept the Hellenistic definition of royalty as including priestly powers. But Old Testament kings had a priestly character, so the emperors could be called the New David or the New Solomon. Moses also was called into service. Eusebius, the first to use such imagery in the Christian cause, makes a comparison between Constantine's victory over Maxentius at the Milvian Bridge outside Rome and Moses' crossing of the Red Sea when Pharaoh's host was drowned.[2] As noted above, Constantine himself used the term 'law' (with its Mosaic overtones) for Christianity. But the Davidic parallel is more important, and there is a good example from the province of Armenia Prima, whose bishops wrote to the emperor Leo I (457–74) in these terms: *pio et Christianissimo principe, quodam secundo David*.[3]

Such terminology is not foreign to Armenian writers. Although the Arsacid dynasty—of Parthian origin—was snuffed out in 428,[4] Lazar makes a series of very direct parallels between the O.T. kings and Vahan Mamikonian, who was made *marzpan* of Armenia by the Sasanian shah in 486.[5] We have also seen the Armenian admiration for the later Maccabees. But these parallels are merely edifying examples. There is no suggestion that Jewish kings or heroes really—or even metaphorically—foreshadowed any Armenian family or institution.

Moses, however, has outdone the general Eastern Christian attitudes to the race of Israel. On behalf of his patrons, he claims a Jewish origin

[1] See references s.v. Ἰσραήλ in G. W. H. Lampe, *A Patristic Greek Lexicon* (Oxford, 1961–8).

[2] *Vita Constantini*, i. 38. The Eusebian authorship of this work has not passed unchallenged; see the extensive discussion in J. Quasten, *Patrology*, iii (Utrecht/Antwerp, 1966), pp. 319–24. None the less, the parallel was well known in the fourth century; see Dvornik (reference in next note), p. 644.

[3] For Byzantine political theory see F. Dvornik, *Early Christian and Byzantine Political Philosophy*, ii (Washington D.C., 1966), esp. ch. 10 ('Christian Hellenism') and ch. 12 ('Imperium and Sacerdotium'). The letter of the bishops from Armenia Prima is in J. D. Mansi, *Sacrorum Conciliorum nova et amplissima Collectio*, vii (Florence, 1762), cols. 587–9.

[4] For the end of the Armenian Arsacid dynasty see R. Grousset, *Histoire de l'Arménie* (Paris, 1947), pp. 182–4.

[5] See Lazar, pp. 178–82, for the long sermon put into the Armenian Catholicos John's mouth at a service of thanksgiving for Vahan's appointment.

for the Bagratuni family, who rose to political pre-eminence in the eighth to ninth centuries.[1] It is not necessary here to elaborate on Moses' literary methods, interesting though these are.[2] The purpose of this curious historical fraud, none the less, is clear enough. The Bagratids needed an honourable pedigree justifying their role as Christian sovereigns of Armenia. So their eponymous ancestor Shambat (a pseudo-Hebrew form for the Smbat of Iranian origin) is put back to the time of the legendary king Hracheay; supposedly Shambat was one of the Jews taken captive by Nebuchadnezzar.[3]

Now the most outstanding feature of these Jewish Bagratids in Armenia, according to Moses, was their constancy to the law and their willingness to die for the faith. Two of Shambat's sons were put to the sword for their refusal to worship idols. These two men Moses compares to the martyred companions of Eleazar Maccabaeus and Anania[4]—though in fact the latter was saved from the fiery furnace! Under pressure in the reign of Tigran, the Bagratunis refused to offer sacrifices themselves, says Moses, but they did agree to eat sacrificial meat and pork.[5] Finally, we should note the interesting twist whereby Moses connects the Bagratunis with the story of Addai/Thaddaeus, the supposed first apostle of Christianity in Armenia. In the earliest version of the story, Thaddaeus, on arriving in Edessa, stayed in the house of Tobias, son of Tobias.[6] The fifth-century Syriac *Teaching of Addai* and the Armenian translation thereof add that Tobias came from Palestine. But Moses says that he was a Jewish prince of the Bagratuni family who faithfully observed the Jewish law until his conversion to Christ.[7] Very neatly it is thus suggested that not only did the Bagratunis have an honourable history of religious steadfastness, but they could also claim Christian origins preceding those of any other Armenian family, including the royal Arsacids who were converted in the fourth century.

This, however, has taken us beyond the main theme of the present article which has been to elucidate one of the literary models used by early Armenian writers in the composition of their histories. It is hardly novel to stress that early Armenian historiography falls within the framework of the Eastern Christian tradition—itself an amalgam of classical, late Jewish, and Christian ideas. But in the field of Armenian scholarship far more interest has been shown in the value of Armenian texts for other disciplines than in Armenian compositions for their own

---

[1] For the rise of the Bagratuni family see Grousset, chs. 9 and 10; and for the Bagratid stemma, Toumanoff, pp. 338–42.
[2] Cf. above, p. 338, n. 4.   [3] Moses Khorenatsʻi, i. 22.
[4] Ibid. ii. 9.   [5] Ibid. ii. 14.
[6] Eusebius, *Church History*, i. 13. 11.
[7] Moses Khorenatsʻi, ii. 33.

sake. Little work has been done on the Armenians' debt to the rhetorical models then in vogue in the Eastern Roman empire, rhetorical models partly known through the great Christian writers like Gregory Nazianzenus or John Chrysostom, and partly through textbooks of rhetoric. Little study has been made of the impact of the mass of saints' lives on the literary techniques of the Armenian historians dealing with non-hagiographical material. The extensive Armenian adaptation of late Jewish apocrypha is only beginning to be explored, while Armenian assimilation of material from Josephus and Eusebius is not fully charted. The influence of Philo, especially on Ełishē and Moses Khorenats'i, has been noted but not exhaustively explored. And even within the Armenian tradition the debt owed by late writers to their predecessors has not always been carefully stated. But before the ideological purposes and often tendentious motivation of Armenian historians can be properly understood, their techniques and models must be elucidated. If we are able to unravel their written sources and piece together their literary background, then we may be able to give sympathetic attention to what the early Armenian writers *themselves* thought important.

VIII

NUMBER SYMBOLISM AND PATRISTIC EXEGESIS IN SOME EARLY ARMENIAN WRITERS

"(Scripture) is to be understood in two ways: one is tangible and visible, the other intellectual [1]." *[Yačaxapatum IX]*

"For God established this world as a school [2], that creatures might learn the Creator's care in fashioning and arranging and (know) that things visible and invisible are sustained through his providence." *[Yačaxapatum VII]*

What follows is an attempt to elucidate the patristic affinities of number symbolism in some early Armenian theological texts [3]. I shall be concerned not with mathematical and mystical symbolism inherited from classical antiquity and the world of late Hellenistic Judaism, but with specifically Christian interpretations of various numbers [4]. Without attempting an exhaustive enquiry into the history of the different interpretations, I shall try to indicate possible sources and parallels in Greek or Syriac texts which were known in Armenia. This article, therefore, is more a study of patristic influence on Armenian theologians than a contribution to the mysteries of number symbolism.

THREE ist the first perfect number. This idea finds its most obvious parallels in the Armenian Philo [5]. Of more specifically Christian interest is the interpretation of the three men who appeared to Abraham (Genesis, ch. 18) as indicative of the Trinity [6]. In early patristic exegesis this passage was explained

---

[1] Cf. Ełišē,, *Matenagrut'iwnk'*, Venice 1859, p. 235: "the words of scripture are as a shadow in a mirror."

[2] The idea of nature as a school could be found in the Armenian Philo, *Questions on Genesis*, iii 27 (Loeb edition, Supplement I, translated by R. Marcus; Armenian text, *Philonis Judaei Paralipomena Armena*, ed. J. B. Aucher, Venice 1826) and in Basil of Caesarea, *Hexameron* I 6 (Migne, *P. G.* 29.16; the Armenian version, Venice 1830, was not available to me). This passage from the Yačaxapatum is echoed by Anania, p. 238 (see references in note 3).

[3] The texts most frequently cited in this article are: Agathangelos, *Patmut'iwn Hayoc'*, ed. K. Ter Mkrtč'ean and St. Kanayeanc', Tiflis 1909; Anania Sirakac'i, *Matenagrut'yunĕ*, ed. A. G. Abrahamyan, Erevan 1944 (notably the tract "On the interpretation of numbers" pp. 237—250) [Although the authorship of this piece has been denied to Anania (see Abrahamyan, p. 237), if the tract "On Easter" (ibid., pp. 292—299) which has similar number speculation is his, there seems to be no *a priori* reason to discount the authenticity of this. It is worth noting that in this tract there are numerous errors in the interpretation of scripture, which makes it unlikely that it was composed by a learned theologian such as Anania of Narek, as "Miaban" supposed]; Ełišē, *History = Vasn Vardanay ew Hayoc' Paterazmin*, ed. E. Ter-Minasean, Erevan 1957, *Matenagrut'iwnk'*, Venice 1859, *Questions et réponses sur la Genèse*, ed. N. Akinian and S. Kogian, Vienne 1928; John Mandakuni, *Čaṙk'*, Venice 1860; John of Odzun, *Opera*, ed J. B. Aucher, Venice 1834; *Yačaxapatum Čaṙk' ew Ałōt'k'*, Venice 1954. For Greek texts I have generally given references to J. P. Migne's *Patrologia graeca* as the most convient source, without attempting to note all the more recent critical editions.

[4] In the spirit of Origen's frequent insistence on number as symbol.

[5] Anania, p. 240, quotes Philo as authority for this statement. The theme is common in Philo's *Questions*, e. g., *On Genesis* ii 5, iv 8; *On Exodus* ii 100.

[6] See Anania, p. 241.

in terms of the Logos and two angels [7], but by the fifth century the Trinitarian interpretation was standard [8].

The significance of the "third hour" is elaborated by John of Odzun in his work on the Offices of the church [9]. It was at the third hour of the day that the first created man was captivated by the devil; that Daniel had his propletic vision (a misinterpretation of Daniel 6.10); that the crucifixion and the descent of the Spirit occurred. In fact the gospel accounts of the crucifixion differ. Only Mark places it in the third hour [10]. But Aphraates, known erroneously in Armenian as Jacob of Nisibis, follows Mark [11]. And the theme of the third hour as that of both the crucifixion and of Pentecost would be familiar to John from the Armenian version of Cyril of Jerusalem's *Catechetical Homilies* [12]. John's ecclesiastical interests are also paramount in his comparison of Noah's ark and the church [13]. The spiritual figure does not interest him so much as the architectural: the ark had three storeys, and likewise the church has three sections, the sanctuary, the nave, the narthex (*gawit'*) [14].

---

[7] See J. Daniélou, *The Theology of Jewish Christianity*, Chicago 1964, p. 138; G. L. Prestige, *God in Patristic Thought*, London 1964, p. 122.

[8] See notably Cyril of Alexandria, *Contra Julianum* I (P. G. 76.532—3).

[9] *Opera*, pp. 212—214.

[10] Mark 15.25, as opposed to Matthew 27.45 and Luke 23.44, who place it at the sixth hour. (The accounts are assimilated in Athanasius, *De virginitate* 12 (P. G. 28.265), by having the cross set up at the third hour, the crucifixion at the sixth and the death at the ninth.)

[11] Aphraates XII 12. Syriac text in *Patrologia Syriaca* I and II, Paris 1894 and 1907; Armenian text in A. Gallandi, *Bibliotheca Veterum Patrum*, vol. 5, Venice 1769, «Sancti Jacobi episcopi Nisibeni Sermones».

[12] XVII 19 (*P. G.* 33.992). Armenian version (*Koč'umn Encayut'ean*), Vienna 1832, p. 379. The Third hour was also celebrated as that of the last supper (Aphraates XII 6), and of the resurrection and the ascension (see J. Van Goudoever, *Fêtes et calendriers bibliques (Théologie historique* 7), Paris 1967, p. 264).

[13] *Opera*, p. 292.

[14] For the storeys of the ark see R. Murray, *Symbols of Church and Kingdom*, Cambridge 1975, pp. 253, 258. The parallel between ark and

The question of the three days that Christ spent in the tomb is discussed by Ełišē. He is, however, unable to reconcile the three days and nights in the heart of the earth — like Jonah in the whale (Matthew 12.40) — with the resurrection on the third day after two evenings, one daytime and two hours. A solution to the problem was available in the Armenian Aphraates [15].

Under the rubric FOUR all writers mention the four elements, either as earth, air, fire and water, or as the hot and the cold, the dry and the moist [16]. But only John of Odzun gives these four elements a religious significance: there are four psalms at evening prayer, "perhaps" in accordance with the four elements [17].

There are also four virtues. John Mandakuni describes several goups of four virtues each: the basic four are silence, humility, the keeping of God's commandments, and tribulation. Then there are four virtues which preserve the soul: alms-giving, not becoming angry, long-suffering, and the keeping of oneself from wandering thoughts. There are four further virtues profitable to a young monk: meditation on the scriptures all the time, vigils and labour, obedience to the father, not considering oneself as anything at all. John Mandakuni then goes on to list various fourfold groups of vices which harm the soul, darken the mind and render the soul unfruitful [18]. Anania's list of four virtues, on the other hand, is that of the classical tradition echoed in the more philosophical reflections of the Greek fathers: the three parts of

---

church is an old theme of patristic exegesis; see J. Daniélou, *Primitive Christian Symbols*, London 1964, pp. 67—70; idem, *The Bible and the Liturgy*, Notre Dame (Indiana) 1966, pp. 82—85.

[15] Ełišē, *Matenagrut'iwnk'*, p. 301; Aphraates XII 7.

[16] Anania, p. 241; Ełišē, *History*, pp. 33—34, *Matenagrut'iwnk'*, p. 321; *Girk' T'łt'oc'*, Tiflis 1901, p. 23; John Mandakuni, *Čaṙk'*, p. 198; *Yačaxapatum*, pp. 33—34, 170.

[17] *Opera*, p. 54. Epiphanius, *Treatise on Weights and Measures, the Syriac Version*, ed. J. E. Dean, Chicago 1935, p. 52, associates the various manifestations of four with the four times of prayer.

[18] *Čaṙk'*, pp. 187—188.

the soul plus virtue (which is acquired and not natural) [19]. Anania also interprets the four rivers that flow from Paradise in a philosophical sense: the Phison is for us the image reason, the Gehon represents the overthrow of evil, in a manly fashion expelling effeminate debauchery; the Tigris is sobriety, warning against desire; the Euphrates is justice. Flowing from Paradise (i. e. the church), they irrigate the four extremities of the rational world [20].

The image of the church as the garden of Paradise leads Anania to consider the second Adam established in the garden of the church, who is preached by the four evangelists. The animals which represent three of the evangelists are then interpreted: the lion of Matthew is an image of royal power over death and hell; the ox of Luke is an image of the sacrifice on behalf of the world; the eagle of John represents the Word flying from the heights as if over prey, for where the dissolution of the body occurs, there the eagle descends. Anania then justifies these images by quoting Isaiah 31.4, adding that all parallels and images refer to Our Lord [21].

The potentially most elaborate of the figures represented by the number four is that of the cross. The foursided wood is mentioned by Eḷišē [22], and in Agathangelos the theme of the four points of the cross receives extended treatment. Two main ideas are found in Agathangelos: the four directions of the points of the cross, and the four corners of the cross indicating an altar. The cross also provides him with three other themes: it is an antitype to the tower of Babel, it is an antitype to wooden idols — and here Agathangelos introduces the concept of the dead Christ on the cross as a dead image — and it is an antitype to the ark. These themes are worth quoting in more detail.

(a) "The principal corner, the top, points upwards... elevating the nature of him who rested on it and indicating the Father... The right hand points to the joy of the just and the blessings prepared for them, while the left indicates the torments of sinners [23]."

(b) "The horns of the altar (as in Psalm 117,27) are an indication of the cross which has four corners." "And the cross is truly an altar since it received the true sacrifice of the Lord's body." (The thought leads on naturally to a consideration of the eucharist [24].)

(c) "The tower is the cross... From the first tower was scattering, but from the cross gathering; from the one, expulsion to torments, from the other, approach to the kingdom [25]."

(d) "Instead of the wood that men worshipped (after the tower of Babel), He set up his cross to send out light to all creatures sitting in darkness and the shadow of death [26]." "Because men like to worship images in human shape skillfully carved from wood, he became the image of men in order to subject to his own image of his divinity the image-makers and image-lovers and image-worshippers. And because men were accustomed to worship dead and lifeless images, he became a dead image on the cross [27]."

---

[19] Anania, p. 241. Cf. Nilus, Epistle I 223 (P. G. 79.164): there are four virtues (φρόνησις, ἀνδρεία, σωφροσύνη, δικαιοσύνη), and the devil has four vices, witness Zechariah 1.18.

[20] Anania, pp. 242—243. Eḷišē, Questions, p. 61, notes that the Phison is either the Ganges or the Danube, and the Gehon is the Nile.

[21] Anania, p. 243; cf. Eḷišē, Questions, p. 12; Epiphanius, Treatise on Weights and Measures, p. 52; and Methodius, De Resurrectione mortuorum, II 10 (P. G. 18.316), referring to Origen.

[22] Eḷišē, Matenagrut'iwnk', p. 271. Cf. Nonnus, Paraphrasis in Joannis evangelium, 19 (P. G. 43.901): δόρυ τετράπλευρον; and the Byzantine poem published in P. Maas, Frühbyzantinische Kirchenpoesie, Bonn 1910, p. 8: τετρακόρυφον δένδρον.

[23] Agathangelos, § 489. For patristic parallels see the discussion to this paragraph in R. W. Thomson, The Teaching of Saint Gregory, Cambridge (Massachusetts), 1970, p. 113. For the four corners of the earth reached by the cross cf. Maas, Frühbyzantinische Kirchenpoesie, p. 8: τετραπέρατον κόσμον. More elaborate is Severian, Orationes in mundi creationem V 3 (P. G. 56.474): the first letters of the Greek words for North, South, East and West spell "Adam".

[24] §§ 488, 490—491.

[25] § 629.

[26] § 585.

[27] §§ 80—81. For the theme of Christ as a dead image in later Armenain writers see S. Der Nersessian, «Une apologie des images au septième

(Again this leads Agathangelos to speak of the eucharist, Christ's body on the cross being food for the universe.)

(e) "The Lord saved Noah from the flood through the crosslike wood and worked salvation through the cross [28]."

John of Odzun elaborates on the four-sided shape of the church as a building. The four sides recall the four corners of the world that has been called to worship God by the one Spirit in Christ. More allegorically, the East looks to Paradise and to the coming of the heavenly king and bridegroom. The window on the East represents the entrance of spiritual light into this world; while the windows to left and right represent the shining virtues, and that to the West represents the light of day [29].

Finally, the theme of the four-cornered fishing net in Ełišē deserves quoting. The idea of the gospel or the church as a net was common in Greek and Syrian writers [30], but Ełišē has combined several numerical themes in his interpretation: "For the apostles are twelve in number and there are two cords to the net and four ends to the cords, by which in threes they take hold of each corner, for double three is perfect stability: one side to the West, the other parallel to it to the East, and two to the North and the South. With a circular spiral motion they enclose the whole world. The do not pull the net to each one's own side, but all together gather everyone to where the bait has been placed, for life and not death. For the food is living and is for those alive and not the dead. The sea is this world; the net the preaching of the Lord; the corners of the net the four gospels; the net-holders the twelve apostles; the prey all the races of the heathen; the bait the body and blood of Our Lord Jesus Christ' and the method the true faith [31]."

The only one of the Armenian authors discussed in this article who offers religious interpretations of the number FIVE is Anania. The five senses are the site of the war of the passions [32]. (Anania does not enumerate the senses, but they are clearly: sight, hearing, taste, smell and touch.) Therefore Moses wrote five books of law with which we combat the passions. David put five stones in his knapsack to oppose the foreign warrior (I Kings 17.40). Five cities of foreigners *(aylazgeac')* were left in the promised land but subjected to tax, like the senses to the mind (cf. Joshua 16.10; 19.49). Anania then links this interpretation to Jesus' remarks about "five in one house divided three against two and two against three" (Luke 12.52). Anania interprets the "two" as sight and hearing, which are capable of spiritual understanding; whereas the "three" are the subject bodily senses of taste, smell and touch. Anania also introduces the five kings mentioned in Genesis 14.8—9; though he misinterprets the passage and thinks that it was the five, rather than the four of the same story, who captured Sodom. Sodom he interprets as "blindness", and Anania thus associates this passage with the bishops at the council of Nicaea who struck down the blindness of the heretics. (Anania does not speculate on the significance of the number of bishops present at that council, traditionally put at 318 after the number of Abraham's servants — Genesis 14.14 [33].)

---

siècle», *Byzantion* vol. 17 (1944—1945), pp. 57—87, esp. p. 61 and note 15 (Reprinted in *Etudes byzantines et arméniennes*, Louvain 1973, vol. 1, pp. 379—403.

[28] § 169. The ark was widely used as a figure for the church, cf. note 14 above. But the emphasis on the cross in Agathangelos seems to point to an early stage in Christian exegesis, see Daniélou, *Theology*, p. 277.

[29] *Opera*, p. 300.

[30] E. g. Cyril of Jerusalem, *Procatechesis* 5 (*P. G.* 33.344; not in the Armenian): "the nets of the church"; or Cyril of Alexandria in J. A. Cramer, *Catenae in Novum Testamentum*, vol. 2, Oxford 1844, p. 40: "the net of evangelical μυσταγωγία". For Syrian parallels see Murray, *Symbols*, pp. 176—177.

---

[31] *Matenagrut'iwnk'*, p. 338. For "bait" cf. Agathangelos, § 81.

[32] Anania, p. 243. Cf. Athanasius, *Contra Gentes* 31 (*P. G.* 25.61—64), a classic exposition of this common theme.

[33] Cf. J. Rivière, «318, un cas de symbolisme arithmétique», *Recherches de Théologie ancienne et médiévale*, vol. 6 (1934), pp. 349—367.

The number SIX is primarily associated with concepts of time. The sixth hour was that of the crucifixion, therefore, says John of Odzun, one must be vigilant at that hour of prayer and beware of the demon of mid-day tedium [34]. There were six days of creation, and Anania stresses the significance of the sixth, that of Man's creation. He also notes that Solomon in the sixth year finished the temple — a pattern of the first man. This temple Christ destroyed and by his resurrection raised a new, spiritual temple [35]. (But as seen above, Anania was not a scrupulous biblical scholar: it was the *second* temple that was finished in the sixth year of *Darius* — Ezra 6.15; Solomon took seven years to finish his temple — III Kings 6.38.)

The most important idea involving six is that of the six ages of this world leading to the seventh, when the Lord will come again. Ełišē draws the customary parallel between the six ages of one thousand years during which this world is subject to corruption, and the six days of creation; the seventh day of rest thus prefigures the seventh age which will be free of corrruption and evil [36]. This idea receives greater elaboration in Agathangelos:

"(God) measured six thousand years of time for the evils and sweat of toils and travail of the world. He measured a thousand years for each day according to the first six days, in which might take place the growth of creation and the trials of the proving of the good. (For this Psalm 89.4 is quoted as authority.) In the first age was the beginning, and in the sixth was the renewal which he effected by his own coming. And in the same thousand will be the end, wherefore it is called the last, in which he is to come again...

And because he calls the seventh day of his own creation rest, therefore he commands the seventh day to be kept holy... For likewise in the seventh age he will give rest to the weary who have worked in the six ages of their time... The Spirit of God appeared in this sixth age to fulfill his predicted promises, the sayings through the mouths of the prophets. The grace of the Holy Spirit was poured out in the last times and was spread over the great variety of peoples [37]."

Agathangelos is thus following the typology which has its origins in Judaism and is represented notably by Irenaeus: the seventh day represents the world to come [38]. On the other hand, some early Christian writers saw the seven ages as representing the time of this world and the eighth day as the eternal rest [39]. Only in Anania is there a reference to the eighth day. He does not elaborate, but indicates that the mystery completed by Christ was foretold by David, who gives the maximum length of our days as eighty years. This is a reference to Psalm 89.10 [40]. John of Odzun specifically states that Christ was crucified in the sixth age [41].

---

[34] *Opera*, p. 216.
[35] Anania, p. 244. Clement of Alexandria, *Stromateis* III 10 (P. G. 9.365) has an interesting explanation of six as the multiple of two and three; the two and three stand for male and female, and are echoed in Jesus' saying at Matthew 18.20: "where two or three are gathered together in my name...". The idea is found in Philo, cf. *Questions on Genesis*, iii 38. (For a different interpretation of "two" and "three" see above under "five".)
[36] *Matenagrutʻiwnkʻ*, p. 324.

[37] Agathangelos, §§ 668—671.
[38] See Irenaeus, *Adversus Haereses* V 28.3 (P. G. 7.1200; Armenian text ed K. Ter-Mekerttschian and E. Ter-Minanssiantz, *Irenaeus gegen die Häretiker*, Buch IV und V, Leipzig 1910). Cf. Methodius, *De Creatis* 12 (P. G. 18.344): the judgement will come in the seven-thousandth year; and Aphraates II 14. In general see A. Luneau, *L'histoire du salut, la doctrine des âges du monde*, Paris 1964; and Daniélou, *Theology*, pp. 396—404.
[39] E. g. Barnabas XV. See in general A. Quacquarelli, «L'ogdoade patristica e sui riflessi nella liturgia e nei monumenti», *Rivista di archeologia cristiana*, vol. 49 (1973), pp. 211—269; and R. Staats, „Ogdoas als ein Symbol für die Auferstehung", *Vigiliae Christianae*, vol. 26 (1972) pp. 29—52. See further note 55 below.
[40] Anania, p. 248. See also at note 89 below.
[41] *Opera*, p. 216. Cf. John Malalas, *Chronographia*, ch .10, Bonn 1831, p. 228, where Christ's birth is dated to 5500 years after the creation of Adam and his resurrection to the year 5533. An alternative tradition places Christ's birth in the year 6000, Ps. Amplilocius, *Vita Basilii* 2. Methodius, *De Creatis* 9 (P. G. 18.344), says that accordnig to those skilled in arithmetic there have been six thousand years "up to now".

Two other ideas involving the number six deserve a brief mention. John of Odzun compares the six faculties with the six morning psalms; added to the four evening psalms, the total is the perfect number ten [42]. The faculties are the modes whereby the spiritual soul operates through the senses, but John does not elaborate. Anania notes that physical bodies have six positions (above and below, to right and left, behind and in front); but unlike some Greek writers he does not draw any religious significance from this [43].

Of all the numbers given special significance by our authors, SEVEN is the most frequently cited. But the biblical references to seven are not often given a symbolic religious meaning. The seventh day of rest and the seventh age of bliss have been discussed above. The next most common reference to seven is to the seven gifts of the Spirit. Quoting Isaiah 11.2, Eḷišē lists the spirit of wisdom, the spirit of understanding, the spirit of counsel, the spirit of power, the spirit of knowledge, the spirit of piety, and the spirit of the fear of God. This sevenfold distinction Eḷišē associates with the seven spheres of the heavens. In those spheres are two sets of seven bodies: the sun, moon and five planets, and the seven immobile stars [44]. (Anania also mentions the seven wandering bodies, but in connection with the seven pillars in the house of wisdom and the seven senses[45].) Anania lists the seven gifts of the Spirit, but without further comment. But John of Odzun with his interest in ecclesiastical ritual, describes the light of the candlestick on the altar shining with "sevenfold luminous grace [46]."

The significance of seven in the ages of children was a theme familiar to Jewish and Christian writers. Anania notes that the child conceived on the seventh day will be a son; children born in the seventh month will be healthy and fecund; teeth begin to grow in the seventh month; in the seventh year the mental aptitudes are advanced enough for children to start school; at twice times seven the reproductive powers are formed [47]. Anania also notes several biblical parallels: the house of wisdom had seven colums (Proverbs 9.1); the ark was closed for seven days against the unbelievers (cf. Genesis 8.10, 12 — but the unbelievers had by then been drowned!); blood was sprinkled seven times before the altar; the leper was cleansed in seven days (Leviticus 14.38; cf. the dipping of Naaman seven times in the Jordan, IV Kings 5.14). Furthermore, evil is punished sevenfold — as Cain in Genesis 4.15, but Lamekh seventy times (Genesis 4.24) [48].

John Mandakuni states that there are seven vices: fornication, love of money, envy, slander, jealousy, vainglory, pride. But he gives no special significance to the numeral seven [49].

In a more physical sense, Anania notes that there are seven apertures for the senses: two eyes, two ears, two nostrils and one for taste through which the deadly (demon?) enters and the immortal rational (soul) leaves. There are also seven different kinds of human moisture: tears, nasal drip, sweat, menstruation, urine, bowel movements, seed [50]. Eḷišē

---

[42] Opera, p. 54.
[43] Anania, p. 244. Cf. Germanus of Constantinople, In Crucem (P. G. 98.244), where the six directions are related to the cross: it reaches towards heaven and below the earth, to left and right, and before and after in time.
[44] Matenagrut'iwnk', pp. 321—322. Cf. Ire-K. Ter-Mekerttschian and E. Ter-Minassiantz, Leipzig 1907), who links the seven gifts with the seven heavens. Aphraates, I 9, speaks rather of the seven operations of the Spirit.
[45] Anania, p. 245. For the seven columns of the house of wisdom (as Proverbs 9.1), cf. Gregory of Nazianzen, Oratio XLI 3 (P. G. 36.432). Anania notes that there are many mysteries involving the number seven and refers to this "discourse on the Spirit" of Gregory's. (Its actual title, however, is "on Pentecost".)

[46] Opera, p. 304. Cf. Irenaeus, Demonstration 9 (with reference to Exodus 25.31—40).
[47] Anania, p. 245. Cf. Clement of Alexandria, Stromateis VI 11 (P. G. 9.308), who refers to Jewish traditions; and Justin, Quaestiones et responsiones 69 (P. G. 6.1309—1312).
[48] But again Anania has misinterpreted the Armenian biblical text, which reads "seventy times seven". Here the Armenian and LXX differ from the "seventy seven" of the Hebrew and Syriac.
[49] Čaṙk, p. 189.
[50] Anania, p. 245.

merely lists the seven apertures [51], but he does note elsewhere that the five senses plus intelligence and (sexual?) desire are parallel to the seven coils of the snake as it crawls along [52]. The theme of the snake reminds Eḷišē (via Moses' bronze serpent, Numbers 21.8—9) of the crucified Christ. And thus we can say that Our Lord figuratively turned himself into the form of a snake [53]. This is a common patristic theme [54].

The only specifically Christian interpretation of the number EIGHT is made by Anania. He comments on three O. T. references involving Solomon, David and Abraham: the eight (cubits) in the measurements of the temple (III Kings 7.10); the ogdoad mentioned in the titles to Psalms 6 and 11; and the covenant of circumcision to be performed on the eighth day (Genesis 17.12). In standard fashion this physical seal is then interpreted as having been rendered a spiritual one by Christ. The covenant was made by God because of Abraham's faith, as a token that the earth would not again be subjected to an immeasurable innundation as in the days of Noah. But Anania does not draw the Christian parallel to the flood — baptism [55]. Nor in Agathangelos when the eight generations of patriarchs up to Noah is discussed, is any symbolism drawn out, either of the number eight in general or of baptism [56].

In interpreting the number NINE Anania merely compares the number of months Jesus was in the womb (adding that this is the normal human term) with the nine beatitudes [57]. Nor is any figurative interpretation offered by John of Odzun. He explains the "mystery" of prayer at the ninth hour by references to Peter and John going up to the temple at the hour of prayer, the ninth hour (Acts 3.1), and to the death of Jesus on the cross (Matthew 27.46 and parallels). He also adds to the biblical text of Genesis by placing the expulsion of Adam and Eve from Paradise (Genesis 3.23) in the ninth hour, parallel to Jesus' words to the thief (Luke 23.43), and by placing the sending of the raven from the ark (Genesis 8.7) in the ninth hour. As the raven brings death, so we receive the olive branch of life from the dove [58]. Here John is following a long tradition of exegesis that contrasts the raven and the dove [59].

Finally the nine orders of angels deserve mention. They are ranked in Eḷišē, *Questions;* most notably, the "thrones" come at the end in the highest rank. Here Eḷišē is following the listing in Dionysius Areopagita, not that of Cyril of Jerusalem or of John Chrysostom [60].

---

[51] *Matenagrut'iwnk'*, p. 321.
[52] *Ibid.*, p. 280.
[53] *Ibid.*, pp. 282—283, 322.
[54] See, for example, Barnabas XII 6, or Germanus of Constantinople, *Oratio* 1, *In vivificam crucem (P. G.* 98.229). In General see Daniélou, *Theology,* pp. 92, 271.
[55] Anania, pp. 245—246. Ps. Athanasius, *De Sabbatis et circumcisione* 5 *(P. G.* 28.139), states that the eighth day of circumcision signifies the regeneration of everything after the seven days. Cf. the idea of the eighth (not seventh) day as that of rest, note 39 above. For circumcision as a figure of baptism see G. W. H. Lampe, *The seal of the Spirit,* London 1967; and Daniélou, *Bible and Liturgy,* pp. 63—69. The earliest Christian parallel between baptism and the flood is found in I Peter 3.20—22, II Peter 2.5.
[56] Agathangelos, §§ 291—295.

[57] Anania, p. 246. John Chrysostom, *Homiliae in I Thess.* IX 2 *(P. G.* 62.449), notes that some people are born in the seventh, some in the ninth month — such is the uncertainty of life!
[58] *Opera,* pp. 218—222.
[59] Cf. Gregory of Nyssa, *De Baptismo (P. G.* 46.421). In general see Daniélou, *Bible and Liturgy,* pp. 81—82.
[60] Eḷišē, *Questions,* p. 11: angels, archangels, զաթոռիք, զպուիք, իշխանք, իշխանութիք, Seraphim, Cherubim, thrones. From the lists in Ephesians 1.21 and Colossians 1.16 it is clear that the իշխանութիք are the κυριότητες and the զօրութիք are the δύναμεις; but both զաթոռիք and իշխանութիք can render either ἀρχή or ἐξουσία. Cyril of Jerusalem, *Catecheses* XXIII 6 *(P. G.* 33.1113; not in the Armenian — but see A. Renoux, «Une versionne arménienne des Catéchèses mystagogiques de Cyrille de Jérusalem?» *Le Muséon,* vol. 85 (1972), p. 147—153) and John Chrysostom, *Homiliae in Genesin Cap I,* IV 5 *(P. G.* 53.44) have identical lists except for the placing of the "thrones" (in seventh place in Cyril, in fourth place in Chrysostom). If one discounts exact verbal parallels with the biblical lists, then Eḷišē's list could

VIII

The number TEN represents the rational sciences: it is the sum of one, two, three and four, which make a triangle. This mathematical commonplace is repeated by John of Odzun. He links it with the number of psalms recited at morning and evening prayer (six and four) and with the ten commandments [61]. Then in a physical sense ten represents the mind and the nine ways in which it operates through the body: the eyes, ears, nostrils, mouth and hands. Here too John is following a theme common to patristic writers, who added in various combinations the five senses (or the parts of the body through which they operate) to other physical and mental faculties [62].

In a more spiritual sense ten is associated with the pascha and with Jesus' baptism. Anania notes that the Passover Lamb is to be taken on the tenth day of the first month and killed and eaten on the evening of the fourteenth (as Exodus 12.3). He also states that Jesus entered Jerusalem on the tenth day (the day of palms) and fasted until the fourteenth, until the evening of the last supper [63]. Ełišē elaborates more precisely on this, indicating that the sacrifice of Christ the true lamb of God is the sacrifice that saves everyone, Jew and Gentile [64].

Anania also brings out another typological parallel between the old and new dispensations. Just as the Hebrews crossed the Jordan on the tenth day (Joshua 4.19), so was Christ baptised on the tenth day. Here we have a reflection of a common patristic theme, but not the earliest exegesis which saw the Old Testament type of baptism in the crossing of the Red Sea [65].

The number TWELVE is associated primarily with the apostles. As Ełišē notes, it was not by chance that they were twelve; the number was revealed long ago in the Old Testament. Ełišē lists three such indications: the twelve sons of Jacob (Genesis 35.22), the twelve rocks of Joshua ch. 4 (where the number is based on the twelve tribes), the twelve baskets of crumbs in the miracle of the feeding of the five thousand (Matthew 14.20 and parallels) [66]. In another context Ełišē speaks of the apostles and the twelve rocks who will build on the cornerstone dishonoured by the Jews [67]. Agathangelos merely notes the parallel between the twelve tribes and the twelve apostles [68]. And not surprisingly, John of Odzun is more interested in the sacerdotal parallels; the twelve gems in the high-priest's robe (Exodus 28.21), and the twelve stones of the temple [69]. These last are not the twelve stones of Elijah's altar (III Kings 18.31—32). John obtains twelve by multiplying three by the four sides. And the three are not the three rows of stone in the description of Solomons's temple in II Kings 6.36; three here is rather a mystical number derived from the three types of the church: the ark, Solomon's temple and the temple restored by Zerubbabel.

Ełišē elaborates on the theme of twelve as applied to periods of time. Day and night

---

render that of Dionysius, *De caelesti hierarchia*, 7—9 (*P. G.* 3.205, 237, 257): angels, archangels, ἀρχαί, ἐξουσίαι, δυνάμεις, κυριότητες. Seraphim, Cherubim, thrones.

[61] *Opera*, p. 52; cf. Anania, p. 246. Clement of Alexandria, *Stromateis* VI 16 (*P. G.* 9.357), speaks of the decalogue as a "heavenly image" representing the sun, moon, stars, clouds, light, spirit, water, air, darkness, fire. Contrasted to this is the "earthly decalogue" of men, beasts, reptiles, animals, fish, whales, two kinds of birds, two kinds of plants.

[62] John of Odzun, *Opera*, p. 52. Cf. Clement of Alexandria, *Stromateis* II 11 (*P. G.* 8.985): ten represents the five senses plus speech, τὸ σπερματικόν, τὸ διανοητικόν and body and soul.

[63] Anania, p. 292.

[64] *Matenagrut'iwnk'*, p. 244.

[65] Anania, p. 294. For Christian exegesis of the O. T. types of baptism see Daniélou, *From Shadows to Reality*, London 1960, pp. 261—275.

[66] *Matenagrut'iwnk'*, pp. 327—328. It is noteworthy that no mention is made of the twelve springs of Elim (Genesis 15.27), often associated with the apostles (or the prophets, as Eusebius, *De ecclesiastica theologia* 3.3, *P. G.* 24.988). Aphraates, IV 6, explains the variation between eleven and twelve disciples, i. e. after Judas' apostasy and before the election of Matthias, by the eleven sons of Jacob mentioned in Genesis 32.22, and the twelve after the birth of Benjamin.

[67] *Matenagrut'iwnk'*, p. 257.

[68] § 612.

[69] *Opera*, pp. 298, 262.

have twelve hours, thus the twelve years' illness of the woman with an issue of blood (Matthew 9.20 and parallels) represents the sickness of this world. Likewise there are twelve sins: abandoning God; worshipping human artifacts; sacrificing to insensible beings; being indifferent to repentence; killing those (created) in one's own image; avarice — which is the root of bitterness; hatred — which is the unfruitfulness of the righteous part; stealing — which is the beginning of the ruin of this world; rapine — which provokes wars; hatred — which is the denial of God; pride — which is the destruction of souls and bodies; the fruit of death — which we inherited for corruption. In these twelve respects the world had fallen into sickness, physically and spiritually. Furthermore, men had looked up to the heavens and worked out in place of God an astral mythology based on the twelve stars. But through the twelve apostles the Lord healed the world, both men and time — the twelve hours and twelve months. Through the distribution of life by the twelve apostles, the following twelve benefits are seen: men are spurred to virtue; they speak truth instead of their former error; they work righteousness; they give godly fruit; marriage in purity; virginity; mercy; kindness to strangers; hope in God; true faith; love without doubting; instead of pouring out blood in impure sacrifices men shed their own as martyrs for the blood of Christ [70].

The number THIRTY gives rise to two lines of thought: the meaning of the thirty pieces of silver (Matthew 26.15, with reference to Zechariah 11.12), and thirty as the age of Adam and Jesus. Eḷišē explains the thirty pieces of silver as representing three tens associated with the Old Testament: the first ten represents the dishonouring of the ten commandments, the second ten the denial of Mosaic salvation, the third ten the disbelief in the promised land [71].

The age of Jesus as thirty (when he began his ministry, Luke 3.23) is explained by Anania as double that of maturity. For at fifteen one can beget one's kind, and at thirty be a grandfather [72]. (This is somewhat at variance with the statement elsewhere in Anania that everything was created perfect and in full stature and maturity, thus man was thirty years old in paradise[73].) But although Anania contrasts such human begetting with the spiritual rebirth granted us through the divinely-begetting water and the Spirit, he has no further biblical or spiritual parallels to draw.

The number FORTY contains many mysteries, says Anania [74], of which only a few examples can be given. Other than the forty cities of refuge (sic! — a misreading of Numbers 35.6—7), all Anania's examples are periods of time. He recalls the forty days of the flood (Genesis 7.12), Moses' forty days before the Lord when he received the ten commandments (Deuteronomy 9.25), Elias' flight of forty days from Jezabel (III Kings 19.8), the purification forty days after childbirth (Leviticus 12.2—4) as in the case of Jesus (Luke 2.22 ff.), who was both presented and presents us all through himself in a priestly manner to the Father. The forty years that Isaac remained unmarried (Genesis 25.22) are explained as necessary so that he might beget the promised offspring Israel by a chaste marriage [75].

Eḷišē discusses Jesus' remarks about the temple (John 3.19 and parallels), noting that

---

[70] *Matenagrutʻiwnkʻ*, pp. 324—327.
[71] *Matenagrutʻiwnkʻ*, p. 250.

[72] Anania, p. 247. But for fourteen as the age of maturity see above at note 47. Aphraates, XXI 9, compares Christ's age at baptism to Joseph's thirty years when he stood before Pharoah (Genesis 4.46). For the contrasting traditions which give Christ thirty or thirty-three years of life on earth see Goudoever, *Fêtes*, p. 288.

[73] Anania, p. 293. Cf. Ephrem, *Diatessaron* IV 1 (Armenian version ed. L. Leloir, *Corpus Scriptorum Christianum Orientalium* vol. 137, *Scriptores Armeniaci* 1, Louvain 1953): the thirty years show Christ's humanity. Eḷišē, *Questions*, p. 30, stresses that Adam and Eve were perfect (*katarealkʻ*). For the tradition that they were children see Murray, *Symbols*, pp. 304—306.

[74] Anania, p. 247.

[75] Cf. Aphraates, XVIII 6: as an illustration of the excellence of virginity Moses abstained from his wife for forty years.

VIII

the temple was built in forty years, whereas God formed man in the womb in forty days and preserved the Jews in the desert for forty years. The reference to the desert naturally leads Eḷišē to the rock which gave water, paralleled in the rock which is the chief cornerstone (Mark 12.10 and parallels). But he does not elaborate on this extremely common theme of Christological exegesis [76].

John Mandakuni is more concerned with the ecclesiastical significance of forty. Noting that Moses and Elias both fasted for forty days, he emphasises the importance of keeping strictly the forty days of the Lenten fast, based on Jesus' forty days of temptation. In contrast to these forty days of suffering are the forty days of life celebrated from Easter to the Ascension [77].

The liturgical parallels of FIFTY are brought out by Anania. It was on the fiftieth day that we (Christians) received the Spirit and were freed from sin. This is our Jubilee as opposed to the old Jewish Jubilee every fifty years (Leviticus 25.10) when slaves were freed and possessions returned [78]. John of Odzun uses the same term for the period between Easter and Pentecost [79]. Anania states that fifty represents the day on which the transgressors received the rescript of death on the stone tablets. This perhaps represents the fifty days from the Exodus to the giving of the law, a period discussed by numerous Christian exegetes [80].

SEVENTY alternates with SEVENTY-TWO in Armenian exegesis, as in patristic writers [81]. Agathangelos refers throughout his *History* to seventy-two patriarchs, seventy-two tongues after the tower, and thus seventy-two disciples to evangelise the world [82]. The same parallel between 72 tongues and 72 apostles is made by John of Odzun [83]. And Eḷišē, discussing the apostles, notes that the Spirit of God who inspired them also inspired Moses to appoint 72 elders [84]. But elsewhere Eḷišē refers to the seventy [85]. Anania says there were 70 elders, excluding Eḷdat and Meḷdat (cf. Exodus 24.1) [86]. His only other reference to 70 is an interpretation of the blessings of the Spirit as numbered by Isaiah, seven times the perfect ten [87].

Anania likewise interprets EIGHTY as eight times ten [88]; it is thus for him a figure of the eighth day. As noted above, Anania is the only one of the authors discussed here to refer to the figure of the eighth day [89]. Anania also adduces the eighty generations from the first to the second Adam in Luke's genealogy, i. e. a count of the names in the Armenian of Luke 3.23—38, including those of God and Jesus.

Only Eḷišē has an explanation of the ONE HUNDRED AND FIFTY-THREE fishes of John 21.11. He divides it into three fifties plus three ones. The fifties are then interpreted as jubilees rescued by Christ from corruption,

---

[76] *Matenagrut'iwnk'*, p. 257. For the theme of the water from the rock see, for example, Daniélou, *Shadows to Reality*, pp. 193—197.

[77] *Čaṙk'*, pp. 35 and 209—211, where elaborate rules for the fast are spelled out. For the fasts of Moses and Elias as types of Jesus' fast cf. Origen, *Fragmenta in Johannem* 79 (*Griechischen christlichen Schriftsteller*, Leipzig, 4, p. 546).

[78] Anania, p. 248.

[79] *Opera*, p. 214.

[80] See Goudoever, *Fêtes*, pp. 199—205 for Jewish exegesis of the fifty days, and *ibid.*, pp. 251—253 for the Christian interpretation of Pentecost and the giving of the Law on the fiftieth day.

---

[81] See in general B. M. Metzger, "Seventy or seventy-two disciples?" *New Testament Studies*, vol. 5 (1958—1959), pp. 299—306.

[82] §§ 503, 579, 612.

[83] *Opera*, p. 294.

[84] *Matenagrut'iwnk'*, p. 320.

[85] *Ibid.*, p. 260.

[86] These names are mystifying corruptions (?) of Nabad and Abiud. (Nabad in the Armenian for Nadab of the Hebrew, Syriac and LXX.)

[87] Anania, p. 248.

[88] Anania, p. 248.

[89] See note 40 above.

but the three ones are given no especial significance [90].

Finally the number SIX THOUSAND picks up the theme of the six days or ages. Anania links the six thousand years of this unredeemed world with the illustration of Babel, which Satan had arranged as a place for his own amusement with musical instruments and harps [91]. But more interestingly, in Ełišē there are two references to Christ's redeeming the world after six thousand years. At one point Ełišē specifically interpolates into Jesus' words to Peter "Were you unable to remain awake one hour?" (Matthew 26.40 and parallels) the following: "For in six days I created heaven and earth and all their order. And now behold this is the six thousandth year since they have fallen into corruption and been ruined; and I have come to save and renew [92]." And in Ełišē's *Questions* there is a reference to "an old wives' tale" to the effect that God had given Adam a rescript in which he promised to come and save him after six thousand years. This deed had eventually passed into the hands of the magi, who brought it with them to Christ in Bethlehem. Ełišē ridicules the story and explains the reference to the rescript abolished by Christ (cf. Collossians 2.14) as a figure [93]. But the tale of this document, signed and sealed by God and given to Adam when Seth was born as a "son of consolation" is widespread in the Armenian elaborations of the apocryphal *Infancy Gospels*. This document was supposedly handed down through Seth's descendants to Noah; he gave it to Sem, whose descendants gave it to Abraham. Abraham gave it to the high-priest Melchisedek, and from him it passed to the Persian king Cyrus. Thenceforth it was kept safely in the Persian archives until king Melchior (Melk'on) brought it to Bethlehem. The whole story is found in two long recensions of the Armenian *Infancy Gospel* and in several shorter texts [94].

---

[90] *Matenagrut'iwnk'*, p. 334. For the jubilees cf. notes 78—80 above. The Armenian Ephrem changes the 153 to 150 in order to equal the number of psalms; see Murray, *Symbols*, p. 176 note 2. On the other hand, the *Logos* on prayer attributed to Nilus (P. G. 79.1165 ff.) is dividied into 153 chapters. St. Augustine, *Letter* LV 17.31 (P. L. 33.220) elaborates on the mathematical interpretation: 153 is the sum of the integers 1 to 17.
[91] Anania, p. 248.
[92] *Matenagrut'iwnk'*, p. 254.

[93] *Questions*, pp. 52—53.
[94] Printed in *Ankanon Girk'* II (Venice 1898); see esp. pp. 46, 51, 127, 276, 294—295, 304. Translation of the long recension in P. Peeters, *Evangiles apocryphes II, L'évangile de l'enfance, rédactions syriaques, arabe et arméniennes (Textes et documents pour l'étude historique du christianisme)*, Paris 1914.

ADDITIONAL NOTE: The popularity of number symbolism—both in the sense of the supposed inherent properties of numbers and in the interpretation of numbers in the bible—was so great among Armenian writers that a full study would require several volumes. Of particular interest is the extensive discussion throughout Grigoris Aršaruni, *Meknut'iwn Ént'erc'uacoc*, Venice 1964 [translated by L.M. Froidevaux, *Grigoris Aršaruni: Commentaire du Lectionnaire*, Venise 1975]. Further comments on this subject may be found in items VIII, XIV, XVIII, and XIX below.

IX

ARCHITECTURAL SYMBOLISM IN CLASSICAL ARMENIAN LITERATURE

THE Continuator to Thomas Artsruni's *History* gives an elaborate description of the palace and church built on the island of Alt'amar in Lake Van by king Gagik at the beginning of the tenth century.[1] The historian found it difficult to express in words his astonishment at the wondrous beauty of these constructions: 'Even if an intelligent man were to examine only one section (of the palace) for several hours on end, on coming out he would be unable to tell anyone of what he had seen.' Commenting on the reliefs that surround the exterior wall of the church, he refers to 'the glorious image of king Gagik, who with proud faith raises the church (i.e. a model of his endowment) on his arms like a gold vessel full of manna, or a golden box filled with perfume; he stands in front of the Lord, depicted as if begging forgiveness for his sins'. In the interior of the church the architect Manuel had 'fashioned the wonderful holy of holies with elegant paintings, with silver doors full of gilt ornaments, with images encased in gold and precious stones and pearl ornaments, and with various notable and splendid vessels which wonderfully show us the second Jerusalem and also the gate of Sion on high'. The historian thus hints at the symbolic representation of the spiritual and immaterial realities of heaven in the material structure and ornament of the church.

On the other hand, numerous Armenian writers are quick to point out that the church in its true meaning is not a material but a spiritual entity. In the homilies attributed to Gregory the Illuminator we read: 'The church is the believing congregation of God.'[2] The same statement is repeated more than once in Khosrov Andzewats'i's *Commentary on the Liturgy*.[3] The mystic poet Gregory of Narek elaborates on the symbolism of the church—that is the congregation (*zholovurd*)—as bride in his

---

[1] *Patmut'iwn Tann Artsruneats'*, Tiflis, 1917, part IV, chs. 7–8, pp. 477–87. For the surviving church see S. Der Nersessian, *Aght'amar, Church of the Holy Cross*, (Cambridge, Mass., 1965).

This paper draws together evidence for symbolic interpretations of a church building found in classical Armenian writers. It is not a study of the origins of such interpretations in Eastern Christianity but an attempt to elucidate certain Armenian literary traditions. Only printed sources have been used; much Armenian homiletic literature and the majority of biblical commentaries (still unpublished) remain to be explored. References to Greek and Syriac parallels have generally been confined to texts translated into Armenian in the fifth century.

[2] *Yachakhapatum* 17 (Venice, 1954), p. 189.

[3] *Meknut'iwn Alōt'its' Pataragin* (Venice, 1869), pp. 42, 53.

ARCHITECTURAL SYMBOLISM 103

Commentary on the Song of Songs.[1] And in the *Canons* attributed to the patriarch Sahak many Old Testament parallels to the church as a group of people are adduced. Here we are taught that the church is a rational and spiritual entity, not built of stone and wood but on the rock of faith.[2]

However, these *Canons* also distinguish between the 'congregation' or 'community' (*zhoḷovurd*) and the place where the people assemble, the *zhoḷovrdanots'* (as in Luke vii. 5; xiii. 10).[3] Such places are buildings (*shinuatsovk' teḷik'*) where priests and people gather together for prayer, the liturgy, and other forms of worship. The distinction between the spiritual and physical senses is brought out more explicitly by John of Odzun: 'But it is necessary to know why the term "church" is applied equally to the church which is built of inanimate stones and wood and to the congregations of the faithful. Now just as we understand "paradise" in two ways, so also we should understand "church" in two senses. For "church" is interpreted from the Hebrew among us as "people"; but the same term is also applied to the meeting-place (*zhoḷovaran*), as this is truly built as the house of God since the Son of God is sacrificed therein. Likewise man too is the temple of God according to Paul because of the cleansing of the font and the purity of his life.'[4] John then proceeds to elaborate on the church as a symbol (*awrinak*)[5] of faith and virtue.

But in addition to such spiritual interpretations, a more material symbolism may be read into the church as a structure. The eleventh-century historian Aristakēs, bewailing the desolated churches of Armenia, says: 'They exemplified the likeness of heaven through their magnificent constructions.' He has in mind primarily the sumptuousness of their

---

[1] *Matenagrut'iwnk'* (Venice, 1840), p. 277; cf. also pp. 281, 303, 305, 330, 351.

[2] *Canon* 36, in *Kanonagirk' Hayots'*, ed. V. Hakobyan, 2 vols. (Erevan, 1964, 1971), I, pp. 386–91. For the use of *ekeḷets'i* in the Old Testament referring to a group of people see especially p. 389.

[3] *Canon* 37, *Kanonagirk'*, I, pp. 391–3.

[4] *Opera* (Venice, 1834), pp. 308–10. But whether the two discourses printed at the end of this book (pp. 256–312) are definitely John's is not certain. For the term *zhoḷovaran*, cf. Nerses of Lambron, *Letters* (included in Grigor Kat'olikos Tḷay, *Namakani*, (Venice 1865)), p. 236; *ekeḷets'in or t'argmani zhoḷovaran*. The theme is elaborated in Nerses' *Commentary on the Liturgy* (*Khorhrdatsut'iwnk' i Kargs Ekeḷets'woy ew Meknut'iwn Khorhrdots' Pataragin* (Venice, 1847)), pp. 120–1. Cf. the definition of the church as συνάθροισις λαοῦ in the *Rerum ecclesiasticarum Contemplatio*, P.G. 98. 384, attributed to Germanos I of Constantinople (see R. Bornert, *Les commentaires byzantins de la divine liturgie du VIIe au XVe siècle*, *Archives de l'Orient chrétien* 9 (Paris, 1966), p. 160), and the συνάθροισμα λαοῦ in F. E. Brightman, 'The *Historia Mystagogica* and other Greek Commentaries on the Byzantine Liturgy', *J.T.S.* ix (1908), p. 257.

[5] For the use of the term *awrinak* as 'symbol' or 'type' see R. W. Thomson, *The Teaching of Saint Gregory* (Cambridge, Mass., 1970), pp. 15–16.

decoration; the worshipper, overawed, might think himself in heaven.[1] But Gregory of Narek in his *Mystic Soliloquy* 75 goes further: § 9, the church is built as the dwelling place of God; § 10, it is a form (*tesak*) of the upper vault (of heaven).[2] Although in this prayer Gregory is mainly concerned with the church as a spiritual entity—the mystical body of Christ— from these two brief quotations two important points emerge: the O.T. parallels (for the 'dwelling place of God' reminds us in particular of a common theme in the Psalms), and the parallels with the structure of the universe as understood by Gregory and his fellow Armenians. This paper will be primarily concerned with the second of these themes; at the end we shall return to some of the corresponding O.T. parallels.

It is not appropriate here to describe in detail early Armenian conceptions of the nature of physical reality, of the composition of the material world from the four elements, and of the ethereal nature of the vault of the sky.[3] But a few ideas derived from the bible are basic to the architectural symbolism.

The *Teaching of Saint Gregory* (the Illuminator) as found in the *History* of Agathangelos opens with a brief description of heaven, earth, and the void.[4] Heaven is domed (*khoranard*), with a firm roof (? *hastayark*), suspended in the void. The adjective *khoranard* is used in Job xxxviii. 38 to render κύβος, while the noun *khoran* renders the σκηνή of Isa. xl. 22 and the δέρρις of Ps. ciii. 3. It is the theme of the tent that is the more important. *Khoran* occurs several hundred times in the Armenian bible, rendering σκηνή, and is one of the key terms used in Armenian architectural symbolism.

In Armenian the basic meaning of *khoran* is 'tent'. Eḷishē glosses its use in Ps. ciii. 3 as *vran*.[5] In a secular sense *khoran* refers to a military

---

[1] *Patmut'iwn* (Erevan, 1963), ch. 10, pp. 55–6. Cf. the wonder of the beholder on entering the church of the Virgin of the Pharos: 'it is as if one had entered heaven itself... one is so amazed' (Photius, *Homil.* X. 5), quoted in C. Mango, *The Art of the Byzantine Empire, 312–1453, Sources and Documents* (Englewood Cliffs N.J., 1972), p. 185.

[2] *Matenagrut'iwnk'*, pp. 187–98. For the term *kamar* (vault) see below.

[3] See, for example, Eznik, III. 1–9; Eḷishē, *Questions et réponses sur la Genèse*, publié par P. N. Akinean, traduit par Dr. P. S. Kogian (Vienne, 1928); Anania Shirakats'i, *Matenagrut'yunĕ*, ed. A. G. Abrahamyan (Erevan, 1944). For a later summary of Armenian ideas about the nature of the physical universe see the first part of the *Chronicle* of Mkhitar of Ayrivank: M. Brosset, 'Histoire chronologique par Mkhitar d'Airivank, XIIIe S.', *Mémoires de l'Académie impériale des sciences de St.-Pétersbourg*, VIIe serie, tome XIII, no. 5 (St.-Pétersbourg, 1869), esp. pp. 5–6.

[4] § 259. These paragraph numbers are those of the Tiflis 1909 edition of Agathangelos. For the *Teaching* see p. 103 n. 5, above, and for the *History* see R. W. Thomson, *Agathangelos, History of the Armenians* (Albany, 1976).

[5] *Questions*, p. 27.

ARCHITECTURAL SYMBOLISM

tent[1] or a domed area, such as the shah's audience chamber.[2] Such a dome is an image (*awrinak*) of the sky;[3] for the sky, in Gregory of Narek's words, is 'the upper, inaccessible dome of ether, outside physical space'.[4] The theme is elaborated by Nerses Shnorhali: heaven is a hemisphere (*kisagund*) like a *khoran*, self-moving and unsupported.[5]

Another term, also found in the Armenian bible, is even more frequently used of the vault of heaven: *kamar*, which renders the καμάρα of Isa. xl. 22.[6] Anania Shirakats'i describes the vault (*kamar*) formed by the fire and air which surround the earth.[7] Gregory Magistros speaks of the firmament above as a *kamar*.[8] Gregory of Narek refers to the 'celestial

---

[1] e.g. Kirakos Gandzakets'i, *Patmut'iwn Hayots'* (Erevan, 1960), pp. 161, 233. Smbat Sparapet, *Taregirk'* (Venice, 1956), p. 238, speaks of the race of Ishmaelites (Arabs) as 'tent-dwellers' (*khoranabnak*). Matthew of Edessa, *Patmut'iwn* (Jerusalem, 1869), p. 160, notes that when the Muslims were about to attack Sebaste in 1059/60, they were at first afraid to enter the city because they thought that the numerous white domes of the churches were soldiers' tents (*vrank'*).

[2] As in Łazar P'arpets'i, *Patmut'iwn Hayots'* (Tiflis, 1904), p. 107[16], [19]. Cf. also Faustos (P'awstos Buzandats'i), *Patmut'iwn Hayots'* (4th edn., Venice, 1933), IV. 54.

[3] As in Nerses of Lambron, *Commentary on the Liturgy*, p. 146.

[4] *Matenagrut'iwnk'*, p. 458 (*On the Church*): *verin anvayr khoran et'ern anmatoyts'*. Cf. Severian, *De Mundi Creatione*, III. 5, *P.G.* 56.452.

[5] *Yałags Erkni* (*On Heaven*), Erevan, 1968, p. 21. Cf. also Theodore K'ṙt'enawor, *Chaṙk' Erek'* (printed in *Yovhannu Imastasiri Awdznets'woy Matenagrut'iwnk'* (Venice, 1833)), p. 170: heaven is a divinely constructed *khoran*.

[6] Cf. Cyril of Jerusalem, *Catecheses*, IX. 5, with *kamar* in the Armenian version (*Koch'umn Ĕntsayut'ean* (Venice, 1832), p. 147).

But the Armenian version of Basil's *Hexaemeron* (*Chaṙk' vasn vets'ōreay Ararch'ut'eann* (Venice, 1830)), I. 8 (p. 15), offers an idiosyncratic version of Isa. xl. 22 quoted by Basil. 'Ο στήσας τὸν οὐρανὸν ὡσεί καμάραν is rendered: *o dzgeats' zerkins ibrew zkonk' gmbet'ard ew hastateats' kangneats' zna ibrew zkhoran i bnakut'iwn*, 'who stretched out heaven like a domed conch and established (and) set it like a *khoran* for habitation'. (The Armenian vulgate reads: 'who set heaven like a *kamar* and stretched (it) out like a *khoran* and established the earth to dwell therein.') The Armenian translator has amalgamated Isaiah with the *konk'* of Ezek. xl. 24 etc.; *gmbet'ard* (domed) is not a biblical term, but cf. p. 108 nn. 5, 9, below. The variant *gmbet'ayard* in Basil, *Hexaemeron* III. 4, renders ἡμικύκλιος. However, this Armenian version of the *Hexaemeron* is widely divergent from the Greek, often expanding, occasionally abbreviating the original text. For the impact of this version on Armenian astronomy see references in R. W. Thomson, 'The Fathers in Early Armenian Literature', *Studia Patristica*, 12 (1975), p. 467, and for a general study of the Armenian text, K. M. Muradyan, *Barseł Kesarats'in ev nra 'Vetsōrean' Hay Matenagrut'yan mej* (Erevan, 1976).

[7] *Matenagrut'yunĕ*, p. 318 (*On the Rotation of Heaven*).

[8] *T'łt'erĕ* (Alexandropol, 1910), p. 171 (*Letter 70*). In his *Poems* (*Tałasats'ut-'iwnk'* (Venice, 1868)), p. 5, Gregory elaborates on the nature of the heavens, the *kamar* and *khoran* unsupported by pillars. *Kamar* and *khoran* are also used more or less as synonyms by Nerses Shnorhali, *On Heaven*.

kamar of heaven not made by human hands'.[1] And the later historian Vardan describes in detail the three spheres (*kamark'*) of fire, water, and air, each above the other, which encircle the earth.[2] (Even more elaborate, but basically similar, is the description of the universe in Mkhitar of Ayrivank'.)[3] The *kamar* of the sky is where God dwells. As John of Odzun explains: 'The Lord's temple is not built in one place, as the Jews had it, but is the supernal vault of heaven at the ends of the world.'[4] Both *khoran* and *kamar* are widely used in descriptions of the symbolism of a church building. The former more particularly reminds us of the many O.T. images of a tent, while the latter has more or less exclusive reference to the physical aspect of the sky and heaven.

Scattered throughout Armenian historical works from the fifth to the fifteenth centuries are hundreds of references to the building, restoration, or destruction of churches. But although the basic idea of the symbolic parallelism between the vaults or dome of a church and the celestial vault of heaven was familiar to Armenian historians, they rarely expand on it in their descriptions of actual buildings. Even when they describe in detail the materials used, the design of the church, or its decoration, their references to the symbolic meaning of the architecture are usually confined to a few stock phrases. Not surprisingly, it is to the theologians that we must look for more elaborate disquisitions on symbolism. But a brief review of the basic ideas in historical texts will provide us with a background for investigation of the theological texts.

The first churches in Armenia were supposedly built at the orders of St. Gregory the Illuminator on the sites of the pagan temples that he and king Trdat had destroyed. These events—enshrouded in legendary detail—are reported by the writer known as Agathangelos, whose *History* in its surviving form dates to nearly a century and a half after the period it purports to be describing.[5] The first church was built at Ashtishat in Western Armenia, on the site of the temple of Vahagn, and it enclosed relics of John the Baptist and the martyr Athenogenes.[6] This became the chief church of the first episcopal see in Armenia, and there the Armenian primates resided through most of the fourth century.

But Agathangelos does not describe this church. The only comments he makes that are relevant to our study concern the chapels erected near

---

[1] *Matenagrut'iwnk'*, p. 396 (*On the Cross*): *vernayark andzeṙagorts erknits' kamar*.
[2] *Hawak'umn Patmut'ean* (Venice, 1862), p. 2.
[3] Reference as in p. 104 n. 3, above.
[4] *Opera*, p. 282.
[5] See the introduction to Thomson, *Agathangelos*.
[6] Agathangelos, §§ 809–14. See also Faustos, III. 3, 14, 19.

Vałarshapat (in north-eastern Armenia) for the nuns martyred by king Trdat before his conversion. These chapels were made of rock, stone, brick, and cedar-wood (§ 757), and adorned with lamps and candelabras (§ 759). The door-posts were made of massive, unhewn stones (§ 767). Inside the chapels the martyrs were buried in caskets. Over their resting places, in the centre of the domed roof (? *i nerk'sagoyn khoranats'n*) Gregory erected crosses, glossed as 'pillars bearing the weight of the edifice of your salvation' (§ 769). 'Pillar' here is used in a metaphorical sense, but the paragraph seems to imply that Agathangelos had in mind a structure with a central dome supported by pillars. However, the imagery is dependent on Gregory's vision (§§ 731–55), in which—among other predictions—he was shown the sites for three future chapels for the martyrs and for the main cathedral.[1]

In the vision the main site was marked with a circular base of gold on which rested a column of fire and capital of cloud, surmounted by a cross of light. The sites for the martyrs' chapels were marked with red bases (the colour of blood), columns of cloud, capitals of fire, and crosses of light; these columns were lower than the column of light. Above all four crosses, vaults (*kamark'*) fitted into each other. The whole was surmounted by a wonderful canopied (*khoranard*)[2] construction of cloud in the form of a dome (*gmbet'adzew*). These architectural features (probably based on the architecture of the cathedral at Vałarshapat) are then interpreted in a metaphorical or spiritual sense. The base is the rock of establishment (cf. Matt. vii. 25); the column is the Catholic church (cf. Eph. iv. 13); the capital of cloud is the cloud that will receive the just when they fly up before the Lord at his coming (cf. 1 Thess. iv. 16); the cross on the tallest column is the image of Christ; the other crosses represent the equality and unity of the Catholic church; the canopy (*khoran*) represents the celestial city—the meeting place (*zhołovaran*)[3] of the kingdom of heaven.

This last is the most important feature of the symbolism, which will be echoed by later writers. The church is the meeting place of the faithful; it is a symbol of the celestial city, the kingdom of heaven; and this symbol is represented in physical terms by the domed or canopied roof supported by vaults that rest on pillars. Agathangelos seems to imply that 'domed' (*gmbet'azdew*) and 'canopied' (*khoranard*) are identical in meaning. Later writers do not distinguish between these two adjectives, nor indeed do they make clear the difference (if any) between the *khoran*

---

[1] For these churches see A. Khatchatrian, *L'architecture arménienne du IVe au VIe siècle* (Bibliothèque des Cahiers archèologiques 7, Paris 1971).
[2] Cf. the description of heaven at p. 104 n. 4, above.
[3] Cf. p. 103 n. 4, above.

and the *kamar*, at least in their architectural as opposed to symbolic sense.[1] Both terms are used to describe the vault of the sky above—the image of heaven.[2]

It is surprising that not until the eighth century are the terms *gmbetʻ-adzew* and *khoranard* found again after Agathangelos, despite the many descriptions of churches in earlier writers, especially Sebēos. John of Odzun uses the two terms to describe the summit of the church which rises up to support the cross on top.[3] But his description of the *khoran* with four pillars on the same page probably refers to the baldacchino over the altar. For the basic meaning of the term *khoran* naturally leads to its use for 'tabernacle', 'sanctuary', and the complex over the altar (*seḷan*). In the following century the historian John Catholicos has many descriptions of the founding of churches, but there is no symbolic imagery to be found in his *History*. The early eleventh-century Stephen of Tarōn, however, is quite explicit. The cathedral of Kars had a circular dome supported by stone columns; the effect was of a dome that resembles heaven.[4] This expression *khoran erknanman* is dear to him as well as later writers. Stephen uses it of the cathedral at Argina: a heaven-like domed *khoran* with firm pillars;[5] of the cathedral at Ani—a heaven-like domed *khoran* on lofty vaults—(the church) was resplendent like the vault of heaven;[6] of the church of St. Gregory at Ani 'wonderfully domed, very lofty and like the sphere of heaven'.[7]

Kirakos uses the term *khoran* in a more restricted sense. He describes the construction of churches with three and five *khorans* (cupolas) in the monastery of Nor Getik. These were domed.[8] Several times he refers to a church being 'domed like heaven'.[9] (But the adjective *khoraneay* in Kirakos refers to a tent church, not to the architectural design of a church's roof.)[10] Stephen Orbelean uses the phrase 'domed like heaven' of the churches at Tsaḷatsʻ-kar[11] and at Tatʻev. At Tatʻev the interior had

---

[1] Cf. the comments of Gregory Magistros and Nerses Shnorhali as cited on p. 105 n. 8, above.

[2] Cf. the reference in Gregory Tḷay, *Elegy on the Capture of Jerusalem*, to the 'sons of Sion and the brides of the upper *khoran*'; Armenian text in E. Dulaurier, *Recueil des historiens des Croisades, Documents arméniens* I (Paris, 1869), p. 272.

[3] *Opera*, p. 311.

[4] *Patmutʻiwn Tiezerakan*, III. 7: *bolorapēs gmbētʻaworeal . . . erknanman khoran.*   [5] Ibid. III. 9: *gmbētʻard khoran erknanman.*

[6] Ibid. III. 30: *bardzraberdz kamarawkʻ gmbētʻaworeal khoran erknanman . . . jahanayr ěst erknayin kamarin katʻoḷikēn surb.*

[7] Ibid. III. 47: *skʻanchʻates tesleamb gmbētʻaworeal gunak gerambardz ew erknanman gndin.*   [8] *Patmutʻiwn*, pp. 222–3.

[9] *Gmbetʻard erknanman*, as at pp. 164, 212, 269.   [10] Ibid., p. 358.

[11] *Patmutʻiwn Nahangin Sisakan* (Tiflis, 1910), p. 71 (ch. 19), where the jemaran was *erknanman hrashakʻartar shinuatsovkʻ erkagmbētʻs* (with two domes) *ew erekʻ khorans* (with three *khorans*).

ARCHITECTURAL SYMBOLISM

been decorated by painters from a distant country of Frankish (*P'rang*) origin; heaven was represented on the main vault above the altar.[1]

If the idea of a church as the symbol of the celestial kingdom, the dome representing the vault of heaven, is well known to Armenian writers,[2] what of the symbolism of other parts of the edifice? Terms such as 'foundation', 'base', 'pillar' are often used in a metaphorical sense of people or aspects of the faith. For example, Gregory Magistros refers to the beatitudes as the base (*khariskh*) and foundation (*himn*) of the faith of the new Israel;[3] John Sarkawag refers to the base (*khariskh*) of God's commandments.[4] Vardan refers to Bartholomew and Thaddaeus as pillars (*siwnk'*) of the church[5]—an expression which Gregory T!ay applies generally to the Armenians of the Northern regions.[6] Kirakos calls Sahak and Mashtots' (among other epithets) the 'pillars' and 'walls' of the church;[7] while Gregory of Narek can speak of the 'rational stones' of the church, meaning her teachings.[8] But the only writer who draws symbolic meaning from the stones, walls, doors, windows, and divisions of the material structure is John of Odzun. Not surprisingly, the rites for the blessing of the foundations and the consecration of the finished edifice provide the occasion for most of his comments.[9]

In the rite for the laying of a church's foundations twelve unpolished stones are used. The number twelve reflects the twelve stones taken from the river Jordan (Joshua iv. 3) and Christ's twelve disciples. The stones are washed with water and wine—as Christ washed the apostles' feet and gave them wine to drink at the Last Supper. The stones are placed at the four corners of the church—signifying the four corners of the world. Then the officiating bishop takes the architect's measuring line and marks out the space of the foundations, thus drawing the contrast between God's immeasureless nature and the bounded, finite nature of man. John draws the parallels of Ezekiel's vision (Ezek. xl. 3) and the passage in Agathangelos that describes Gregory laying out the foundations of the martyrs' chapels with an architect's *lar* (§ 758). Three

---
[1] *Patmut'iwn Nahangin Sisakan*, pp. 256–7 (ch. 44).
[2] Cf. the hymn of censing in the Armenian liturgy, where the church is addressed as: *harsn pantsali erknanman lusachem khoran*.
[3] *Letter* 36, p. 89.
[4] *Yałags K'ahanayut'ean, Sop'erk' Haykakank'* 3 (Venice, 1853), p. 97.
[5] *Hawak'umn*, p. 84. Cf. Gal. ii. 9.
[6] *Namakani* (Venice, 1865), p. 84.
[7] *Patmut'iwn*, p. 27.
[8] *Mystic Soliloquy* 75, § 14 (*Matenagrut'iwnk'*, p. 201). Cf. Nerses of Lambron, *Synodal Letter* (*Atenabanut'iwn*), (Venice, 1812), p. 36: the stones of the spiritual temple are the various nations of Christendom.
[9] The rites are in the *Mashtots'*. I am here following the commentary thereto in *Opera*, pp. 256–78.

times the line of the foundations is drawn out, indicating the three types of the church in the Old Testament: the ark of the covenant, the temple of Solomon,[1] and the temple restored by Zerubabel. The number three has further significance in that there are three of the twelve stones to each side; and twelve is not only a symbol of the apostles, it is the number of the principal limbs of the body and also has certain unique mathematical properties. John also notes that the twelvefold anointing of the altar reflects the mystical words of the twelve prophets. The doors of the church, however, are anointed four times, recalling the composition of the human body from the four elements.[2]

More significant, though, is John of Odzun's threefold division of the church into sanctuary (*khoran*), nave (*tachar*), and narthex (*gawit'*), for such a division was mystically prefigured by Noah's ark with its three decks. The three decks of the ark are the *nerk'natun, mijnatun*, and *vernadzeḷun* ('ground floor', 'first floor', and 'attic').[3] The last term is reminiscent of the description of heaven in Eḷishē's *Questions*: God made the firmament like the ceiling of a house (*ibrew zdzeḷun tan*) over the earth.[4] The same term *dzeḷun* occurs in Genesis viii. 13, where Noah opens the 'roof' of the ark and sees that the flood is diminishing. The threefold division of the ark (*eṙamasneay*) is also noted by Gregory Magistros,[5] but he draws no comparison with the division of the church.[6]

The structure of the church is oriented towards the East—whence we await the second coming. Furthermore, Paradise is in the East.[7] The window on the East indicates the entry of spiritual light into the world and the just who shine like the rising sun. [In this regard it is interesting to note the change in the number of windows from one to three in the

---

[1] For parallels between the church and Solomon's temple, cf. Gregory of Narek, *Mystic Soliloquy* 75, § 12 (*Matenagrut'iwnk'*, p. 200) and *On the Church*, *Matenagrut'iwnk'*, p. 458. Cf. also Ephrem Syrus on Hebrews 8 (Armenian text in *Srboyn Ep'remi Matenagrut'iwnk'* III (Venice, 1836), p. 214) and John Chrysostom, *In Psalmum* 133, *P.G.* 55.386 (for the Armenian version see references in M. Geerard, *Clavis Patrum Graecorum* II (Turnhout, 1974), p. 519; but the fragments published by Akinean do not include the text of Ps. cxxxiii). Nerses of Lambron, *Synodal Letter*, p. 24, speaks of Constantine as the new Solomon building the splendid temple of the faith of the church; and p. 14, describes the council of Nicaea as Constantine's spiritual temple.

[2] On such number symbolism in early Armenian writers see further R. W. Thomson, 'Number Symbolism and Patristic Exegesis in some early Armenian Writers', *Handes Amsorya* 90 (1976), cols. 117–38.

[3] *Opera*, p. 292.   [4] *Questions*, p. 27.   [5] *Letter* 76, p. 221.

[6] Cf. the threefold division of the Temple as interpreted by Philo and Josephus; J. Daniélou, 'La symbolique du temple de Jérusalem chez Philon et Josèphe', *Le symbolisme cosmique des monuments religieux*, Serie Orientale Roma XIV (Roma, I.S.M.E.O., 1957), pp. 83–90.

[7] John of Odzun, *Opera*, p. 300. Cf. Gregory of Narek, *Mystic Soliloquy* 75, § 14 (*Matenagrut'iwnk'*, p. 202).

eastern apse of the church of St. Rhipsimē, built in 618. Churches with three windows in the main apse are rare in Armenia. This alteration has been plausibly connected with Chalcedonian influence.][1] The side windows figure the humbler contemplation of the mind and the fact that our side (members?) to right and left are illuminated by virtue. The window to the West indicates the light which goes from East to West. The rectangular form of the building summons the four corners of the world to one hope of the calling in Christ to offer worship to the sole God.

John is thus at some variance from the symbolism in the famous Syriac hymn on the church at Edessa.[2] In the Syriac hymn (strophe 7) the four corners of the world are symbolized by the arches (or vaults, kap'e). Three sides of the building (strophe 12)—i.e. the north, south, and west—represent the Trinity; while the light of the windows on those three sides (strophe 14) represents the apostles, prophets, martyrs, and confessors. The three windows in the chancel represent the Trinity (strophe 13).

The nave where the faithful gather, says John, indicates our equality with the angels when we shall all stand before Christ's tribunal (bem). The bema itself is the image of heaven, for on it is raised the altar with the priests standing around—as Jesus is raised above the surrounding angels who sing his praises.[3] The altar reflects the mystery of the consubstantial Trinity, while the side chapels (khorhrdanots'k') to right and left indicate that the church's vessels are always ready to give merciful gifts to the poor. Likewise the part of the sacrament remaining on the altar shows that the church never lacks the propitiating body of Christ. Furthermore, the sacrament is first placed in the side chapel because Christ first came to us secretly and rested in the Virgin's womb, and then was openly brought to the altar of the cross.

Summarizing the symbolism of the building, John ends by

[1] See A. B. Erémian, 'Sur certaines modifications subies par les monuments arméniens au VIIe siècle', *Revue des Études arméniennes*, N.S. 8 (1971), pp. 251–66 (translated with revisions from the Armenian in *Patmabanasirakan Handes*, 1966, no. 4, pp. 151–70).

[2] For the Syriac text see H. Goussen, 'Über eine "Sugitha" auf die Kathedrale von Edessa', *Le Muséon*, 38 (1925), pp. 117–36; there is a revised translation in A. Dupont-Sommer, 'Une hymne syriaque sur la Cathédrale d'Edesse', *Cahiers archéologiques*, 2 (1947), pp. 29–39, and an English version in C. Mango, *The Art of the Byzantine Empire*, pp. 57–60. For a general study of the symbolism involved see A. Grabar, 'Le témoignage d'une hymne syriaque sur l'architecture de la Cathédrale d'Edesse au VIe siècle et sur la symbolique de l'édifice chrétien', *Cahiers archéologiques*, 2 (1947), pp. 41–67.

[3] For the parallel between the clergy in the *bema* and *khoran* of the church and the heavenly *khoran*, cf. Nerses of Lambron, *Commentary on the Liturgy*, pp. 309 ff.

emphasizing that the sanctuary and nave thus have symbolic meaning.[1] The four columns (which support the dome) indicate the four virtues. The junction of the vaults (*kamarats'*) indicates the coupling of love to virtue. The twelve foundation stones indicate the twelve limbs of rational beings, while the juxtaposition of large and small stones indicates the union in piety of men and women—for in Christ there is no distinction of sex. The bonding of the rubble and other materials is a sign of the faithful who are united in one hope of Christ's calling. The edifice which rises in the form of a dome is then crowned with a purple cross, the colour of the divine blood, whereby God brings his children to the supernal Jerusalem. There they will rejoice and exult in the *khoran* of light, and enjoy eternal sustinence.[2] 'Such,' says John, 'is the symbolic meaning of the building as taught by the holy Spirit.'

John also emphasizes that the 'foundations' of the church are to be found in the Old Testament.[3] We may now turn to a more detailed investigation of such O.T. themes in Armenian writers, confining the discussion to parallels for the church as a structure. For although these parallels do not add further light on Armenian architectural symbolism, it may be interesting in the wider context of Eastern Christian thought to note the major themes of Armenian exegesis in this regard.

A very common theme is that of Noah's ark (*tapan*) as a type (*awrinak*) of the church. The threefold division of ark and church in John of Odzun has already been noted. A more general comparison is elaborated at some length by Gregory of Narek,[4] Gregory Magistros,[5] and Nerses Shnorhali.[6] The parallel with a ship is brought out in the *Canons of*

---

[1] *Opera*, pp. 310–12. Cf. ibid., p. 288: everything in the church 'has symbolic reference to heavenly things' (*zerknaynots'n berē ts'oyts' awrinaki*). But we are not here concerned with the symbolism of ecclesiastical ornaments, vessels, and robes to which John devotes much attention.

[2] The *khoran* of light may be a reminiscence of the liturgical expression quoted in p. 109 n. 2, above. For the heavenly *khoran* cf. also Łazar, *Patmut'iwn*, p. 132: God brought the holy Vasak to himself and settled him in the *khorans* of the kingdom, with the angels in heaven. Very different is the symbolism of the struggle between light and darkness reflected in the black and white stones in the fourteenth-century church in the monastery of St. Thaddaeus (Iran); see V. A. Khachaturjan, 'Simvolika cveta b odnom armjanskom arkhitekturnom pamjatnike XIV veka', *Patmabanasirakan Handes*, 1977, no. 2, pp. 191–8.

[3] *Opera*, p. 262: *himunk' ekełets'woy en awrinakk'n ařajink'*.

[4] *Mystic Soliloquy* 75, § 12, *Matenagrut'iwnk'*, pp. 199–200.

[5] Especially in *Letter* 77 (pp. 224–5). In his *Poems*, p. 80, Gregory Magistros compares the ark with the cross.

[6] *Opera* (Venice, 1833), II, p. 285. Cf. in general John Chrysostom, *De Lazaro* 6. 7, *P.G.* 48.1037: μυστήρια δὲ ἦν τὰ λεγόμενα, καὶ τῶν μελλόντων τύπος τὰ γινόμενα· οἷον, ἡ 'Εκκλησία κιβωτός. Armenian text in *Chaŕk* (Venice, 1861), p. 546: *khorhurd ēr gortsn ar̄ i yapay linelots' awrinak: ekełets'woy awrinak ēr tapann, ew Noy Kristosi, ew aławnin surb Hogwoy*.

ARCHITECTURAL SYMBOLISM

Sahak, where the incarnate Word of God is described as the ship's captain (*nawapet*) and the apostles, prophets, and teachers as the sailors (*nawavarkʻ*).[1] Similar terminology is found in a homily ascribed to Sahak: the church is the harbour (*nawahangist*) and the bishop is the captain.[2]

More directly relevant to the tent-like structure of the dome are the O.T. parallels involving the term *khoran*. Gregory Arsharuni notes that Christ bids us dwell as sojourners (*pandkhtabar*) in the *khorans* of his church as in tabernacles (*taḷawars*)—an allusion to the feast of tabernacles (as Leviticus xxiii. 42).[3] More frequent are allusions to the tents of Abraham and Moses. John of Odzun directly compares Abraham's tent which God and the two angels entered (Genesis xviii) to the sanctuary where the Trinity mystically dwells.[4] (In this connection Gregory Magistros only refers to the angels.)[5] Referring to the same episode Gregory of Narek uses the noun *taḷawar* instead of the biblical *khoran*.[6] The latter word is also used for the ark of the covenant. John of Odzun and Gregory Magistros specifically refer to the mention of this ark on Sinai (e.g. in Exodus xxxiii) as a mystical parallel to the church.[7]

Other parallels with buildings, though somewhat removed from architectural motifs, include the church as tower and as winepress. John of Odzun compares at some length the tower (*ashtarak*) constructed by presumptuous men which led to the scattering of the races, with the tower constructed of firmly secured stones (*hastaheḷoys vimawkʻ*) which is the Catholic church.[8] Of particular Armenian interest is his reference to the Titan Bēl who built the tower, reminding readers of the legends in Book I of Moses Khorenatsʻi and in the *Primary History*.[9] However,

[1] *Canon* 36, *Kanonagirkʻ*, I, p. 388. Cf. the *Constitutiones Apostolorum* II. 57.2: ὡς ἄν κυβερνήτης νηὸς μεγάλης μετ' ἐπιστήμης πάσης κέλευε ποιεῖσθαι τὰς συνόδους, παραγγέλλων τοῖς διακόνοις ὡσανεὶ ναύταις τοὺς τόπους ἐκτάσσειν τοῖς ἀδελφοῖς καθάπερ ἐπιβάταις . . . (ed. F. X. Funk, Paderborn, 1905, p. 159).

[2] *Sopʻerkʻ Haykakankʻ* 2 (Venice, 1853), p. 117. Cf. the *Canon of the Holy Ark* (*Sharakankʻ*, Venice, 1907, p. 407), where it is described as the 'harbour of the just'. For the theme of the harbour see E. R. Hambye, 'The Symbol of the "Coming to the Harbour"', *Symposium Syriacum 1972*, *Orientalia Christiana Analecta* 197 (Rome, 1974), pp. 401–11. For the theme of church and ark see in general J. Daniélou, *From Shadows to Reality* (London, 1960), pp. 69–112, and idem, *Primitive Christian Symbols* (London, 1964), pp. 58–70.

[3] *Meknutʻiwn Ëntʻertsʻuatsotsʻ* (Venice, 1964), ch. 28 (p. 176).

[4] *Opera*, p. 294.

[5] *Letter* 77, p. 225.

[6] *Matenagrutʻiwnkʻ*, p. 458 (*On the Church*).

[7] John, *Opera*, p. 296; Gregory, *Letter* 77, p. 225.

[8] *Opera*, p. 294. For the Syriac symbolism see R. Murray, *Symbols of Church and Kingdom* (Cambridge, 1975), pp. 219–24.

[9] i.e. the first section of the *History* attributed to Sebēos. For an English translation of Moses and the *Primary History*, see R. W. Thomson, *Moses*

more usual in Armenian is the parallelism between the tower and the cross—a major theme in the *Teaching of Saint Gregory*.[1]

The idea of the church as a winepress is widely attested in patristic exegesis (with especial reference to the headings of Psalms viii, lxxx, lxxxiii).[2] In Armenian an example is Theodore Kʻṙtʻenawor's reference to the Virgin Mary as a wondrously divine winepress (*hntsan*), source of the wine of Christ in the church which is built as a winepress (*hntsanashēn ekeḷetsʻi*).[3] But the most interesting use of this theme occurs in the *History* of Agathangelos: when Rhipsimē and her companions—whose martyrdom becomes the occasion for the Armenian king's conversion—arrive in Armenia as they flee from Diocletian, they take refuge outside the Armenian capital in the vat-stores (*hndzanayarks*, the buildings that house the winepresses).[4] The Greek version of the Armenian has merely εἰς τὰς ληνούς.[5] In view of the role of these nuns in the story as the source of conversion to Christianity, and the vat-store as the site of one of the chapels built by Gregory, a more symbolic hiding-place would be difficult to find.

Khorenatsʻi, *History of the Armenians* (Harvard Armenian Texts and Studies, 4, Cambridge, Mass., 1978).

[1] See especially §§ 581–6, 628–31. Cf. also Gregory Magistros, *Poems*, p. 80, and Ephrem, *Commentary on the Diatessaron* 14.2 (Armenian text edn., L. Leloir, *CSCO* 137 (*Arm.* 1), Louvain, 1953). For parallels in Greek patristic literature see G. W. H. Lampe, *A Patristic Greek Lexicon* (Oxford, 1961–8), s.v. πύργος.

[2] See the references in Lampe, *Lexicon*, s.v. ληνός, and for Syriac evidence see Murray, *Symbols*, pp. 100, 122.

[3] *Charkʻ Erekʻ*, p. 178.

[4] § 150. (*Hndzan* is a frequent variant spelling of *hntsan*.)

[5] For the Greek version of the surviving Armenian text (as opposed to Greek versions of Agathangelos not derived from the extant Armenian) see G. Lafontaine, *La version grecque ancienne du livre arménien d'Agathange*, Publications de l'Institut Orientaliste de Louvain 7 (Louvain-la-Neuve, 1973). For the other Greek versions see the references in Thomson, *Agathangelos*, pp. xxii, 436–7.

X

MUHAMMAD AND THE ORIGIN OF ISLAM
IN ARMENIAN LITERARY TRADITION [1]

The military impact of Muslims was felt in Armenia as early as the 640's, and Islamic influences came to have profound significance for many aspects of Armenian life — political, social, artistic, and literary. But the Armenians were slow to develop any coherent understanding of the nature of Islam as a religion. Not until Gregory of Tatʿev in the fourteenth century was any elaborate and detailed discussion of the beliefs and rituals of Muslims attempted (2). There are, however, accounts of the origin of Islam to be found in earlier Armenian sources. These were polemical in intention, but they are interesting for the light that they shed on the sources available in Armenia. And although many of the stories have their parallel in Greek, Syriac, or Arabic Christian writing, there are also idiosyncratic Armenian elaborations and traditions which are worth bringing together.

---

(1) I am indebted to Professors Wolfhart Heinrichs and Wheeler Thackston for several helpful references to Islamic literature.

(2) See G. M. De Durand, «Une somme arménienne au XIVe siècle», *Etudes d'histoire littéraire et doctrinale*, 4e série, *Publications de l'Institut d'études médiévales*, XIX, Montréal — Paris, 1968, pp. 217-277; and *idem*, «Notes sur deux ouvrages de Grégoire de Tathew», *REArm.*, 5 (1968), pp. 175-197. The article by F. Macler, «L'Islam dans la littérature arménienne d'après la publication récente du 'Livre des Questions' de Tathewatsi», *Revue des études islamiques*, 6 (1932), pp. 493-522, is not what the title might suggest but gives merely a summary of sixteen errors of the Muslims as indicated in the work of B. Kiwlēsērean (for which see note 48 below). There is no discussion of the Armenian texts which form the subject of this paper.

X

What follows is an attempt to survey Armenian traditions concerning Muhammad and the origin of Islam down to the thirteenth century.

The first serious encounter between Armenians and Muslims occurred in 637. Numerous Armenian nobles, fighting in the Iranian army, were slain at the battle of al-Qādisiyah (near Sāmarra). The first irruption of Muslim armies into Armenia proper took place four years later. Details of the destructive expedition, culminating in the sack of Dvin, are given by the seventh-century historian known as Sebēos. He then describes the final destruction of the Sasanian forces, the defeat and death of Yazkert III in 651, and the agreement between the caliph Muʿāwiyah and Theodore, prince of the Řštunikʿ, preparatory to the caliph's grand expedition against Constantinople.

Some doubt has been thrown on the authorship of the *History* attributed to «Sebēos». The text as we have it is preceded by several sections that have no relevance to the main part, the so-called «History of Heraclius». And this main section is not entirely devoted to Heraclius, but gives a résumé of Iranian history from the mid-fifth century to the 590's, then a detailed account of the wars between Byzantium and her Sasanian and Muslim foes down to the caliphate of Muʿāwiyah. However, there is little doubt that this main part was written in the late seventh century, even if the text is not to be attributed to «Sebēos» (3). This *History* is important for our theme since it is the first Armenian source to mention Muhammad (4): He was an Ismaelite, a descendant of Abraham from the bond-servant Hagar (5), a merchant well versed in the history of Moses. It was by God's command that he appeared to the Ismaelites as a preacher, teaching them to recognise the God of Abraham; since the command «came from above», the Ismaelites immediately abandoned their vain cults and turned to the God of Abraham. But Sebēos has little further to say about the origin of Islam or the person of Muhammad. He is much more interested in

---

(3) On the question of whether the «History of Heraclius» as now known was written by «Sebēos» or a different author see G. V. Abgaryan, *Sebeosi Patmutʿ-yunə ev Ananuni arelcsvacə*, Erevan, 1965; and *idem*, «Remarques sur l'histoire de Sebéos», *REArm*, 1 (1964), pp. 203-215.

(4) *Patmutʿiwn Sebēosi Episkoposi i Herakln*, Tiflis, 1913, Ch. 30; there is a French translation by F. Macler, Paris, 1905.

(5) In this regard Sebēos quotes Gen. 16.12, which refers to Ismael.

the military conquests of the Muslims, whose success he attributes to two factors: the newly found unity among the Arabs, and the urging of the Jews (6).

Sebēos' comments on the early military success of the Muslims are repeated by the later Armenian historian Łewond, writing at the end of the eighth century. Łewond elaborates somewhat on the Jewish alliance, but says nothing about the origin of Islam as a religion or about the person and career of Muhammad (7). However, in his *History* has been interpolated an exchange of letters between the caliph ʿUmar II and the emperor Leo III — at least these documents purport to be such. But they do not date to the eighth century and will be discussed below.

Other original Armenian writers of the eighth century do not give information about the person of Muhammad, although they sometimes offer a few generalised comments on Islam as a religion. The catholicos John of Ojun (717-728) may be referring to the Muslims in *Canon 28*; here he exhorts the Christian Armenians not to flinch at martyrdom by the heathen *(hetʿanosacʿ)* for worshipping the cross (8). But as so often with theologians, it is the enemies long dead who are the most in mind. For in his treatise against the Paulicians the «heathens» are the ancient pagans, not the Muslims; and John is still concerned with the «obscene» practices of the Mazdaeans. Nonetheless, the later law-codes do legislate on the problems of social relationships between Christians and Muslims (9).

Nor are the accounts of eighth century Armenian martyrs helpful. Vahan of Gołtʿn was martyred in 717, but in his *Vita* there is no exchange

---

(6) As this paper is concerned with literary traditions concerning Muhammad, no attempt will be made to comment on the military or political events described by Sebēos or other writers quoted below. For the reaction of Sebēos and other early Christian writers to the Muslim invasions see W. E. Kaegi, «Initial Byzantine Reactions to the Arab Conquest», *Church History*, 38 (1969), pp. 139-149.

(7) *Patmutʿiwn Łewondeay meci Vardapeti Hayocʿ*, St. Petersburg, 1887, Ch. 1; there is a French translation by G. Šahnazarean, Paris, 1857.

(8) See *Kanonagirkʿ Hayocʿ*, ed. V. Hakobyan, I, Erevan, 1964, p. 533. Armenian text with Latin translation in *Johannis Ozniensis Opera*, Venice, 1834, p. 74.

(9) See in particular: *The Penitential of David of Ganjak*, ed. C. J. F. Dowsett. CSCO 216, 217, Louvain, 1961, §§ 10, 16, 45, 56; Mxitʿar Goš, *Girkʿ datastani*, Erevan, 1975, Section A Intr. §§ 9, 10, Chs. 101, 161, 163; J. Karst, *Sempadscher Kodex*, Strassburg, 1905, §§ 1, 12, 15, 26, 28, 29, 40, 72, 115, 116, 117, 125, 143, 170.

of views on the nature of Islam (10). Hamazasp and Isaac Arcruni were martyred in 785/6. In their *Vita* we read that their brother Merhujan accepted the Muslim faith *(lit.* legislation — *awrensdrutʿ- iwn)* (11) and was immediately circumcised, a rite frequently stressed in later Armenian authors (12). But the Muslim faith is merely described as «impious *(amparišt)*», or «fictitious *(karcecʿeal)*, or «born of death *(mahacin)*». Nor in the martyrdom of Isaac and Joseph at Karin (Erzerum) ca. 808 do we find anything but opprobrious epithets describing Islam *(molor snoti usmunkʿ)* (13).

The first Armenian author to give a detailed account of Muhammad's life is Thomas Arcruni, writing at the beginning of the tenth century. He begins with the story of the Jews inviting the Ismaelites to share their inheritance, as in Sebēos, but then continues with a circumstantial description of Muhammad's career and teachings.

(10) *Vahanay Goltʿnacʿwoy vkayabanutʿiwn,* in *Sopʿerkʿ Haykakankʿ,* Vol. 13, Venice, 1854. Cf. also John Catholicos Drasxanakertcʿi, *Patmutʿiwn Hayocʿ,* Tiflis, 1912, p. 99.

(11) It renders the $\nu o\mu o\theta\varepsilon\sigma i\alpha$ of Rom. 9.4. Used in Elišē (ed. E. Tēr-Minasean, Erevan, 1957), p. 29, for Christianity; it is very frequent in later writers for Islam. Muhammad is often called *awrēnsdir,* as in Thomas Arcruni, III, 6 — the $\nu o\mu o\theta\varepsilon\tau\eta\varsigma$ of James, 4.12 or Ps. 9.21. For the use of *awrēnkʿ* in Armenian as «religion» see R. W. Thomson, «The Maccabees in Early Armenian Historiography», *Journal of Theological Studies,* N. S. 26 (1975); pp. 329-341, esp. pp. 336-7.

(12) *Vkayabanutʿiwn srbocʿ isxanatcʿn Hamazaspay ew Sahakay,* in *Sopʿerkʿ Haykakankʿ,* Vol. 12, Venice, 1854, pp. 61-80. For circumcision required of converts to Islam cf. John Catholicos, *Patmutʿiwn Hayocʿ,* Tiflis, 1912, pp. 129ff., and Thomas Arcruni, *Patmutʿiwn Tann Arcruneacʿ,* Tiflis, 1917, III, 6. Cf. Evodius on the 42 Martyrs of Amorium (V. Vasilevskij and P. Nikitin, «Skazanie o 42 Amoriiskix Myčenikax», *Zapiski Akademii Nauk,* St. Petersburg, 8th series, vol. 7, no. 2 [1905], p. 66), § 17: $\pi\varepsilon\rho\iota\tau\mu\eta\theta\eta\tau\varepsilon\ \varkappa\alpha i\ \tau\tilde\omega\ \pi\rho\omega\tau o\sigma\upsilon\mu\beta o\upsilon\lambda\omega\ \sigma\upsilon\nu\varepsilon\upsilon\xi\alpha\sigma\theta\varepsilon,\ \varkappa\alpha i...$

(13) *Vkayabanutʿiwn srboyn Sahakay ew Yovsēpʿay,* in *Varkʿ ew Vkayabanutʿ- iwnkʿ,* II, Venice, 1874, pp. 266-271. Similar expressions in Thomas Arcruni, III, 6, describing the martyrdom of bishop John, prince Gregory Arcruni, and the priest Gregory.

Thomas Arcruni, II, 4 (14):

   How the wicked kingdom of the Persians came to an end and was succeeded by the even more wicked (kingdom) of the Ismaelites

   In the time of the Byzantine emperor Heraclius the Persian kingdom reached its end. And at that time there came and gathered in the city of Edessa 12,000 men from all the tribes of Israel. As they had seen that the Persian army had left and abandoned the city, they entered (Edessa), closed the gates, fortified themselves therein, and began to rebel against Roman rule.
   But the emperor Heraclius commanded them to be besieged. The king's brother Theodore and the host of the army wished to slaughter them, but the king commanded them to go from his territory. They took the desert road and went to Arabia to the sons of Ismael, to the city called Madiam, which Israel had destroyed on leaving Egypt in its war with Bałak, king of Moab. And because the Persian power had become very weak, they fearlessly entered the city of Madiam and dwelt in it.
   They sent messengers to the sons of Ismael, indicating their close relationship: «We are sons of Abraham, we and you, brothers. You must come to our help, and we shall take the land of our inheritance». But although the latter were persuaded, yet there was a great division among them, because they were divided by the worship of idols according to each one's desire.
   At that time there were some despotic brothers in the regions of Arabia Petraea in the place (called) Pʿaṙan, which is now called Makʿa — warlike chieftains, worshippers of the temple of the Ammonites of the image called Samam and Kʿabar. It happened that one of them, called Abdla, died leaving a son of tender age called Mahmet. His uncle Aputalp took and raised him until he reached puberty. On attaining a sufficient age he dwelt with a certain wealthy man from among their kin. He served him faithfully, pastured camels, and was the steward of his house. When some time had passed, the master of the house died. Seeing that Mahmet was a faithful man and very judicious in all wordly affairs, the wife (widow) married him and turned over to him all the supervision of the house and property. So he became a merchant by trade and skilled in commerce. He undertook distant journeys on mercantile business, to Egypt and the regions of Palestine. And while he was engaged in this business he happened to meet in the regions of Egypt a monk called Sargis Bhira, who had been a disciple of the mania of the Arians. Becoming acquainted with him and in the course of time becoming friendly, he taught (Mahmet) many things, especially concerning the old testaments and that God has by nature no Son. He tried to persuade him to follow the former faith of the Israelites: «For if you accept this, I predict that you will become a great general and the leader of all your race». He reminded him of God's promise to Abraham and of the rites of circumcision and sacrifice and all the other

---

(14) There is a French translation by F. M. Brosset, *Collection d'historiens arméniens*, I, St. Petersburg, 1874, but this chapter is in complete.

things which it is not necessary to mention here in detail. On these the Ismaelites speculate to the very end (i.e. the *n*th degree).

It happened one day when he was departing from him that a strange voice, an inspiration fearsome and demonic, fell upon him and drove him out of his senses, as is now appropriate to indicate according to the following example. For they say of the woman from whom Antichrist will be born, that journeying from Egypt to the land of Palestine and desiring to see the column of David's wife, she went and lingered there quietly. And as she dozed, a strange spirit cried out from the mouth of the woman turned into stone: «You will bear a son who (will) conquer the world». And indeed a daughter of the tribe of Dan conceived from fornication. Such things also occurred in his (Mahmet's) time. For when his travelling companions asked why he had lost his wits, he said: «Some fearsome angel's voice fell on me and ordered me to go as a messenger to my nation, to show (them) God the Creator of heaven and earth, to take upon myself the title of leadership and to refute and destroy the false faith in idols». Coming to Pʿaṙan he repeated these same words to his uncle called Apḷjēhr. He said: «What is this new faith which is now being revealed by you? If you say any more you will be responsible for your own safety». Grieved, he went to his own house, for he was continuously oppressed by the demon; perhaps God allowed him to suppose that his loss of reason (was caused) by an angel. And many of them believed him when he said he was a messenger of God.

One day, when he was depressed from his uncle's threats, Ali son of Aputalip came in and said to him: «For what reasons do you sit depressed»? He said: «I preach God the creator of heaven and earth, but they reject me with threats». Now Ali was a valiant man. He said to him: «Arise, let us go out, for there are many men with us. Perhaps there may be some good solution to this matter».

When they had gone outside, Mahmet began to speak the same words publicly. There was a great outcry among them and such a dispute that many of them drew their swords. Mahmet's side was defeated; many on both sides were wounded, and Mahmet and Ali fled with about forty men. They came to the city of Madiam which we mentioned above. On hearing the cause of their flight the Jews, like zealots for God and as sons of Abraham and mutual brothers, were emboldened to unity and to proclaim that his words were true. They joined him and made a pact, gave him a wife from their nation, and made ready to support him in whatever way his wishes might dictate. So one could say that it was by a command of God that this undertaking began. The Jews joined with the Ismaelites, forming a large army. Attacking Pʿaṙan, they inflicted a great defeat on their opponents, killed Apḷjēhr and many of the Ammonite and Moabite troops, destroyed the images of Samam in his temple, and dared say that the temple was the house of Abraham. They subjected all the inhabitants of the neighbouring regions and wiped out by the sword all resistance.

When Mahmet saw the success of this venture and the concord of the Jews, he proclaimed himself head and leader of them all. He appointed as his officers and generals Ali and Apubikʿr and ʿAmr and Utʿman. He sent a message to Theodore, the brother of Heraclius, in that the Jews had cooperated:

«God promised this land to Abraham and his seed, and it was in their possession for a long time. And if God was disgusted with their wicked deeds and gave it into your hands, let the period you have held it suffice for you. Now we are the sons of Abraham and you know the promise made to Ismael our father. Give to us our land peacefully, otherwise we shall take it by war — and not only that (land) but also many others». He (Theodore) wished to show it to the king, but Heraclius died in those same days. His son Constans did not agree to respond as he (Theodore) had wished, but simply ordered caution and not to wage war against them until he saw the outcome of events. But the army of Ismael was vigorously straining for war. So wishing to defend the country (the Byzantines) went out against them. Leaving their horses, they opposed them on foot. The latter, having been at rest, attacked them. Exhausted by the weight of their arms, the great heat of the sun, the density of the sand which gave no support to the feet, and their tramping on foot, and distressed in every way, they fell into the hands of the enemy who slew them with their swords. Reaching the site of their camp, (the Muslims) seized a great amount of booty, and began fearlessly to spread over the land because they had no worries of any battle.

Then the inhabitants of Jerusalem, seeing the perilous situation with no hope of help, took the divine holy symbol of the Lord with their church ornaments and brought them in flight to the imperial capital to Constans. And Ismael ruled over all Judaea.

Now the Arian monk whom we mentioned above, Mahmet's teacher, on seeing his success rose up and went to Mahmet (to ask for) his kind favour, as if he had attained such things on being instructed by his teacher. But since (Mahmet) said he had a message from an angel and not from a man, he was very vexed at this and killed him secretly.

At this very time there was a certain hermit in the regions of Persia who had a pupil called Salman. At the hour of his death the hermit gave him these instructions: «My son, on my death do not remain in this land lest you lose your faith among the infidels, but go to the regions of Egypt to dwell in the numerous company of brethren (monks) so that you may gain your soul». When the hermit died, Salman intended to carry out his intructions. On his journey he happened to come to the city of Madiam; he had knowledge of the scriptures, though not a perfect one. When Mahmet saw him, he summoned him and attached him to him, and ordered him to write a book of laws for his nation by the hand of Abut'uraba the Ismaelite; for he himself did not know writing or reading. Salman agreed to write for him and composed a fictitious book, some of it from accurate memory, other parts being imaginary sayings. But Mahmet himself, moved by a raving spirit, had him write perverse (things), of which we shall give brief extracts.

He said that he was the Consoler whom the Lord Christ had promised to send to his disciples; he said he was equal to the Saviour, his travelling companion — in the words of Isaiah: «riding one on a donkey, and the other on a camel». All this he applied to himself. Instead of holy baptism (he prescribed) continual washings with water, and reckoned this was sufficient for purification. The heavenly gifts which the Lord has promised for the future, the ineffable and angelic renewal, he said were vast quantities of food and drink; should one wish to eat insatiably one would find them (already) prepared. And there would be continual and insatiable intercourse with women who remained virgins. It is too long to repeat all his impure sayings, for they are many and opposed to God. And all this he affirmed and set down for his nation, calling it the Kuran.

Now come and I shall tell you with what laments the old author bewails them, saying: «Woe to you, alas for you, nation of Arabs *(Tačik)*, men and women of all the cirties by the sea, for the impiety of your tongue and filthiness of habits, whereby opening your mouth you spoke impious things, you have come before the mighty God. And now with new and amazing wounds he will judge you more than the whole world for the filthiness of your tongue, which you sharpened against the mighty king. He will slay you with heavy blows. The whole world will see you smoking, and fire will never leave you for ever. Like a potter's furnace will you burn, and you will have no rest».

All these evils he accomplished, and even more laws than these he established for his nation in his multifarious wickedness. Having lived for twenty years in this fashion he died, and appointed Apubakʿr to the leadership of the Arabs.

The immediate source of Thomas' account is not clear. Although there are a few parallels with the later account in Mxitʿar of Ani, which is even more elaborate, Mxitʿar took his material more or less word for word from the Armenian version of a document in Karshuni (15); but no such written source for Thomas has yet come to light. Living in Southern Armenia, Thomas was familiar not only with earlier Christian traditions about Islam but also with native Muslim ones as well.

There are parallels between Thomas and some Byzantine writers, notably John of Damascus (675-749?), many of works were translated into Armenian (16). John, like Thomas, begins his account of the origin of Islam with the assertion that the Saracens were idolators, worshippers of the idol of Venus called Khabar (17). The Ammonite connection adduced by Thomas is mentioned in Theophanes (early ninth century) (18) and George Hamartolus (late ninth century) (19).

(15) See below, p. 16.
(16) See G. Zarpanalean, *Matenadaran Haykakan Tʿargmanutʿeancʿ Naxneacʿ*, Venice, 1889, pp. 575-580. For a general presentation of the Byzantine evidence see A.-Th. Khoury, *Polémique byzantine contre l'Islam (VIIIe-XIIIe s.)*, Leiden, 1972; and idem, *Les théologiens byzantins et l'Islam, Textes et auteurs (VIIIe-XIIIe s.)*, Louvain, Paris, 1969.
(17) *De Haeresibus Compendium*, 101 (*Patrologia Graeca* 94, col. 764). See also the Abjuration (note 20), p. 153.
(18) *Chronographia*, s.v. A.C. 622 (*Patrologia Graeca* 108, col. 685).
(19) *Chronicon*, CCXXXV (*Patrologia Graeca* 110, col. 865).

But in addition to information possibly taken from written sources available in his own time, Thomas also had direct knowledge of Islam. For he knows the name of Muhammad's uncle, information not repeated in Greek until the eleventh/twelfth century in the texts attributed to Bartholomew of Edessa, or in Syriac until the twelfth century historian Michael (20).

Muhammad's mercantile journeys to Palestine and Egypt are known to Theophanes and George Hamartolus, as is his marriage to his master's widow. As early as John of Damascus we hear that Muhammad became acquainted with an Arian monk, but the name Sargis Bhira, which becomes standard, is not known in Greek before «Bartholomew» (21). The story in an elaborate form appears in Arabic in Ibn Isḥāq (d. 753 A.D.) (22). The demonic possession which Muhammad attributed to an angel is mentioned frequently in the Greek sources beginning with the Abjuration; they claim that Muhammad persuaded his wife to believe in his mission by asserting that Gabriel had appeared to him.

The support of ʿAlī is not mentioned in the Christian sources before Thomas, nor is the alliance with the Jews of Medina following the hegira. Interestingly enough, the Syriac text of Michael's *Chronicle* says nothing about a Jewish wife for Muhammad, but the Armenian translator (or more accurately, adaptor) repeats the story found in Thomas (23). Encouraged by this alliance, says Thomas, Muhammad sent a message to the emperor Heraclius' brother Theodore, warning him to evacuate Palestine. This seems to be a reflection of the famous

(20) Muhammad's father ʿAbdullāh is mentioned by name in the Greek abjuration; see E. Montet, «Un rituel d'abjuration des Musulmans dans l'église grecque», *Revue de l'histoire des religions,* 53 (1906), pp. 145-163. This has been dated to the late seventh century by F. Cumont, «L'origine de la formule grecque d'abjuration», *Revue de l'histoire des religions,* 64 (1911), pp. 143-150. A later date is regarded as more probable by several scholars; see D. J. Sahas, *John of Damascus on Islam.* Leiden, 1972, pp. 125-6.

(21) Bartholomaeus Edessenus (anno incerto), *Confutatio Agareni, Patrologia Graeca,* 104, col. 1396 etc. On Bhira see A. Abel, art. «Baḥira», *Encyclopedia of Islam,* New edition, I, Leiden, 1960, pp. 922-923.

(22) A. Guillaume, *The Life of Muhammad, A Translation of Isḥaq's Sīrat Rasūl Allah,* Oxford, 1955, pp. 78-81. The Armenian traditions are collected and discussed in R. W. Thomson, «Armenian Variations on the Baḥira Legend», *Harvard Ukrainian Studies,* 3/4 (1979-80), pp. 884-895.

(23) *Žamanakagrutʿiwn Tearn Mixayēli,* Jerusalem, 1871, p. 293; French translation by V. Langlois, *Chronique de Michel le grand,* Venice, 1868.

apocryphal letter of Muhammad to Heraclius himself, not found in the early Byzantine chroniclers but attested in Islamic tradition (24). The refusal of the Byzantines to respond led to their defeat on the battlefield, as already described in the *Histories* of Sebēos and Łewond.

Thomas then states that Muhammad killed his teacher, the Arian monk (Bhira), because the latter wished to be acknowledged for what he had taught Muhammad. Quite a different story is found in the late Greek source Euthymius Zigabenus, who ascribes the murder to drink — hence Muhammad's ban on wine (25). The only other Armenian author to mention the murder of Bhira, Moses Dasxuranc'i, implies a similar motive as that made explicit in Thomas (26).

Unique to Thomas among early Christian critics of Islam is the attribution of the Qur'ān to a Persian called Salmān. This, however, was an important feature of the Muslim tradition found as early as Ibn Isḥāq (27). Again, Thomas shows his familiarity with Muslim tradition in stating that Muhammad claimed he was the rider on the camel mentioned in Isaiah 21.7. This proof-text adduced by Muslims to show that the Old Testament prophets foretold Muhammad's mission does not figure in Greek polemic (28). The carnal delights of Muhammad's paradise are a commonplace of Byzantine writing. But the specific contrast between Muslim ritual washings and Christian baptism is not brought out in Greek writers until well after Thomas, by an imitator of Euthymius Zigabenus (29).

There is as yet no critical text of Thomas Arcruni whereby we could judge the textual reliability of this section on Muhammad and Islam. Several of the stories reported by Thomas have no parallels in foreign sources until much later, nor is there anything comparable in Armenian until the thirteenth century. Even then some of Thomas'

(24) See L. Caetani, *Annali dell' Islam,* I, Milan, 1905, pp. 731-734.

(25) In the Controversy attributed to Euthymius, *Patrologia Graeca,* 131, col. 36.

(26) See below, p. 12.

(27) For details see G. Levi Della Vida, art. «Salmān al-Farīsī», *Encyclopedia of Islam,* IV, Leiden, 1924, pp. 116-117.

(28) But it is known in Syriac; see A. Mingana, *Timothy's Apology for Christianity, Woodbrooke Studies,* 2, Cambridge, 1928, p. 37. For further Armenian references see below, pp. 22, 27. Also absent from Greek tradition is the story of Hagar as Pharaoh's daughter; see Max Grünbaum, *Neue Beiträge zur semitischen Sagenkunde,* Leiden, 1893, p. 104.

(29) *Patrologia Graeca,* 131, col. 28.

claims remain unknown — or at least are never repeated. The original text of Thomas' *History* was extended twice by later chroniclers, the latest section being dated to 1303. Whether or not all the apocryphal legends found in Book II, ch. 4 form part of the original text composed at the beginning of the tenth century, Thomas was clearly familiar with material in Arabic as well as Greek. But it is difficult to tell whether he could read the texts in the original or whether he derived his information from oral sources.

Thomas Arcruni (II 4) is the first Armenian writer to refer to correspondence between the caliph 'Umar and the emperor Leo. He does not say that this was included in Łewond's *History*, and indeed the Armenian text of the letters shows evidence of being a much later composition than the time of Łewond (30). Furthermore, Thomas' description of 'Umar's letter as a *tʿultʿ havatocʿ* (letter of faith) is hardly compatible with the cursory rehearsal of questions that had been prefaced to Leo's long response. Gero's suggestion that it is the work of the Armenian redactor of the Christian apologia is convincing, as is his demonstration that the letter of «Leo» in its Armenian form is the work of an Armenian (31). The correspondence to which Thomas refers is not extant. One is equally unconvinced that Thomas is right in claiming that after receipt of Leo's response ʿUmar rejected the most fabulous parts of the Qur'ān.

However, the letter of «Leo» is not particularly helpful in our present enquiry. There is nothing on the life of Muhammad and little on the source of his religious knowledge and inspiration, but a few points are worth noting.

ʿUmar asks why Leo does not believe the Muslim interpretation of Isaiah's reference to two riders. Leo responds with the fullest explanation of the «real» meaning found in Armenian. This prooftext is first found in Armenian in the account of Thomas Arcruni. Leo also refers to the charge that Salmān the Persian (with ʿUmar and Abū Turab) was responsible for the composition of the Qur'ān, but he does not adduce any of the fanciful details found in Thomas. He

---

(30) Armenian text in Łewond, pp. 42-98. English translation in A. Jeffery, «Ghevond's Text of the Correspondence between 'Umar II and Leo III», *Harvard Theological Review*, 37 (1944), pp. 269-332.

(31) S. Gero, *Byzantine Iconoclasm during the Reign of Leo III*, CSCO, Sub-sidia, 41. Louvain, 1973, Appendix 2: The Authenticity of the Leo-'Umar Correspondence.

charges that Muslims venerate the pagan altar of sacrifice which they call the house of Abraham, though scripture does not associate Abraham with Mecca, and he mentions the seduction of Zayd's wife by Muhammad. The only other Armenian source to refer to these last two points is Moses Dasxuranc'i, a tenth century author whose work shows signs of retouching as late as the twelfth century (32). But they figure already in John of Damascus (33). And the only Armenian source other than «Leo» to suggest that Muhammad was influenced by Nestorian ideas is Ps. Šapuh Bagratuni (34). However, this claim is found in Greek as early as George Hamartolus (35), and in Arabic in the *Apology* of al-Kindī at the court of the caliph al-Ma'mūn (813-833) (36).

Thomas Arcruni's younger contemporary John Catholicos Drasxanakertc'i has little new to say. His comments about Islam are all opprobrious, but in attenuation one might note that he did suffer personally in the struggle between the Bagratid kings of Armenia and the emirs of Azerbaijan. The only interesting point is the claim that Muhammad was raised or born in servitude (37). But this does not mean more than the statement in Theophanes that Muhammad was a hired servant: $\mu\iota\sigma\theta\omega\tau\acute{o}\varsigma$ (38).

The next Armenian historian to interest himself in Muhammad and the origin of Islam is Moses Dasxuranc'i, author of the *History of the Caucasian Albanians (Aluank^c)*. As noted above, it is not certain whether he wrote in the same century as Thomas Arcruni and John Catholicos; the last hand in the compilation of his *History* dates to the beginning of the twelfth century. Reference has already been made to his agreements with Thomas and «Leo», but many of the details in his account are unparalleled in Armenian. However, since this *History* has recently been translated into English (39), it does not seem necessary to quote the text again here.

(32) See two paragraphs below.
(33) *Patrologia Graeca*, 94, col. 770.
(34) See below, p. 28ff.
(35) *Patrologia Graeca*, 110, col. 868. In Islamic sources the monk is often named «Nestor».
(36) W. Muir, *The Apology of Al-Kindi*, London, 1882, p. 23.
(37) Tiflis ed., p. 81: *cneal* (born); Jerusalem 1867 ed., p. 104: *sneal* (raised).
(38) *Patrologia graeca*, 108, col. 686.
(39) *The History of the Caucasian Albanians by Movsēs Dasxuranci*, translated by C. J. F. Dowsett, *London Oriental Series* 8, Oxford, 1961.

MUHAMMAD AND ISLAM IN ARMENIAN TRADITION 841

The first Armenian to engage in formal correspondence with a Muslim on religious topics was the eleventh century Gregory Magistros, who was unusually well versed in Greek learning for Armenians of his time (40). Gregory composed a verse defense of Christianity (41), but the only document relevant to this study is his *Letter 70*. For the first time we hear in Armenian that what Muhammad wrote in the Qur'ān about the Old Testament prophets is not to be found in the Bible. Muhammad claimed, according to Gregory, that the Jews had altered the scriptures, and also that the Christians altered the Gospel after Christ's ascension. These accusations were familiar to the Byzantine writers, beginning with John of Damascus. Also familiar to these writers is the accusation reported by Gregory that Muhammad said someone other than Christ was crucified. This charge is elaborated in the later Armenian writer Mxit'ar of Ani *(see below)*.

The chronicler Samuel of Ani, writing at the end of the twelfth century, introduces a few new points. According to him Muhammad was learned not only in the heresy of Arius, having been instructed by Bhira, but was also versed in the heresy of Cerinthus. This is repeated by the historians Vardan and Kirakos. As Cerinthus was a Jewish gnostic, the introducting of his name may be a curious interpretation of the common statement in Byzantine sources that Muhammad met both Christians and Jews on his journeys to Palestine. But since Cerinthus was not known to Armenian heresiologists for *Jewish* ideas but for his distinction between the heavenly Christ and earthly Jesus (42), it is more likely that he was introduced to explain the Muslim

(40) See M. Leroy, «Grégoire Magistros et les traductions arméniennes d'auteurs grecs», *Annuaire de l'Institut de Philologie et d'Histoire orientales et slaves*, 3 (1935), pp. 263-294. The letters were edited by K'. Kostaneanc', *T'łt'erə*, Alexandropol, 1910. For a summary of their contents see V. Langlois, «Mémoire sur la vie et les écrits du prince Grégoire Magistros», *Journal Asiatique*, 6ᵉ série, tome XIII (1869), pp. 5-64. See also H. Thorossian, «Grigor Magistros et ses rapports avec deux émirs musulmans, Manoutché et Ibrahim», *Revue des études islamiques*, 15 (1941-46), pp. 63-66, which contains a brief summary of Letters 70 and 71.

(41) Printed in his *Tałasac'ut'iwnk'*, Venice, 1868. There is nothing in early Armenian literature comparable to the Syriac *Apology* of Timothy (see note 28 above) or the text published by F. Nau, «Un coloque du patriarche Jean avec l'émir des Agaréens (AD 639)», *Journal asiatique*, 11ᵉ série, tome VI (1915), pp. 225-267. (Lammens corrects the date of this to 644; see *Journal asiatique*, 11ᵉ série, tome XIII [1919], pp. 97-110).

(42) See R. W. Thomson, «An Armenian List of Heresies», *Journal of Theological Studies*, N.S. 16 (1965), pp. 358-367, especially pp. 362, 363, 366.

842

account of Jesus' crucifixion. Samuel is also the first Armenian writer, save for the undated letter of «Leo», to mention female circumcision, a ritual already known to John of Damascus (43).

Of more local Armenian interest is Samuel's claim that Muhammad himself made a pact with the Armenians, guaranteeing the free observance of Christianity. The claim is repeated by Mxitʿar of Ani, Kirakos, and the Armenian Ĵuanšer. But it is not particularly surprising that Muhammad himself was credited with an arrangement only worked out under his successors.

Samuel of Ani, p. 78 (44)

    615. In those days appeared the false prophet of the Saracens, a sectary of Cerinthus and the Arians, called Mahmet, from the race of Ismael, son of Hagar. He was instructed by a solitary called Bxira, of the sect of Arius, in the Sinai desert, where they (the Ismaelites) had settled and multiplied when Sarah expelled the hand-maiden from her sight.

...

    618. Some historians say the exodus (*eln* = hegira?) of Mahmet the false prophet (occurred) in the sixty-fifth year (= 616), others in the sixty-second, and others in the sixty-eighth.

...

    647. ... Now in the days of Constans, son of Heraclius, Dvin was taken by the Arabs, says the historian, and on the day of the holy epiphany in the holy martyrium of saint Sargis 20,000 were killed; the holy altar and font were covered with the blood of the slain. They also took captive more than 30,000 others. Then the patriarch Nersēs gathered the corpses of those who had fallen in the battle and buried them in the same martyrium which he restored for them. Here resides the chief of the race of Ismael whose first name is Kałartʿ, as scripture relates: «The sweet-lipped people shall sate their swords with blood» (Sirach, 12.16 ff, with a pun on *kalcʿr*). He lived for eight years then died. After him Amaran (was chief) for twelve years. When Kałertʿ reached Damascus in Mesopotamia, he ravaged and plundered as far as the city of Amida. Then he sent out three (generals): one to Rome (Constantinople), called Yaz, with Yovēl as advisor; they slaughtered 70,000 of the Romans. To the region of Persia he sent the emir Otʿman and the general Mawiē. They defeated Miwrdat with 20,000 and Mušeł the *sparapet* of Armenia with his army. Then they ruled over the whole land of Armenia, Persia, Egypt, Media, Parthia and Palestine.

    (43) *Patrologia graeca*, 94, col. 774.
    (44) Samuel Anecʿi, *Hawakʿmunkʿ*, Vałaršapat, 1893; there is a French translation by F. M. Brosset, *Collection d'historiens arméniens*, II, St. Petersburg, 1876.

Now the reason for their rule is the following. There was a certain prince of the regions of Damascus called Sargis. He used to rob the Ismaelite traders of many possessions. Three times Kłertʿ implored him and he ceased. Then he gathered the cavalry of his own race, and raiding three times, captured his own and theirs. And when he dominated Armenia then he began to circulate their faith, but they did not accept it. So the Ismaelite prince found a certain confidant called Mahmet, the chief of the traders, an Egyptian who knew a little of the laws of Moses but was grounded in the heresy of Arius and Cerinthus, in that he spoke of a bodily kingdom on earth, food for the belly, and marriage after the resurrection. He taught laws opposed to the old and new legislations, with unworthy thoughts and twisted words. Very derisively he corrupted the covenant of Abraham, as it is written: «Every one of your males shall be circumcised on the eighth day». But he (ordered to be circumcised) not only males but even females, thereby detestably mocking the token of the Lord's pact. And with simple water (he said they were) to wash always, instead of the font of baptism. And many other unworthy and erring traditions (he instituted) — and most ridiculous ones. This man he (Kełertʿ) acquired as lawgiver, messenger and general for twenty years. They destroyed Bznunikʿ, Ałiovit and Tarōn.

Then Mahmet stayed the sword, and by the word of his instruction they subjected to themselves the greater part of the universe. With an eternal oath he sealed a deed for the land of Armenia, (that) they could freely observe Christianity. And he sold *(vačareacʿ)* them their faith, taking from every household four drachmas, three bushels of *xorbal,* one nose-bag, one cord of hair, and one gauntlet (45). But from the priests, nobles and cavalry he ordered no tax to be taken.

To the same period of Samuel's *Chronicle* belongs that of the Syrian Patriarch Michael, which was translated into Armenian in 1248. As noted above, the Armenian text — but not the Syriac original — claims that Muhammad married a Jewish wife following his alliance with the Jews. The Armenian version of Michael also provides for the first time in Armenian an etymology for the term «Saracen», deriving it from the name of Abraham's wife Sarah. This etymology was familiar to Greek writers as early as John of Damascus: $\dot{\varepsilon}\varkappa\ \tau\tilde{\eta}\varsigma\ \Sigma\acute{\alpha}\varrho\varrho\alpha\varsigma\ \varkappa\varepsilon\nu o\acute{\upsilon}\varsigma$ (46). Curiously enough, the only other Armenian text to offer an etymology for «Saracen» is also a translation — the Armenian version of the Georgian chronicler Ĵuanšēr. But here the

---

(45) On this passage involving taxes paid by the Armenians see H. A. Manandian, *The Trade and Cities of Armenia in Relation to Ancient World Trade,* trans. N. G. Garsoïan, Lisbon, 1965, pp. 130ff.

(46) *Patrologia graeca,* 94, col. 764.

meaning given is quite different: instead of the Georgian «dogs *(dzaglt'a)* of Sarah» the Armenian reads «servants *(spasawork˜)* of Sarah» (47).

The most elaborate account by far of Muhammad's life in Armenian is that found in the chronicler Mxit˜ar of Ani, writing at the turn of the twelfth and thirteenth centuries. The source for most of Mxit˜ar's information was discovered by Babgen Kiwlēsērean and published in 1930 (48). It is an Armenian translation of a Karshuni document which purports to be based on a written account of a converted Muslim who knew an eyewitness of Muhammad's career. The Armenian text is first found in a manuscript dated to 1273 A.D. (Jerusalem MS 1288). An eighteenth century copy (Jerusalem MS 888) associates it with the thirteenth century scholars Vanakan and Vardan. But this is because Jer. 1288 begins with theological works by Vanakan, and because the historian Vardan repeats some of the material found in Mxit˜ar (49).

Like most chroniclers, Mxit˜ar of Ani culled his information from a variety of sources without indicating what came from where. The long section in chapters 25 and 26 was copied from an Armenian version of the Karshuni text that was very close to but not identical with the text dated to 1273 (though Mxit˜ar himself may have been responsible for the minor differences). But later in his chronicle, in ch. 27, Mxit˜ar quotes Łewond by name and copies details from him of the early Muslim conquests. On the other hand, Mxit˜ar's references to Kałert˜ and Emran derive from Samuel of Ani. Also based on Samuel is a third section, which was probably an addition to the original chronicle. The author of this attributes the taxes payable

---

(47) Juanšēr, *Patmut˜iwn Vrac˜*, Venice, 1884, p. 98. Georgian text in *K˜art˜lis Tskhovreba*, ed. S. Qaukhchishvili, vol. 1, Tiblisi, 1955, p. 230; French translation in M. F. Brosset, *Histoire de la Géorgie*, vol. 1, St. Pétersbourg, 1849, p. 234. The Georgian depends on a misreading of κενούς as κύνας.

The Armenian version of Michael claims that the Midianites are descendants of Abraham's third wife, Ketura, following the biblical text. But earlier Armenian tradition emphasizes that the Parthians are the descendants of Ketura. See Movsēs Xorenac˜i, II, 1. For Syriac evidence see Aphrahat, *Demonstrationes* XI 9 (ed. I. Parisot, *Patrologia syriaca*, I, Paris, 1894).

(48) B. Kiwlēsērean, *Islamə Hay matenagrut˜ean mēj*, Vienna, 1930, pp. 189-222. For a précis in English see A. Jeffery, «Gregory of Tathew's 'Contra Mohammedanos'», *The Muslim World*, 32 (1942), pp. 219-235. See also note 2 above.

(49) For a full description of the manuscripts see N. Połarean, *Mayr C˜uc˜ak jeragrac˜ srboy Yakobeanc˜*, Vols. III and IV, Jerusalem, 1968, 1969.

in Armenia as described by Samuel to Muhammad's legislation for all Christians, and elaborates on the various ways of dating the Muslim era — an expansion of Samuel *s.v. anno* 618.

There are several unique features in Mxitʿar, which though repeated by later Armenian writers are not found in Greek or Syriac. Although the Muslim association of Mecca with Abraham was known to the Christians from the earliest times, Mxitʿar is the first to give the story of Abraham's visit to Ismael's wife. With some variations it is found in the historians Masʿudi (50) and Ṭabari in Arabic (51). The story of the idol of the Damascene god Raman has no parallel in Christian sources; that it was stolen by Ethiopian traders for its gold, thus sparking war between Ethiopia and Arabia, must be a reflection of that sixth century conflict. Mxitʿar is also the first Armenian to offer any details of the rituals associated with the *hajj*. But his account and explanations differ from what is found in the Greek sources. Also for the first time in Armenian Mxitʿar tells of Muhammad's claim that he was snatched by an angel to Mecca and of various miracles worked by the prophet (52). Mxitʿar then expounds the Muslim theory of Christ's crucifixion. The suggestion that Christ was not really crucified had been attacked in earlier Greek and Syriac writers (53). Absent from earlier Armenian tradition is the story of Muhammad affixing a paper to a heifer's horn claiming that it was the Qurʾān. But this, like the story of Muhammad's death, is found in Syriac (54). As the Armenian text of Mxitʿar of Ani has never been translated, I offer here a rendering of the relevant passages into English, noting the major variants in the Armenian version of the Karshuni text.

---

(50) Masʿūdi, *Les Prairies d'Or*, trad. Barbier de Meynard et Paret de Couteille, revue et corrigée par Charles Pellat, Paris, 1962 —, § 941 (vol. 2, III, 91).

(51) Ṭabari, *Chronique*, trad. H. Zotenberg, Vol. 1, reprint Paris, 1958, I, 51.

(52) Several of these miracles are mentioned by Ibn Saʿd (d. 845 A.D.); see Tor Andrae, *Die Person Muhammeds in lehre und glauben seiner gemeinde*, Upsala, 1917, p. 47 (water), p. 49 (tree), p. 56 (poisoned ram). Arabic text ed. E. Sachau, *Biographieen Muhammeds*, Leiden, 1905.

(53) E.g. Abjuration, p. 132; John of Damascus (*P.G.* 94), col. 765; Timothy's Apology, pp. 40, 41.

(54) See the texts published and translated by R. Gottheil, «A Christian Bahira Legend», *Zeitschrift für Assyriologie*, 13 (1899), pp. 189-242, 14 (1900), pp. 203-268. It was also known (via Arabic sources) in the West; see N. Daniel, *Islam and the West*, Edinburgh, 1960, p. 5.

Mxit'ar of Ani, Ch. 25 (55).

Concerning the fables of the impious Mahmet and his falsehood, which his disciple corrupted

Now that we have arrived (at the place) to tell of the impious Mahmet, let us set out the multitude of his error so that you may completely hate and flee his name, O Christ-loving soul. To this very day they still ignorantly go on pilgrimage to Mecca, offer gifts to demons, and thoughtlessly perform the rite of the former idolatrous devil-worship, not knowing what they are doing. Now you can know their deeds, as they ignorantly reckon the worship of demons to be worship of God.

There was at that time, he [a] says, a man called Mahmet from the tribe called Kureš, from the sons of Kedar (Ketura?) of the twelve tribes of Ismael. Coming to the holy mountain of Sinai, he studied with a certain hermit who knew the Ismaelite tongue and also Persian [b]; ha was called Bxira [c]. Receiving him, he wished to inform him about everything. Beginning from creation, he read to him in progressive order the book of Genesis and all the others, the New Testament and the book which they call the *Childhood of Jesus* (56).

While he only heard the divinely inspired scriptures and did not comprehend them correctly, he had reason to go to the innermost desert, and thereafter never returned to his teacher. His mind did not love Christianity, but his thoughts were seeking to know what Judaism was. Meeting a certain Jewish merchant, he learned from him their rites and faith. He despised that also. And he began of his own invention to proclaim a new faith, opposed to the truth and false.

Scorning all cults like Antichrist, he decreed (laws for) only his own [d].

---

a. I.e. the informant of the author of the Karshuni text which begins:
In the time of Mahmed there came to us a truthful man, who left us in writing (this) account from the beginnings of the faith of Mahmed. For, following many world-histories, he said thus concerning the man who went around after Mahmed (namely that) he reported what he had seen with his own eyes. This I decided to write to you, so that you might learn and not believe their words, or suppose them to be worshippers of God because they always mention God.

b. Ismaelite tongue and Persian] Arabic, K
c. Bxira] Sargis, an Arian, K
d. decreed ... own] honoured only his own religion *(den)*, K

(55) Mxit'ar Anec'i, *Patmut'iwn*, St. Petersburg, 1879.

(56) For the Armenian versions of the *Infancy Gospel* see *Ankanon Girk'*, II, Venice, 1898, pp. 1-312. There is a translation of the long recension in P. Peeters, *Evangiles apocryphes*, II, *L'évangile de l'enfance, rédactions syriaques, arabe et arméniennes (Textes et documents pour l'étude du christianisme)*, Paris, 1914.

Coming to the village ^{e} of Mecca, which is beyond Yathrib (Ep'crip') Medina, their capital, he preached in accordance with his own whim and pleasure, proclaiming the house of their tribal gathering, that is of the cult of snakes, was the house of God and ^{f} the house of Abraham; he called it *al-K'aaba*. And he said that Ismael married a wife, and this is his house. When Abraham longed to see him, he said to Sarah: «Let me go that I may go and see my son». But Sarah was suspicious that perhaps he might approach the handmaiden ^{g}. She imposed an oath by God on him: «Do not descend from your beast to the ground, but remaining on it see your son and return here». When he arrived he did not meet Ismael because he was hunting. So he questioned his wife: «Where has your husband gone»? But she insulted and scorned him, saying: «O mad and tottery old man, for what purpose do you seek my husband»? He replied: «Tell your husband that the doors of your house are not in good shape; change it by making other doors».

When Ismael returned from the hunt, his wife did not tell him, neglecting Abraham's command. But Ismael, perceiving his father's odour, questioned his wife: «Did some stranger (come) here»? She said: «An old man». Ismael asked: «What did he say»? When his wife informed him, Ismael knew that he had referred to his wife. He dismissed her and took another wife. In like fashion, he (Abraham) met the second wife and the third, as far as the seventh. And she said to Abraham: «Welcome father, come down from your beast that I may anoint your head». But he said: «I do not consent». When the wife entreated him, Abraham descended — not to the ground because of the oath to Sarah, but he put one foot on a rock and kept the other astride (the beast). The rock gave way to his foot, showing the imprint.

This he so taught from fables, and he ordered (people) to come from every region to offer worship to that stone and house. And inside the house, he ordered them to worship as they circle the stone ^{h}, which is the other stone and a hole for their feet ^{i}. Furthermore, he ordered them to circle the outside stone where Abraham's footprint is, skipping on one foot and saying: «*Lbayk', lbayk',*» as if replying to someone: «*Yay, yay, awas, awas*» (57).

Then crossing the valley which they call *Vordn al haram* ^{j}, they slaughter animals there. And riding a beast, they rush without turning back as far as the hill near Mecca. As they flee, if anyone's coat falls or (the horse) throws its rider, they do not turn back to raise him up. After that they run on foot

---

e. village] ditch, *K*
f. + he called it, *K*
g. his hand-maiden Hagar, *K*.
h. walls, *K*
i. which ... feet] which, furthermore, (is) a hole for snakes, *K* (i.e. corruption in Mxit'ar, *ōdzic'n* > *otic'n*)
j. *Vodn al hamam, K*

(57) Cf. Ibn al-Kalbi, *The Book of Idols,* trans. N. A. Faris, Princeton, 1952, p. 5. n. 16.

between two rocks which they call Safa and Emran; they run from rock to rock seven times without a pause as energetically as they can. Then they run to another place which they call *Makʿa al has*. Seven times they run and throw stones, and it is not clear at whom they throw stones ᵏ. But they merely say that Mahmet did thus. And he gave a command, saying: «Abraham did likewise». This was said imprudently (?) by him, for he said: «He did not descend from his mount», and later he belied it (saying): «He ran and threw stones» ˡ. And they do not slaughter in that spot reptiles, crawling things or wild beasts because of the snakes which dwell in the house, mingling with the humans but not harming any of those they call *muslims* — that is, «believers». And they cover over the house with seven draperies, and kissing the drapery they place it on their eyes.

Now the erring deceit of their silly nonsense is not obvious to us. For many who do not know all this, see those races of men engaged in all these rituals and assiduous at prayer and continually saying «by God», and they suppose them to be believers. Therefore I considered it important to reveal the secrets of their deceit.

The house which they call Abraham's, neither Abraham nor Ismael ever went to, as the divine histories testify. But it is a house of idols and of the cult of snakes. For the tribal gathering takes place in the house, where they raise snakes up to the present time, as we have said. But the idols were removed by a foray of Egyptians at the time of Trajan. For the statues were of bronze, and with other deities they set them up in Alexandria. Then the Arabs found other idols, that is the idols of *Dimaskos Riman*, in some desert. At the coming of Christianity its priests were afraid that it might fall into the hands of Christians and be broken up, so they took it and fled into the desert. Later the idolatrous Arabs found it and took it to Mecca with its priest to that house, wishing to set it up in the famous site of their first idols. But the snake-worshipping priests did not agree to setting up the idols of foreign priests in their own house and persuaded the crowd that the house was sufficient for the snakes only, on the grounds that the snakes would not like the foreign priests in their own dwelling. On this pretext they set it outside the door on the rock, standing on one foot and holding up the other ᵐ, as if the image of Raman was like the image of Hephaistos or as if this itself was Raman, called Hephaistos by the Damascenes ⁿ. Hollowing it out with iron, and bonding it with lead, they set it on one foot on the rock. In the time of Theodosius ᵒ through the neglect of the ministers, since it was standing outside the building, it was stolen by Ethiopian merchants for its gold. Therefore there was a war between the two (countries), (as) they relate in Egypt by tradition down to today. This is the footprint on the rock which Mahmet said was Abraham's — which the

---

k. + similarly they do not know the other things that they do, *K*
l. for ... stones] with the second saying he annulled the first, *K*
m. and holding up the other, *om. K.*
n. + I do not know, *K*
o. + the great, *K*

MUHAMMAD AND ISLAM IN ARMENIAN TRADITION   849

Arabs circle on one foot, imitating the one-footed Raman. And they worship its demon and cry out, and do not know *p*.

Likewise they do not understand for whom they slaughter animals in the valley *q* or from whom they flee. But after investigating we discovered that Mahmet, going aside from the multitude of people into the valley, sacrificed to all the demons. Rushing to him, the demons appeared to him in human form, and terrified by them Mahmet fled. The same (story) he handed down *r*.

But as for their running between the rocks, the rocks were their cults before the former idols, like that rock which is inside the house. And the demons forced the cult of themselves on Mahmet from the two rocks. For this reason he ran fast hither and yon in his frenzy; and the same he legislated.

Furthermore, as he was going out in haste to the cult of the house, some mad dog followed him in to seize him. But Mahmet escaped by throwing a stone. Thinking this (?) to be strange and obstructive to his worshipping *s*, he handed down the same. But as for their saying that Abraham went there seven times, they greatly lie *t*. And those who do not kill reptiles and creeping things and wild beasts, render honour and reverence to the snakes *u*. Just as did the chief magi in Yazkert's letter to the Armenians (58), the same they legislated: that snakes and lizards and other insects/reptiles are not to be killed, because they were gods and their cults (were observed) among them *v*. All this the blessed man, who was very knowledgeable and came from the island of Crete, believed and revealed and made known *w*.

---

p. + why Abraham ran or why there was the place of one foot on the rock and not of two, K

q. + and throw them out as carrion, K

r. + to them. This is why they slaughter animals and flee, K

s. thinking ... worshipping (Mxit'ar is corrupt)] it went on foot there and prevented his worship, but through his stone-throwing he got away from it, K

t. he handed down ... lie] likewise he handed down in his allegations about Abraham, but from their own sayings they are destroyed and annulled. He says Abraham went there five times; the sixth he did not descend from his beast, the seventh he stood on the stone. But when did Abraham do all this? K

u. render ... snakes] the reasons are clear, because of the cult of the snakes which they previously worshipped, K

v. just as ... them, *om. K* (Cf. Ełišē, p. 53).

w. all ... known] all this one of Mahmed's disciples revealed to us, who had been himself an eye-witness of it all. And terrified by the appearance of the demons, he fled to the island of Crete; and there he became a Christian and believed in Christ, K

(58) The letter in short form is found in Łazar P'arpec'i, *Patmut'iwn Hayoc'*, Tiflis, 1904, pp. 43-4, and in expanded form in Ełišē, *Vasn Vardanay ew Hayoc' Paterazmin,* Erevan, 1957, pp. 24-27. Mxit'ar is referring to Ełišē's version. The letter was not written by the shah Yazkert II himself, according to the Armenian historians, but by his grand-vizier Mihrnerseh.

850

Ch. 26. Now we shall tell of his death — truly worthy of derision.[x]

For when Mahmet died, they wrapped him and placed him in his garden; they did not bury him because he had promised that[y] on the third day he would rise, like Christ. And when the guards[z] were asleep, dogs entered and ate the face of the corpse (59). Consequently it was prescribed by his disciples to kill dogs in that month. Observing this custom up to the present day, they kill dogs in that month.

And there is more for me to say about his religion and rites and laws, full of folly. He suggested the idea to his followers that just as the prophets had foretold about Christ, so also they had foreseen about Mahmet, indicating the prophetic declaration: Jesus on an ass and he on a camel, taking as their testimony the vision of Isaiah: «I saw, he says, one riding an ass and one riding a camel»[aa]. This he said in his city Medina while sitting in the crowded square. And while he was speaking he disappeared from sight for a long time, and great astonishment seized them all. Then, while they were talking, he stood among them and greeted them, saying: «Peace (be) with you, and mercy and grace». Awestruck, they were lost in wonder and said: «Where have you come from, and what is this greeting of yours, and from what gods have you brought such a saying of mercy and grace?» He replied: «Behold, while I was speaking with you, I was snatched up by an angel and found myself in Mecca, in the house of our fathers Abraham and Ismael, which they had built as a house of God and as an inheritance for us; just as once the Jews and prophets built Jerusalem as a dwelling for the sons of Israel. For he had heard of the snatching of Ambakum from Jerusalem to Babylon to Daniel, and attributing the same to himself so told them. But his words were never true. He hid from them that he had seen Mecca[bb] and told them the des-

---

x. ch. 26 ... derision] but we shall narrate another tale, truly worthy of derision, *K*

y. because ... that] saying that, *K*

z. the guards] the drowsy disciples, *K*

aa. and there is ... camel] I know that I have made you greatly shake with laughter, but there is still more for me to tell you about his religion and judgments and legislation. But now I shall interrupt in order (to tell) the story of the accursed Jews which he put in their mouth, to boast that just as the prophets had foretold about Christ, so also they had foretold about Mahmed, indicating the calling of his prophethood: Jesus on an ass and he on a camel. For they took as their testimony the vision of Isaiah, the passage which says: «I saw two riders, one on an ass, the other on a camel», wickedly and falsely interpreting the vision, *K*

bb. but his ... Mecca] but he had never gone to Mecca *(sic)* nor informed anyone that he had seen it, *K*

(59) This story (repeated by Vardan) is not found in the Greek tradition but was known in Syriac; see ref. in note 54 above. It was also known in the West; see Eulogius, Archbishop of Toledo (martyred 859), *Liber apologeticus martyrum, Patrologia latina*, 115, col. 860. Cf. Daniel, *op. cit.,* p. 39.

cription of the place, of the sites and buildings, and all the distinguishing features of the region he reported to them by magic ^{cc} just as he had known them from his youth ^{dd}. Therefore they were all astonished and said he was a prophet. When he heard this from their mouths he was emboldened to preach and say: «Bear witness that there is no God save only He, and He has no companion, and Mahmet is his servant and apostle» ^{ee}. In such fashion did he reason, announcing one God according to the Jewish (faith) ^{ff}. But by saying that He has no companion, he thereby divided the Son and Spirit from the Father. And thus he taught them: «The God whom our fathers and the prophets worshipped, I am preaching to you». Thereby he persuaded the people. And furthermore he distinguished them from the Jews who said that Christ was only a man and the son of Joseph, and crucified by themselves. But he called Jesus the Word of God and the Spirit sent from God to Mary, and he took from her a body in human fashion. And he adduces the word of God as testimony, saying: «Thus said God, that we have sent our Spirit to her, who took the form of a man». And he said that the Jews did not crucify him, but he counterfeited (himself) to them ^{gg}. And he did not reckon them able to crucify the Word of God or (for him) to be crucified by them. And he was not subject to death, but remains alive and will come to the world in the latter times ^{hh}. And he praised Christians and accepted the gospel and the prophets. And he anathematised the Jews, since they denied Christ and abjured him, and killed the prophets ^{ii}.

Now Mahmet made his legislation from the old laws and the gospel, but changed by willing inventiveness what he liked, as laid down by himself and not taken from someone else, whatever he legislated for his people ^{jj}. And he performed apparent miracles in front of the people like a present (manifestation of?) the future Antichrist, of whom our Lord Jesus Christ warns.

---

cc. by magic] in full, *K*

dd. just ... them] as if he had been raised there from his youth and had taken all the details in a moment of time. I do not know if by magical art he arrived there suddenly, or whether by investigation he had stored the others up in his mind, *K*

ee. + and prophet, *K*

ff. + as (scripture) says: «I am God and there is no other God except Me», *K*

gg. + as if he likened someone else to himself, and they crucified him — whom they call Simon Kyrenatsʻi. And this for the reason that, *K*

hh. and he did not reckon ... times] he did not regard him able to be crucified as the Word of God; and the other was crucified by them. And he was subjected to death, but lives and will come to the world at the last time to judge all nations, *K*

ii. since ... prophets] and said thus: God anathematized the Jews because they denied Christ and rebelled against him and killed the prophets and all the apostles, *K*

jj. now Mahmed ... people] now he took legislation from the gospel, but changed from the two whatever he could in order to establish laws by himself; in his own name and not from other laws he legislated (for) his people, *K*

852

As the harbinger of Antichrist he prepared a road for him, for ^{kk} at that time he called trees from the forest by name. And departing from their midst, it came walking and stood before them. Then he ordered it to go back to its place. And he made men think mountains moved. And lifting up his hands, from his five fingers he made a stream flow apparently. A mortal poison, they say, was prepared for him. A kid having been roasted and set before him, he wished to eat. But the kid spoke in the hearing of many: «Do not eat of me, for a mortal poison has been prepared in me for you» ^{ll} (60).

And when robbers fell on him in a caravan wishing to despoil him... *(lacuna)*... and them ^{mm}. But they gathered in one place, camped ^{nn} in the dry plain and made the sea encircle him. The robbers were held at the edge of the sea, and after remaining three days went away empty. And these saw themselves on the dry land, where there was no moisture. This they say his uncle did, and learning from him, he (Mahmet) did likewise. But many of his people did not believe his fabulous nonsense ^{oo}. They say also that he showed to men the moon divided into four parts distinct from each other, then gathered it back into one full circle. But as for the throwing of stones which we mentioned above, they invent the following story ^{pp}: when God expelled Adam from Paradise, he settled him in this world. And when he saw Satan in that spot where we throw stones, he recognised that he was the one who had deprived us of life ^{qq}, and takingst ones he threw them at him ^{rr}. Therefore we do the same.

Now when he had told them what he had to say and had proclaimed himself a messenger ^{ss}, then they begged him to lay down laws for themselves. He promised them to ask God the next day what he might command, and

---

kk. and he performed ... for] but earlier we spoke to you about his miracles. Now I shall tell you again from the beginning further (things), *K*

ll. + now thus they say a miracle was worked by him, which is not confirmed by any of the miracles that were clearly (?) worked later, but seems now to be an apparent semblance, *K*

mm. and when ... them] and he came across violent men in a caravan, wishing to despoil them, *K*

nn. in one place camped, *om. K*

oo. but many ... nonsense] now some say many did not believe that it was by magic and in appearance and not really. This has been told us by believers in him, *K*

pp. + which they themselves do not know, but at our insistence those who suppose they know say thus, *K*

qq. who ... life] who had deceived us and expelled us from the garden of life, *K*

rr. + and he fled from him, *K*

ss. now ... messenger] similarly I shall tell another thing. When they had testified that there is no other God save one and Mahmet is God's messenger, then, *K*

(60) Cf. Daniel, *op. cit.*, p. 32, 74.

MUHAMMAD AND ISLAM IN ARMENIAN TRADITION   853

dismissed them. He had a heifer that had just given birth brought to that public square and the calf kept at home. And whatever he himself desired he wrote down and fixed to the heifer's horn, then led it to the desert. Then at the time of the assembly, he ordered the heifer to be released. He and the assembly awaited its arrival, as if for some visitation from above. When the heifer appeared making an uproar, he offered up thanks. Taking the writing he read it with veneration and ceremony, as the law that had come from heaven *tt*.

All this his disciple revealed to us, unmasking the deceit of those heretical fables. He came and was baptised on the island of Crete by the inspiration of the providential will of God. And we wrote down his fable and obscene deceit for the information and warning of fearers of Christ, that they might flee and detest that hater of God.

---

tt. then led it to the desert ... heaven] he gave the heifer to trusted servants at night clandestinely, sent it far away and ordered his servants to release the heifer at dawn and themselves to return by another route. He himself at the coming of dawn gathered the people in the place where he had separated the mother and her offspring from each other. While they were talking (the heifer) arrived roaring, dazed and sweating, as if forcibly led by someone, burst into the crowd and came up to Mahmet. He ordered it to be held, and himself took the paper from its horns. Kissing it he placed it on his eyes and said it had been sent from God. They write this down in the Qur'ān as the introduction, which they call *Surat al-Bakara,* that is «discourse of the cow, or laws». Then he opened (the paper) and read it in the hearing of the people. And they supposed that the very cow with the paper had been sent from heaven, *K*

(The Karshuni text [in its Armenian version] continues from where Mxiʿtar ends:)

They write this down in the Qur'ān as the introduction, which they call *Surat al-Bakara,* that is, «discourse of the cow, or, laws». Then he opened (the paper) and read it in the hearing of the people, and they supposed that the very cow with the paper had been sent from heaven.

And he ordered them to perform the ritual of prayer seven times a day, with washing of the hands and feet and face at morning and night. And instead of the Jewish trumpets and lyres at the time of psalm-singing or our bell-ringing *(žamaharutʿiwn),* he ordered them to build a tall *mnira* in the middle of the city. He selected someone with a loud voice and called him *modin,* that is, «he who bears (witness to) the faith». And he ordered him to go up, on the grounds that God so ordered the prophets: «Go up to the heights, O evangelist of Sion. Raise up powerfully your voice, O evangelist of Jerusalem». And he ordered him to call out loudly three times.

O honourable readers, when you read the history of the false prophet Mahmed, curse him and loudly praise God. And make a worthy recollection of this unworthy scribe Mxitʿar and my parents, and remember (them) in the eternal day, Amen. (End of K)

854

The historian Vardan (thirteenth century) repeats in abbreviated form much of Mxitʿar's information. More interestingly, he is familiar at first hand with the same Armenian translation of the Karshuni document. For Mxitʿar names no sura from the Qur'ān, nor does he refer to the daily ablutions or the call to prayer, all of which are mentioned at the end of the Karshuni text and by Vardan. But Vardan does not follow his source so closely as Mxitʿar had. He is also indebted to other Armenian sources: Sebēos for the twelve tribes of Ismael, the Byzantine defeat, and the removal of relics from Jerusalem; Samuel (or Mxitʿar, Ch. 27) for the reference to Kalertʿ.

Vardan, Ch. 34 (61):

> At that time there was a man from among the sons of Ismael whose name was Mahmatʿ, a merchant. He was born in the city of Madina, a two days' journey away from Makʿa, from the tribe called Korēš, the son of Abdlay, who died leaving him an orphan. He joined a certain merchant, and made progress in his house. When the merchant died, he gained control of his master's house, marrying his wife (widow). He used to go with camels to Egypt. And there met him a certain hermit named Sargis, of the sect of Arius and Cerinthus, who taught him (about) God from the old books and (taught him) the book of the *Childhood of Our Lord* (62). On his return home he preached what he had heard. But his family persecuted him. So he went to the desert of Pʿaran. And when the 12,000 Jews arrived, using them as a pretext, he preached the God of Abraham to the sons of Ismael; and he assured them that if they worshipped him they would inherit the land that God had given to Abraham.

After describing the Muslim success against the Byzantine army, Vardan continues:

> It was the year of our era 67 (63). And because the advice of Mahmed had succeeded, they asked him for laws. And he called the site of the temple of the snakes that they worshipped *al-Kʿayuba*, which is, «gate of God». And he called the city where he lived «house of Abraham». Because Christianity was strong (there?) they took the idol of Damascus, Ṙemana — which is

(61) Vardan Vardapet, *Hawakʿumn patmutʿean,* Venice, 1862; there is a more critical text of this section and a French translation in J. Muyldermans, *La domination arabe en Arménie,* Louvain, 1927.
(62) Cf. note 56 above.
(63) I.e. 618 A.D.

bald Hephaistos — and threw it into the desert. Finding it, the Arabs brought it to the temple of snakes. But the priests of the snakes did not wish to place it there; taking it outside, they made a site for one of its feet on a rock and set it there. The Ethiopian merchants stole it for the gold that the Ismaelites had cast it in. So there was a serious war between the two nations until they forgot (the cause?). About it (the site?) he said: It is the footprint of Abraham, when he came to see his son Ismael. And because Ismael was out hunting he asked his wife: «Where is your husband»? She said: «Go away, you, decrepit old man». Then Abraham said: «When he comes home, tell your husband: Change the door of your house». Now when Ismael came (home) and perceived the odour of his father, he questioned his wife, and she told him what she had been instructed. On learning this, Ismael divorced his wife and took another, as far as a seventh. This one begged Abraham to descend from his donkey so she might anoint his feet. He put down one foot, said (Mahmet?), and placed it on the rock, and the rock yielded to his feet *(sic)*. The other foot he did not put down from his beast. For he had sworn to Sarah that he would not dismount, as she feared that he might be with Hagar. This is the fable of Mahmet. And he ordered that they should (come) there from every region to worship, and said they should go around the rock on one foot and say: «*Lbayk‛, lbayk‛*», and as if replying to someone: «*Ay, ay, awas, awas*».

Crossing the valley they slaughter an animal, then mounting a beast they flee as far as the hill of Mak‛a. And if in their flight some clothing falls or comes out of place (?), no one is allowed to look behind. Running between the two rocks which they call Safa and Emra, they go from rock to rock seven times without pausing, and throw stones. They say Mahmet did so, and so taught. But the running on one foot is because of the single footprint. The slaying of an animal in the valley and the fleeing, they say, (are because) Mahmet offered sacrifice to all the demons so that they might show him visions, but when they appeared to him he fled. The going round the two rocks and throwing stones (are because) their rocks were worshipped before the idols. And while Mahmet was worshipping according to his custom a mad dog attacked him, and he threw stones at it; so he ordered the same thing to be done. Snakes and serpents are not killed because they were worshipped by them. And the slaughter of a dog, they say, is because when Mahmet died they did not wish to bury him, expecting that he would rise up on the third day like our Lord Jesus Christ, and dogs devoured his face. When they realised this, they slew the dogs, and ordered the same to be done on the same month (of each year).

He taught (them) to say God is one and that no one is companion to him, and Mahmet is his servant. As for those who say, on the word of some Jew, that the prophets spoke about Mahmet as they did about Christ — in this regard they say that Isaiah saw two people riding, (one) on a donkey, (the other) on a camel. And one day, suddenly by magic Mahmet disappeared, and a little later reappeared, saying: «Peace be with you and the mercy and grace of God». In astonishment they said: «Whence do you come, and what is this new greeting of yours, and which god's grace did you bring us»? He said: «God took me to Mak‛a, to the house of my father Abraham, and explained his wishes. And tomorrow he will send us laws». Taking a heifer that had given birth, on the public square he separated it from her calf; then he wrote whatever he wished, fixed it to her horns, and sent it out to the desert with trusted (friends). He ordered it to be released the next day, while he himself remained (behind) and gathered the crowd. The cow arrived mooing and sweating, and bursting into the crowd, sought its calf. He ordered it to be seized, and taking the piece of paper, kissed it and said that it came from God.

Up to today it is written about this at the beginning of the Qur'ān: *Surat῾ al-Bakara*, which is: laws of the cow. And he ordered (them) to pray five times with ablutions, and instead of the trumpets of Israel, to summon (the faithful) from high up, taking as witness (the saying): «Go up on the mountain of Sion, O evangelist». And they call the crier *Modin*, which is «he who bears (witness to) the faith». And the putting of the finger in the ear, they say, is because one hears with the ear, willy-nilly. And he called Christ the Word of God and Spirit. And they say that he performed a miracle: bringing the moon down, they say, he divided it into four parts; then making it whole again, he sent it back to heaven.

Kirakos of Ganjak, writing in the second half of the thirteenth century, has nothing new to add. He takes his information from various earlier sources, drawing primarily on Thomas Arcruni (for the stories of Muhammad's demonic possession, ῾Alī's support, Muhammad's ideas about heaven, female circumcision and the constrast between Muslim ablutions and baptism) and Samuel of Ani (for Cerinthus, Kałert῾ and the Muslim military compaign and the taxes levied on Armenia). He does not know, or chooses not to use, the material from the Karshuni document in Mxit῾ar or Vardan (64).

The final text to be considered here is the most idiosyncratic. It is the «History of the Birth and Upbringing of Anti-Christ Mahamat and His Reign», which appears as a preface to an anonymous work commonly known as the *History* of Pseudo-Šapuh Bagratuni. Although quotations from an historical work by Šapuh Bagratuni dealing with the seventh and eighth centuries do appear in later Armenian historians, his own *History* has been lost. A text published in 1921 and attributed to him bears no relation to what is known of his *History* from other sources (65). In a second edition of 1971 the preface was for

---

(64) Kirakos Ganjakec῾i, *Patmut῾iwn Hayoc῾*, Erevan, 1961, pp. 56-60; there is a French translation by F. M. Brosset, St. Petersburg, 1870.

(65) *Patmut῾iwn Šaphoy Bagratunwoy,* ed. G. Tēr-Mkrtč῾ean and Mesrop Episkopos, Ējmiacin, 1921.

the first time published in full (66). But the earliest manuscript containing this section dates only from the sixteenth century. The origin and date of the passage dealing with Muhammad remain a mystery. There are two main themes. The first is that the monk Sargis (Baḥira), having cured Muhammad of demon-possession, fraudulently plans to «discover» him as a prophet thus assuring his later acceptance. Parallels exist in other Christian polemical sources, where it is claimed that Muhammad suffered from demon-possession, that the monk was a healer and that as prophet Muhammad was an imposter (67). But that Sargis plotted with Muhammad before «recognizing» him as a prophet seems unique to this Armenian text.

Much more difficult to explain, however, is the assertion that Muhammad was a Persian, born near Rayy, who fled from the last Sasanian king and built the city of Baghdad. That Baghdad was a Sasanian city — rather than a Muslim one built in the eighth century — was supposed by some later chroniclers. The Georgian Ĵuanšēr, for example, claims that Abū-Bakr captured Baghdad on invading Persia (68). (The Armenian version of Ĵuanšēr renders Baghdad as «Babylon» (69).) A clue to the association of Muhammad with Baghdad may lie in the emphasis in Ĵuanšēr and other sources that Baghdad/Babylon was a center of idol-worship and that the Persians were idolators *par excellence*. The preface to Ps.-Šapuh also claims that Muhammad was an idolator and a magus. Furthermore, the epic *Sasuncʻi Davitʻ* opens with a reference to the idolatrous caliph of Baghdad (70), the Muslim who is Armenia's chief enemy. Perhaps the author of the strange preface to Ps.-Šapuh, identifying Baghdad with the idolatrous enemies of his country and recognizing Muhammad as the first leader of these «idolators», assumed that he must have built their capital city. But it is not certain that this text was originally composed by an Armenian, since the last Sasanian king is given his name in its Arabic rather than Armenian form *(Kasre* instead of

(66) *Patmutʻiwn Ananun zrucʻagri (karcecʻeal Šapuh Bagratuni)*, ed. M. H. Darbinyan-Melikʻyan, Erevan, 1971. For a translation of the relevant passage see Thomson, ref. in note 22 above.
(67) Cf. Khoury, *Polémique* (as note 16 above), pp. 82-3.
(68) *Kʻartʻlis Tskhovreba* (as note 47 above), p. 230; Brosset, I, p. 234.
(69) Ĵuanšēr, p. 98.
(70) E.g. D. Čʻitʻuni, *Sasunakan*, Paris, 1942, p. 78: *kar krapaštʻ-tʻagawor m' al, Baldat-Məsər kənsatēr*. For a translation of the standard Armenian text published in Erevan see *David de Sassoun*, trad. F. Feydit, Paris, 1964.

Khosrov). In the Armenian popular tradition Muslims and Sasanians became somewhat confused, so Baghdad could be identified with Persia. But that Muhammad himself was a Persian is a conclusion that no other writer on Islam ever seems to have adopted.

In conclusion, it is perhaps strange that the Armenians did not develop a more precise and coherent understanding of the religion of their enemies or engage in dialogue with them as did the Byzantine Greeks and the Syriac speaking Christians. Only Gregory of Tatʿev in the fourteenth century made any elaborate attempt to understand Islam as a religion. Even he has nothing much to say about the person of Muhammad or the origin of Islam. But his work is the closest Armenian equivalent in the Muslim era to the work of Eznik in the Sasanian era.

ADDITIONAL NOTES

It is noteworthy that the Armenian Juanšēr [*Hamaŕōt Patmutʿiwn Vracʿ*, Venice 1884, 102] adds the story of Kałert, which is not in the original Georgian. On Bahira see R.W. Thomson, 'Armenian Variations on the Bahira Legend', *Eucharisterion: Essays Presented to Omelyan Pritsak, [Harvard Ukrainian Studies*, 3/4 (1979–1980)], 884–895.

This article does not tackle the question of Armenian knowledge of Muslim religious practice. There are interesting comments on that in Nersēs Šnorhali, *Ołb Edesioy* [translated by I. Kechichian, *Nersēs Šnorhali: La complainte d'Edesse*, Venise 1984] and in Mxitʿar Goš, *Girkʿ Datastani*, ed. X. Tʿorosyan, Erevan 1975, esp. 21–22.

XI

"Let Now the Astrologers Stand Up": The Armenian Christian Reaction to Astrology and Divination

Armenian enthusiasm for Byzantine learning can be clearly attested in many Armenian authors—even if it was tempered by a healthy mistrust of Byzantine politics.[1] But Byzantium was honored by the Armenians more as a depository of Christian learning than as a source of original and continuing scholarship. Over the centuries many Armenians came to Constantinople to seek out Greek texts and make translations, but remarkably little Greek literature composed after the end of the sixth century (i.e., after the rupture between the churches) was rendered into Armenian.

Byzantium was a Christian empire, and the classic works of patristic Greek writers remained the prime goal of Armenian translators. But the secular traditions of late antiquity were also of interest to them and Armenian versions of basic textbooks in such subjects as grammar, rhetoric, philosophy, and science were of great significance in promoting the development of original Armenian scholarship in those areas.[2] Such secular traditions included topics that were not entirely welcome to the ecclesiastical authorities, who were the major sponsors of learning in Armenia. There are also modern scholars who think some of these subjects unworthy of the attention of a serious Byzantine.

Discussing the ninth-century philosopher Leo's knowledge of Plato, a recent commentator states: "Less creditable to our way of thinking is his ownership of Paul (of Alexandria)'s Introduction to Astrology."[3] Alas, part of this too found its way into Armenian.

The editor of the Armenian version notes that the date of the translation is not certain, but may be put in or before the seventh century.[4] The rendering is in the style of the "hellenizing school," which is a general term for translations of an extreme literalness, but the texts in this style cannot be dated absolutely.[5] Needless to add, such learned works were not the first intimation in Armenian of the existence of astrology. The Bible has numerous references to a wide range of "curious arts." And patristic literature, of which so much was translated at an early period, abounds in diatribes against astrology, magic, and other undesirable practices.[6] Interest in the subject was frequently condemned in canon law, and homilists were liberal in their warnings. So it may be of interest to examine some early Armenian texts in order to see the atmosphere in which Paul's work would have been received.

---

[1] Title quotation from Isaiah 47:13. This paper discusses the early Christian Armenian literature concerning astrology. The pre-Christian situation, exemplified by Trdat I's reputation as a "magus" (Pliny, *Natural History*, bk. 30, ch. 6, sec. 16), is not our concern; it had no echo in Armenian literature. For a discussion of the earlier period see N. G. Garsoïan, "Prolegomena to a Study of the Iranian Aspects in Arsacid Armenia," *Handes Amsorya* 90 (1976), 177–234, repr. in her *Armenia between Byzantium and the Sasanians* (London, 1985).

[2] For a general overview see R. W. Thomson, "The Formation of the Armenian Literary Tradition," in *East of Byzantium: Syria and Armenia in the Formative Period*, ed. N. G. Garsoïan, T. F. Mathews, and R. W. Thomson (Washington, D.C., 1982), 135–50.

[3] N. G. Wilson, *Scholars of Byzantium* (Baltimore, 1983), 84. For the place of Paul in antique tradition see W. Gundel and H. G. Gundel, *Astrologumena: Die astrologische Literatur in der Antike und ihre Geschichte* (Wiesbaden, 1966), 236–39.

[4] H. Bart'ikyan, "Aratos Solac'u ev Połos Ałek'sandrac'u astłbašxakan erkeri hin hayeren t'argmanut'yunĕ," *Banber Matenadarani* 12 (1977), 137–62. The Armenian renders the prologue and the chapter on the zodiac.

[5] For a general view of this style with references to previous literature see Ch. Mercier, "L'école hellénistique dans la littérature arménienne," *REArm* 13 (1978–79), 59–75; and A. Terian, "The Hellenizing School: Its Time, Place, and Scope of Activities Reconsidered," in *East of Byzantium*, 175–86.

[6] For Greek patristic literature on the topic of astrology see U. Riedinger, *Die heilige Schrift im Kampf der griechischen Kirche gegen die Astrologie* (Innsbruck, 1956).

Reprinted form *Dumbarton Oaks Papers*, 46 (1992), pp. 305-312. Copyright © Trustees for Harvard University. Reprinted by permission.

Original Armenian texts will be our prime concern,[7] but it is impossible to disregard completely texts translated from Greek or Syriac. On the one hand, biblical terminology was so pervasive in Armenian writing that an author describing an Armenian phenomenon would naturally dress it in familiar garb, thereby laying many a trap for later critics. And on the other hand, themes from patristic texts might prove popular to Armenian authors, even if there was no local phenomenon. For example, a homily against attendance at immoral theatrical productions might be appropriate in Constantinople and come naturally to the lips of a John Chrysostom, but an Armenian homily on the same subject would hardly be good evidence for social mores in Armenia of the fifth or sixth centuries.[8] Similarly, references to magic in the standard account of the conversion of Armenia tell us nothing about the secret strength of the Christians. It was a hagiographical commonplace for the persecutors of the martyrs to call them sorcerers.[9]

In this regard the comment of an earlier investigator of western evidence for roughly the same period has relevance also for Armenia: "There is the unfortunate tendency ... in both official and unofficial references to astrology to group it with magic, augury, divination, and other pagan rites and superstitions."[10] In what follows we also shall find references to astrology mingled with extraneous matters.[11]

Armenian writing is not contemporaneous with Armenian Christianity.[12] The first historians, writing in the fifth century, looked back over the past century with a viewpoint, as well as a vocabulary, different from that of the time described. So when P'awstos describes the shah's consultations with soothsayers, astrologers, and Chaldaeans, he uses terms familiar from the Armenian version of the Old Testament.[13] The exact role of these persons at the Sasanian court is thus obscured. It is somewhat ironic that their main guarantee of the arrival at court of the Armenian king was a gospel on which Christian priests had sworn an oath, and which the shah kept securely chained up in his treasury.[14]

P'awstos does not mention astrology as such, but he does once refer to prognostication by the casting of dice (k'uē). When the apostate Meružan was pursuing the Armenian general Manuēl, he boasted of the latter's imminent capture. But worried by confusing directions as to the road to be followed, he resorted to "Chaldaean spells" and "cast dice."[15] Despite his reputation as a magician

---

[7] Armenian names and terms are transliterated according to the system used in the REArm.

[8] Cf. the 17th homily attributed to John Mandakuni titled "Concerning impious and demonic theatres (Vasn anōrēn t'aterac' diwakanac')," in Yovhannu Mandakunwoy Čaṙk' (Venice, 1860), 131–37, although John Chrysostom's Contra ludos et theatra is not attested in Armenian. More relevant to the present theme would be the works on Fate (περὶ εἱμαρμένης) by John Chrysostom and Gregory of Nyssa, but neither is attested in Armenia. But Basil of Caesarea's Hexaemeron, of which the sixth homily is particularly relevant, was well known in Armenia. There is a recent edition by K. Muradyan, Barseł Kesarac'i: Yałags Vec'awreay Ararč'ut'ean (Erevan, 1984), but he did not take sufficiently into account the fact that the Armenian was translated from a discursive Syriac rendering, not directly from the Greek original.

[9] Armenian kaxard; see Agat'angełos, Patmut'iwn Hayoc', ed. G. Ter-Mkrtč'ean and St. Kanayeanc' (Tiflis, 1909); repr. Delmar, N.Y., 1979), 203–4, trans. R. W. Thomson, Agathangelos: History of the Armenians (Albany, 1976). See further Ełišē, Vasn Vardanac' ew Hayoc' Paterazmin, ed. E. Ter-Minasean (Erevan, 1957), 42, and references in R. W. Thomson, Ełishē: History of Vardan (Cambridge, Mass., 1982), note 5 ad loc.
Other historical works have to be treated with equal circumspection. A long description of a visit by a doctor to a patient in Ełišē's History of Vardan comes directly from Philo and cannot be used in a study of Armenian medical practice; Thomson, Ełishē, note 2 to p. 172 of the Armenian text.

[10] M. Laistner, "The Western Church and Astrology during the Early Middle Ages," HTR 34 (1941), 251–75, p. 253 note 5.

[11] There is not a great deal of secondary literature on this subject. Modern scholars have tended to devote their attention either to texts dealing with "scientific" astronomy or to superstitious practices. B. E. T'umanyan, Hay Astłagitut'yan Patmut'yun (History of Armenian Astronomy) (Erevan, 1964), deals with calendars and astronomical instruments. J. R. Russell, Zoroastrianism in Armenia (Cambridge, Mass., 1987), has valuable information on magic based on a wide range of sources. The older work by Ł. Ališan, Hin Hawatk' kam Het'anosakan Krōnk' Hayoc' (The Old Faith, or Pagan Armenian Religion) (Venice, 1910), has useful evidence from later sources, but—as so often in works by Ališan—exact references to those sources are not always given.

[12] For the stages of the conversion of Armenia see R. W. Thomson, "Mission, Conversion, and Christianization: The Armenian Example," Harvard Ukrainian Studies 12–13 (1988–89), 28–45.

[13] P'awstos, Buzandaran Patmut'iwnk' (St. Petersburg, 1883; repr. Delmar, N.Y., 1984), IV 54, trans. N. G. Garsoïan, The Epic Histories (Cambridge, Mass., 1989): the Persian shah Šapuh summoned the diwt's and asteła gēts and k'awdeays. Astełagēt, "astrologer," only occurs in the Bible at Isa. 47:13, but the term gēt occurs some twenty times, with diwt', "soothsayer," at 2 Chron. 35:19, with the verb diwt'el at 1 Kings 28:8–9, and with k'ałdeay at Dan. 2:2. This last, "Chaldaean," is variously spelled k'awdeay or k'ałdeay.

[14] P'awstos, ibid.

[15] P'awstos, V 43: Meružan tried to find his way by "Chaldaean divination, hmays k'ałdēut'ean," by "casting dice, zk'uēs harc'anēr," and by "magic charms, yuṙut' kaxardanac'n." Later in the same chapter he is described as a "magician, soothsayer, and diviner, kaxard, diwt', k'uēic'n kaxard." Meružan resorted to divination because he was given an enigmatic reply to his question about the road: "The road lies through the Horns." This was the name of local mountains. But the term also refers to the points of the

THE ARMENIAN CHRISTIAN REACTION TO ASTROLOGY AND DIVINATION 307

and sorcerer, and in spite of his disguise, he was recognized by Manuēl in the ensuing encounter and slain.

Other early Armenian historians have little to say about Armenian practices. Ełišē refers to "Chaldaeanism" as equivalent to magism, and to the shah's "Chaldaeans" as a group similar to the magi.[16] But these were Iranian officials. Łazar, who continues Ełišē's account of Armenian-Iranian relationships into the second half of the fifth century, does not mention these "Chaldaeans." His references to magic are traditional insults against Christianity put into the mouths of Persians.[17]

The antiquarian Movsēs Xorenacʻi offers rather more information, though his evidence for ancient practices must be balanced by his later date. He once refers to astrology as such, indicating that in Persian tales Biwrasp Aždahak gained his strength from *astełabanutʻiwn*.[18] Although this is an exact calque on ἀστρολογία, it is quite a rare word in Armenian. Movsēs also knows of Persian stories concerning Papag and the prophecy of the "astrologers." Here he uses the term *axtarmol*, an even rarer word, which he glosses as "Chaldaeans," his only use of either term.[19] For Armenia proper Movsēs refers to various kinds of magic, and he describes divination by plane trees at Armavir.[20]

But he has nothing to say about the stars foretelling fate or fortune.[21]

More information comes from the fifth-century writer Eznik. Basing his work on a wide range of patristic and pagan Greek sources, he sought to refute those who supposed that evil had an existence in and of itself. His themes are the nature of God and man's free will; his opponents are pagan philosophers, Zurvanite Persians, and Marcionites.[22] His closely reasoned treatise offers a wealth of information about popular beliefs and erroneous ideas that Satan and the demons have introduced to mankind. But it is not always clear whether Eznik has in mind contemporary Armenian practices, or is elaborating on a foreign source. However, this work, which has brought him fame in modern times, was untypical of early Armenian literature. Eznik was not at all involved in those questions of Christian theology that were the hot issues of the fifth century. It would not be difficult to suppose that his obvious themes—paganism, Zurvanism, Marcion—were soon considered dead issues, and that his basic motif of free will was thought irrelevant to the christological controversies that came to divide Christendom.

Eznik devotes several pages to the question of predestination: Are men's life-spans fixed in advance by a decree (*hraman*)? This is what the Chaldaean astrologers say, in that the position of the planets relative to the zodiac at the time of a person's birth determines his fate.[23] Eznik has no difficulty in showing the illogical conclusions to which such ideas would lead—his usual method of refutation—though his actual exposition of the theories attacked is somewhat confused.[24] More interesting is the fact that the term "astrologers" occurs only once in his book. Eznik uses the very rare

---

arc of the moon. Since in Armenia divination by the moon is attested (see *lusnaxtirkʻ* below, p.310), perhaps Meružan thought that there was more to the response than a statement of geography.

[16] P. 15, 18 of the Armenian text.

[17] Łazar Pʻarpecʻi, *Patmutʻiwn Hayocʻ*, ed. G. Ter-Mkrtčʻean and St. Malxasean (Tiflis, 1904; repr. Delmar, N.Y., 1986), 79, 81, trans. with commentary in R. W. Thomson, *The History of Łazar Pʻarpecʻi* (Atlanta, 1991). Cf. also Yovhannēs Mamikonean, *Patmutʻiwn Tarōnoy* (Venice, 1889), 54, trans. by L. Avdoyan, *Pseudo-Yovhannēs Mamikonean's History of Tarōn* (forthcoming): the Persians taunt the Armenian soldiers, calling them *kaxardasar* (as Acts 19:19), who hope to conquer by magic.

[18] Movsēs Xorenacʻi, *Patmutʻiwn Hayocʻ*, ed. M. Abełean and S. Yarutʻiwnean (Tiflis, 1913; repr. Delmar, N.Y., 1981), "From the Fables of the Persians," which is a short section between books 1 and 2 of the *History*, p. 91 of the Armenian text. The date of Movsēs' *History* remains disputed. The arguments for an 8th-century date, not in the 5th century as the author of the work claims, are presented in the introduction to the translation by R. W. Thomson, *Moses Khorenatsʻi: History of the Armenians* (Cambridge, Mass., 1978).

[19] *History*, II 70. The plural noun *axtarkʻ* is used in the sense of "horoscope" (for which see note 95 below), though it is also rare in early texts; cf. the Armenian version of Ephrem, "On the Entry of the Lord into Jerusalem," *Matenagrutʻiwnkʻ* (Venice, 1836), vol. 4, p. 52: "You abandoned the Trinity and loved vain gods, demons and horoscopes (*axtars*) and material likenesses."

[20] See I 20 for divination, *hmaykʻ*. He uses the same term to describe Eruand's "evil eye," II 42, and for the reason for the Persians' plundering of the bones of the Armenian kings at Ani, III 27. For *hmaykʻ* see further below, p. 309.

[21] Movsēs is the prime authority for Armenian traditions about Bēl, whom he identifies with Nimrod, I 5. The parallel version of the settlement of Armenia, the "Primary History" published as a preface to the work of Sebēos, notes that Bēl used "apparent magic" (*aṙ acʻawkʻ kaxardutʻeamb*) to attain his ends (*Patmutʻiwn Sebēosi*, ed. G. V. Abgaryan [Erevan, 1979], 49; trans. of the "Primary History" in Thomson, *Moses Khorenatsʻi*, 357–68). But there is no trace in these stories of Nimrod's repute as an astronomer; cf. Ch. Haskins, "Nimrod the Astronomer," *The Romanic Review* 5 (1914), 203–12.

[22] Eznik de Kołb, *De Deo*, ed. L. Mariès and Ch. Mercier, PO 28, 3, 4 (Paris, 1959). For analysis of the themes and discussion of the sources see L. Mariès, "Le *De Deo* d'Eznik," *REArm* 4 (1924), 1–213.

[23] Eznik, 216.

[24] Note 522 to the French translation of Mariès, as in note 22.

word *astełanšmar,* a compound with biblical overtones.[25]

That the Chaldaeans invented astronomy was a commonplace known from earlier sources.[26] David the "Invincible" Philosopher indicates that the clear sky in that part of the world enabled the Chaldaeans to comprehend easily the movements of the heavenly bodies.[27] A different idea is found in the Scholia to Ps.-Nonnus: the Babylonians invented astronomy through Zoroaster.[28]

Ełišē, in the *Questions on Genesis,*[29] picks up the theme of the stars controlling men's fate. "Moses said in Gen. 1:14: God created (the stars) to be for signs. Can what the astronomers (*astełabašxkʿ*) say be true?" In response, Ełišē indicates that men's fate and destiny bear no relation to the movements of the stars. God is indeed responsible for their movement, but they serve as signs only in the sense that they indicate the weather. What a man does for good or evil is within his own capacity and free will. Ełišē, however, is more concerned with magic and incantations, and this text has no other reference to astrology or any other method of foretelling the future. In another homily attributed to Ełišē, "On the Souls of Men," references to astrology only elaborate themes from the Old Testament.[30] Nor is a "Questionnaire" attributed to Gregory the Illuminator (which has certain parallels with Eznik) very helpful. It deals with the abilities of magicians (*kaxardkʿ*), beginning with references from the Old Testament, and goes on to list the weapons of Satan: *kaxardutʿiwn, tʿovčʿutʿiwn, diwtʿutʿiwn, astełagitutʿiwn,* and "similar things."[31]

The most important source for early Armenian practices of divination is one of the homilies attributed to John (Yovhannēs) Mandakuni. John was Catholikos in the second half of the fifth century.[32] He is praised by the historian Łazar, who ends his *History* with a long sermon purportedly given by John on the occasion of Vahan Mamikonean's appointment as *marzpan* of Armenia.[33] However, the collection of homilies published under his name is of uncertain authorship. They have also been attributed to a later John, Mayragomecʿi, of the seventh century.[34] The latter was a fierce opponent of reunion with the Greek church. The homilies deal with matters of more general pastoral interest than the technical christological issues that so stirred Mayragomecʿi, and their editor has noted that some appear in Armenian collections of homilies attributed to Ephrem the Syrian.[35] Their precise origin remains unclear.

In homily 26 John deals with divination in a multitude of forms.[36] He is also interested in—or rather, opposed to—spells, amulets, false expectations from relics, dreams, and similar matters, in which even the clergy might indulge. Magic is not here our concern, but his comments on various kinds of foreknowledge by divination are valuable and rare evidence.

The stars are only mentioned once in a long list of divinatory practices. It may be helpful to list these terms (in the order in which they appear) and to indicate evidence in other early Armenian sources for their use:[37]

---

[25] Isa. 47:13: "Astrologers who observe the stars of heaven, *astełagētkʿn or nšmaren zastełs erknicʿ.*"

[26] Known in Armenia, for example, was Philo's *Quaestiones in Genesin* (Armenian text in *Mnacʿordkʿ,* ed. M. Awgerean [Venice, 1826]), III 1, IV 88.

[27] David, *Sahmankʿ ew Tramatutʿiwnkʿ Imastasirutʿean,* ed. S. S. Arevšatyan (Erevan, 1960), repr. with English trans. and notes as *Definitions and Divisions of Philosophy,* by B. Kendall and R. Thomson (Chico, Calif., 1983), ch. 17.

[28] "Nonnos: Die Scholien zu fünf Reden des Gregor von Nazianz," ed. A. Manandian, *Zeitschrift für armenische Philologie* 1 (1903), 220–300, I 63 (I 70 in the Syriac: S. Brock, *The Syriac Version of the Pseudo-Nonnos Mythological Scholia* [Cambridge, 1971]).

The 13th-century Vardan refers to Abraham learning astronomy (but there *astełagitutʿiwn* in place of the *astełabašxutʿiwn* of Philo, David, and Ps.-Nonnos), *Hawakʿumn Patmutʿean Vardanay Vardapeti,* ed. Ł. Ališan (Venice, 1862), 16 (trans. and commentary in R. W. Thomson, "The Historical Compilation of Vardan Arewelcʿi," *DOP* 43 [1989], 125–226). But Vardan is indebted to the *Chronicle* of Michael the Syrian; and here the theme goes back to Jubilees. See further Riedinger, p. 110–16. Vardan, ibid., defines Chaldaeanism as "soothsaying of the stars, *hmayutʿiwn astełacʿ.*"

[29] Elisée Vardapet, *Questions et réponses sur la Genèse,* publiée par P. Nerses Akinian, traduit par P. Sahak Kogian (Vienna, 1928), Question 32, pp. 33–36.

[30] Ełišē, *Matenagrutʿiwnkʿ* (Venice, 1859), 375–76. Here he also equates the magi, the Chaldaeans, and astrology.

[31] N. Adontz, "Le questionnaire de saint Grégoire et ses rapports avec Eznik," *ROC* 25 (1925–26), 317.

[32] G. Garitte, *La Narratio de Rebus Armeniae,* CSCO, Subsidia 4 (Louvain, 1952), 426.

[33] Łazar, *Patmutʿiwn,* 179–82.

[34] References in Garitte, *Narratio,* 348.

[35] Introduction to the Armenian text (note 8 above), 5.

[36] This homily has been translated in part by F. Feydit, "La XXVIe homélie de Jean Mandakouni," in *Mélanges offerts à Jean Dauvillier* (Toulouse, 1979), 293–306, but without comparison with other Armenian texts. In his discussion of this homily Ališan, *Hin Hawatkʿ,* ch. 11, notes some parallels with later authors, but does not collate the earlier evidence. Not available to me was the general study on John Mandakuni by B. Sargisean, *Kʿnnadatutʿiwn Mandakunwoy* (Venice, 1896).

[37] Pp. 193–94 of the Armenian text. Where expressions are rare or unusual I have also added some references to authors writing in the 10th or later centuries, but without attempting a full study of that evidence.

THE ARMENIAN CHRISTIAN REACTION TO ASTROLOGY AND DIVINATION

xtirkʿ: "soothsaying, augury." This does not appear in the Armenian Bible. In the translation of the *Teaching of Addai* attributed to Labubna,[38] it renders the Syriac *nexše*. The two compounds *lusnaxtirkʿ* and *seljaxtirkʿ* are noted below.

hmaykʿ: "divination, spell." This is more usual than the abstract from *hmayutʿiwn*, which appears below.[39] It occurs frequently in the Bible, in Pʿawstos, Movsēs, and Eznik, as noted above, and in the canons.[40] The form *hmayeak*, "amulet," is found in Gregory of Narek, where he describes myron as a "destroyer of hmayeaks,"[41] and in the canons.

kewos: "divination." In Labubna this renders the Syriac *qeṣme*, but generally in Armenian it occurs in combination, with stem spelled *kiws: kiwsahmay*, Zech. 3:8 and Jer. 27:9, and *kiwsakertoł* in Gregory Magistros, Letter 4.[42]

diwtʿutʿiwn: "sorcery." This is a very common term. In the Bible the noun *diwtʿ* occurs once (2 Chron. 35:19), but the verb *diwtʿel* and the abstract noun are common. It is also found in Pʿawstos, Movsēs Xorenacʿi, Eznik, the Scholia to Ps.-Nonnus, and numerous canons. The noun *diwtʿaran*, which indicates the place where soothsaying took place, is found in the Scholia[43] and Gregory Magistros, Letter 61.[44]

tʿovčʿutʿiwn: "wizardry." This is also found in the Bible, Eznik, Ełišē's *Questions*, and canon law.

hataharcʿutʿiwn: "divination by grains." This is found only in the Armenian version of John Chrysostom, *On Ephesians*, homily 6, where the Armenian expands on the Greek.[45]

However, in David of Ganjak the term *hatahmayutʿiwn* (for *hmayutʿiwn* see below) is found.[46] The person who threw the grains was called *hatēnkēcʿ*, and this term occurs in another work attributed to John Mandakuni[47] and in Letter 4 of Gregory Magistros.[48] A parallel may be found in David of Ganjak, ch. 95, who refers to consultation of the *garēnkēcʿs*, "crithomancers (those who threw barley)."[49]

hawahmayutʿiwn: "divination by birds." The parallel nouns *hawahmaykʿ* and *hawaditutʿiwn*, and the nouns for the diviner, *hawaharcʿ*, and *hawagēt*, occur in the Bible. *Hawahmaykʿ* renders ὀρνεοσκοπίαι in the Armenian version of Cyril of Jerusalem, *Catecheses*, IV 37.[50] But the term is not common in Armenian. Vardan, in his *Chronicle*, claims that Maniton discovered *hawahmayutʿiwn*.[51]

małabaxutʿiwn: "divination by sieve." The only other attested use of this term in early Armenian is in the passage from John Chrysostom, *On Ephesians*, quoted above,[52] where the Armenian expands on the Greek and precise parallels are not clear.

kʿuaharcʿutʿiwn: "divination by throwing dice." This seems to be the only use of the abstract noun. *Kʿuē* occurs in Pʿawstos,[53] in the Bible (only at Hos. 4:12), and in the canons. Movsēs Dasxurancʿi refers to Bishop Israyēl burning the "destructive magical dice" (*zkʿuēs korusičʿs hmayicʿ*) of the Huns.[54]

hełaharutʿiwn: "divination by water"(?). The term is not found elsewhere, so various corrections have been proposed. Feydit suggests *-harcʿutʿiwn*, "interrogation," for *-harutʿiwn*, "striking," and Ačaṙean suggests that the first syllable might be *her*, "hair." Baronian and Conybeare propose *hołaharutʿiwn*, which they associate with *razmarkutʿiwn*, "an

---

[38] Labubna, *Tʿułtʿ Abgaru*, ed. Ł. Ališan (Venice, 1868), 33; Syriac text in W. Wright, *Ancient Syriac Documents* (London, 1865; repr. Amsterdam, 1967).
[39] For its etymology see Russell, *Zoroastrianism*, 443.
[40] The evidence from the canons is discussed below.
[41] Grigor Narekacʿi, *Girkʿ Ołberguṭʿean* (Buenos Aires, 1948; repr. Delmar, N.Y., 1981), no. 93.18, trans. in I. Kechichian, *Grégoire de Narek: Le livre de prières*, SC 78 (Paris 1961). *Hmayeak* is also a fairly common personal name; twelve examples are listed in H. Ačaṙean, *Hayocʿ anjnannuneri Baṙaran*, 5 vols. (Erevan, 1942–62; repr. Beirut, 1972), s.v.
[42] Grigor Magistros, *Tʿłtʿerē*, ed. Kʿ. Kostaneancʿ (Alexandropol, 1910), 14.
[43] But there, IV 12, it refers to the oracle at Dodone.
[44] Gregory Magistros, p. 139.
[45] John Chrysostom, *Commentary on the Pauline Epistles*, Armenian version, *Meknutʿiwn Tʿłtʿocʿ Pawłosi* (Venice, 1862), 734; cf. PG 62, col. 48. The Armenian reads: *i hmays ew i kaxardutʿiwns ew i małabaxutʿiwns ew i hataharcʿutʿiwns ew i tʿovčʿutʿiwns*, where the Greek has merely: οἰωνιζομένους, καὶ φαρμακείαις καὶ κληδονισμοῖς καὶ ἐπῳδαῖς.

[46] *The Penitential of David of Ganjak*, ed. and trans. C. J. F. Dowsett, CSCO, Scriptores Armeniaci 3, 4 (Louvain, 1961), ch. 95 (p. 82).
[47] See below in the discussion of canon law, p. 311.
[48] P. 14.
[49] Russell, *Zoroastrianism*, 442, quotes the same term from Siméon of Ałjnikʿ and Vardan Aygekcʿi.
[50] *Kočʿumn Ēncayutʿean* (Vienna, 1832), 71.
[51] P. 9.
[52] See note 45.
[53] See above, p. 306.
[54] Movsēs Dasxurancʿi, *Patmutʿiwn Ałuanicʿ Ašxarhi*, ed. M. Emin (Moscow, 1860; repr. Tiflis, 1912), II 41, trans. by C. J. F. Dowsett, *The History of the Caucasian Albanians by Movsēs Dasxurançi* (London, 1961).

Arabic word meaning 'sand'." Divination by sand is attested, but the word is *raml*.[55]

hmayut'iwn: "divination." More usual than this abstract noun is the form *hmayk'*, discussed above.[56]

mijagitut'iwn: The meaning is unclear; *mēj* (giving *mij* in combination) means "middle," and *gitut'iwn* is the abstract noun from *gēt*, "knower, savant," used of astrologers in the Old Testament. Cf. the equally obscure *t'iknagēt* in the canons.

grararut'iwn: "making of phylacteries." This is also found in the canons. John Mandakuni and David of Ganjak also refer to phylacteries.[57]

astełagitut'iwn: "astrology." The abstract noun is not common in Armenian; it occurs once in the canons, and in Labubna (where it renders *kukbe*, "stars"). The form *astełagēt*, "astrologer," occurs once in the Bible (Isa. 47:13), the more common biblical expression being simply *gēt*. It is also found in P'awstos and Ełišē's *Questions*. As noted above, Eznik uses the rare form *astełanšmar*, based on the quotation from Isaiah.

diwaharc'ut'iwn: "consultation of demons." This term is not attested elsewhere. The *Nor Bargirk' Haykazean Lezui* (*NBHL*)[58] gives one reference to a similar term, *diwahmayut'iwn*, in a collection of homilies. If the stem *harc'* has been confused with *har* (cf. *hełaharut'iwn* above), then *diwaharut'iwn* means simply "demon possession." The adjective *diwahar* is very common in the Bible and elsewhere.

awrahmayk': This is a hapax: *awr*, "day," and *hmayk'*, as above. On p. 199 of his homily John expands on those who distinguish days, and on p. 210 he quotes Gal. 4:10, where Paul castigates those who distinguish (*xtren*, cf. *xtirk'* above) days, months, and times.

lusnaxtirk': "auguries by the moon." This and the following compound with *xtir* seem not to be attested elsewhere.

šełjaxtirk': "auguries by (observing) heaps or piles." This is a hapax in Armenian.

ozotnahmayk': This too is a hapax. *Hmayk'* is discussed above but *ozotn* is not an Armenian stem.

dełahmayk': "divination by potions." The text reads *gełahmayk'*, but Feydit proposes this simple correction.[59] The word is otherwise unattested. *Deł* is "potion, medicine, or poison," and *dełatu* is discussed below.[60]

snnikon: "amulet, phylactery." The term appears in John Chrysostom, *On I Timothy*, homily 10,[61] in a long list: *hmayk', kiwsk', xtirk', cnnundk', patahark', snikonk', diwt'ut'iwnk', t'ovc'ut'iwnk'*. The Greek text (PG 62 col. 552) reads: οἰωνισμοὺς καὶ κληδονομισμούς, παρατηρήσεις, γενέσεις, σύμβολα, περιάμματα, μαντείας, ἐπῳδάς, μαγείας. In Chrysostom, ibid., homily 13,[62] περίαπτα is rendered by *snikons*. The meaning is also clear from John Mandakuni's own homily 9, p. 83, where it is linked with *paharan*.[63]

yuŕut's: "talisman." This appears once in the Bible (2 Macc. 12:40), but is common in Armenian. It is found in P'awstos, Movsēs Xorenac'i, Eznik, and the canons. Gregory of Narek, 75.12 and 93.18, indicates that the cross and myron are effective antidotes. The person casting such spells is *yuŕt'oł*, a term found in the canons, and in the title to this homily by Mandakuni. David of Ganjak, ch. 95, refers to *juruŕt'oys*, "hydromancers."[64]

baxts: In the singular this means "fate." Eznik, § 174, emphasizes that this has no existence of its own, but is merely an attribute. However, the plural in Isa. 65:11 gives the impression that something personal is involved. Gregory of Narek uses the plural, 51.4, as parallel to *hmayk'*.

cakatagir: "fate, what is decreed" (lit., written on the forehead). Eznik, §206, associates this term with *baxt* and the hopes of those who gaze at the stars.[65]

---

[55] H. Wehr, *A Dictionary of Modern Written Arabic*, ed. J. M. Cowan (New York, 1976), s.v. *raml*. Feydit, "La XXVIe homélie," note 25; H. Ačaŕean, *Hayeren Armatakan Baŕaran*, 4 vols. (Erevan, 1971–79), s.v.; S. Baronian and F. C. Conybeare, *Catalogue of the Armenian Manuscripts in the Bodleian Library* (Oxford, 1918), 235 (describing MS no. 113).
[56] P. 309 above.
[57] Mandakuni, p. 192, *gir paharan*; David, ch. 95, *pahapan*.
[58] *NBHL* = *Nor Baŕgirk' Haykazean Lezui*, ed. G. Awetik'ean, X. Siwrmēlean, and M. Awgerean, 2 vols. (Venice, 1836–37; repr. Erevan, 1979, 1981).
[59] Feydit, "La XXVIe homélie" (as note 36), p. 305 note 28. The letters *g* and *d* are similar in Armenian script.
[60] P. 312.
[61] P. 85 of the Armenian text.
[62] P. 105 of the Armenian text.
[63] In a text "On the Nicaean Faith" in the Armenian Evagrius, ed. B. Sargisean (Venice 1907), 139, *snikon* renders φυλακτήριον (PG 28, col. 837B); but the Armenian was translated from the Syriac, not directly from the Greek. See I. Hausherr, "Les versions syriaque et arménienne d'Evagre le Pontique," *Or Chr* 22 2 (no. 69) (Rome, 1931).
[64] Cf. also Russell, *Zoroastrianism*, 443–44.
[65] Movsēs Xorenac'i, III 15, uses the participle *cakatagreal* in the heading of a letter supposedly sent by Emperor Julian, "destined (for immortality)."

THE ARMENIAN CHRISTIAN REACTION TO ASTROLOGY AND DIVINATION 311

bzzankᶜ: "talismans or amulets." This term only occurs in the Bible at 2 Macc. 12:40 (cf. *yuṙutᶜs*), but is found in the canons. Gregory of Narek, 66.4, links these last two terms: prayer is the antidote to the devil's attempts at magic worked through *bzzankᶜ inčᶜ yurtᶜicᶜ*.

harcᶜuk: "oracle." (This occurs earlier in John's homily, at p. 190, not in the list just discussed.) Movsēs Xorenacᶜi, II 13, uses the term for the Pythian oracle; it is frequent in the Bible and the canons.

jeṙnacu: "sorcerer, conjuror." (This occurs after the list just discussed, on p. 195, where it is applied to women.) It is not common in Armenian. It is found in the canons; and in his eulogy to myron, holy oil, Gregory of Narek mentions that it repels many kinds of magicians, including *jeṙnacus*,[66] whom he condemns without further explanation.

This list in John Mandakuni does not have any clear logic to it. The same is true of similar lists in patristic authors, some of which contain several of the practices mentioned by John. Texts in John Chrysostom and Cyril of Jerusalem have been cited above. Such lists also appear in scripture, the longest at Deut. 18:10, where seven terms are found: *diwtᶜutᶜiwn, hmayel, hawaharᶜ, kaxardel, vhuk*,[67] *nšanagēt*,[68] *zmeṙeals harcᶜanel*.[69]

The closest parallels to the divinatory practices attacked by John Mandakuni may be found in the collection of Armenian canon law. The first Armenian council whose canons were set down in Armenian was that held at Šahapivan in 447.[70] (The various gatherings of the fourth century described by Pᶜawstos have not left a written record of their resolutions.) Canons 8, 9, and 10 of Šahapivan deal with magic or the casting of spells. Precise forms of magic are not described; it is simply declared that *kaxardutᶜiwn* is worse than "mere" (*lok*)

---

[66] Gregory, 93.18.
[67] See below, p. 311.
[68] Lit. "knower of signs." The only reference in the *NBHL* is to a commentary on Deuteronomy by Vardan (unpublished).
[69] "To interrogate the dead." The noun *meṙelaharcᶜuac* occurs in the Armenian version of Cyril of Jerusalem, *Catecheses*, IV 37, rendering the Greek νεκυομαντεία. The only parallel in Armenian authors noted by the *NBHL* is *meṙelaharcᶜuk*, found in a commentary on Isaiah by the 13th-century George of Skevṙa; the passage is quoted by Ališan, *Hin Hawatkᶜ*, 423.
[70] The canons to be discussed are found in the two-volume collection *Kanonagirkᶜ*, ed. V. Hakobyan (Erevan, 1964, 1971). The canons of Šahapivan have also been published by N. Akinean in *Mxitᶜar Tōnagirkᶜ* (Vienna, 1949), 79–170.

diwtᶜutᶜiwn.[71] Not a word is said about astrology. Canon 9 indicates that those who frequent *harcᶜuks* or engage in sorcery (*diwtᶜel*) have to pay a fine. If they are bishops or priests, then they are also unfrocked.

Of less certain date are canons attributed to an earlier period. Those ascribed to Gregory the Illuminator condemn *tᶜovičᶜs* to five years of excommunication, and the *jeṙnacu*s to one;[72] those ascribed to Thaddaeus, the legendary founder of Christianity in Armenia in apostolic times, state that magicians (*kaxard*) are to be treated as apostates;[73] and those attributed to Nersēs Catholicos impose five years' penance on believers in the spells worked by amulets (*hmayicᶜ bzzankᶜ*).[74] A later work on repentance ascribed to John Mandakuni lists among sinners those who are *tᶜovičᶜ* and those who frequent *vhuks* and *hatēnkēcᶜs*.[75] These last were mentioned in his homily on spells. *Vhuk*, "sorcerer," is very common in the Old Testament and in translated texts, both from Greek and Syriac.[76] Movsēs Dasxurancᶜi includes them among those who led opposition to Christianity among the Huns: *kaxardkᶜ, kawdeaykᶜ, vhukkᶜ, kᶜrmapetkᶜ* (pagan priests), who performed incantations (*diwtᶜutᶜiwns*) and spells (*uṙutᶜs*).[77]

The foreign canons translated into Armenian very frequently inveigh against various kinds of astrology and magic. But as with homilies, such evidence from outside must be used with caution as regards actual Armenian practice. Specific references to the stars are rare, but other means of foretelling one's fate are more common. The fifteenth of the Apostolic Canons (translated from Syriac)[78] condemns those who go to *kaxards, harcᶜuks, kᶜawdeays, vhuks*, or who believe in horoscopes (*cnundkᶜ*)[79] and astrology (*astełagitutᶜiwnkᶜ*, in the plural).[80] The thirty-sixth canon of Laodicaea[81]

---

[71] Canon 10, in vol. I, 442; in canon 8 *kaxardutᶜiwn* is equated with apostasy.
[72] Canons 12, 27 in vol. I, 246, 249.
[73] Canon 22, in vol. II, 35.
[74] Canon 26, in vol. II, 261.
[75] Vol. II, 300–301.
[76] In Labubna it renders the Syriac *zakure*. Movsēs Xorenacᶜi, I 15, uses the abstract noun *vhukutᶜiwn* of Semiramis' magic arts. See also Gregory Magistros, Letter 61, p. 139, where he refers to those who have recourse to *vhuks*. See Russell, *Zoroastrianism*, 442, for the etymology.
[77] *Patmutᶜiwn Ałuanicᶜ*, II 41.
[78] *Kanonagirkᶜ*, I, 37.
[79] Lit. "births." In Labubna it renders the Syriac *bet yalda*.
[80] The fortieth canon of the Apostolic Canons, which were rendered from Greek, forbids clergy from being involved in dice (*kᶜuē*). But since this is linked with drunken revelry (*ginarbu*), this canon may have no relevance for soothsaying!
[81] *Kanonagirkᶜ*, vol. 1, 237.

forbids priests or monks from acting as *mogs*, *tʿovicʿs*, *diwtʿs*, *vhuks*, or from making *hmayeaks ew pahpans* (charms and phylacteries). The thirty-ninth canon of Basil[82] also condemns those who pay attention to *hmays* and *harcʿuks*.

A second set of canons attributed to Basil repeats some of the terms already familiar from John Mandakuni and introduces new ones. Canon 197[83] warns especially against *jeṙnacus*, *delahats*,[84] *lerdahmays*,[85] *tʿiknagēts*,[86] *uṙtʿoɫs*, *hatēnkēcʿs*. Canon ninety[87] gives in abbreviated form the content of the tenth canon of Šahapivan. Canon 253[88] anathematizes those who consult the books of demons or the "tables (*cʿoycʿ*) of the moon and stars." Similarly, canon seventy-six[89] condemns those who in pagan fashion distinguish (*xtrē*, cf. *xtirkʿ* above) days and hours, or the old and new moon.

Talismans are mentioned only once. The second canon of those attributed to Epiphanius[90] condemns people who cast *uluns* for the sake of soothsaying (*hmayutʿiwn*), and those who engage in the making of phylacteries (*grararutʿiwn*, as above).

The secular code of Mxitʿar Goš has no reference to astrology, but two laws concerning divorce are worth noting. Canons 145 and 195 forbid a man from divorcing or abandoning his wife without cause. However, fornication or other wicked deeds, such as magic (*kaxardutʿiwn*) and the giving of philters (*delatuutʿiwn*) are grounds for divorce.[91] It is precisely those two crimes of magic and philters that are linked together in the canons of Basil[92] and Nersēs Šnorhali's *General Epistle*. Nersēs addressed that section of his long pastoral letter specifically to women.[93]

The name of Paul of Alexandria is absent from all these texts, nor is astrology in the technical sense often mentioned. In general the Armenian sources of the early period are not very informative about the practices condemned by canon law. Indeed, in Armenia, as in the medieval West, "prohibition of magic, augury, and other superstitious customs and beliefs is found frequently in the penitential literature. Yet astrology and astrologers as such are mentioned infrequently."[94] The Armenian terminology is not always clear, and when patristic sources are used, the application to Armenia of the practices mentioned can on occasion be more rhetorical than historical. Even the earliest attested horoscope does not predate the thirteenth century.[95] Nonetheless, although the evidence is not abundant, it remains clear enough that Armenians were no less interested in prognostication than other people of the time, and that such popular traditions were hard to eradicate.

[82] *Kanonagirkʿ*, vol. 1, 354.
[83] *Kanonagirkʿ*, vol. 2, 102.
[84] Cf. *delahmaykʿ* above.
[85] I.e., divination by means of the liver. It occurs in the Bible at Ezek. 21.21, and in Ełišē, *Matenagrutʿiwnk*ʿ, 375, where he refers to that biblical passage. The Scholia of Ps.-Nonnos I 15 refer to *lerdahmayutʿiwn*, but I have found no other attestations in Armenian.
[86] This seems to be a hapax, *tʿikn-* meaning "back." Cf. *mijagitutʿiwn* above.
[87] P. 122.
[88] P. 171.
[89] P. 119.
[90] P. 62.
[91] *Girkʿ Datastani*, ed. X. Tʿorosyan (Erevan, 1975), 92, 113.
[92] *Kanonagirkʿ*, vol. 1, 351; vol. 2, 102.
[93] *Ĕndhanrakan Tʿułtʿ srboyn Nersisi Šnorhalwoy* (Jerusalem, 1871), 82 (Latin translation in *Sancti Nersetis Clajensis Opera*, I (Venice, 1833).

[94] Laistner, "Western Church and Astrology," p. 265. Thus a study such as B. E. Tʿumanyan, *Hay Astłgutʿean Patmutʿyun* (History of Armenian Astronomy from the Oldest Times down to the Beginning of the Nineteenth Century) (Erevan 1964), has no information on the topic of this paper.
[95] It is noteworthy that only one actual horoscope is clearly attested before the 15th century: in MS no. 1999 of the Matenadaran in Erevan. Of the 10,408 manuscripts listed in the general catalogue (*Cʿucʿak Jeṙagracʿ Maštʿocʿi anvan Matenadarani*, ed. O. Eganyan, A. Zeytʿunyan, and Pʿ. Antʿabyan, 2 vols. [Erevan, 1965, 1971]), 173 are classified as horoscopes (*axtarkʿ*). MS 1999 is dated to the 13th century, but its place of writing is unknown. It is a general miscellany of 277 pages, containing various works on calendars as well as homilies attributed to Armenian, Greek, and Syrian authors. No horoscopes are dated to the 14th century; five are dated to the 15th century, one to the 16th, and all the rest to the 17th century or later. In Jerusalem, of the 3,235 manuscripts catalogued so far (*Mayr Cʿucʿak Jeṙagracʿ srbocʿ Yakobeancʿ*, ed. N. Połarean, 9 vols. to date [Jerusalem, 1966–79]), only one horoscope is listed (in MS no. 3110 of the 17th century). Nor are horoscopes earlier than the 17th century attested in the indices to other published collections. But the second book published in Armenian (Venice, between 1511 and 1513) was a horoscope; R. H. Kévorkian, *Catalogue des "Incunables" arméniens*, Cahiers d'Orientalisme 9 (Geneva, 1986), 24.

For Armenian horoscopes see H. A. Anasyan, *Haykakan Matenagitutʿyun*, I (Erevan, 1959), 424–67, "axtarakan grakanutʿiwn." Of interest is also F. Feydit, *Amulettes de l'Arménie chrétienne* (Venice, 1986). For an Armenian text on the magical properties of numbers and modern survivals, see J. R. Russell, "The Book of the Six Thousand: An Armenian Magical Text," *Bazmavēp* 147 (1989), 221–43.

Additional Note: For the influence of stars see also the Homily on the Passion attributed to Ełišē in *Ełišēi vardapeti Matenagrutʿiwnkʿ*, Venice 1859, esp. 325–327.

XII

The Fathers in Early Armenian Literature

The purpose of this paper is to discuss the significance of the church fathers in early Armenian literature and scholarship. I shall not be interested in assessing the value of Armenian translations for the study of the texts of non-Armenian writers. At this conference there is no need to dwell on the importance of the oriental versions of patristic works. Rather I wish to discuss some problems that arise in the study of *Armenian* literature. I would like to pose such questions as: which fathers were read, studied and translated by Armenian scholars; what patristic texts were available in Armenia; did these circulate in Armenian or in the original; and, most important of all, what texts influenced early Armenian writers – either directly as source material, or indirectly as models to be imitated.

The subject is, of course, enormous, for since classical Armenian literature was almost exclusively the domain of ecclesiastical interests the influence of the fathers was all pervasive. And even in the realm of supposedly "scientific" studies like astronomy, ideas taken from patristic writers played a rôle. To do justice to the title one would have to write the history of early Armenian literature in general. So in order to bring the present discussion within manageable bounds I shall restrict my comments to the Greek fathers and to the major Armenian texts in the first three centuries of Armenian literature, with only occasional forays into later times. Nor shall I be concerned with the questions of biblical or liturgical texts.

Although Eusebius tells us of a letter written by Dionysius of Alexandria in the mid-third century to the otherwise unknown Meruzanes, bishop of the Armenians,[1] it is not until the fourth century that the Armenians themselves began to show interest in the Greek fathers. But we cannot speak of Armenian literature until the fifth century, after the invention of a script for the Armenian tongue by the monk Mashtots. From the time of Gregory the Illuminator, whose consecration at Caesarea may be plausibly dated to

---

[1] Eusebius, H. E. VI 46. 2. This cannot be Greater Armenia. For various identifications see L. Duchesne, "L'Arménie chrétienne dans l'Histoire ecclésiastique d'Eusèbe," Mélanges Nicole, Geneva 1909, p. 105–7; H. Gelzer, "Die Anfänge der armenischen Kirche," Berichte der königlichen sächsischen Gesellschaft der Wissenschaften, Leipzig, 47 (1895), p. 109–174, esp. p. 172; N. Adontz, Armenia in the Period of Justinian, translated by Nina Garsoian, Louvain 1970, p. 271.

314¹, until the beginning of the following century Greek and Syriac were the languages of the church. And as we learn from Faustos of Buzand – the later historian who describes the conflict between church and state in 4th century Armenia – the number of those converted in more than name during that century was small: only those who knew some Greek or Syriac really grasped the Christian gospel.² The three most significant patriarchs of the 4th century, Gregory, Nerses and Isaac (Sahak), had all received a good education in Greek literature, as had Mashtots himself. And Armenians who desired a more traditional and secular education attended the famous schools of the Eastern Roman empire; several studied with Libanius in Antioch, for example.³ So although some Armenians in the 4th century studied the Greek fathers, although schools for Greek were founded and Greek books circulated,⁴ we can hardly yet speak of the influence of Greek on Armenian literature. Nonetheless during this time a trend was set which proved extremely significant. It was to the Greek world, especially Constantinople, that the Armenians looked: first for authoritative teaching, and then, after the break in the 6th century, for learning and scholarship. However, as time went on the Armenian attitude towards Constantinople became increasingly ambivalent; respect and distrust were inextricably intertwined.⁵

The history of Armenian literature proper begins with Mashtots, who left a promising career in the government at the end of the 4th century in order to become a hermit.⁶ He attracted a number of disciples and began a series of missionary journeys to the wilder parts of Armenia and the Southern Caucasus. Though it was nearly 100 years since the establishment of Christianity in Western Armenia, the gospel had hardly yet penetrated to these outlying regions. In connection with his missionary activity Mashtots realised the need for a script to bring the gospel in the local tongue to these

---

¹ Cf. P. Ananian, "La data e le circostanze della consecrazione di S. Gregorio Illuminatore," Le Muséon, 74 (1961), p. 43–73 and 317–360. This date has gained wide acceptance (cf. M.-L. Chaumont, Recherches sur l'histoire d'Arménie, Paris 1969, p. 162, and C. Toumanoff, "The Third Century Armenian Arsacids," Revue des études arméniennes, N. S. 6 (1969), p. 272), but not universal approval (cf. B. MacDermot, "The Conversion of Armenia in 294 A. D.," Revue des études arméniennes, N. S. 7 (1970), p. 281–359).

² Faustos, III 13.

³ Cf. A. J. Festugière, Antioche paienne et chrétienne, Paris 1959, p. 108–9, and further references p. 522.

⁴ Cf. Faustos IV 4 (Nerses founds schools) and Moses Khorenatsi III 36 (Greek books are destroyed and the use of Greek is forbidden in favour of Persian by Merujan Artsruni).

⁵ For the ecclesiastical relations between Armenia and the Byzantine empire see G. Garitte, La Narratio de Rebus Armeniae, CSCO 132, Louvain 1952, and the copious bibliographies provided in his commentary.

⁶ The biography of Mashtots was written by his disciple Koriun in the 440's. The longer (more authentic) version and the shorter (a later rewriting) are printed

unhellenised areas[1]. He had in fact been forestalled in the invention of a script for Armenian by a Syrian bishop Daniel – an interesting sidelight on the activities of Syrian Christians in Armenia[2]. But this script, based on a semitic alphabet, proved inadequate and Mashtots fashioned a more satisfactory one based on Greek. The details of this new invention do not concern us here. What is significant is that, as Mashtots' pupil and biographer Koriun puts it: Armenia now for the first time became aware of the law of Moses, of the Prophets, of the Gospels and of the Pauline epistles in the Armenian tongue[3].

The first efforts of Mashtots, the patriarch Isaac, and their disciples were directed towards providing Armenian translations of the bible (the book of Proverbs being the first text translated with the new script)[4] and of the liturgy; soon followed the canons of the major councils and the fathers of the church. Pupils were set to learning the new script and a foreign language, and they were then sent abroad, to Edessa or Constantinople, in order to make translations.[5] But although Koriun mentions several of these first translators by name, he gives no details of the books that they translated. He does say that the false books of Theodore (of Mopsuestia) began to circulate in Armenia and were thrown out by the Patriarch Isaac and Mashtots.[6] Further light is thrown on this episode by another of Mashtots' pupils, Eznik, who had been sent to Edessa and then on to Constantinople as part of his training. The controversy over Theodore's theology had not reached Armenia until Acacius of Melitene had taken it upon himself to warn the Armenians after the council of Ephesus, at which no representative from Eastern Armenia had been present. While in Constantinople Eznik urged the patriarch Proclus to send an authoritative exposé of the teaching of Ephesus to Armenia, the famous *Tome to the Armenians*. But we are not so much concerned with the dogmatic controversies as with the influence of the Greek fathers. And in the correspondence surrounding this episode no mention is made of the orthodox fathers and their writings which might have been available in Armenian.[7]

---

together in the Lukasean Matenadaran vol. 13. Tiflis 1913. N. Akinean has produced a critical edition with commentary (Mechitar Festschrift, Vienna 1949 = Handes Amsorya vol. 63, reprinted as vol. 1, fasc. 1 of Texts and Studies in Early Literature, Vienna 1952), but he has taken many liberties with the order of the text.

[1] Koriun, ed. of 1913, p. 11–12.
[2] Ibid., p. 12. For the missionary activity of Jacob of Nisibis in Armenia cf. Faustos III 10.
[3] Koriun, p. 19.
[4] Ibid., p. 15. Koriun adds that this was the text he used as a pupil when learning to write.
[5] See especially Koriun, p. 30–31.
[6] Ibid., p. 37.
[7] These letters and the replies are preserved in the Book of Letters (cf. below p. 461), Tiflis 1901. For a translation and commentary on those of Acacius and Proclus see M. Tallon, "Livre des Lettres, 1er groupe: documents concernant les relations

One of the few early Armenian writers who does mention by name the Greek fathers whom he had studied is Lazar P'arpetsi. He was a very self-opiniated and cantakerous clergyman who ran into opposition at Etchmiadzin and was forced to leave the country. At the turn of the 5th and 6th centuries he wrote a defence to his patron, Vahan Mamikonian, the governor of Persian Armenia. In this self-righteous epistle[1] Lazar speaks of his education in the land of the Greeks (i. e. the Byzantine empire) and of the Greek fathers whom he had studied: these were Athanasius, the two Cyrils of Jerusalem and Alexandria, Basil and Gregory Nazianzenus.[2] Lazar also contrasts his knowledge of the scriptures, which his teachers had made him repeat three or four times, with the ignorance of those who did not even know the number of the canonical books. But unfortunately Lazar does not name the books that he considered canonical, nor does he mention their number.[3]

Lazar claimed to be familiar with the fathers he mentions in the original Greek. But it is possible on grounds of style to date the translation into Armenian of many patristic works to the fifth century.[4] However, it is difficult to dicover whether or not all such books were read by Armenian students or used by Armenian authors. In the following century also, little direct information can be gleaned. The historian Elisaeus, who wrote an account of the unsuccessful Armenian revolt against Sassanian Persia that was crushed in 451,[5] makes much of the rôle of the church and casts the whole episode in a religious mould. The book contains long speeches and letters which defend the Armenian Christian faith and which borrow extensively from other Armenian writings and from John Chrysostom and Eusebius.[6] But Elisaeus never mentions any of his sources, Greek or Armenian, by name. [The only book to which he refers explicitly is Maccabees, to the heroes of which he likens the Armenian soldiers.][7]

---

avec les grecs," Mélanges de l'Université saint Joseph, vol. 32, fasc. 1, Beirut 1955. Cf. also M. Richard, "Acace de Mélitène, Proclus de Constantinople et la Grande Arménie," Mémorial Louis Petit, Bucarest 1948, p. 393—412.

[1] This is usually printed after his History of the Armenians; critical edition by G. Ter-Mkrtchean and St. Malkhasean, Tiflis 1904.

[2] Lazar, ed. of. 1904, p. 192.

[3] Ibid., p. 201. With regard to the canon, it is interesting to note that the Armenian version of the 60th canon of Laodicaea omits Esther, Baruch and Lamentations, but adds Maccabees (no number of books is given) after Daniel. See Kanonagirk' Hayots I, ed. V. Hakobyan, Erevan 1964, p. 241. This compilation of canon law is attributed to John of Odzun, Catholicos of Armenia in the early 8th century. On the importance of Maccabees in other Armenian writers see note 7 below.

[4] See, for example, N. Akinean, "The golden age of Armenian literature," Handes Amsorya, 46 (1932), col. 105—128 (in Armenian).

[5] But the History may not have been written before the early 7th century. See N. Akinean, Elishe (in Armenian, three volumes, German summaries to vols I and II), Vienna 1932, 1936, 1960.

[6] Cf. Akinean, op. cit., vol. II, p. 627—643.

[7] Critical edition by E. Ter-Minasean, Erevan 1957, p. 105. There are also many reminiscences of Maccabees in the History of Agathangelos.

The most important source for the 6th century is the *Book of Letters*.[1] This is a compilation of a later date which brings together much of the official correspondence between the Armenian patriarchs and bishops and the Greeks, Syrians, and Georgians. Of particular interest to our present enquiry is the correspondence between the Armenians and the Syrians at the time of the two councils of Dvin (505 and 555) when the Armenian attitude to the council of Chalcedon crystalized. In these letters we have a plethora of reference to the heretics, most frequently the so-called "Nestorians" who followed the teaching of Diodore, Theodore, Theodoret, Ibas and other misguided fathers.[2] (In 555 the *Tome* of Leo and Severus are also anathematized.)[3] Only Cyril of Alexandria's *Twelve Chapters* and the *Henotikon* of Zeno are mentioned by title in this correspondence as containing authoritative teaching,[4] but we have a long list of other blessed fathers which is of some interest: Ignatius, Athanasius, Basil, Gregory the Great (i. e. Nazianzenus) and his two homonyms, Julius, "leader of the Western road to life", Ambrose, John (Chrysostom), Atticus, Theophilus, and Proclus.[5] This is a curious list. Athanasius, Basil, the Gregories, John Chrysostom and Cyril of Alexandria are often mentioned and were already well known in Armenia. Atticus was patriarch of Constantinople when Mashtots visited the Byzantine capital,[6] and Proclus, his successor, was revered for the letter concerning the council of Ephesus and Theodore of Mopsuestia.[7] Ignatius and Theophilus (of Alexandria?) are rarely mentioned by Armenian writers, though translations of some of their works in Armenian are known.[8] The reference to Julius is presumably to the Apollinarian forgeries which were attributed to him and included in Timothy Aelurus' florilegium.[9] But the reference to Ambrose is unique and most puzzling.

In the same letter that contains this list, written in 505 by Babgen patriarch of Armenia, there are also references to the authoritative writing of Ampelis of Cherson and Anatolius the pious priest. This may be a confusion of Timothy Aelurus' brother Anatolius who accompanied him on his exile to Cherson; the writing would then be the famous *Refutation of the Council of*

---

[1] Cf. note p. 459, note 7.
[2] Book of Letters, p. 46.
[3] Ibid., p. 56.
[4] Ibid., p. 49.
[5] Ibid., p. 50–51.
[6] Koriun, p. 25.
[7] Cf. p. 459, and note 7.
[8] Cf. G. Zarphanalean, Catalogue des anciennes traductions arméniennes, siècles IV–XIII (in Armenian), Venice 1889, s. v. Ignatius and Theophilus.
[9] The compliment paid to Julius may be paralleled in the remark in Elisaeus, p. 72: "... the Christian faith which was received from the patriarch of Rome." But here the reference is probably to the New Rome, since Tiridates "who was brought up in the land of the Greeks" is mentioned immediately preceding.

462

Chalcedon by Timothy.[1] Whether this identification is correct or not, the anti-Chalcedonian florilegium was translated into Armenian fifty years later in connection with the second council of Dvin.[2] This translation proved most significant for later Armenian literature, not only in providing a source book, but especially because it served as a model for similar florilegia in Armenian.

The first such original Armenian collection, the *Seal of Faith*, was put together in the early 7th century, during the pontificate of the Catholicos Komitas.[3] The *Seal of Faith* has often been ransacked for the fragments of lost works that it contains (e. g. Irenaeus);[4] the texts it quotes have been used as valuable early witnesses to the text of known works; and studies have been made of the tendentious alterations that many of these texts underwent.[5] But the question that is of most concern to our present enquiry does not seem to have been discussed. Did the Armenian compiler take his fragments from earlier collections of the same ilk, or did he make his own selection from the texts in his library? And if he followed the latter procedure, at least in some cases, did he translate that passage from a Greek manuscript, or did he have a previously existing Armenian translation before him? The *Seal of Faith* included extracts from 10 works composed in Armenian[6], from two Syrian writers, Ephrem and Philoxenus, and from 25 authors whose works were originally composed in Greek. From these 25 we have to exclude Timothy Aelurus, whose *Refutation* was quoted from the Armenian translation, and those other texts taken from the same florilegium. But we are left with quite an impressive list. A comparison of the quotations with the Armenian translations of the complete texts reveals that the following Armenian texts were used by the compiler. The list does not contain many surprises, but it does offer confirmation of the use of Armenian versions rather than Greek originals in the early 7th century.[7]

---

[1] This is the theory of the editor of the Seal of Faith, p. lxiiff. (On this work see note 3 below). The Armenian version of Timothy's Refutation was published by K. Ter-Mekerttschian and E. Ter-Minassiantz, Timotheus Aelurus Widerlegung, Leipzig 1908.

[2] For bibliography on the date of this translation see Garitte, Narratio, p. 163—5.

[3] Knik' Hawatoy, ed. K. Ter-Mkrtchean, Etchmiadzin 1914. Cf. J. Lebon, "Les citations patristiques grecques du *sceau de la foi*," Revue d'histoire ecclésiastique, 25 (1929), p. 5—32.

[4] Cf. H. Jordan, Armenische Irenaeusfragmente, Texte und Untersuchungen, Band 36, Heft 3, Leipzig 1913.

[5] Cf. R. W. Thomson, "The Transformation of Athanasius in Armenian Theology," Le Muséon, 78 (1965), p. 47—69, esp. p. 59.

[6] There are quotations from nine authors (Agathangelos, Eznik, John Mandakuni, Sahak, Babgen, Nerses, John II Catholicos, Abraham, John Mayragometsi) and one refutation of heretics in credal form.

[7] In what follows the references to the Greek texts will be found in the article of Lebon; see note 3 above. For the Armenian versions of the various texts see Zarphanalean, p. 461, note 8. The article by M. Djanachian, "Les Arménistes et les

Athanasius: Of his authentic works, only the *Letter to Epictetus* (quoted in its entirety) is a worked over form of an earlier Armenian version. The extracts from the *Letter to the Antiochenes* and the *Contra Arianos III* are taken from Timothy's *Refutation*. Of the unauthentic works the entire *Dialogus IV de sancta Trinitate* is cited, but under the name of Basil. The text is less complete than that of the other MSS of this work in Armenian. The origin of the extracts from the *Contra Apollinarium I* is obscure; no complete Armenian text of this book is known, though *C. Apollinarium II* exists in several MSS. These extracts diverge from the Greek text. The extracts from the *De Cruce et Passione* bear no relation to the complete Armenian translation, though this is attributed to the "first translators."[1]

Basil of Caesarea: The compiler of the *Seal of Faith* drew on previous translations of the *Homilia de fide*, the *Homilia de gratiarum actione* and the *Homilia quod Deus non est auctor malorum*. These were drawn from an Armenian collection of Basil's homilies in the same order as they appear in the MSS. The quotation from the homily on Julitta also probably comes from this collection, but I have been unable to check this.

Cyril of Alexandria: Several works of Cyril's are quoted from Timothy's *Refutation*, but the entire *Explicatio XII capitum Ephesi* and part of *Letter LV* are taken from previous Armenian translations. The most interesting item by Cyril in the *Seal of Faith* is the *Commentary on the Epistle to the Hebrews*, which is quoted very extensively and which preserves more of the text than the extant Greek fragments[2].

Cyril of Jerusalem: The extracts from the *Catecheses* are all taken from the Armenian version made in the fifth century.

Dionysius the Areopagite: The *Seal of Faith* contains two quotations from the Areopagite which are taken from a previous translation; these are from the *Mystica theologia* ch. 4 and the *Epistle to Gaius*. Part of this second item is repeated again in a corrupted form. Also from ps. Dionysius is a quotation attributed to Hierotheus; again the Armenian version served as the source. Parts of this passage are repeated twice; once from the longer extract and

---

Mekhitaristes," Armeniaca, Mélanges d'études arméniennes, Venice 1969, p. 383 – 445, is helpful and gives references to the more recent literature though it naturally concentrates on the work of the Mechitarists. The bibliographies in J. Quasten's Patrology (Utrecht/Antwerp) are more inclusive and wide-ranging. By far the most complete reference work is H. S. Anasyan, Haykakan Matenagitut'iun (Armenian Bibliology), which gives full references to manuscripts as well as published texts, but to date only the first volume (A to Ar, Erevan 1959) has appeared. There is no "Armenian Patrology" to compare with what we have for Syriac or Georgian.

[1] According to a colophon cited in Zarphanalean, op. cit., p. 287. Cf. R. P. Casey, "Armenian manuscripts of St. Athanasius of Alexandria," Harvard Theological Review, 24 (1931), p. 43–59, esp. p. 52.

[2] Cf. J. Lebon, "Fragments arméniens du commentaire sur l'épitre aux Hébreux de saint Cyrille d'Alexandrie," Le Muséon, 44 (1931), p. 69–114 and 46 (1933), p. 237–246.

once from a completely different version. This second version was known to Stephen Imastaser, who quotes a longer passage containing the same fragment in his florilegium on the *Incorruptibility of the Flesh* in the early 8th century.[1]

Epiphanius: From Epiphanius there are several quotations of the *Ancoratus*. But as no Armenian version of this has yet been reported, it is impossible to say whether these extracts were culled from a Greek or an Armenian text. One fragment is also quoted in Timothy Aelurus' *Refutation*, but the two Armenian texts diverge widely, Timothy's being closer to the Greek.

Gregory Nazianzenus: The *Seal of Faith* gives many extracts from Gregory's *Orationes*. These were all taken from a previous Armenian translation which was carelessly done. The translator seems not to have understood Greek very well, and when one adds the corruptions that have crept into the transmission of the *Seal of Faith* to the obscurities of the first translation, the result is sometimes incomprehensible. Attributed to Gregory Nazianzenus are also two extracts from the *Oratio de deitate Filii et Spiritus sancti* of Gregory of Nyssa. What is interesting is that this work was included among the *Orationes* of Nazianzenus in at least some manuscripts of the original translation.

Gregory the Wonderworker: The *Seal of Faith* quotes the *De fide capitula XII* in its entirety, but I do not know whether the translation was made by the compiler. There are some extracts from this work in Timothy's *Refutation*, but the Armenian texts have no relation to each other. Of the κατὰ μέρος πίστις, an Apollinarian work attributed to Gregory, the extracts are all taken from the Armenian version of Timothy.

Gregory of Nyssa: From Gregory of Nyssa the *Seal of Faith* gives extracts from a previous Armenian translation of the *De hominis opificio* and the *De oratione dominica*. Extracts from other works are copied from Timothy.

Irenaeus: The quotations from the *Demonstratio* and the *Adversus Haereses* are from the previous translation, but the *Seal of Faith* also offers four quotations from unidentified works attributed to Irenaeus.

John Chrysostom: From John the *Seal of Faith* gives many extracts. There are quotations from the *Commentary on Isaiah* which probably come from an earlier Armenian translation of the whole. Most of the Greek has perished, so it is not always clear whence the compiler of our florilegium took his text, for in places his extracts make better sense than the printed Armenian edition. On the whole the extracts and the full text are close, but in the quotations from scripture there are wide variants. With the *Commentary on Matthew* the situation is more complicated. The Armenian version represented by the published text is a very free rendering, but the translation in the *Seal of Faith* is much closer to the Greek. Two of the five

---

[1] Published by G. Ter-Mkrtchean, "Stephanosi Imastasiri Vasn Anapakanutʻean Marmnoyn, Ararat (Etchmiadzin), vol. 35 no. 3–4 (1902), p. 368–400.

extracts are also found in Timothy, and although the Armenian texts have variants between them they are too close to be entirely different translations. So unless the compiler of the *Seal of Faith* made his own translation, basing himself partly on the Armenian version of Timothy, there were already two different Armenian versions of this commentary circulating before the 7th century. The extract from the *Commentary on John* is too short for conclusions to be drawn with confidence, while for those from the commentaries on the *First Epistle to the Corinthians*, the *Epistle to the Hebrews*, and the *homilia VII dicta in templo Anastasiae* I have found no Armenian parallels. (The extract from the commentary on Romans is taken from Timothy.) The extracts from the two spurious homilies, *de fide* and *in crucem*, are taken from previous Armenian translations. Other spurious works attributed to Chrysostom are put under the name of John of Jerusalem in the *Seal of Faith*. These have no Armenian parallels, save one extract from the *expositio fidei*. This is quoted in its entirety by Timothy, and the same fragment is quoted in the 8th century by Stephen of Siunik in his florilegium on the *Incorruptibility of the Flesh*. But the three Armenian versions of this paragraph differ greatly.

Peter of Alexandria: The same short quotation as appears in Timothy, but the translations are quite different.

Proclus of Constantinople: The *Seal of Faith* gives an extensive quotation from Proclus' famous *Letter to the Armenians*. Unfortunately the Armenian text of this epistle in the *Book of Letters* is incomplete and lacks the first part from which these quotations are taken. There is no reason to suppose that the Armenian translation was not originally complete. To the *Homily on Easter*, from which two quotations are given in the *Seal of Faith*, there is no Armenian parallel.

Severian of Gabala: There are many quotations from the *Homilies* of Severian; these are taken from the previous Armenian translation. Another quotation from the homilies of Severian is attributed to Eusebius of Emesa, which is hardly surprising in view of the confusion between the works of these two fathers in Armenia.

After the early seventh century our information about the fathers studied in Armenia increases. In Sebeos the historian, who wrote soon after 661, there are quotations which perhaps show knowledge of the *Seal of Faith*.[1] Sebeos also refers to a writing of Gregory, used by the Armenians in a dogmatic controversy with Syrian and Georgian representatives before the Great King Khosrov in Ctesiphon.[2] Although one is tempted to associate

---

[1] Sebeos (Armenian text of Tiflis 1913, Lukasean Library no. 7) gives three quotations from Cyril's anathemas (p. 218) which may be taken from the Seal of Faith. But the texts have significant differences. Those texts found in the Armenian version of Timothy and the printed Armenian version of Cyril offer quite different translations.

[2] Sebeos, p. 197.

this with the work of Agathangelos, some Armenian scholars have equated this "writing" of Gregory with the *Seal of Faith*.[1] Sebeos repeats the familiar names of Athanasius, Basil, the three Gregories and others; and we find another such list of orthodox fathers in the canons attributed to John Mandakuni.[2] But only after the 7th century, beginning with Stephen of Siunik, have colophons survived attributing the translation of specific texts to specific scholars. In later times, as surviving colophons, letters and other sources become more plentiful, we can begin to reconstruct the libraries of certain individuals and of the monasteries and scriptoria where they worked. The 12th century is a particularly fruitful period to study in this regard as it was a time of renewed enthusiasm for the translation of Greek texts and a time of new and close contacts with the Latin West. Armenian monks and scholars mingled with the Greeks, Georgians, Syrians and Latins on the Black Mountain outside Antioch, and many colophons testify to the hunting down and translating of texts hitherto unknown in Armenian.

Unfortunately we lack such detailed information for the earlier period. And although we know some of the texts because they were used in dogmatic controversies, it is impossible to reconstruct the entire library of Greek fathers available in Armenian translation by the 7th century. Furthermore it is risky to rely on the names and titles quoted in the florilegia, for in these compilations, as in apologies and official letters, the same texts tend to recur, often with deliberate alterations. One may legitimately doubt whether the compilers of such documents were usually acquainted with the original texts. In the case of Athanasius, for example, the quotations and the complete texts circulated independently, and no one seems to have bothered to check the former against the latter. Had he done so, he might well have wondered if there were not two Athanasius, one a writer of the 4th century, the other an anti-Chalcedonian of Julianist tendencies.[3]

There is another type of Armenian compilation which so far has not been greatly explored. I refer to the catenae of biblical exegetical texts. These take various forms. Sometimes they are in the manner of questions and responses, with quotations from Greek, Syrian and Armenian writers thrown in. Others follow the biblical text more closely and intersperse the verses with commentaries from the fathers. In this way we have Armenian frag-

---

[1] See the discussion in the Preface to the Seal of Faith, p. xiiff. The later Stephen of Taron (Universal History, 2nd edition, St. Petersburg 1885, p. 94) adds that the History (*patmut'iun*, not writing, *gir*, as in Sebeos) of Gregory served as a proof for the Armenian position in the debate over the council of Chalcedon. The only council to which reference is made in the History of Agathangelos is Nicaea, but the theology of the Catechism in that work does support a rejection of "two natures." See R. W. Thomson, The Teaching of Saint Gregory, Cambridge, Mass. 1970, p. 19—20.

[2] Kanonagirk' (see p. 460, note 3), p. 496—7.

[3] Cf. p. 462, note 5.

ments of lost works (e. g. Apollinarius on Genesis and Leviticus).[1] But such collections are later than the period we are discussing and the question of their originality remains to be explored.

When we turn from the question of which patristic texts were available in Armenian to the question of which texts exercised a direct or indirect influence on original Armenian compositions, we find that surprisingly little work has been done. And even when patristic borrowings have been detected, we are often left with the problem whether the Armenian author was acquainted with the fathers in the original Greek (a language of which all educated Armenians had some command), or whether he relied on translations. As an example of the latter we may cite a treatise on meteorological signs attributed to the Armenian astronomer and mathematician Ananias of Shirak. In fact this tract is an almost verbatim rewriting of the Armenian version of Basil's *Hexaemeron*.[2] But such clear cut borrowings are rare. In Lazar and Moses Khorenatsi we find verbal reminiscences of the Armenian version of Eusebius' *Chronicle*. In Elisaeus there are verbal reminiscences of the Armenian translations of John Chrysostom and of Philo. But in most cases the borrowings have been so reworked that it is practically impossible to tell whether the author took his ideas from the original or from an Armenian version.

This problem arises in the study of the two works in 5th century Armenian literature that depend the most on patristic texts. The best known and most studied of these is the treatise of Eznik, a pupil of Mashtots whom we have already mentioned. This treatise survived in a single MS without title. By its first editor it was named "Refutation of the Sects", while in his more recent edition the late L. Mariès renamed it *De Deo*[3]. Eznik's theme is the problem of evil in a creation that is by nature good. He develops his argument by refuting the major philosophical and religious systems that gave evil an independent existence: gnostic philosophy, the Zurvanite interpretation of Zoroastrianism, and Marcion's theology. What is of particular interest to us is the way in which Eznik used and adapted a wide range of Greek and Syriac sources. He never mentions these by name, but studies over many years have shown that they include Methodius and Adamantius, Aristides, Basil, Diodore of Tarsus, Epiphanius, Hippolytus and Ephrem. There are also reminiscences of other Greek writers[4]. But Eznik was acquainted with his sources in their original languages. And although he may also

---

[1] As in Venice, Mechitarist library, no. 219, where the fragments show no correlation with those in the catena published by Nicephorus, Leipzig 1772.

[2] Cf. H. T'orosean in Bazmavep, 54 (1896), p. 214—221, and G. V. Abgaryan, "Concerning the work *On Clouds and Signs* attributed to Shirakatsi," Patmabanasirakan Handes (Erevan), 1971 no. 1 (= no. 52), p. 77—94.

[3] L. Mariès, Eznik de Kolb, De Deo, Patrologia Orientalis, vol. 28, fasc. 3 and 4, Paris 1959.

[4] See L. Mariès, Le *De Deo* d'Eznik de Kolb, études de critique littéraire et textuelle, Paris 1924, extrait de la Revue des études arméniennes, vol. 4, fasc. 1.

have been the translator of some of these texts from Greek into Armenian, his book in no way promoted the study of these Greek writers in Armenia. In fact his treatise was little known, it was rarely quoted by later Armenian authors, and in nearly every respect it was not only unique but unrecognised in Armenian literature.

More interesting from our point of view are the theological sections in the *History* of Agathangelos. This *History* purports to describe the conversion of Armenia to Christianity and the activity of Gregory the Illuminator. The longest section of this curious book takes the form of a sermon or catechism supposedly preached by Gregory to the Armenian court. It rapidly surveys the creation of the world, the origin of sin, the prophecies of and O. T. parallels to the life of Christ, the birth, death and resurrection of Christ, and the life of the spirit in the church. This text may be dated to the mid-5th century, a decade or two after Eznik's work. Because it purported to be the traditional and authoritative teaching of Saint Gregory the Illuminator, this long sermon was frequently quoted by later writers and it played a significant rôle in the formulation of a specifically Armenian theology.

Like Eznik, Agathangelos never mentions his sources by name, nor does he quote them verbatim. But it can be shown that he is indebted to a number of the better known Greek fathers. For his exposition of the creation of the world the *Commentaries on Genesis* by John Chrysostom and the *Hexaemeron* of Basil provided much information. In his discussion of O. T. prophecies and parallels Agathangelos drew on the *Catecheses* of Cyril of Jerusalem. Athanasius, Eusebius of Caesarea, the two Gregories of Nazianzen and Nyssa, and especially Cyril of Alexandria all had an influence on the theology of this catechism[1]. Unfortunately, however, we cannot tell whether Agathangelos was using Armenian translations of these fathers or was acquainted with the originals. Even more than Eznik he has reworked his borrowings so that one cannot compare his text directly with the known Armenian versions. For example, of 32 close parallels between Agathangelos and Cyril of Jerusalem, not one has identical wording with the Armenian version. But extensive knowledge of Greek literature (and of Syriac also) in the original texts was usual amongst Armenian writers of the early period, most of whom had lived and studied abroad for considerable periods of time.

The influence of Greek patristic writers was not confined to providing ideas and interpretations which Armenian authors could adapt to their own purposes. The fathers also provided Armenian authors with models – or perhaps it would be more accurate to say, a specific outlook and attitude towards the basic source material. We cannot here survey all the various kinds of early Armenian literature. Even leaving out of consideration all the technical, scientific, philosophical and grammatical texts which are based on Greek sources and Greek methods, we still have a large amount of homil-

---

[1] See the Introduction to the Teaching of Saint Gregory (as p. 466, note 1).

etic and exegetical literature, as well as all the dogmatic treatises. But the most interesting and original compositions in early Armenian literature are undoubtedly the various histories. The Armenians may not have produced a Thucydides, but they can boast of a large number of creditable historians who are of more than parochial interest.

The self-avowed purposes of the Armenian historians were basically two: to present an ordered narrative of the worthy and glorious deeds of past generations, and to offer their readers an edifying narrative which would deter men from following impious ways and show them the eventual blessings that are enjoyed by those who suffer for the sake of Christ and his church. In both regards they were heavily indebted to Eusebius. For the idea of history as a profitable and edifying narrative we could quote Elisaeus' final sentence: "This memorial has been written concerning him (i. e. the villain of the book, Vasak), in order to reprove his sins, so that everyone who hears and learns of this may heap curses on him and not become an admirer of his deeds." Lazar in his Introduction explains that he wishes to expound how many of the most illustrious Armenians gave up their lives for the church, how the clergy were martyred for their faith, and how those who apostatised inherited the eternal fire prepared for Satan and his companions. Such motives are in the spirit of Eusebius' *Ecclesiastical History*, one of the first books to be translated into Armenian, and can be paralleled not only in Eusebius' preface but even more clearly in Book VIII 2.3: "We shall add to the general history only those things that may be profitable, first to ourselves and then to those who come after us."

Of equal significance was Eusebius' *Chronicle*, though this was perhaps not translated until the end of the 6th century.[1] After that time it was quoted repeatedly, and it formed the basic source for the sections in Moses Khorenatsi and later writers that deal with the ancient past of the world outside Armenia. The influence of Eusebius' emphasis on strict chronology finds its classic expression in the dictum of Moses Khorenatsi: "There is no true history without chronology."[2] The *Chronicle* of Eusebius also served as a mine for curious antiquarian information. One example will suffice. In the *History* of Agathangelos there are some brief references to the heroic exploits of king Tiridates while he was in exile, before his restoration to the Armenian throne and his conversion to Christianity. Amongst other things Tiridates is supposed to have distinguished himself at the Olympic games. Moses elaborates on this by comparing Tiridates to two earlier athletes and by claiming that his hero could subdue with one hand twice the number of bulls that they could subdue with two hands. The names of these athletes were taken (at random) from the list of Olympic victors given in Eusebius' *Chronicle*.[3]

---

[1] Cf. J. Karst, Die Chronik des Eusebius, GCS 20, Leipzig 1911, p. xxxiv–xxxviii, though he admits that Lazar was familiar with it.

[2] Eusebius, Chronicle, par. 2; Moses, II 82.

[3] Agathangelos, § 202; Moses, II 79.

The influence of the fathers in early Armenian literature is thus all pervasive and goes beyond what one might be tempted to call "strictly theological" texts. The reasons are clear. The Armenian alphabet was invented as an aid to missionary activity. The first generations of translators and writers were monks and bishops; and though their interests were wide, they brought to their work a religious viewpoint and a religious training. Except in the scientific field, there were no lay authors for many hundreds of years. It is perhaps curious that the interest shown in Greek literature during the first century B. C. by Armenians should have borne no fruit. The son of Tigranes the Great, Artavazd, who ruled after him, had quite a reputation as a Greek writer.[1] But this Hellenistic veneer was as artificial as it was thin.

No school of pre-Christian Armenian literature ever developed. When in the 5th century A. D. a native Armenian literature burst into sudden bloom we find the Armenian writers thinking in Christian terms and using Christian models in their descriptions of a society that was basically Iranian. So, although Armenian literature has preserved many texts of interest to the patristic scholar, even more important is a knowledge of the Greek and Syriac fathers for those who would study the Armenian writers for their own sake.

---

[1] Cf. Plutarch, Crassus, 33. On the whole question of Armenian literature before the invention of the Armenian script see G. Kh. Sargsyan, "Historiography in the pre-Mesrop period," Patma-banasirakan Handes (Erevan), 1969 no. 1 (= no. 44), p. 107–126.

Additional Note: The influence of Basil of Caesarea's *Hexaemeron* in Armenia has been studied by K.M. Muradyan, *Barseł Kesarac'in ev nra 'Vec'orean' hay matengrut'yan mej*, Erevan 1976. The same author published a critical edition of the Armenian text, *Yałags vec'awreayArarč'ut'ean*, Erevan 1984, without acknowledging that this Armenian text had been translated from the Syriac version, not directly from the Greek. This had long been suspected and was first demonstrated conclusively by L. Ter-Petrosyan. See now R.W. Thomson, 'The Syriac and Armenian Versions of the *Hexaemeron* by Basil of Caesarea', *Eleventh International Conference on Patristic Studies*, Oxford 1991, Studia Patristica XXVII [1993], 113–117.

XIII

THE TRANSFORMATION OF ATHANASIUS
IN ARMENIAN THEOLOGY
(A TENDENTIOUS VERSION OF THE *EPISTULA AD EPICTETUM*)

Athanasius enjoyed a high reputation among Armenian theologians. His authority was as great as that of Basil of Caesarea, the two Gregories of Nyssa and Nazianzen, Cyril of Alexandria or John Chrysostom, and he was invariably included in lists of orthodox Fathers and of those whose teaching refutes the impieties of Nestorius, Eutyches, Paul of Samosata and other heretics [1]. Many of his works were translated, some in the earliest period of Armenian literature, and quotations from them figure prominently in catenae and apologetic writings. The value of these early translations for the study of the original Greek text was recognised long ago [2]; but it does not seem to have been noticed that the Athanasius known to the Armenians was different from the Athanasius familiar to modern Patristic students. He was known as one who had spent his life fighting the dyophysites, dedicated to the cause : « one nature of the incarnate Word ».

From soon after Athanasius' death his works were handed down in two groups, the Ἀπολογίαι and the Λόγοι [3]. The former do not seem to have been translated into either Syriac or Armenian, nor are there Oriental versions of all the Λόγοι. On the other hand, a vast mass of spurious documents was attributed to Athanasius, and the Syriac and Armenian literatures abound in forgeries, both translations from Greek and original compositions. The history of these curious documents (which include a « vision » of Athanasius and the like) has not yet been written, but it was largely on the basis of such works that Athanasius' reputation in the East was founded.

---

[1] Cf. the frequent references to Athanasius as an authority in the documents in the *Book of Letters* (Tiflis, 1901).

[2] Cf. F. C. CONYBEARE, *On the Sources of the Text of St. Athanasius*, Journal of Philology, XXIV (1895), p. 284-299; J. LEBON, *Pour une édition critique des œuvres de S. Athanase*, Revue d'Histoire ecclésiastique, XXI (1925), p. 524-530.

[3] The basic work on the Greek manuscripts of Athanasius' works is H.-G. OPITZ, *Untersuchungen zur Überlieferung der Schriften des Athanasius* (*Arbeiten zur Kirchengeschichte* 23), Berlin, 1935; see esp. p. 142.

The Λόγοι circulated in collections rather than singly. In Armenian three *corpora* of Athanasian writings are known, but they bear no relation to the Greek *corpora* [4]. Like the only known collection of *Athanasiana* in Syriac [5], they were compiled from individual versions already made and not translated as complete collections. This is clear from the diversity of style and vocabulary in the different items in these *corpora*, some being idiomatic and careful renderings of the Greek, others slavishly literal, and others paraphrases rather than direct translations. Some pieces exist in more than one version and the differences between these versions point to the contemporary tendencies and allegiances of the Armenian translators. One text in particular illustrates the changes which polemic considerations might effect, even in a genuine work. This is the version of the Letter to Epictetus found in the collection of *Athanasiana* published by Tayezi [6]. We are unusually fortunate with this letter in that a critical edition of the Greek has been made [7] (though more Greek manuscripts have come to light since it appeared) and the Syriac version [8] and the literal Armenian version [9] have also been published. So we are able to assess the idiosyncrasies of the Armenian and isolate individual characteristics. The entire letter is also included in the *Seal of Faith* [10], a

[4] These are described by R.P. CASEY, *Armenian Manuscripts of Athanasius*, Harvard Theological Review, XXIV (1931), p. 43-59.

[5] Cf. R. W. THOMSON, *The Text of the Syriac Athanasian Corpus*, in Biblical and Patristic Studies in Memory of R.P. Casey, Freiburg, 1963, esp. p. 252-253.

[6] Ս. Աթանասի Հատոր, Venice, 1899, p. 324-343.

[7] G. LUDWIG, *Athanasii Epistula ad Epictetum*, Jena, 1911.

[8] The text is in the Ms. British Museum Add. 14557 and has been published by P. BEDJAN, *Nestorius, Le Livre d'Héraclide*, Paris, 1910, p. 577-593. Cf. J. LEBON, *Altération doctrinale de la Lettre à Épictète de S. Athanase*, Revue d'Histoire ecclésiastique, XXXI (1935), p. 713-761. The Syriac text with English translation of the *Ad Epictetum* will be included in the first volume of my *Athanasiana Syriaca* to appear this year.

[9] Published from the two Vienna corpora 629 and 648 by R.P. CASEY, *An Armenian Version of Athanasius' Letter to Epictetus*, Harvard Theological Review, XXVII (1933), p. 127-150.

[10] Կնիք Հաւատոյ, Ejmiacin, 1914, p. 57-70. Cf. H. JORDAN, *Armenische Irenaeusfragmente (Texte und Untersuchungen, 36. Band, Heft 3)*, Leipzig, 1913, p. 108-120; J. LEBON, *Les citations patristiques du « Sceau de la Foi »*, Revue d'Histoire ecclésiastique, XXV (1929), p. 5-32; G. GARITTE, *La Narratio de Rebus Armeniae* (CSCO 132, Subsidia 4), Louvain, 1952, p. 277.

THE TRANSFORMATION OF ATHANASIUS 49

seventh century catena of Julianist tendency, and this text is very close to that published by Tayezi. It does, however, show signs of having been worked over, and a few deliberate alterations may be discerned. As it appears to be secondary to the other Armenian text, its particular variants will be noted after the more important divergences from the Greek of both copies have been set forth.

Tayezi's version has been described as « loose and paraphrastic » [11]. In fact the whole text is an adaptation of the Greek rather than a strict translation, which makes it impossible to give a collation of the two. So the most notable divergences are given below in quotation. These quotations are typical in that they show how the original Greek (for the Armenian bears no relation to the Syriac) has been expanded; the extra length of the Armenian text was obtained not only by the stylistic device of using two or more words to render one of the Greek, but primarily by the insertion of new material. The translator had regard only to the general sense of the Greek and reset its periods as he fancied, elaborating some ideas and more rarely omitting a few phrases. So any theological tendency in the Armenian which diverges from the thought in the Greek text is not to be attributed to an unknown Greek manuscript which may have served as the translator's original, but to the translator himself. This is all the more certain as the other Armenian translations of the whole text and the Armenian version of Timothy Aelurus' quotations (in his *Widerlegung*) [12] render faithfully the known Greek text.

Here follow the major differences of the Armenian. The English translation has been made from Tayezi's text and the Greek references are to the pages of Ludwig's edition and the columns of J. P. MIGNE, *Patrologia Graeca*, vol. 26.

(1) § 2. (Ludwig 4.10-5.1; P.G. 26.1052C-1053A; Tayezi 326.17-32)

$\tau a\hat{v}\tau a\ \delta\hat{\epsilon}\ \pi\acute{o}\theta\epsilon v\ \dots\ o\dot{v}\sigma\acute{\iota}a\ \tau\hat{\eta}s\ \sigma o\phi\acute{\iota}as$:

But this fire of wrath, whence has it come and sprung forth, or what Hell has belched forth to say that the body from Mary and the Word of God are one nature, or that the Word changed into flesh and bone or in every way

---

[11] CASEY, *An Armenian Version*, p. 128.
[12] Timotheus Älurus' *Widerlegung*, ed. K. TER-MEKERTTSCHIAN und E. TER-MINASSIANTZ, Leipzig, 1908. Cf. F. CAVALLERA, *Le dossier patristique de Timothée Aelure, Bulletin de Littérature ecclésiastique*, XI (1909), p. 342-359.

50

into the nature of a body, or was altered from his own nature? Or who has heard in the church or amongst all the believers that the Lord put on falsely the likeness and nature of our body? And <who> has been so impious as to say or suppose that the nature of the divinity, which was equal with the Father, was circumcised and became imperfect from perfection; and that what was nailed on the cross was not the body, but the very creative nature which was the wisdom of the Father?

(2) (Ludwig 5.11.12; P.G. 26.1053B; Tayezi 327.20-21)

ὁ ἐκ Μαρίας ⋯ τοῦ Θεοῦ ἐστιν:

. . that He who was born of Mary, Lord and Son, is equal with the Father according to the nature of the essence of the Godhead . .

(3) Ludwig 5.14-15; P.G. 26.1053B; Tayezi 327.24-26)

ὥστε εἰπεῖν τὸν Χριστὸν ⋯ μὴ εἶναι Κύριον:

. . so that they said of Christ, whose body suffered and was crucified, that He is not Lord . .

(4) § 4. (Ludwig 8.6; P.G. 26.1057A; Tayezi 330.12-13)

τροπὴν + and corruptibility.

(5) § 5. (Ludwig 8.19; P. G. 26.1057B; Tayezi 331.3)

ὅμοιον ἡμῖν σῶμα:

a body of our nature.

(6) (Ludwig 8.20; P.G. 26.1057B; Tayezi 331.5-7)

τοῦτο λάβῃ καὶ ὡς ἴδιον:

. . take the body of our nature from her and uniting it with the Word as his own . .

(7) (Ludwig 9.19-22; P.G. 26.1060A; Tayezi 332.14-22)

ἀλλ' ἐν τῷ περιτμηθέντι ⋯ τοῖς ἐν φυλακῇ πνεύμασιν:

But it appeared that it was the same true nature, the body which was circumcised and taken in arms (by Simeon — cf. Lk. 2.28), and which ate and drank and laboured and was nailed on the wood of the cross and suffered; and in the body was the impassible and incorporeal Word of God. This was the body which was placed in the tomb, and with it was God the Word who preached the deliverance and remission of sins to the spirits . .

THE TRANSFORMATION OF ATHANASIUS

(8) § 6. (Ludwig 10.6-10; P.G. 26.1060B; Tayezi 333.5-10)

καὶ τοῦτο Θωμᾶς ... ὁ Λόγος ὁ ἀσώματος:

And this body risen from the dead Thomas touched, and saw in it the places of the nails; but the Word Himself remained impassible, although He saw his own flesh being nailed, which He could have prevented — the nails and the sufferings of his own body — and He Himself was the invisible and impassible Word.

(9) (Ludwig 10.11; P.G. 26.1060B; Tayezi 333.13-14)

καὶ ἄψαυστος ὢν τῇ φύσει

and the untouchable and incomprehensible nature of the Word, considering as his own the condition of his own body . .

(10) (Ludwig 10.13-14; P.G. 26.1060C; Tayezi 333.16-19)

ἃ γὰρ τὸ ἀνθρώπινον ... εἰς ἑαυτὸν ἀνέφερεν:

. . because the Word's own body suffered, the Word who was united with the body considered it all as his own.

(11) (Ludwig 10.18-11.4; P.G. 26.1060C-1061A; Tayezi 333.26-334.16)

καὶ αὐτὸς μὲν ... τὸν Ἀπόστολον εἰπεῖν:

And the Incorporeal Himself was united to his passible body, and the impassible Word of God had the body united to Himself. He erased and destroyed the weakness of the corruption of the body's nature and clothed the body with incorruption. And having done this, and taking the body which was from us into union with Himself, bringing immortality to mortals by the immortal (Word), and offering his body as a sacrifice, He erased and destroyed death from the body and clothed the mortal with immortality. For the mortal could not restrain the immortal in death; but the immortal eliminated death, and uniting the mortal with the immortal made it immortal. And giving us through his own body such immortality, He lets his Apostle say . .

(12) § 7. (Ludwig 11.6-8; P.G. 26.1061A; Tayezi 334.20-26)

ὥς τινες πάλιν ... σωτηρία ἐγίνετο:

. . as some of the heretics say that the body was a likeness and not nature; but our Saviour really became a true man, and the Word of God united to Himself all our nature and granted salvation to the whole and complete nature of man.

XIII

52

(13) (Ludwig 12.10-11; P.G. 26.1061C; Tayezi 336.3-6)

ἀλλ' αὐτὸς ἔχων ... εἶναι πιστευθῇ:

But the Word Himself was in his body, united to the same flesh of ours both before death and after the resurrection; and thus was clearly preached to all believers by the Apostles.

(14) § 8. (Ludwig 12.13-16; P.G. 26.1061C; Tayezi 338.7-15)

τοῦ γὰρ σώματος ... ἐν σαρκὶ γενομένου:

For the body was united to the Word, and the divinity of the Word and the body were not one nature, but it was truly born from the holy Mother of God, Mary; and it was not that the Word of God was altered and changed into a body, but the Word was indissolubly united to his body which He took from the Virgin; and the uniting (*միաւորիլն*) shows the indissolubility and unity of the natures.

(15) (Ludwig 13.1-2; P.G. 26.1064A; Tayezi 338.26-29)

ἀλλ' ὅτι ... γέγονεν ἄνθρωπος:

. . but because the Word of God, taking a body for our sake, united it to Himself and became man; for this reason it was said that « the Word became flesh. »

(16) § 10. (Ludwig 16.9-15; P.G. 1068 A; Tayezi 340.11-31)

ναὸς δὲ ... γέγονεν ἄφθαρτον:

The body of God the Word suffered, and was filled and united with the Godhead of the Word. And the only begotten Son of God reckoned the sufferings of his body as his own, and was Himself unaffected and impassible in his own suffering body. Therefore the sun, seeing his creator, that is the Word, being crucified and the Lord's body being insulted, restrained the light of his rays and made the whole land dark. And again (regarding) the body of the Word of God which was a mortal body by nature; the Word who was in the body made his own body immortal and incorruptible above the nature of the mortal body, and united it <to Himself> and extirpated from the body natural death and corruption. Because the Word of God put on and united <to Himself> a body which was above human nature, therefore the corruptible body became an incorruptible body, and death was conquered in the nature of a mortal body, because by the Word of God life reigned in it.

(17) § 12 (Ludwig 17.18; P.G. 26.1068C; Tayezi 341.36)

ἄνθρωπος + perfect.

THE TRANSFORMATION OF ATHANASIUS 53

These quotations give an indication of the way in which the Armenian translator has rehandled his material. Although the Greek style of this letter is compressed in comparison with some of Athanasius' more discursive writings, it is clear that the expansions in the Armenian do not serve a merely literary purpose, nor do they only elucidate obscurities in the text. They take up and stress certain ideas which the translator considered important. What are these ideas?

The Word is equal with the Father in nature and essence [13]; He is by virtue of this divine nature impassible and incorruptible [14]. But the body was a true body born of Mary, and was no likeness or phantom [15]. This body and the Word Himself are not of the same nature [16], therefore the Trinity is not made a Quaternity. The Word did not change into a body [17], thereby becoming altered from his own nature (which is divine); rather He united the body to Himself, and considered its bodily affections and sufferings as his own [18]. This union of the two natures, of God the Word and the truly human body, is indissoluble [19].

The first proposition needs no demonstration. Athanasius' whole theology has as its basis the unity of the Trinity; the Son and the Holy Spirit are God, not created beings but co-eternal, co-essential and consubstantial with the Father. The testimony of the *De Incarnatione*, the *Contra Arianos* and the Letters to Serapion is conclusive.

The Word took a truly human body. This again is one of the cardinal points in Athanasius' theology, the corollary of the perfect divinity of the Logos. For at the basis of Athanasius' doctrine of redemption lies the understanding that if the body which the Word assumed had not been really human, of our $\varphi\acute{v}\sigma\iota\varsigma$ or $o\grave{v}\sigma\acute{\iota}\alpha$ (Athanasius considered these terms synonymous), then man would not have been saved. Redemption had to come from within man's nature and could not be effective if merely imposed on it from without.

[13] Cf. quotations 1 and 2 above.
[14] Cf. quotations 11 and 16.
[15] Cf. quotations 1, 12 and 14.
[16] Cf. quotations 1 and 14.
[17] Cf. quotations 1 and 14.
[18] Cf. quotations 6, 9, 10, 11, 12, 13, 14, 15 and 16.
[19] Cf. quotation 14.

XIII

54

Only one expression in the Armenian of the *Ad Epictetum* betrays a non-Athanasian expression in this particular connection. In § 12 to the phrase ἐκ δὲ Μαρίας αὐτὸς ὁ Λόγος ἑαυτῷ σάρκα λαβὼν προῆλθεν ἄνθρωπος is added «perfect» (...ծնունդ մարդ կատարեալ). Athanasius never used this expression [20]; it occurs in the printed text of the *De Incarnatione et contra Arianos* (P.G. 26.996 C), but is the result of an interpolation in many Greek manuscripts. All the versions (Armenian, Syriac, Latin) omit ἄνθρωπος τέλειος as do the Greek manuscripts A B F K W Z c [21].

The humanity of Christ being thus assured, Athanasius thought that it would be quite ridiculous to suppose that the body of Christ was a phantom or illusion. For example, in the *De Incarnatione*, § 18, he wrote: ὅταν τοίνυν ἐσθίοντα καὶ πίνοντα καὶ τικτόμενον αὐτὸν λέγωσιν οἱ περὶ τούτου θεολόγοι, γίνωσκε ὅτι τὸ μὲν σῶμα, ὡς σῶμα, ἐτίκτετο καὶ καταλλήλοις ἐτρέφετο τροφαῖς... (περὶ τούτου is omitted by the Syriac version). Nor could it be said that the Word *was* the body or had turned into the body. For Athanasius, the divine and the human are radically opposed. The body is not the Word; if it were also divine there would be a Quaternity in place of the Trinity.

So far the elaborations of the Armenian text have been in accord with Athanasius' own ideas. But the same cannot be said of the stress laid on the Word's *uniting* the body to Himself or of the *union of the two natures*. Athanasius was never so precise in defining the connection between the Word and the body as our Armenian version would have us suppose. He spoke generally in vague terms: the word took (ἔλαβε, συνεστήσατο, πλάττει, κατασκευάζει) a body from the Virgin; He put it on (πεφόρηκεν, ἐνεδύσατο) and dwelt in it (ἐνοικεῖ, συνῆν) as if it were a temple (ναός), and used it as an instrument (ὄργανον) [22]. Somewhat more precise is the expression συναφή (*Contra Arianos* II, PG.

---

[20] Athanasius did use the expression τελείωσιν of the body of the Word (*c. Arianos*, III, § 22), but ἄνδρα τέλειον in the same paragraph is a quotation from Eph. 4.13 and does not refer to Christ Himself (cf. *c. Arianos*, II, § 74).

[21] Cf. THOMSON, *Text*, p. 257.

[22] These expressions are too frequent in Athanasius for complete references to be given here; see the various entries in G. MÜLLER, *Lexicon Athanasianum*, Berlin, 1944-1952.

26.296 B) [23], but to Athanasius ἰδιοποιεῖσθαι was more congenial. He uses this word frequently both of the body directly (e.g. *De Incarnatione*, P.G. 25.109 C and D) and of the properties of the body (e.g. *Contra Arianos* III, P.G. 26.393 B; *Ad Epictetum*, P.G. 26.1060 B).

What is particularly instructive, however, is the number of expressions describing the junction or union of the Word with the body found in books which are generally included among Athanasius' works, but which are almost certainly not by his own hand. In the fourth book of the *Contra Arianos*, for example, we find σύναψις (P.G. 26.501 B) and συναφθείς (P.G. 26.517 B) used of the union between Word and body. This term also occurs in the *Contra Apollinarium* II (P.G. 26.1145 B), but Athanasius himself only used it of the connection between men and the Father or Logos (e.g. *De Incarnatione* P.G. 25.140 A). Similarly the terms ἕνωσις or ἑνωθείς only occur in spurious works, the *Contra Arianos* IV (P.G. 26.524 B), the *Contra Apollinarium* I (P.G. 26.1100 A) and the *De Incarnatione et contra Arianos* (P.G. 26.996 C). (These last two works are probably to be ascribed to disciples or close followers of Athanasius) [24].

Therefore when the Armenian version stresses repeatedly the union of Word and body and mentions the union of the two natures, it is clear that the translator (or perhaps he should rather be titled adaptor) was influenced by the later development of this term. It was not until after Athanasius' death that the widespread use of this expression began to cover conflicting dogmatic positions. Irenaeus' phrase ἕνωσις... καθ'ὑπόστασιν φυσική [25] was taken up by Cyril of Alexandria. According to him, the humanity and divinity of Christ united to form a ἑνότης φυσική, although in normal speech and to mortal understanding the divine and the human are incompatible. This ἑνότης φυσική or ἑνότης καθ'ὑπόστασιν was sharply opposed by Cyril to the ἕνωσις κατὰ συν-

---

[23] But in the *De Incarnatione*, § 17 (P.G. 25.125 C), Athanasius denies that the Λόγος συνεδέδετο τῷ σώματι; he adds : μᾶλλον αὐτὸς ἐκράτει τοῦτο, ὥστε καὶ ἐν τούτῳ ἦν.

[24] Except once in the *Ad Epictetum* § 9. But it was clearly not a technical term for Athanasius since he combined it with κοινωνία.

[25] Fragment 28, P.G. 7.1244 C.

άφειαν²⁶, the expression preferred by the Antiochenes, and the classic expression of his mode of thinking is the μία φύσις τοῦ Θεοῦ Λόγου σεσαρκωμένη. This Cyril made his own, mistakenly supposing the *De Incarnatione Dei Verbi* from which it was taken to be by Athanasius ²⁷.

Both Cyril and the Antiochenes could refer to the two φύσεις of the one Christ, but there was a basic difference between them in their understanding of the meaning of φύσις and the relation between the ἕνωσις (or incarnation) and the two natures. Both recognised the full divinity and full humanity of Christ, but in opposition to Cyril's conception of a hypostatic or natural union of the two, Theodoret, for example, denied that two natures could be so joined. For the refutation of those who said that the divinity and humanity were one nature he composed his *Eranistes*, where he wrote in no uncertain terms : μία δὲ φύσις πρὸ τῆς ἑνώσεως ἤγουν σαρκώσεως ἦν, μετὰ δέ γε τὴν ἕνωσιν, δύο λέγειν προσήκει, τὴν τε λαβοῦσαν καὶ τὴν ληφθεῖσαν. Theodoret's position rested on the basic assumption that Christ is Θεὸς φύσει καὶ ἄνθρωπος φύσει. But Athanasius had always been careful to say only that Christ took human nature upon Himself or to employ kindred expressions; he never said Christ *is* human by nature. His guarded references to the divine nature of the Word were reinforced by the explicit declarations in the forgeries attributed to him. So, secure in the assumed authority of Athanasius, Cyril proclaimed the μία φύσις τοῦ Θεοῦ Λόγου σεσαρκωμένη and later monophysite writers followed his example. Yet the Antiochenes could also claim Athanasius' authority, for he had used συνάφεια ²⁸, the favourite expression of Nestorius.

The expressions « united » and « union of the two natures » were thus employed by both sides in the Christological controversies, but the variants in the Armenian text of the *Ad Epictetum* tend towards the interpretation of Cyril's. It seems unlikely that

---

[26] Cf. *Epistola 17*, anathema *3* (P.G. 77.120 C) and *Homilia Paschalis* 17, § 3 (P.G. 77.784 A).

[27] In the *De recta Fide ad Reginas*, quoting from the περὶ σαρκώσεως Λόγου attributed to Athanasius (P.G. 76.1212 A).

[28] But unlike συναφή or συνάψις, συνάφεια was only used by Athanasius of the union between the Logos and the Father (*De Sententia Dionysii*, P.G. 25.504 D; also in the (pseudo-) *c. Arianos*, IV, PG. 26.492 B). The Arians assumed a διάστημά τι μεταξὺ τῆς συναφείας (*De Synodis*, P.G. 26.733 B).

the translator would have introduced his tendentious emphasis on the indissoluble union of the two natures until this had become a serious theological issue in Armenia, yet the term « united » in a Christological context was not unknown to the early Armenian theological tradition. It occurs in the *Teaching of Gregory* which is probably to be dated before Chalcedon, but there is usually coupled with the more common word « mingled »[29]. A little later John Mandakuni (Catholicos 478-490) wrote in his discourse on the Trinity : « God became man... the Word and the man were united in the flesh and divinity, the Word being God by essence (բուն էութեանն) »[30]. He echoed the same thought in his Demonstration, defining the nature of the Word as the divinity[31]. John composed this *Demonstration* to prove that one could only speak of one nature in Christ after the union; the humanity of Christ might be called human nature, but Christ is a single person[32]. He therefore did not distinguish between φύσις and ὑπόστασις in the manner defined at Chalcedon. The influence of Cyril is most noticeable in the title of this work, but Cyril is not mentioned personally. His name is quoted as an authority only after the first council of Dvin (505)[33].

Although the term « united » was traditional in Armenian theology, not until John Mandakuni do we hear of « two natures ». As for the expression « union of the two natures », it first occurs in the anathemas composed by Abdisho after his consecration as bishop in 555[34]. If, then, the Armenian translator was deliberately altering his original, as seems impossible to doubt, he was doing so to gain a show of authority for expressions which had but recently gained currency. Since it was not until the council of 505 that the Armenian

---

[29] The *Teaching* forms the longest section of the history of Agathangelos; cf. G. GARITTE, *Documents pour l'étude du Livre d'Agathange* (Studi e Testi 127), Vatican, 1946; R. W. THOMSON, *Some Philosophical Terms in the Teaching of Gregory*, Revue des Études arméniennes, N.S. I (1964), p. 41-46. In the *Teaching* the terms միացաւ and խառնեալ occur frequently (e.g. § 369, 385, 515, 592, 679) and the combined expression խառնեալ միայոյց ընկղմեալ զմարմին յԱստուածութեան իւրում in § 378.

[30] Յովհաննու Մանդակունւոյ Ճառք, Venice, 1860, p. 213.
[31] *Book of Letters*, p. 33.
[32] *Ibid.*, p. 35.
[33] *Ibid.*, p. 49.
[34] *Ibid.*, p. 67, 68.

58

church found its rallying point in a national theology of monophysite tendency and such expressions were officially adopted, it is unlikely that this adulterated translation of the *Ad Epictetum* was made before that date. It was certainly in circulation before the next century when an adapted version of it was included in the *Seal of Faith*.

The Armenian version of the *Ad Epictetum* represented by the texts in Tayezi (T) and the *Seal of Faith* (K) is totally dissimilar from the literal translation found in the two Armenian corpora of *Athanasiana* (A and B — Vienna 627 and 648), but one difference in terminology has some relevance to the present discussion: this is the way in which οὐσία and ὁμοούσιος are rendered. Where οὐσία stands alone, all four texts translate it by բնութիւն (e.g. Ludwig, 5.2; 9.15; 14.2); this term is also used for φύσις (Ludwig, 4.13 etc.). Since for Athanasius οὐσία and φύσις were synonymous, no obscurity arises from the single term in Armenian. Where the Greek has οὐσία and φύσις together, then both Armenian versions distinguish them in the same way: բնութիւն and էութիւն. At 5.12 բնութիւն stands in place of οὐσία and էութիւն for φύσις, while at 17.18 the reverse is the case; but this is not significant, for in Armenian there were no fixed equivalents for these Greek technical terms (though էութիւն generally stood for οὐσία or ὑπόστασις rather than for φύσις). The important difference between AB and TK is in the way they render ὁμοούσιος; the former employ մբանական (4.11; 7.4; 8.8 etc.) or համաբնական (4.16). This latter is a literal translation of ὁμο-ούσιος, while մբանական was a traditional Armenian term. But TK render ὁμοούσιος by մի բնութիւն (one nature) and occasionally by հաւասար (equal), or by both terms together. At 14.8 it is translated by TK as մի բնութիւն և էութիւն ; but since Athanasius is here referring directly to Nicea, the expansion is probably due to a reminiscence of the Nicene creed and anathemas. In general when TK wish to translate ὁμοούσιος, the Greek is converted and becomes « one nature of the body and the Word » (4.11) or « one nature of the Word and the Father » (7.15). This periphrasis is most unusual; in Armenian ὁμοούσιος was rendered by a variety of words but the Greek phrasing was retained, so this variant reflects a conscious alteration. It seems most likely to have been adopted by a translator familiar with the Cyrillian μία φύσις and it fits in well with the general tendency of the variants in TK discussed above.

The version of the Letter to Epictetus in the *Seal of Faith* is basically the same as that published by Tayezi, but it has not suffered so much in transmission (though neither text is free from corruptions). However, there are a few passages where K has tendentious variants from both the Greek and the Armenian of T; these variants appear to have arisen as deliberate alterations to a previous Armenian text similar to T rather than to reflect a separate translation from the Greek. Since the compiler of the *Seal of Faith* was a theologian of the Julianist persuasion, it is not surprising to find that these variants concern the problem of the suffering of Christ.

The first of these variants is the most revealing. In § 2 K reads : (Ludwig 5.2; P.G. 26.1053 A; Tayezi 327.2; Seal of Faith 59.11) « Who heard it said that not from Mary but from his own nature the Word changed and made for Himself an *impassible* body...?» In § 6 (quotation no. 8 above, Seal of Faith 63.25) before the Armenian of Tayezi « and He Himself was the invisible and impassible Word », K adds : « and He was able to prevent the sufferings of his body or not prevent them, but He counted and considered as his own the sufferings of his own body ». The first phrase is exactly parallel to a fragment of Julian preserved in Severus' *Apologia pro Philalethe*[35]; the second phrase may be paralleled in the Armenian of T (quotations 9 and 10 above) and here may be simply an expansion of the Greek ἰδιοποιεῖτο τὰ τοῦ σώματος ἴδια ὡς ἑαυτοῦ. But the force of the expression « considered as his own » is much weaker than Athanasius' own words and may echo another idea of Julian's — the willingness of Christ to accept the sufferings implied by the incarnation, rather than the necessity of such suffering as a consequence of the human nature He took. The variant in § 6 (quotation 10 above), where instead of « the Word's own body suffered » K reads : « because the body suffered in the Word », is a curious inversion of the thought expressed just below by Athanasius : καὶ αὐτὸς μὲν ὁ ἀσώματος ἦν ἐν τῷ παθητῷ σώματι.

These alterations to the already tendentious version of the *Ad Epictetum* suggest that apologetic or polemic considerations might

---

[35] No. 77 in R. Draguet, *Julien d'Halicarnasse*, Louvain, 1924, p. 27*; cf. also p. 188.

prevail over strict faithfulness to the original texts and accuracy in copying them. We must now turn to later Armenian dogmatic works to see how these texts were respected, and which renderings proved most suitable for the purposes of their authors.

*
* *

The Armenian tradition concerning the translation of Athanasius' works is preserved in a colophon of unknown origin [36]. It states that seventeen treatises were rendered into Armenian by « the first translators » and a further five by Stephen, bishop of Siunik, at the order of John Odznetsi. These five are : the *De Incarnatione Dei Verbi* (P.G. 28.25) ; the *Ad Jovianum* (P.G. 28.532) ; the *Quod Unus sit Christus* (P.G. 28.121) ; the Homily on John 12.27 (P.G. 26.1240) ; and the *Contra Apollinarium II* (P.G. 26.1132). It has been suggested that these were translated as part of the preparation for the synod of Manazkert [37]; as the works of Julian of Halicarnassus were translated for that council [38], the suggestion is plausible. However, it seems that the evidence of this colophon may be questioned. The fact that the seventeen translations attributed to the « first translators » betray differences of style and idiom, and that some must be placed no earlier than the seventh century, does not of itself invalidate the tradition of the colophon, as, in Casey's words, « it seems likely that they were texts current in Armenia before the eighth century, which a natural but mistaken enthusiasm assigned to the golden age of Armenian literature » [39]. More serious, however, is the fact that three of the translations supposedly made by Stephen are quoted in Armenian before he became bishop of Siunik and before John of Odzun became Catholicos.

[36] It is quoted by G. ZARBANALIAN, *Catalogue des anciennes traductions arméniennes* (Հայկական թարգմանութիւնք նախնեաց) Venice, 1889, p. 287, but he gives no indication from which Ms. he took it. The colophon is reproduced in translation by Casey (*Armenian Manuscripts*, p. 52-53) and the order of the treatises mentioned in it compared to the three known Armenian corpora (*ibid.*, p. 55).

[37] CASEY, ibid., p. 53, note 21.

[38] According to the letter of Photius; cf. GARITTE, *Narratio*, p. 284-285.

[39] CASEY, *Armenian Manuscripts*, p. 57.

John's predecessor but one, Sahak III (Catholicos 678-705), composed a treatise against the dyophysites, a lengthy work of importance not only for the views of Sahak, who supported the Julianist ideas on the ἀφθαρσία of the body of Christ, later opposed by John, but also for the very large number of quotations from «orthodox» fathers, Greek, Syrian and Armenian. There are ninteen reminiscences of Athanasius in this letter, but not all can be paralleled with known Greek texts. Of most interest for our present purpose are the following [40]:

1. *Ad Jovianum,* P.G. 28.532B, πρῶτον μὲν ... πολέμιος. [41]
There are the following variants:
μετ'αὐτῆς θεϊκῶς: Theotokos
διὸ καὶ ... ἡ ἁγία Μαρία omitted.
This is not the same text as the Armenian found in Tayezi (T) or the two corpora in Vienna (A and B), nor is this passage quoted in the *Seal of Faith* or by Timothy Aelurus.

2. *De Incarnatione Dei Verbi,* P.G. 28.25A-28A, ὁμολογοῦμεν δὲ εἶναι ... μία προσκυνήσει [42]. The Armenian is very different from the Greek and from the text in T A B and Timothy; it seems to have been conflated with part of the *Quod unus,* P.G. 28.125C. It reads: "We confess him to be God and the Son of God according to the Spirit, and the son of man according to the body; not two natures, nor two persons, nor two adorations, but one nature and one person of the incarnate Word of God, with one adoration".

3. *Contra Apollinarium II,* P.G. 26.1148C, καὶ ἐγεννήθη ἐκ γυναικὸς ... μορφῆς τῆς ἀνθρωπίνης [43]. This is different from the Greek and from the Armenian of T A B; it is not quoted in the *Seal of Faith* or Timothy. It reads: "God the Word was born of a woman to establish the first created form of mankind in himself; he was revealed in the body without human will and human mind, for an image of renewal, in the will of the deity only, because the whole nature of the Word was in the manifestation and form of human flesh."

4. *Ad Arianos IV* (?) [44]. This has its closest affinities to § 6-7 of the *Ad Arianos IV,* but is not the same text. The *Ad Arianos IV* is not in T A B,

---

[40] Sahak's letter is preserved in the *Book of Letters,* p. 413-482. Cf. E. TER-MINASSIANTZ, *Die armenische Kirche in ihren Beziehungen zu den syrischen Kirchen* (*Texte und Untersuchungen,* N.F., 11. Band, Heft 4), Leipzig, 1904, p. 136-142.
[41] *Book of Letters,* p. 442.
[42] *Ibid.,* p. 443.
[43] *Ibid.,* p. 447.
[44] *Ibid.,* p. 449.

nor is it quoted in the *Seal of Faith* or Timothy; nor is this piece identical with the Armenian *Contra Arium* (P.G. 28.440; Tayezi 134) or the short *Ad Arium* (Tayezi 235). It reads: "The blessed Athanasius says in his fourth treatise to Arius: The Word had again the weakness of the body as his own, for his was the body, the co-worker of divine deeds, for it was by him because it was the body of God; and again: if the works of God the Word were not done through the body, then the body would not have been deified; and again: because he effected the work of the Father through the body"

5. *Ad Adelphium*, P.G. 1081B, χεῖρα γοῦν ... τὸν Λάζαρον. This text omits γοῦν σωματικήν [45]. T A B have a different Armenian translation of the same underlying Greek text.

6. *Ad Epictetum* [46]. This extract from the *Ad Epictetum* does not come from the Greek text, but can be compared with the altered text of § 10 quoted above: "The Word who was in the body ... therefore the corruptible body became an incorruptible body." However, this last phrase is altered in Sahak's quotation to read: "Therefore the body which was from corruptible things, became incorruptible." This quotation does not agree exactly with either the known Armenian versions or the text in the *Seal of Faith*. This latter composition, however, is only known in one manuscript; it is quite possible that the copies circulating in the seventh and eighth centuries had significant variants among them.

7. *Contra Apollinarium I*, P.G. 26.1105A, καὶ ὅπερ 'Αδὰμ ... ἀνέδειξεν [47] There is no Armenian translation of the complete work, though it is quoted in the *Seal of Faith*. This passage does not agree with the Greek. It reads: "Adam cast the sinless flesh into condemnation and corruption, but Christ showed it incorruptible and insusceptible of death and saving for mortals. Death was not able to destroy the spirit of Christ, nor was corruption able to take captive his body ... (the three last lines are illegible).

8. *Quod Unus sit Christus*, P.G. 28.124C, καὶ ἐχώρησαν ... καὶ ἔσχατον [48]. Here the Armenian follows the Greek, only omitting καὶ συνθέσεως. But compared with the three Armenian versions of the complete work, there is one interesting difference. Instead of աննձնաւորութիւն (hypostasis) Sahak always writes էնթակայութիւն [49]. The former is the traditional expression, the latter was invented in the Philhellene period of translation.

---

[45] *Ibid.*, p. 449.
[46] *Ibid.*, p. 452.
[47] *Ibid.*, p. 453.
[48] *Ibid.*, p. 470.
[49] In the letter of Photius this term is equated with դէմ and աննձն, while in a commentary inserted before the text of the Armenian reply, էնթակայութիւն is equated with զոյացութիւն and բնութիւն, while the phrase « unity hypostatised (էնթակայացեալ) in one personality »

Although at first sight the fact that Sahak quotes from works of Athanasius which Stephen of Siunik is said to have translated seems to invalidate the claim of the colophon, yet closer investigation shows that in no case did Sahak use the text of any of the known Armenian versions. Therefore these translations as they have come down to us may still be attributed to Stephen, while the problem of Sahak's sources remains unsolved. The mines of Patristic quotations already available in Armenian, the *Seal of Faith* and Timothy Aelurus' *Widerlegung*, do not contain these particular extracts, with the exception of that from the *Ad Epictetum*. But as we have just seen, here also Sahak was not quoting from the text as we now have it. The problem of the source of these Athanasian quotations seems linked to the question of Sahak's sources in general; further light may be thrown on it when the provenance of all of Sahak's citations is discovered.

It is noteworthy that later Armenian authors usually repeated well known quotations in their apologetic works, borrowing large sections from previous writers. So one is not surprised to find that Stephen of Siunik, quoting the same four extracts from the *Contra Arianos* and the *Ad Adelphium*, follows them with the same quotations as Sahak from Gregory of Nyssa, Julius of Rome, John Chrysostom, Cyril of Alexandria, etc.[50]. We are not here concerned with Armenian quotations of Athanasius in general, but rather with the fate of the *Ad Epictetum*; yet it would be misleading to consider quotations from this one work in isolation, for the very reason that once a quotation became fixed in a catena or authoritative letter (such as Sahak's or Stephen's) it was nearly always copied from that catena without reference to the complete and original text. The *corpora* of Armenian *Athanasiana* existed alongside these collections of quotations, but neither influenced the other.

Further evidence for such borrowing comes from the letter of the Catholicos Khatchik (972-991) in reply to the accusations of

---

is applied to the unity of Logos and flesh (the Armenian texts, edited by A. PAPADOPOULOS-KERAMEUS, in *Pravoslavnyi Palestinskii Sbornik*, XI (1892), p. 179-226. On Photius' letter, see GARITTE, *Narratio*, p. 370-375).

[50] In his letter to Germanos of Constantinople, *Book of Letters*, p. 373-395. These four quotations are on p. 377. Stephen also gives the same quotation as Sahak from the *c. Apollinarium II* (p. 379 = Sahak quotation no. 3 above) but begins four lines earlier at διὰ τοῦτο ἦλθεν.

heresy levelled at the Armenians by the Metropolitan of Sebastea. This letter has been preserved by Stephen of Taron and is one of the most valuable documents for a knowledge of contemporary Armenian dogmatics. All the quotations from Athanasius included in the apology, save one, are taken from the letters of Sahak or Stephen (the sole exception being from an apocryphal discourse on the Nativity)[51]. The quotation from the *Ad Epictetum* does not exactly follow Sahak's version or that of Tayezi, but agrees word for word with the text of the *Seal of Faith*. This interesting fact shows that Khatchik and his vardapets might borrow the schema of their quotations from one writer and the text from another.

The last text to be considered in this connection is the *Root of Faith*, as yet unpublished[52]. It contains selections from the Bible and from Greek, Syrian, Latin and Armenian authors. A work entitled Հաւատարմատ was attributed to Anania of Narek by the historian Oukhtanes, but this cannot have been the *Root of Faith* as we have it, for the latter contains quotations from Nerses of Lambron (who is referred to as the last Armenian Catholicos). Although no copy of Anania's work now exists, it was suggested by Jordan that it formed the basis of this fuller version[53]. This

---

[51] Stephen (Ասողիկ) of Taron, ch. 21. Unfortunately I could find no copy of the Armenian text, but the quotations are easily recognisable from the translation of F. MACLER, Paris, 1917. The quotations are : p. 87 of the French text, from the « c. Apollinarium » (a mistake in the Armenian for the *De Incarnatione Dei Verbi*) quoted by Stephen, *Book of Letters*, p. 375; p. 89 from « On the Birth of Christ », full text in Tayezi, p. 258-263, this section on p. 260; p. 92 from « The Epiphany » (i.e. *c. Apollinarium II*) quoted by Stephen p. 379; p. 96 from *c. Arianos IV* and *Ad Adelphium*, quoted by Stephen p. 377 and Sahak p. 449 (quotations 4 and 5 above); p. 100 from *c. Apollinarium I*, quoted by Sahak p. 453 (quotation no. 7 above); p. 101 from *Ad Epictetum*, quoted by Sahak p. 452 (quotation no. 6 above); p. 106 from *Quod unus sit Christus*, text in Tayezi 56-63, this section on p. 59 (cf. Sahak p. 443, quotation no. 2 above).

[52] Three manuscripts are known : Paris 153, Vatican 31 and Ejmiacin 1500 = 1538, now 2080. I am grateful to the authorities of the Bibliothèque Nationale and of the Biblioteca Apostolica Vaticana for providing me with microfilms of this text. On the *Root of Faith*, see H. JORDAN, *Irenaeusfragmente*, p. 160-63; for a description of the Vatican Ms., E. TISSERANT, *Codices Armeni Bibliothecae Vaticanae*, Rome, 1927, p. 51-53.

[53] JORDAN, *Irenaeusfragmente*, p. 161, note 3.

is not very likely, however, for Anania was not unfriendly to the Byzantine church[54], whereas the *Root of Faith*, like the *Seal of Faith*, is of pronounced monophysite tendency. Its title gives the tenor of the collection : « Book of consolidation and root of faith and reply to the Arians; for the heretics say that the divinity was not united to the body, but they confess the divinity separate from the body. God forbid that the orthodox should think anything similar, but they must courageously bring forward as witness the prophets and gospel and apostles, and with frankness reply to the dyophysites. » Furthermore the *Root of Faith* is devoted to the refutation of those who supposed that the body of Christ was corruptible, a further indication of the continuing influence of Julianist ideas.

This catena contains eighteen quotations from Athanasius[55]. After the last (from the *Ad Epictetum*) the compiler added a most revealing interpretation of Athanasius' condemnation of those who say « one nature », explaining how Athanasius, that « lifelong champion of the monophysites », intended this phrase to be understood.

1. *Ad Jovianum*, P.G. 28.532B μίαν τοίνυν ⋯ πολέμιος.
The Armenian title reads: "From the letter to the emperor Claudius(!)" and the text is very different from the Greek.
"We confess one will, we say rather one nature and hypostasis of the Word, perfectly incarnate. And who does not say thus, fights with God and against the holy Spirit and the holy fathers."

2. *Ad Jovianum*, P.G. 28.532B πρῶτον μὲν ⋯ ὁ αὐτός.
"First the Lord was with the Virgin divinely, then the same (came forth) from her. Who says two natures or two persons, worships a Quaternity instead of the Trinity."

3. Unidentified: "Just as it is impossible to say that a king and the purple are two kings, so it is impossible to say that God the Word and his body are two natures."

4. *De Incarnatione Dei Verbi*, P.G. 28.28A ἀλλὰ μίαν φύσιν τοῦ Θεοῦ Λόγου σεσαρκωμένην. The Armenian title reads: "Apology against Apollinarius." This is not the title in the complete Armenian versions (T A B), but Stephen of Siunik quotes "one nature of the incarnate Word of God"

---

[54] Cf. the preface by J. MÉCÉRIAN to I. KÉCHICHIAN, *Grégoire de Narek, le Livre de Prières (Sources chrétiennes 78)*, Paris, 1961, esp. p. 20, 24.
[55] Paris 153, ff. 30b-35a; Vatican 31, ff. 113a-116a.

under the title "Letter to Apollinarius" (*Book of Letters,* p. 375). The Armenian text differs from the Greek.

"But according to all the divinely inspired testaments, one nature of the incarnate Word of God was declared."

5. Unidentified: "He did not say that the Word became God, but he said that the Word is God. God always existed, he says, and the same God became flesh, that the flesh might become God the Word, according to Thomas who called his flesh 'Lord and God'. Therefore we confess one nature of the Word of God who became flesh, and the body is worshipped by the angels; not like the Arians who say that they are different."

6. Unidentified (but cf. *Ad Adelphim,* § 5, P.G. 26.1077D):

"But he says that the body of the Spirit was born from the Virgin. Who divides the Word from the body, denies the grace which was bestowed by him on us, because the blessed Stephen saw the same body at the right hand of the Father. Therefore we do not say that the Word is outside the body for you to worship. At the time of the crucifixion the earth shook because the Word was united to the body on the cross."

7. *Quod unus sit Christus,* cf. P.G. 28.124C-D. The quotation is entitled "Against the Samosatene," the usual title in Armenian for this work, but the text differs from the Greek.

"Who understand two natures in Christ after the union, wish to call the Lord a slave and make the Trinity a Quaternity, because one must understand and say 'one nature of God the Word incarnate.' And if any one says they are different, he is anathema."

8. *Quod unus sit Christus,* cf. P.G. 28.125C. The order of the Greek is inverted in the Armenian.

"We know Christ born from the seed of David; the same they called God, the same man, the same Son of God, the same son of man, the same from heaven, the same from earth, the same passible (and impassible); not different, nor two persons, nor two natures."

9. *Ad Adelphium,* P.G. 26.1081B. This is a conflation of the quotation from the *Ad Adelphium* and the last of the three from the *Ad Arianos IV* found in Sahak's Letter (nos. 4 and 5).

"The works of the Father he effected through the body, because with his hand he raised the one ill with fever, and with his voice the dead. For the light of the divinity shone out in the mutable body, and in the same was the child who had sprung from the womb, pure and immaculate; and the incomprehensible who had left the heights of divinity was with him."

10. *De Incarnatione Dei Verbi,* P.G. 28.25A-28A, ὁμολογοῦμεν δὲ εἶναι ... σεσαρκωμένην. This follows Sahak's quotation (no. 2) rather than the Greek or the complete Armenian versions.

"For we confess that he is God and Son of God according to the Spirit, and son of man according to the flesh; one nature and one person of the Word of God who became man."

11. *Ad Epictetum,* cf. the version of § 10 found in Tayezi (quotation no. 16).
"The Word who was flesh, above the nature of mortal flesh made his body immortal and incorruptible, for the Word of God put on and united to Himself the body.

12. *Against Arius.* This is similar to the quotation which Sahak (n°. 4) attributes to the *Contra Arianos IV*. But here only two of the three short quotations are combined; the third goes with the quotation from the *Ad Adelphium* (no. 9 in the *Root of Faith*.)
"The Word had the weakness of the flesh as his own, because the body was his, and by it were the divine works accomplished. Because if the deeds of God the Word were not done though the body, he (i.e. man) would not have become God."

13. Unidentified: "Because the spittle was divine, although it had human power for healing; and the human feet walked divinely on the sea, because the Word was united to the body without confusion or division."

14. *Contra Apollinarium II,* cf. P.G. 26.1148C. This quotation is entitled « Manifestation »; the usual title of this work in the Armenian versions is "Concerning the saving manifestation of our Lord Jesus Christ." The Armenian does not follow the Greek exactly.
"The body of the Saviour had a divine will only after the union, and the human mind disappeared from the divine body at the incarnation of the Word."

15. *From the Saying of Peter the Apostle.* Unidentified [56]: "The suffering of Christ in the body was not the suffering of the nature of the Word Himself, but of the nature of the body. But if the body was in another, then the suffering must be attributed to another. But if the Word became flesh and the body was the Word's, then one must say that the sufferings are the Word's, because on account of the indissoluble union the Word considered the sufferings of the body as his own. Opposed to 'why do you strike me?' he also said: 'I turned my back on the blows' ".

16. Unidentified: "They babble who say that the sufferings were of his divinity. Because God did not suffer through the body but through God, the sufferings were in the body. But because of the Word united to Himself, he considered the sufferings of the body as his own. But he was free from sufferings as a man, and being by essence God (and therefore) immortal, he willingly accepted death and suffering."

17. Unidentified: "When the Word accepted his body, he bore it as his

---

[56] A commentary on the two Epistles of Peter attributed to Athanasius is found in the Armenian Ms. Erevan 1408 and is described by H. A. ANASYAN, Հայկական Մատենագիտություն, Part I, Erevan, 1959, col. 360.

own and not as if by force. And he teaches you hunger and thirst which (he endured and) after forty days gave up."

18. *Ad Epictetum*, P.G. 26.1052C, ποῖος ᾅδης ... Λόγου θεότητι. This is the same version as that found in Tayezi (quotation no. 1).

"Whence came and sprang forth this fire of wrath, or what hell has belched forth to say that the body from Mary and the Word of God are one nature?"

To these distorted quotations the compiler (or perhaps an earlier gloss) has added a commentary on the last:
"One must understand wisely this saying, why saint Athanasius said it. Do not think that he has undertaken to invalidate what he built up earlier against the dyophysites and that he opposes himself and establishes two natures, against which he combatted all his life. God forbid! But it was necessary to place this saying here, that you might know why Athanasius said that one must not say 'one nature of the Word and body,' because the ignorant hear this, who do not understand the meaning of the remark and say the opposite, like the dyophysites, that Athanasius anathematised those who say 'one nature.' Now Valentinus and Marcion and Eutyches and many others said that the Lord brought his body from heaven, and others that the Lord moved as a phantom on earth, and others that the body existed before the coming into being of the world, that it was with the Father, equal to the Word and co-eternal with him, and that the Word and the flesh were one nature. But Athanasius says against them: The holy Fathers in Nicaea said that the Word was equal to the Father, and defined the Word and the Father as one nature. And afterwards He took a body from the Virgin and united it with Himself ineffably. So all the holy Fathers said that (if) there is one nature of the Word and flesh before the taking (of the body) from Mary then it would have been superfluous to mention Mary and to say that He was born from her or to say that there was any necessity for Him to bring the body from heaven and to put on a second nature of man from Mary. He could not be in the body without being born from Mary, nor could He put on his own nature twice. Again the heretics say that when we say 'one nature of the Word and flesh before He took it from Mary' then the Trinity remains (intact). But if we say that He took the body from Mary, in place of the Trinity a Quaternity is made, from which they wish to flee in ignorance. With the same ignorance they thought that there was one nature of the Word and flesh before the world was created, and that it was co-eternal and equal to Him. Oh, you wicked ones, who speak of a Quaternity! How do you say that the body of the Word was associated with and equal to the Father before the birth from the holy Virgin and not younger in time than the Word, and that He did not take it from Mary the Mother of God in the last (days)?"

The transformation of Athanasius is now complete. The struggle with the Arians has been replaced by the struggle with the dyophysites; the cause of the divinity of the Logos and his unity with the Father has been replaced by the cause of «one nature of the Word incarnate» and the union of the human and divine in one nature. Although there existed undistorted versions in Armenian of Athanasius' dogmatic works, they went unheeded by the theologians concerned with defending orthodoxy against the heretical «Nestorians», but this is not a feature unique to Armenian writers. In Byzantium and the other Oriental churches the authority of the Fathers was more often felt at second hand than directly; their works were not widely studied, but commentaries and abbreviations, universal encyclopaedias and collections of purple passages were the books perused and assimilated by lesser mortals, each copying his predecessor. For Athanasius' own thought one had recourse not to his own works but to the compendia of Patristic quotations. Once started this practice gained fatal momentum.

Only the first translators of such tendentious versions as that of the letter to Epictetus discussed above can be accused of deliberate fraud; and in the sixth century few had such strict ideas of literary propriety as are fashionable today. Sahak, Stephen, Khatchik and the compiler of the *Root of Faith* were victims of a universal tendency; they accepted the doctored texts in good faith, but the cumulative effect of such credulity was disastrous. The honest convictions of these Armenians who clung tenaciously to the traditional faith were based on distorted premises. To what extent such frauds encouraged the perpetuation of mutual misunderstanding between the Armenian and other churches is a question beyond the scope of our present enquiry, but a study of the sources on which Armenian theologians based their interpretation of tradition may explain some of the inconsistencies in their claims to represent that tradition.

Additional Note: For quotations of Athanasian Texts in Armenian see also M. de Durand, 'Citations patristiques chez Etienne de Taron', *Armeniaca. Mélanges d'études arméniennes*, Venise 1969, 117–118, and R.W. Thomson, 'Quotations from Athanasius in the *Root of Faith*', *Armenian and Biblical Studies*, ed. Michael E. Stone, Jerusalem 1976, 182–203.

XIV

THE ARMENIAN VERSION OF PS.-DIONYSIUS AREOPAGITA

The purpose of this paper is not to elucidate the mystery of the real author of the corpus of writings ascribed to Dionysius the Areopagite, but to describe the Armenian version of those works and to offer a few comments on their influence on Armenian authors.[1]

There are well over one hundred Armenian manuscripts that contain a translation of the Ps.-Dionysian corpus — that is, all or part of the treatises: On the Heavenly Hierachy, On the Ecclesiastical Hierarchy, On the Divine Names, On Mystical Theology, the Letters.[2] There were in fact two Armenian renderings of these works: One by Stephen of Siunik' in the early eighth century, and one by Stephen of Poland (Step'anos Lehats'i). The latter was a seventeenth century monk who translated several texts from Latin into Armenian.[3] He was prompted to translate Dionysius again because of the obscurity of the earlier rendering. But it is with this first translation, by Stephen of Siunik', that the present paper is concerned.

Armenian tradition — both in the manuscripts of Dionysius and in the historical texts — is unanimous in attributing the first translation to Stephen of Siunik', bishop of that province before his death in 735. There is, however, one Armenian text composed before the eighth century that has quotations from Dionysius, namely the K'nik Hawatoy (Seal of Faith) which is often ascribed to Komitas, Catholicos from 615 to 618, but which may well, in its present form, be a somewhat later composition.[4] The Seal of Faith is a florilegium containing extracts from numerous Greek and Armenian theological writings. But the quotations from Dionysius evince a text quite different from that of the corpus in the manuscripts. The short excerpts in the Seal of Faith were translated directly for that florilegium, either from a full Greek text of Dionysius or from a Greek florilegium. So they have no relevance for the study of the translation attributed to Stephen of Siunik' — though, of course, they are of importance for the study of the influence of the theology of Dionysius in Armenia.

Stephen's scholarly activities and travels are mentioned by several Armenian historians, beginning with Moses Daskhurants'i (whose work re-

Reprinted from *Acta Jutlandica*, 27 (1982), pp. 115-124. Copyright © 1982 by Aarhus University Press, Denmark. Reprinted by permission.

ceived its present form at the turn of the eleventh and twelfth centuries).[5] But only in the fourteenth century is the translation of Dionysius' works explicitly described. According to Stephen Orbelean the translation of Dionysius was made in Constantinople at the urging of the consul David, who himself explained obscure passages.[6]

It may be worthwhile to give here the gist of Stephen Orbelean's account of the travels of Stephen of Siunik', which is somewhat lengthier than earlier accounts.[7] Stephen of Siunik' was prompted to go abroad to learn Greek and Latin and to study philosophy because he had been worsted in a theological debate with a pro-Chalcedonian Armenian prince. Following the pattern of earlier Armenian scholars, he went to Athens and Constantinople. Athens, by the eighth century, was hardly a great centre of philosophical study; but I do not wish to raise here the question whether Stephen Orbelean really thought that his hero went there, or whether Athens had become part of the traditional grand tour attributed to earlier scholars, and was really only a literary *topos*. The scholarly activity of Armenians abroad was solidly rooted in historical fact, but many legendary accretions distort the picture in individual cases – as with Moses Khorenats'i's travels to Egypt.[8] In Constantinople Stephen of Siunik', though originally denounced as a heretic, mollified the emperor and made the acquaintance of the patriarch Germanos, who gave him a letter to take back to Armenia. (Stephen's later response will be mentioned below.) At this time, with the encouragement of the consul David, Stephen translated writings by Dionysius and Gregory of Nyssa. Titles are not given by Stephen Orbelean, but colophons attribute the rendering of the *De Opificio Hominis* to Stephen of Siunik'.[9] Then the emperor sent him to Rome to find books that enshrined the true, orthodox faith. Reaching there, Stephen found works by Cyril of Alexandria, Athanasius and Epiphanius; but he returned directly to Armenia.

Stephen's activity as translator is also mentioned by the 13th century historian Kirakos Gandzakets'i, but he does not refer specifically to the translation of Dionysius. However, Kirakos does note that the famous mystic poet Gregory of Narek (d. 1010) wrote homilies in the style (*och*) of Dionysius.[10] But Gregory of Narek makes no explicit reference to Dionysius in his prayers or homilies.[11]

As noted above, there are more than one hundred Armenian manuscripts containing all or part of the Dionysian corpus, of which more than half have the version by Stephen of Siunik'. I am not at the moment in a position to describe the relationship of all these manuscripts to each other, as I have not yet seen most of them. The comments that follow are based on an analysis of the two earliest manuscripts. These are Matenadaran 49 and 167 in Erevan. The former was written in 1282 and corrected soon thereafter by the renowned grammatical scholar Isaias Nch'ets'i, abbot of Gladzor. The second manuscript, Matenadaran 167, is not dated; but it was commissioned by the same Isaias and was perhaps written at the monastery of Halbat.[12] It may, of course, turn out that these early manuscripts are untypical; it is not unknown for much later manuscripts to have preserved a better text. But at least one can say that we have the text of Dionysius as known and used in the late thirteenth century. From before that time only scattered fragments and quotations, a few quite long, survive in Armenian.

These two manuscripts are related in that Isaias corrected the one (Mat. 49) from a manuscript with a text very close to, but not exactly identical with, the other (Mat. 167). It is the latter which is the more faithful to the Greek text, although both have errors explicable only from corruptions within an Armenian tradition or confusion of Armenian letters.[13] Before the corrections introduced by Isaias, Matenadaran 49 generally had an inferior text. For example, it follows the Armenian biblical text in the quotation from James 1.1 that opens the treatise on the *Celestial Hierarchy*, rather than the text of Dionysius; and it has clear corruptions within an Armenian context.[14] But since Matenadaran 167 is not without mistakes, the readings of 49 are significant. And more importantly, since 167 has been damaged, especially at the top or bottom of the page, the lost passages can be restored from Matenadaran 49.

Narrowing the field even further, I should also say that my collations are restricted to the first item in the Dionysian corpus, the treatise on the *Celestial Hierarchy*. The reason is not because this is the first item in the Armenian manuscripts, but rather because we have a critical Greek text of this treatise — unlike the others — so that comparison between the Armenian and Greek textual traditions is easy.[15] For there is no question of the Armenian having been made from a Syriac version. The Armenian never agrees with a Syriac text against all other Greek manuscripts; it is a very literal translation of the original Greek.[16]

The Greek manuscript tradition of the Dionysian corpus falls into two main groups: one is closer to the original text but full of grammatical errors; the other reflects a revision by Byzantine grammarians, who corrected the grammar and orthography.[17] The later manuscripts that do not belong to either of these groups but reflect a mixed text are not relevant for the Armenian version made in the early eighth century. The oldest example of the first group of Greek manuscripts, Parisinus 437, was given by the emperor of Constantinople Michael II to Louis the Pious in 827. Very closely related to this is a tenth century manuscript, the Vallicellianus 69 in Rome. These are conveniently known as M and Va respectively. It so happens that in ch. 4, par. 2 of the *Celestial Hierarchy* these two manuscripts have a striking misplacement of several lines, attested by no other Greek manuscript or the Syriac, but followed by the Armenian. This is a sure indication that the Armenian text was rendered from a Greek manuscript reflecting a Constantinopolitan text, as tradition claims.

Elsewhere also Armenian follows other idiosyncrasies of M or Va (or both). For example in I 2 ἐνδότητος is rendered by *miut'iwn* ("unity"), as M and the Syriac; and in III 3 the Armenian follows MVa in reading διάδοσιν in place of μετάδοσιν. On the other hand the Armenian does not have all the errors or omissions of MVa. Thus in II 3 it includes the phrase ἐπὶ τῶν ἀοράτων; in II 4 it reads ἕξιν; and in III 2 it does not have the addition αὐτοτέλεως found in M. The Armenian translation (though not the surviving Armenian manuscripts) predates the earliest surviving Greek manuscript, so the actual manuscript or manuscripts used by Stephen of Siunik' cannot be identified. However, it is clear to which general text type the Armenian translation belongs.

The two Greek manuscripts M and Va do differ in that Va contains the scholia on Dionysius attributed to Maximos and M does not. Since these scholia are also found in the Armenian text, clearly we should look to Va — or rather, to an earlier manuscript from which Va was copied in the tenth century — for the origin of the Armenian rendering. But it should be noted that the Armenian manuscripts do not name the author (or authors) of the scholia.

The two thirteenth century Armenian manuscripts on which the present investigation is based differ with regard to the scholia. Matenadaran 49, written in 1282 and corrected by Isaias Nch'ets'i, integrates the scholia into the text in order to make a continuous running whole. On the other hand, Mat. 167, commissioned by the same Isaias, clearly separates the scholia from the text in traditional fashion by placing the scholia in a separate column and by using a somewhat smaller script. A later hand has added some additional notes, usually very brief, that are not found in Mat. 49. But the tradition of Armenian scholia to the Dionysian corpus and their relation to the Greek of Va remain to be investigated.

The Greek text of Pseudo-Dionysius is not the most limpid prose imaginable, nor do the obscurities become any clearer in the Armenian rendering. Indeed, the translation is done in that very literal fashion commonly known as "Hellenizing" where the word order of the original is followed very closely — regardless of whether that would be natural Armenian order — and where compound words are broken down into their component parts, each part is translated separately, and then they are reassembled.[18]

However, it is only fair to point out that Stephen in his rendering of the Greek has not always slavishly translated it by a one-to-one equivalent in Armenian. To take some examples, just from the first few chapters of the *Heavenly Hierarchy*. According to context ἀνάγω can be rendered by *elanem*, *veraberem* or *veranam*; and ἀναγωγή is *imanali tesut'iwn* (spiritual vision) or *verambardzut'iwn* (elevation). Οἰκεῖος can be *ink'ean* (self) or *entani* (family). Ὑπερουράνιος is *erknayin* (heavenly) or *ger i veray k'an zerkins* (above heaven). Σύμβολον is *nshanak* or *awrinak*.

Conversely, *awrinak* can render σύμβολον or αἴνιγμα. *Kartsem* can render οἴομαι or φαντάζω. *Kerparan* can render ἀπεικόνισμα, μόρφωμα or μόρφωσις. *Nmanut'iwn* renders ἀφομοίωσις, μίμησις or ὁμοιότης. It is not necessary to prolong the list in order to indicate that the Armenian is not entirely mechanical.

Stephen made several mistakes in his translation. But we must remember that the Greek text as represented in Contantinople in the eighth century was, in Heil's words: "un texte en désaccord avec les règles de la grammaire, plein de fautes d'orthographe." So, for example, ὑπερκόσμιος (transcendant) and the adverb ὑπερκοσμίως are rendered by *gerazard*, as if the stem κόσμος here meant "order" or "arrangement". For when κόσμος in the sense of "world" stands alone and not in compound form it is rendered by *ashkharh*.

The term μύστικος is important to Dionysius. It is rendered sometimes by *khorhrdakan*, the adjective from *khorhourd* which means μυστήριον. But sometimes μύστικος is rendered by *bch'olakan*, an adjective derived from the particle from the verbal stem *bch'em*, which is used of animals "roaring" or "bellowing". Now the adjective μυκητικός is used of beasts' voices by Dionysius in II 2 and there rendered by *bch'olakan*. Did Stephen of Siunik' think that μύστικος was related to μυκητικός, or was his Greek text defective? This curious term *bch'olakan* is also attested in two later Armenian writers in the sense of "mystical", no doubt due to the influence of the Armenian translation of the Dionysian corpus.[19] Finally, one funny mistake in an otherwise rather humourless text is worth noting. The word θιασώτης, "follower, member of a group", is used often by Dionysius. In the accusative plural it becomes θιασώτας; but that was read as if it were θείας ὤτας (sic) and always rendered in the Armenian as "divine ears" (*astuatsayin akanjs*)! It is perhaps not surprising that in the seventeenth century Stephen of Poland found the first translation of Dionysius "obscure".

We may now briefly note some passages in Armenian texts where the influence of Dionysius is most evident. Sometimes Dionysius is included in lists of theological authorities without much elaboration. Thus Sebēos, writing in the late seventh century, includes Dionysius the Areopagite in Athens as an example of a bishop who received ordination from the apostles, just as did Clement in Rome, Timothy in Ephesus, or Simon in Jerusalem. This passage occurs in a response sent by the Catholicos Nerses III (642-662) and the Armenian bishops to the emperor Constans II (642-668), rejecting the Greek Chalcedonian position.[20] In a letter by Stephen of Siunik' himself to the patriarch of Constantinople Germanos (715-730), Dionysius of Athens is credited with having seen a vision of the Saviour, as "the history relates" [21] This is a reference to the so-called *Autobiography* of Dionysius, which was not translated into Armenian until the ninth century but which would have been known to Stephen in Greek.[22] Here it is worth noting that another text attributed to "Stephen the Philosopher" quotes Dionysius directly. The work is a theological treatise of Julianist tendency *On the Incorruptible Flesh of Christ*. It is in large part of florilegium where numerous authorities are cited; the quotation from Dionysius is in fact borrowed from the *Seal of Faith*. So whether or not Stephen of Siunik' is the author, as the editor of the text Tēr Mkrtch'ean thought, it is no evidence for the Armenian translation of Dionysius.[23]

The Catholicos Khach'ik I (973-992) in a letter to the Metropolitan of Melitene mentions Dionysius as one of the theological authorities respected by Armenians.[24] And in a letter to the Metropolitan of Sebaste, quoted in Stephen of Tarōn (Asolik), ch. 21, the same Khach'ik quotes Dionysius and also refers to his vision of the Saviour. What is significant about the quotation in Asoḷik is that, although the passage is the same as that used in the *Seal of Faith*, the Armenian text is not that of the florilegium but has been taken from Stephen of Siunik''s translation.

As an authority for the nine orders of angels Dionysius is explicitly quoted in some detail by Nersēs Shnorhali in the twelfth century.[25] Equally often Nersēs makes reference to these celestial hierarchies without mentioning Dionysius by name.[26] The *Law-code* of Mkhit'ar Gosh, compiled later in the same century, expounds these matters in specific detail, quoting as source the writings of saint Dionysius the Areopagite — "the pride of Athens".[27] In the following century, Smbat in his *Law-code* takes up the tradition of the nine ranks of clergy within the church as being parallel to the nine ranks of angels. But he does not quote Dionysius explicitly. On the other hand, he expands this parallelism to the nine ranks of courtiers in the imperial palace of Constantinople. The ranks are: Silentarii; Vestitores, Candidati; Prosecutores; Excubitores; Stratores, Scholarii; Decani; Cursores.[28]

But of all texts dating to this period it is the *Commentary on the Liturgy* by Nersēs of Lambron that quotes Dionysius as authority the most frequently. Dionysius teaches us that the church is the image (*patker*) of heaven, so the ranks within the church reflect the heavenly orders.[29] Nersēs goes on to claim that it was the blessed Dionysius who set the rules for basic rituals, from minor matters such as censing to rules for the making of *myron* and questions of ordination, topics indeed discussed in the treatise on the *Ecclesiastical Hierarchy*.

The thirteenth century historian Kirakos Gandzakets'i quotes Vanakan Vardapet using Dionysius as an authority for the procession of the Holy Spirit.[30] And in the following century the influence of Dionysius is strongly attested in Gregory of Tat'ev, in whose massive *Book of Questions* a whole chapter is devoted to angelology. This has been reviewed fairly extensively by Dom Dedurand, who indicates that Gregory has introduced significant changes into the theology of Ps.-Dionysius.[31]

The most noteworthy claim for the authority of Dionysius is in an earlier document where he is cited in support of the doctrine of one nature in Christ. The document in question is an "Exposition, in accordance with apostolic tradition, of the true orthodox faith against the dyophysite Nestorians by Sahak the Armenian Catholicos and Great Translator." It runs to sixty-nine pages in the collection of letters and documents known as the *Book of Letters*.[32] Although the title "translator" is designed to make one associate the treatise with Sahak I, colleague of Mashtots in the early fifth century, the contents of the document point to a later date since Pope Leo, Theodoret of Cyr and Cyril of Alexandria are quoted. Its Julianist tendencies have been noted by earlier scholars, and Tēr Minassiantz ascribed it to Sahak III (677-703).[33] But the text is probably later than that. For in discussing the earliest Armenian Christian traditions, the author quotes (without so acknowledging) from Moses Khorenats'i's version of the story of Abgar, not the version in Eusebius or Labubna.[34] And the role of Bartholomew as a missionary in Armenia is stressed, whereas that apostle's work in Armenia seems to be unknown before the eighth century, being first mentioned by Stephen of Siunik' himself.[35] Be that as it may, the important point is that Dionysius is associated with sources like the Apollinarian frauds attributed to Athanasius which stress the theme: "one nature of the Word incarnate".[36] Furthermore, states Sahak, Dionysius did not mingle water with the wine at mass. For had he done so, he would have indicated a dual nature. The uncorrupted wine (*anapakan*, which has Julianist overtones) indicates the single nature of Christ.[37] But Sahak's claim conflicts with the use of ἡ τοῦ οἴνου κρᾶσις in Dionysius, *Epistle* IX 6 (*ginwoyn kharnumn* in the Armenian of Stephen of Siunik'). Here one is reminded of the famous refusal of the Catholicos Moses II (574-604): "I shall not cross the Azat; I shall not eat leavened bread; I shall not drink hot water," quoted in the *Narratio*.[38]

However, it is not my intention here to raise questions of Christology or ritual. The importance of the text of the Dionysian corpus in Armenia is indicated not only by the large number of surviving manuscripts and by the allusions in Armenian writers to Dionysius. More important for the history of ideas are the commentaries written on that corpus in its Armenian version. The earliest seems to be that of Hamam in the tenth century.[39] More elaborate is that of David and Jacob of the thirteenth century. Isaias Nch'ets'i also is credited with a commentary on Dionysius. But the investigation of the commentaries and scholia will have to await the establishment of the Armenian text as rendered by Stephen of Siunik', to which edition I hope that these comments may be relevant.

Notes

1. According to S. S. Arevshatyan, "Davit' Anhalt'ᵉ ev hin Hayastani P'ilisop'ayakan Mitk'ᵉ", *Patma-banasirakan Handes* 88 (1980, part 1), 21-39, the Ps.-Dionysian corpus was put together by a consortium of scholars that included the elusive "David the Invincible Philosopher" — *obscurum per obscurius*! Although it is tempting to think of this theory as but an Armenian riposte to the idea that Dionysius was Peter the Iberian, it does at least draw attention to Armenian interest in the philosophical schools of the Eastern Mediterranean in the fifth and sixth centuries.
2. In addition there are numerous manuscripts containing the Armenian version of the *Autobiography* of Dionysius the Areopagite. This has been published by N. Akinean in his *Niwt'er Hay Vkayabanut'ean Usumnasirut'ean hamar*, Vienna 1914. It is noteworthy that the Armenian version, made in 880 in Jerusalem, was rendered via Georgian. On this, and on the question of the origin of the Georgian version itself, see P. Peeters, "La version ibéro-arménienne de l'autobiographie de Denys l'Aréopagite", *Analecta Bollandiana* 39 (1921), 277-313.
3. A brief account of Stephen of Poland's activity may be found in N. Polarean, *Hay Grolner*, Jerusalem 1971, 548-9. Numerous copies of colophons describing his translation of the Dionysian corpus will be found in the catalogues of the major collections of Armenian manuscripts (e.g., J. Dashian, *Catalog der armenischen Handschriften zu Wien*, Vienna 1891, no. 255).
4. *Knik' Hawatoy*, ed. K. Tēr-Mkrtch'ean, Ējmiatsin 1914. Cf. J. Lebon, "Lés citations patristiques grecques du *Sceau de la foi*", *Revue d'histoire ecclésiastique* 25 (1929), 5-32.
5. Moses Daskhurants'i, *Patmut'iwn Aluanits'*, III 17. For the date of this work see the Introduction to C. J. F. Dowsett, *The History of the Caucasian Albanians by Movsēs Dasxuranci*, London Oriental Series 8, London 1961.
6. Stephen Orbelean, *Patmut'iwn Tann Sisakan*, ch. 31.
7. For a full discussion of these accounts see S. Gero, *Byzantine Inconoclasm during the Reign of Leo III*, CSCO Subsidia 41, Louvain 1973, Appendix C.
8. Moses Khorenats'i, *Patmut'iwn Hayots'*, III 61-62. Moses' sources for the description of his travels are elucidated in the commentary *ad loc*. in R. W. Thomson, *Moses Khorenats'i, History of the Armenians*, Cambridge, Mass. 1978.
9. G. Zarp'analean, *Matenadaran Haykakan T'argmanut'eants' Nakhneats'*, Venice 1889, 371.
10. Kirakos Gandzakets'i, *Patmut'iwn Hayots'*, ed. K. A. Melik-Ōhanjanyan, Erevan 1961, 72-74, 120.
11. Gregory of Narek, *Matenagrut'iwnk'*, Venice 1840.
12. See the description in the Catalogue of the Armenian manuscripts in the Matenadaran: Ō. Eganyan, A. Zeyt'unyan, P'. Ant'abyan, *Ts'uts'ak Dzeragrats' Mashtots'i Anvan Matenadarani*, vol I, Erevan 1965. I am grateful to the authorities of the Matenadaran for providing me with microfilms of these two manuscripts.
13. For example, in the *Celestial Hierarchy*, II 2, σύνθεσις is rendered by *sharzhadrut'iwn* in Mat. 167 and by *sharagrut'iwn* in Mat. 49. Both are corruptions of **sharadrut'iwn*, which is an exact translation of συν (*shar*) and θεσις (*drut'iwn*).
14. For example, in the *Celestial Hierarchy*, I 3, σχῆμα is correctly rendered by *dzew* in Mat. 167, but corrupted to *dzeṙ* in Mat. 49.
15. R. Roques, G. Heil, M. de Gandillac, *Denys l'Aréopagite, La Hiérarchie céleste*, Sources chrétiennes 58 bis, Paris 1970. This is a reprint of the 1958 edition with only a few additional notes.

16. For the Syriac version in Sinaiticus Syrus 52 of the seventh century see Heil (as note 15), 51-53. For other Syriac texts see J.-M. Hornus, "Le corpus dionysien en syriaque", *Parole de l'Orient*, 1 (1970), 69-93; and G. Wiessner, "Zur Handschriftenüberlieferung der syrischen Fassung des Corpus Dionysiacum", *Nachrichten der Akademie der Wissenschaften in Göttingen*, Phil.-Hist. Klasse, 1972, no. 3. A comparison of the Syriac texts provided by Hornus and Wiessner with the Armenian, and a collation of the readings given by Heil indicate very clearly that the Armenian does not follow the Syriac renderings.
17. See the Introduction by Heil (as note 15).
18. As, for example, with σύνθεσις; see note 13 above. On the classification of Armenian texts in the "Hellenizing" style see H. Manandean, *Yunaban dprots'e ew nra zargats'man shrjanner*^{e}, Vienna 1928.
19. See G. Awedik'ean, Kh. Siwrmēlean, M. Awgerean, *Nor Bargiŕk' Haykazean Lezui*, Venice 1836, s.v.
20. Sebēos, *Patmut'iwn*, ed. G. V. Abgaryan, Erevan 1979, 154.
21. *Girk' T'łt'ots'*, Tiflis 1901, 380.
22. See above, note 2.
23. K. Tēr-Mkrtch'ean, "Vasn anapakanut'ean marmnoyn, Step'annosi Imastasiri asats'eal", *Ararat*, 35 (1902), 368-400.
24. *Girk' T'łt'ots'*, 306.
25. Nerses Shnorhali, *Opera*, trans J. Cappelletti, Venice 1833, vol. II, 214, 276.
26. *Ibid.*, 219; *Yisus Ordi (Jésus, fils unique du Père*, trans. I. Kéchichian, Sources chrétiennes 203, Paris 1973), stanzas 816, 880.
27. Mkhit'ar Gosh, *Girk' Datastani*, ed. Kh. T'orosyan, Erevan 1975, 132, 139.
28. J. Karst, *Armenisches Rechtsbuch*, Strassburg 1905, § 60.
29. Nerses Lambronats'i, *Meknut'iwn Khorhrdots' Pataragin*, Venice 1847, 33.
30. Kirakos (as note 10), 344.
31. M. Dedurand, "Une somme arménienne au XIVe siècle", *Etudes d'histoire littéraire et doctrinale, Quatrième série*, Université de Montréal, Publications de l'institut d'études médiévales XIX, 1968, 217-277.
32. *Girk' T'łt'ots'*, 413-482.
33. See G. Garitte, *La Narratio de Rebus Armeniae*, CSCO Subsidia 4, Louvain 1952, 354.
34. *Girk' T'łt'ots'*, 414; cf. Moses Khorenats'i, II 26.
35. *Girk' T'łt'ots'*, 323.
36. *Ibid.*, 442.
37. *Ibid.*, 479.
38. Garitte, *Narratio*, 242-4.
39. E.g., Matenadaran 6362, dated to A.D. 1181.

ADDITIONAL NOTES

Page 123, note 28: The extensive discussion of the nine ranks found in Smbat is already in Mxit'ar's *Lawcode*. See also R.M. Bartikjan, 'O vizantijskom Klitorologii v Sydebnike Mxitara Gosha i ego armjanskom perebodchike', *Patmabanasirakan Handes* 126 [1989, pt. 3], 197–204.

The Armenian text of the Dionysian corpus has now been published: R.W. Thomson, *The Armenian Version of the Works Attributed to Dionysius the Areopagite*, Corpus Scriptorum Christianorum Orientalium 488 [text] and 489 [translation] [Scriptores Armeniaci 17 and 18], Louvain 1987.

XV

The Armenian Version of David's *Definitions of Philosophy*

This paper has a double theme. On the one hand, I shall concentrate on a single book written by David Anhaghtᶜ, the *Definitions of Philosophy*. It was written in Greek and translated into classical Armenian, whether by David himself or someone else is unknown.¹ My interest will center on the Armenian rendering and the changes the translator made when he adapted the original for his Armenian readers. On the other hand, I shall also try to bring out some of the more general themes in Armenian literature and scholarship to which this translation of David's *Definitions* bears witness. In other words, I hope to illustrate by specific examples taken from this one text some general characteristics of early Armenian literary culture.

The figure of David himself is very shadowy and obscure. Details of his career do not enter the Armenian historical record until after the year 1000, for Stephen of Tarōn (Asoghik) is the first historian to put into coherent form traditions about David and other prominent Armenian scholars and historians.² The most noteworthy aspect of Stephen's account is that he associates David with Moses Khorenatsᶜi, making him

---

¹The Greek text was published by A. Busse, ed., *Davidis Prolegomena et in Porphyrii Isagogen Commentarium, Commentaria in Aristotelem Graeca*, XVIII/2 (Berlin, 1904), pp. 1-79. The Armenian text was published by S. S. Arevshatyan, ed., *Dawitᶜ Anhaghtᶜ, Sahmankᶜ Imastasirutᶜean* (Erevan, 1960), reprinted in S. S. Arevshatyan, ed., *Dawitᶜ Anhaghtᶜ, Erkasirutᶜiwnkᶜ Pᶜilisopᶜayakankᶜ* (Erevan, 1980).

²Stepᶜanos Tarōnetsᶜi, *Patmutᶜiwn Tiezerakan* (St. Petersburg, 1885), Book, II, ch. 2, p. 20.

one of the pupils of that renowned historian. To the same circle, according to Stephen, also belonged Eghishē and other figures who are as elusive as David the Invincible Philosopher. The important point is that these very significant authors, whose works are among the finest and most enduring of Armenian classics, are associated with Mashtots^c *in person*. The desire to see a tangible rather than a spiritual link with the founder of Armenian literature has bedeviled the dating of Moses, Eghishē, and David from the time of Stephen to the present.

A more elaborate account of David's career than that given by Asoghik was published by F. C. Conybeare from a colophon of a manuscript he saw at Ejmiatsin.[3] The manuscript is now in Jerusalem (no. 1303 of the collection at the Armenian Patriarchate); it was written between 1297 and 1307. Not only does the colophon bring David to Constantinople as a companion of Moses Khorenats^ci and others, but David is said to have been invited to occupy the chair of philosophy in Athens by Gregory of Nyssa and Gregory of Nazianzen, the famous fourth-century theologians. Here one is reminded of the eleventh-century fictitious *Life* of Cyril of Jerusalem, which brings another Armenian, the patriarch Nersēs, into contact with the two Gregories.[4] But such fantastic elaborations do not concern us here.

David—that is, the author of commentaries on Aristotle's *Categories* and *Analytics*, Porphyry's *Introduction*, and of the original text *Definitions of Philosophy*[5]—belonged to the school of Olympiodorus.[6] There are several direct references to Olympiodorus in the *Definitons*. This is picked up later by Gregory Magistros, who in his *Letter 21*, describing the books of philosophy that he knew existed in Armenian, notes the "Book of Olympiodorus that David mentions."[7] Olympiodorus was born at the beginning of the sixth century, was a professor in Alexandria by the year 541, and was still teaching in 565. He was a pagan who lectured on the philosophy of Plato and Aristotle as interpreted in the Neoplatonic tradition. The sixth-century date makes it difficult to entertain seriously the idea recently proposed in Erevan, that David was one of a

---

[3]F. C. Conybeare, *A Collation with the Ancient Armenian Versions of the Greek Text of Aristotle's Categories*, Anecdota Oxoniensia I, 6 (Oxford, 1982), pp. x-xii.

[4]E. Bihain, "Une vie arménienne de saint Cyrille de Jérusalem," *Le Muséon*, 76 (1963), 319-348.

[5]For a recent bibliography see S. S. Arevshatyan, *Davit^c Anhaght^c, Matenagitakan Ts^cank* (Erevan, 1980).

[6]R. Vancourt, *Les derniers commentateurs Alexandrins d'Aristote: L'école d'Olympiodore, Etienne d'Alexandrie* (Lille, 1941).

[7]Grigor Magistros, *T^cght^cerē*, ed. K. Kostaneants^c (Alexandropol, 1910), p. 66.

consortium of scholars who together composed the corpus of Neoplatonic Christian texts ascribed to Dionysius the Areopagite.[8] Probabilities of a consortium aside, that corpus was already in existence by the early sixth century.

It is not at all surprising that the pupils of Olympiodorus should have included an Armenian. For even before Mashtotsͨ had deliberately sent his pupils abroad to study and make translations, Armenians had been frequenting the universities of the great cities of the eastern Mediterranean. Constantinople was to become the prime focus of scholarly research for Christian Armenians; but we also know of many Armenians who studied in Antioch in the fourth century,[9] and in Beirut in the fifth;[10] and the lure of Alexandria is echoed by Anania Shirakatsͨi and Moses Khorenatsͨi. Antioch was famous for rhetoric, Beirut for law, and Alexandria for philosophy. The texts used in those universities were studied by Armenians and some were translated into the Armenian language. The technical nature of their subject matter—grammar, logic, and other more scientific topics—led to a more literal style of translation than that used in the earliest period of Armenian literature.[11] But the linguistic problem is not our concern here. What we should emphasize is that Armenians played a role in the intellectual life of the Eastern Roman empire, and that they brought to Armenian scholarship in its formative stage a wide range of scholarly disciplines that went beyond the more strictly ecclesiastical interests of Mashtotsͨ and his immediate circle of pupils.

By the time David was studying and writing in Alexandria, more Armenians had become familiar with various aspects of Greek culture through translations or through original books written in Armenian, such as the work of Eznik, than had had the opportunity to study abroad themselves. Nonetheless, when David's *Definitions of Philosophy* was translated into Armenian, the translator realized that many of its allusions to things well known in Alexandria would not necessarily be immediately comprehensible to the readership in Armenia, where the cultural background was significantly different. So he introduced a

---

[8] S. S. Arevshatyan, "Davitͨ Anhaghtͨě ev hin Hayastani pͨilisopͨayakan Mitkͨě," *Patma-Banasirakan Handes* (1980), part 1, pp. 21-39.

[9] P. Petit, *Les étudiants de Libanius* (Paris, 1957).

[10] Zacharias Rhetor, *Vita Severi*, ed. M. Kugener, Patrologia Orientalis II, 1 (Paris, 1904), p. 57.

[11] A bibliography of earlier Armenian scholarship on this so-called Hellenizing School will be found in A. N. Muradyan, *Hunaban dprotsͨě* (Erevan, 1971). See also H. Lewy, Introduction to *The Pseudo-Philonic De Jona, Studies and Documents*, 7 (London, 1936).

number of changes in order to make the book easier to understand. The changes do not involve the basic ideas of David's philosophy, but some are interesting in that they draw attention to Armenian themes.

Let us begin with some of the minor variations. For example, in chapter 20 David discusses images made in wax: The wax cannot take the imprint of a different image unless that of the first image is destroyed. David uses Hector as an example of a person whose image might be made in wax; but the Armenian text reads "Tigran," a figure who would come to the Armenian mind more readily than the Greek hero.[12] It is worth noting that other works by David were similarly altered in their Armenian versions. Thus, in the translation of his commentary on Aristotle's *Categories*, Helen is rendered as "Tigranuhi." And elsewhere Vardan is introduced as an example of bravery. More amusingly, the example of Socrates as a philosopher becomes, in Armenian, "David."[13]

Many other allusions to classical lore that would have been familiar to a Greek audience are either omitted or explained. For example, Alcibiades is usually expunged,[14] and references to gymnastics, not a typically Armenian sport, are omitted.[15] Epicureans or Pythagoreans, however, are explicitly named on occasion, when the reference would not be obvious to an Armenian,[16] as is also Homer when the Greek merely reads "the poet."[17] The *Theaetetus* of Plato is defined as "a dialogue."[18] When David refers to Argives and Boeotians, the Armenian translator adds: "and all the other Greeks,"[19] for these two peoples would not be familiar to an Armenian reader. And to a list of natural disasters the Armenian adds "earthquake."[20]

Actual mistakes in rendering the Greek are very rare. There are only two clear examples. One is in a quotation from the poet Theognis and involves reading a rough breathing in place of a smooth breathing: κατ' ἠλιβάτων is rendered by *yaregnakokh*,[21] that is, the Armenian stem -*kokh* correctly renders -βατ-, but ἡλι- was read instead of ἠλι-, so "sun" in the Armenian takes the place of "high." The other mistake is

---

[12]Greek, p. 62²⁰; Armenian, p. 130³⁴. References are to Busse's and Arevshatyan's editions of David's *Definitions*; see n. 1 above.

[13]For changes in the Armenian version of Aristotle's *Categories* see A. Vardanian, "Hay Tarrner Aristotēli Storogutʿeantsʿ tʿargmanutʿean mēj," *Handes Amsorya*, 34 (1920), 292–295. For the use of Vardan see Conybeare, p. vi (see n. 3 above).

[14]Greek, p. 7⁸, 15⁸. But not on p. 136 of the Armenian.

[15]Greek, p. 19³⁵.

[16]Armenian, pp. 18³³, 96¹⁵.

[17]Greek, p. 14³⁵, 31¹⁰; Armenian, pp. 34³⁴, 72⁷.

[18]Greek, p. 37³; Armenian, p. 86¹.

[19]Greek, p. 75¹; Armenian, p. 150²⁰.

[20]Greek, p. 33²²; Armenian, p. 76³⁰

[21]Greek, p. 32²²; Armenian, p. 74²².

reading "Plato" for "Plotinus" on two occasions.[22] The second time, three of the five manuscripts used for the Armenian edition have garbled renderings of Plotinus (Platinios, Platonios, Planios). This indicates that the translator probably wrote Plotinus on that occasion, but the name was totally unfamiliar to later scribes.

In addition to being able to distinguish Plotinus from Plato, the translator was clearly familiar with the actual writings of the latter. For when David quotes the *Timaeus* in chapter 1, the Armenian adds that the demiurge is here addressing "the spiritual powers," though they are not mentioned in the Greek text.[23]

But these changes are not particularly significant. Let us turn to adaptations that are more complex. For example, in the first chapter David deals with the problem of giving names to things that have no real existence. Some philosophers had claimed that if something can be named it must exist. But David gives three examples of Greek words that describe nonexistent things: the τραγέλαφος (goat-stag—a fantastic animal often mentioned in classical Greek literature), σκινδαψός (which can refer to a stringed musical instrument but more generally stands for a meaningless word) and βλίτυρι (the twang of a harp string and hence a meaningless sound). The Armenian renders the "goat-stag" more or less literally by *eghjernakʽagh* "horned goat." But in place of the other two Greek words the translator has put *aralēz*, the mythical creature of Armenian lore that supposedly restored life by licking.[24] (The most famous example comes in the story of Ara and Semiramis, as reported by Moses Khorenatsʽi. Alas, the Assyrian queen's sorcery was ineffectual and Semiramis was cheated of her desired Armenian hero.)[25] The word *aralez* is variously spelled in Armenian sources. Faustos Buzand (V, 35) refers to the *aṛlezkʽ*. Moses Khorenatsʽi (I, 15) does not actually name the creature, but by referring to *Ara* and using the verb *lizel* he implies a form *aralēz*, as in David. Eznik writes both *aṛlez* and *aralēz*.[26] More significant from our point of view is the fact that Eznik uses this word of

---

[22]Greek, pp. 30[31], 59[17]; Armenian, pp. 70[22], 124[19]. Similarly at p. 9[22] of the Greek (Armenian, p. 22[14]) the Armenian text reads "Phaedo" for "Phaedrus," but three manuscripts have the correct title.

[23]Armenian, p. 2[17].

[24]Greek, p. 1[17]: Armenian, p. 2[22].

[25]Moses Khorenatasʽi, *Patmutʽiwn Hayotsʽ* (Tbilisi, 1913) I, 15.

[26]Eznik, §§122, 124. The references are to the edition and translation by L. Mariès, *Eznik de Koghb, De Deo, Patrologia Orientalis,* vol. 28, fasc. 3 and 4 (Paris, 1959); they correspond to pp. 98 and 100 of the Venice 1826 edition. There are further references to these creatures in Eghishē, *Questions et réponses sur le Genèse,* ed. N. Akinian (Vienna, 1928), p. 18, and in N. Adontz, "Le Questionnaire de Saint Grégoire," *Revue de l'Orient chrétien,* 25 (1925/26), 319. See also the *Primary History,* text in *Patmutʽiwn Sebēosi,* ed. G. V. Abgaryan (Erevan, 1979), p. 51.

"names that do not refer to persons (*anuankʿ arantsʿ andzantsʿ*)." Did the Armenian translator of David have this passage in mind when he added the reference to the *aralēzkʿ* as an example of things that can be named but have no real existence?

A much stranger variation occurs in chapter 12 where David cites the natural attributes of certain animals: the dove is prudent, the lion brave, the fox sagacious, the stork just. Here the Armenian text renders "fox" by "camel."[27] It is not very likely that the Armenian *aghuēs* (fox) has been corrupted in the entire manuscript tradition to *ught* (camel). But there is no suggestion in Armenian fables (for example, in those attributed to Vardan or in the Armenian version of the *Physiologus*) that the camel is renowned for its sagacity. More in keeping with that animal's character is the epithet "vindictive" found in the *Hexaemeron* by Basil of Caesarea, the Armenian version of which was widely read and influential.[28]

In chapter 20, David, discussing number and proportion, refers to music and mentions as examples of musical instruments κύμβαλοι (cymbals) and αὐλοί (flutes). But the Armenian text has *pʿandrunkʿ* (stringed instruments), *pʿoghkʿ* (trumpets), and *tsntsghaykʿ* (cymbals).[29] The first, *pʿandirn* in the singular, is a particularly important instrument in Armenian life, used to accompany the singer of traditional tales (e.g., Moses Khorenatsʿi, I, 6, 24, 31). It was also a feature in the pagan funeral practices against which the Armenian clergy protested so violently. Thus Faustos Buzand (V, 31) contrasts the calm, Christian behavior with which the dead were buried during the pontificate of Nersēs I (tears, psalms, lighted candles), with the wild habits after Nersēs's death: "They buried them dancing their laments with trumpets (*pʿogh*) and lyres (*pʿandirn*) and flutes (*vin*), cutting their arms and tearing their faces, men and women dancing together in filthy lasciviousness and clapping their hands." Conversely, cymbals are associated with biblical themes, and trumpets even more so. But since in the Armenian Old Testament "lyre" is rendered by *kʿnar* and the word *pʿandirn* never appears, the Armenian translator of David's *Definitions* was probably not thinking of biblical parallels when he rendered "cymbals and flutes" by the three Armenian terms *pʿandrunkʿ*, *pʿoghkʿ*, and *tsntsghaykʿ*.

It is difficult to imagine any non-Christian writing in, or making translations into, Armenian. The Christian nature of early Armenian litera-

---

[27]Greek, p. 39[7]; Armenian, p. 90[26].

[28]Basil, *Hexaemeron*, 71A. On the Armenian version see K. M. Muradyan, *Barsegh Kesaratsʿin ev nra ʿVetsʿoryanʾ hay matenagrutʿyan mej* (Erevan, 1976).

[29]Greek, p. 64[20]; Armenian, p. 134[7].

ture is all pervasive. Of course, Christian writers had interests beyond what we might call Christian texts, for some writers of pagan antiquity were read and translated. But in view of the numerous variations in the Armenian rendering of David's *Definitions*, it is noteworthy that little effort was made to infuse Christian ideas into the text. At the very end, when David summarizes the purposes of philosophy, the Armenian translator expands a little to say: "God granted philosophy."[30] And when the Greek text speaks of the control of one's desires, the Armenian translator says: "so that we should not receive any false knowledge from our reflection nor work any evil deed."[31] Earlier, in chapter 3, the Armenian text slightly expands the Greek to include a reference to God as creator.[32] And in chapter 6 the nymphs of classical mythology are rendered by "angels and demons."[33] But there are no explicit or implicit references to Christianity as such.

In general the Armenian text of David's *Definitions* abbreviates the original, especially in the second half, which is more of an adaptation than a translation of the Greek. But there are a few additions of some length, not just of an explanatory word or phrase. For example, in chapter 20 David, having cited Orpheus, makes a reference to the power of music over animals and men. At the end of that section the Armenian translator adds: "just as some tell the tale (*vipasaneal*) about Alexander: that when he was feasting, the musician played a martial tune, and he straightway armed himself and went out to the attack; then when the musician played melodies of jollity, he returned to join the guests."[34] This story does not occur in the Armenian version of the *Alexander Romance*, where the only reference to the power of music over Alexander (when the bard Ismenias tried to turn him to pity) indicates that Alexander was not beguiled.[35] Nor do references to Orpheus in the works of rhetoric available in Armenian mention this tale. The translator of David's text was thus himself familiar with Greek traditions beyond what was available in Armenian texts—as we have already noted with regard to Plato.

Greek was not the only literature with which Armenians were familiar. Syriac had been used in the Armenian Church before the time of Mashtotsʿ, and translations of Afrahat, and more especially of Ephrem, had

---

[30] Greek, p. 79^{24}; Armenian, p. 158^{10}.
[31] Greek, p. 79^{26-28}; Armenian, p. 158^{13-14}.
[32] Greek, p. 8^{15}; Aremenian, p. 18^{35}.
[33] Greek, p. 16^2; Armenian, p. 38^{12}.
[34] Armenian, p. 134^{16-23}.
[35] *Patmutʿiwn Aghekʿsandri Makedonatsʿwoy* (Venice, 1842), §131.

exerted a profound influence on early Armenian Christian literature. Furthermore, numerous works of Jewish origin were translated into Armenian and had a wide vogue. This helps explain another addition in the Armenian version of David's *Definitions*.

Chapter 14 of the Armenian is a very abbreviated rendering of chapters 16 and 17 in the Greek and omits most of the complicated discussion concerning numbers. At the very end of the chapter the translator adds some comments about the number seven: "Children born in the seventh month have a better chance of survival, in the seventh month children produce their first teeth, and in the seventh year they change them."[36] This has parallels in the curious speculations in Anania Shirakats'i, who notes that the child conceived on the seventh day will be a son; children born in the seventh month will be healthy; in the seventh year the mental aptitudes are advanced enough for children to start school; and at twice times seven the reproductive powers are formed.[37] This is not the place to investigate the number symbolism found in Armenian whose origins are to be sought in Christian interpretations of Jewish traditions.[38] What is interesting from our point of view is that the translator did not think such notions incompatible with the philosophical theme of David's *Definitions*. But then, neither were these speculations ignored by Philo, whose works in Armenian translation had a profound influence on numerous Armenian writers.

In the preceding remarks attention has been focused on how an Armenian translator wrought certain changes in his text in order to make it more meaningful for an Armenian audience. Some works of a more technical nature than David's *Definitions of Philosophy* required even greater adaptations when translated into Armenian. Such, for example, was the case with the *Ars Grammatica* of Dionysius Thrax; not only were references to classical motifs omitted, but the grammatical examples were adapted and expanded to fit the structure of the Armenian language.[39]

One could also point to historical works written in other languages, but adapted for an Armenian readership. Both the Georgian chronicles known in Armenian as *Juanshēr* (of which the Georgian *Juanshēr* is only a part) and the Syriac history by the patriarch Michael were translated

---

[36] Armenian, p. 114[11-14].

[37] Anania Shirakats'i, *Matenagrut'yunĕ*, ed. A. G. Abrahamyan (Erevan, 1944), p. 245.

[38] See R. W. Thomson, "Number Symbolism and Patristic Exegesis in Some Early Armenian Writers," *Handes Amsorya*, 90 (1976) 117-138.

[39] The Greek and Armenian texts are juxtaposed in N. Adontz, *Dionysii Frakiiskii i Armyanski Tolkovateli*, Bibliotheca Armeno-Georgica 4 (St. Petersburg, 1915); French translation, *Denys de Thrace et les commentateurs arméniens* (Louvain, 1970).

into Armenian. But not only are the translations shorter than the original, the translators also introduce new Armenian material into their adaptations.⁴⁰ Then there are translations which have been doctored for a tendentious purpose. This occurs most frequently in theological texts in which the authority of earlier writers is claimed for later dogmatic positions. There is nothing peculiarly Armenian about this very general phenomenon; but I might mention in passing that by a series of subtle changes in the Armenian texts Athanasius of Alexandria was transformed from an anti-Arian champion to an opponent of Chalcedon—which council was held about seventy years after his death.⁴¹ However, this is taking us away from our theme; for there is no suggestion that the Armenian adaptation of David's *Definitions of Philosophy* was made with any ulterior motive save that of simplification.

Sometimes the Armenian translations of technical works such as this, made in the so-called "Hellenizing" style, are condemned for their slavishness to the original texts and for lacking the literary polish of earlier translations, such as that of the Bible (the "queen of versions," as it has been named). I do not think that many would deny that the effort to render technical texts in Armenian was sometimes taken to extremes. But it was necessary to create a specialized vocabulary, totally new in Armenian, and precise verbal equivalence was considered vital in works of logic or rhetoric. In the hands of inexpert translators the results were often ungainly, sometimes incomprehensible, and occasionally ludicrous. For example, the Armenian rendering of the texts ascribed to Dionysius the Areopagite, mentioned earlier, abounds with obscurities which can be explained by the fact that the translator (in this case, Stephen of Siwnikʿ) looked at syllables separately and not at whole phrases.⁴²

But although there were excesses, I wish to conclude by suggesting that a blanket verdict of slavishness is unjustified. In the case of David's *Definitions* there was a clear desire on the part of the translator to make his text more meaningful for the Armenian reader than a perfectly literal rendering would have been. Such freedom, such willingness to adapt in a creative fashion, is a sign of vitality; it evinces an intellectual awareness of the problems involved. This also comes out in the Armenian rendering of Basil's *Hexaemeron*, to which I referred earlier when discussing

---

⁴⁰*Hamaṛōt Patmutʿiwn Vratsʿ ěntsayeal Juanshēri Patmchʿi* (Venice, 1884); *Zhamanakagrutʿiwn Tearn Mikhayēli Asorwotsʿ Patriarkʿi* (Jerusalem, 1871).

⁴¹R. W. Thomson, "The Transformation of Athanasius in Armenian Theology," *Le Muséon*, 78 (1965), 47-69.

⁴²R. W. Thomson, "The Armenian Version of Ps.-Dionysius Areopagita," *Acta Jutlandica*, 57 (1982), 115-123.

the camel. Here the translator has frequently expanded the original in order to make the arguments clearer to his Armenian readers. So the great influence of David's works on later Armenian thinkers is not only explained by the fact that he was a significant expositor of the philosophy of late antiquity. I suggest that the sympathetic adaptation of his works into Armenian played a large role in the emergence of David as "the Invincible Philosopher."

Additional Note: Arevshatyan's text of 1960 (see above n. 1) has been reprinted with English translation, Introduction and commentary in: B. Kendall and R.W. Thomson, *Definitions and Divisions of Philosophy by David the Invincible Philosopher*, University of Pennsylvania Armenian Texts and Studies 5, Chico, Calif., 1983.

XVI

THE ARMENIAN VERSION OF THE GEORGIAN CHRONICLES

Armenian literature is rich in historical writing. For more than two centuries scholars in various fields have combed these texts for what Armenian sources have to say about the history and culture not only of Armenia but also of the many neighboring countries. Armenian studies have greatly profited from these investigations, even if they were not always prompted by an interest in things Armenian for their intrinsic value. Just as recent non-Armenians have translated Armenian sources for their own purposes, so early Armenian scholars translated foreign works into their own language for what these could contribute to the broader picture of Armenia in relation to her neighbors. Before discussing the particular example of the Georgian *Chronicles*, it may be useful to look briefly at other historical works translated into Armenian to see in what ways these were relevant to Armenian purposes.

The motivation for the earliest translations following the invention of the Armenian script is clear enough. Armenian literature begins with Masht'ots'; and although *ipsissima verba* have not been recorded, all sources agree that the first effort at translations was directed to aiding the church in its evangelizing role.[1] The Bible and the church fathers were needed in the native tongue. (Curiously little is said about liturgical texts, which were just as essential for the regular operations of church ritual.) So in the first instance we might expect to find Armenian versions of those histories which had described the origin and progress of the church militant.

If we omit the role of the Bible itself as a historical record, pride of place belongs to the *Ecclesiastical History* of Eusebius of Caesarea. This was among the first works translated into Armenian, at the express command of Masht'ots' according to Movsēs Khorenats'i. But he does not indicate that the rendering was made from an exemplar in Syriac, not from the original Greek.[2] This indirect path is not particularly surprising, for numerous disciples of Masht'ots' were sent to Syrian territory to learn Syriac, while others learned Greek (and some learned both). Since Edessa figures prominently in Eusebius's *History*, and since it was to Edessa that Masht'ots' had first gone in his quest for a script, it is very likely that a copy of the book in Syriac came easily to hand in those first days of literacy. And other Greek books not so immediately essential for ecclesiastical purposes, such as the *Hexaemeron* by Basil of Caesarea, also came into Armenian via their Syriac renderings.³

A second historical work by Eusebius was also translated into Armenian, his *Chronicle*. This dealt primarily with pre-Christian history and demonstrates how the old dispensation described in the Bible correlated with the history of the great empires of the ancient world as known from non-Christian sources. The *Chronicle* was not rendered into Armenian as early as the *Ecclesiastical History*, and it came directly from the Greek.⁴ Although Movsēs Khorenats'i has no reference to the *Chronicle*, it was in fact one of his most important sources and enabled him to set the long past history of Armenia into perspective alongside the great civilizations of antiquity.⁵ Later Armenian historians are equally familiar with Eusebius's *Ecclesiastical History* and his *Chronicle*; from the latter come most of their citations of earlier historians.

However, given the number of works translated into Armenian from Greek and Syriac and adapted to Armenian needs, it is surprising that few other foreign histories were translated.⁶ Not until the late seventh century was the *History* of Socrates Scholasticus rendered into Armenian, long after the development of a native tradition of historiography.⁷ Socrates' *History* was of some importance in the development of Armenian theories concerning the antiquity of their patriarchate,⁸ and it is served as a source for the history of the Arian controversy. But those were past events; the translator, Philo of Tirak, was not interested in contemporary matters. Nor are there Armenian renderings of the Byzantine historians, despite the familiarity of Armenian historians with events in the empire and the many visits of Armenians to Constantinople. Numerous translations of Greek works were made in the imperial capital, but these were works of the patristic period not yet available in Armenian.⁹ One looks in vain for Armenian versions of Procopius, Theophanes, Psellus, or other noted Byzantine historians.

The only non-Christian historian influential in Armenia was the Jewish writer Josephus. Since he dealt with events close to the time of Christ,¹⁰ and since the Maccabees whose revolt he describes in his *Antiquities* were an important model for Armenian authors,¹¹ it is not surprising that he is frequently mentioned. But only his *History of the Jewish Wars* was translated into Armenian, though the first version is lost. The many quotations of Movsēs Khorenats'i are so close to the known Armenian version that it is hardly conceivable that Movsēs used a Greek text and happened to render it in the same fashion as the translator. Yet the only surviving version dates from the seventeenth century. This rendering, by Stephen of Lvov, is to be seen as a revision of a lost earlier Armenian translation.[12] This supposition not only elucidates the use of Josephus by Movsēs, it parallels another work by Stephen of Lvov—his rendering of the Pseudo-Dionysian corpus. This had first been translated into Armenian from Greek in the early eighth century. But Stephen found it so obscure that he revised it from a Latin rendering.[13]

Josephus, Eusebius, Socrates, and some lesser Chronicles of Christian origin,[14] fitted the Armenian interest in Christian origins and the development of their own Christian traditions. This attitude is also reflected in the adaptation of two foreign works which date to a much later period. It was not their version of twelfth-century history that prompted these renderings, but rather the importance of these two works for their antiquarian information and their contribution to the period when the Armenians were developing their own national traditions. These texts are the *Chronicle* of Michael, patriarch of the Syrian Jacobite church who died in 1199, which was rendered into Armenian in the following century,[15] and the Armenian version of the Georgian *Chronicles*, which was made a little earlier.[16] These translations demonstrate Armenian interest in the history of other countries. But neither is a strict rendering of the original. The Georgian *Chronicles* were greatly abbreviated, and into both a good deal of Armenian material was interpolated. For example, the translation of Michael's *Chronicle* elaborates on the story of King Abgar of Edessa (who was claimed as an Armenian by Movsēs Khorenats'i), on the role of the Armenians at the ecumenical councils, and on the accounts of Persian invasions into Armenia.[17] The elaborations on the original Georgian *Chronicles* are the main focus of the following investigation.

The Armenian version of the Georgian *Chronicles* (transliterated as *K'art'lis Ts'khovreba*) ends in midsentence. Having described the death of King David II (the Builder) in 1125, it refers to the installation of his successor (*nstuts'* . . .) and then breaks off. Since all manuscripts end at the same point, it is unclear whether the original continued any further. An anonymous Armenian chronicler refers to the "Georgian History" continuing to 1151 in an Armenian version, but such a text is not otherwise known.[18] In the early thirteenth century Mkhit'ar of Ani was familiar with the Georgian *Chronicles*, but in the original version, not the Armenian. Step'anos Ōrbēlian refers to this earlier historian in flattering terms. In chapter 66 he states that the *K'art'lis Ts'khovreba* presents a confused account of Georgian history compared to the accurate version in Mkhit'ar of Ani. Unfortunately, the latter is lost.[19] The Armenian version of the Georgian *Chronicles* was used by Vardan, whose own *Chronicle* ends in 1267.[20] and by the later Mkhit'ar Ayrivanets'i.[21] But that leaves a gap between the early twelfth and late thirteenth centuries for the actual composition of the Armenian version. For the earliest surviving exemplar is in Matenadaran 1902, written between 1279 and 1311 for Hamazasp Haghbatets'i. But there is no particular reason to place the translation at that famous monastery. The translator remains unknown.

The date of the adaptation (within a generation or so either side of 1200) makes it the earliest witness to the original, for no extant manuscript of the Georgian predates the late fifteenth century.[22] Its value for the state of the text of the Georgian collection in the thirteenth century is thus considerable—though the greatly abbreviated nature of the Armenian makes its evidence difficult to assess. But the present inquiry is concerned with the innovations introduced into the Armenian by the adapter. For although the text is very much shorter than the original, there are many changes. Some are meaningful, while others have little significance.

Mistakes as such are rare, though scribal confusions played havoc with numbers, and the similarity of certain letters in the Georgian cursive "ecclesiastical" hand led to errors—for example *b* for *sh*. Thus Arshak becomes "Arbak." But the correct rendering of technical terms indicates that the translator was very familiar with literary Georgian, though occasionally proper names have been misinterpreted. Later scribes ignorant of Georgian, however, introduced many curious variants into the Armenian text, and the original translator cannot be blamed for all anomalies in the printed editions.

The translator was not rigid in his rendering. He might translate compounds with clear Armenian equivalents always in the same way. For example, Dedats'ikhe is rendered as Mayraberd, Rkinis-khevi as Erkat'adzor, *mamasakhli* as *tanutēr*. But other Georgian terms might be rendered in different ways according to the context. For example, *eristavi* has no precise calque in Armenian, so the translator uses *nakharar, sparapet, koghmnakal, gawaṙapet*. Not infrequently the Armenian gives a transliteration of the original term and then adds a gloss. Whether all of these go back to the translator is not clear. But typical is the addition of a phrase such as: "which means." Thus we find Up'lis-Ts'ikhe plus "which means lord's castle."[23] Conversely, the Armenian adapter adds a note that the Kushans are not to be confused with the inhabitants of Kush, which is Abyssinia.[24] Sometimes the Armenian and Georgian both offer etymologies, but these differ. Thus the meaning of "Saracen" is given as "servants of Sarah" in the Armenian, but "dogs of Sarah" in the original.[25] Not all explanations give

The Armenian Version of the Georgian Chronicles 85

an etymology. For example, the Qipchaqs are explained as "Huns."[26] And the identification of Chronus with Bel and Nebrot is a reminiscence of the earlier Armenian historian Movsēs Khorenats'i. There are some minor variations in the quotation of scripture. The Armenian will sometimes identify the book for which the Georgian gives only a vague reference to "scripture"; or a person in scripture may be identified. Other minor differences in the Armenian include the addition of dating: "at the time that."

But such differences between the two texts do not amount to significant variations. By far the most interesting divergence between them is the addition of new material to the Armenian, especially given the greatly abbreviated nature of the rendering. These additions may be divided into two general groups: additions of particular Armenian interest, and additions that are neutral with regard to Armenia. The second category deals mainly with religious or biblical material.

P. 16 of the Armenian (Georgian, p. 14). The Armenian elaborates on Moses—called "the friend of the great God," which Vardan copies[28] —and the crossing of the Red Sea. The twelve tribes are said to have been 60,000 strong (instead of the 600,000 of Exod. 12:37); and manna is described as "bread that came down from heaven" (as Exod. 16:15).

P. 17 (Georgian, p. 16). Pagans are said to eat "crawling reptiles and worms." This is not so much a reflection on the eating of carrion in Armenia before the "reforms" of Artashēs (described by Movsēs Khorenats'i, II 59), as a parallel to the many references in Eznik to worms, which are associated with paganism and evil.

P. 51 (Georgian, p. 96). Daniel's prophecy is explained as referring to the Son of God, which prophecy was fulfilled in the days of Augustus—a reference to Luke 2.

P. 51 (Georgian, p. 98). To the story of the magi is added a reference to their finding "as a guide a rational and wise star in the desert." This is an unusual description of the star, which has no parallel in patristic literature known to me. "Rational" and "wise" would more normally be used to describe human nature.

P. 57 (Georgian, p. 107). God is described as "driver and controller" (*karavar, yawrinich'*). These attributes are common in theological literature, and in Armenian are first found in Eznik.

P. 77 (Georgian, p. 153). Vakht'ang makes the sign of the cross before going out to battle, and adds a quotation from David's words to Goliath (I King = Sam. 17:47). These are commonplace in Armenian descriptions of combat.

P. 80 (Georgian, p. 162). The story of the tower of Babel is elaborated. Those who climbed to the top understood the meaning of the seven spheres of the stars. These spheres are described in several Armenian texts.[29] With the tower is associated Christ's cross, it also being a stairway to heaven. This is a major theme of *The Teaching of Saint Gregory* (in the *History* of Agat'angeghos).[30]

P. 90 (Georgian, p. 196). The authority of the see of Antioch over Georgia is stressed. Also at p. 95 (Georgian, p. 207), when the Georgians installed their own Catholicoi, the Georgian text notes that these no longer came from Greece. But the Armenian adds that this happened without the permission of Antioch.

P. 102 (Georgian, p. 244). There is a long elaboration on Kaghert' and the rise of Muhammad. This is closely parallel to the account in Samuel of Ani, but not to any of the many other versions of the origin of Islam found in Armenian historians.[31]

P. 117 (Georgian, p. 117). There is an elaboration of scripture with a simile of fish cast out. This is based on the image of the kingdom of heaven in Mat. 13:48.

In addition to these expansions of a theological nature, there are others with a clear Armenian interest.

P. 11 (Georgian, p. 10). The Armenian adds that the unity of the sons of T'orgom prevented their being defeated in war. The theme of unity is central to the classic descriptions of the Armenian resistance to Sasanian aggression found in Eghishē and Ghazar; when that unity was ruptured, then Armenia was defeated.

Pp. 17-18 (Georgian, p. 16-17). The Georgian text indicates that six languages were originally spoken in Georgia: Armenian, Georgian, Khazar, Syriac, Hebrew, and Greek. But the Armenian adapter says that the Georgian tongue is merely a combination of the other five!

P. 41 (Georgian, p. 65). At the beginning of his reign King Mirian agrees to Persian demands that he worship both Persian and traditional gods. But the Armenian changes this to indicate that the Georgians refused to abandon their traditional religion. "It is better for us to die, they said, than to be separated from the rites of our fathers." Again this is a reminiscence of a major theme in Eghishē, curiously changed to reflect defense of paganism. The main point is the appeal to ancestral custom.

P. 50 (Georgian, pp. 95-96). Although the Georgian speaks of a threefold division of Israel, the Armenian adds that Romans, Greeks, and Armenians ruled over Israel. This change may reflect the description of Tigran's conquests in Palestine as described by Movsēs Khorenats'i, II 14.

P. 53 (Georgian, p. 101). To an expansion describing Old Testament prophecies of Christ, the Armenian adds a reference to the Georgian king hearing of the miracles (i.e., conversion) that had occurred in Armenia. This is reminiscent of news of these miracles reaching Georgia as described by Movsēs Khorenats'i, II 86. There are other additions referring to Armenia's conversion at p. 66 (Georgian, p. 125) and p. 79 (Georgian, p. 161). This last has added details from the text of Agat'angeghos.

P. 56 (Georgian, p. 105). To a description of idols and fire in Georgian paganism the Armenian text adds "sun" and "Aramazd." Again this seems to be a reminiscence of Eghishē, for he stresses the Persian worship of sun and fire. Aramazd figures prominently in all early Armenian descriptions of paganism.

P. 72 (Georgian, p. 138). The Persians are described as establishing fire temples following their invasion of Georgia. Again there are parallels with Eghishē's description of the Persian invasion of Armenia.

P. 97 (Georgian, p. 224). The Armenian adds that Heraclius stopped in Bznunik' on his way to Georgia. There is no exact parallel in Armenian descriptions of Heraclius's campaigns, though his presence in Armenia is described by them.[32]

P. 103 (Georgian, p. 245). The Armenian adds an explanation of the origin of Kamakh, a name for Ani not found in Armenian before the eleventh century. Surprisingly, the Armenian addition gives the fortress a Georgian origin, claiming that it was founded by Georgian princes fleeing from Muslim depredations.

P. 111 (Georgian, p. 289). The miracle of the Catholicos Peter is added. This occurred on the feast of the Epiphany, near Trebizond, in the presence of the Byzantine Emperor Basil II. The story is first found in Aristakēs.[33] The wording in the Armenian version of the Georgian is closer to the version in Kirakos (who was writing after the adaptation had been made).

At the end of the book the relationship of King David to Yovhannēs Sarkawag is elaborated. This was known from Sarkawag's own *History* (now lost), and was picked up by Vardan in his *Chronicle*. The opprobrious comments about Armenians "who imagined that they had attained the summit of all learning and science," however, are omitted!

The influence of the Armenian version of the Georgian *Chronicles* on later Armenian writers deserves a separate study. Here my intention has been to demonstrate how a foreign text was not merely made accessible to Armenian readers, but was in minor ways altered in the process. The adapter was more interested in early Georgian history and in themes common to Georgian and Armenian traditions than in events closer to his theme. So the rendering becomes increasingly more abbreviated. Various explanatory notes were added—as was not uncommon in Armenian translations.[34] But more interesting are the modifications that subtly boost the role of the Armenians or draw unacknowledged parallels with Armenian history.[35]

NOTES

1. Koriwn (M. Abeghyan, ed., [Erevan, 1941; repr. Caravan Books: Delmar, NY, 1985, with Introduction by K. H. Maksoudian], pp. 40 ff.). Ghazar P'arbets'i (G. Tēr-Mkrtch'ian and St. Malkhasian, eds., [Tiflis, 1904; repr. Caravan Books: Delmar, NY, 1985, with Introduction by D. Kouymjian], pp. 13-14). Movsēs Khorenats'i [M. Abeghian and S. Yarut'iwnian, eds., [Tiflis, 1913; repr. Caravan Books: Delmar, NY, 1981, with Introduction by R. W. Thomson], III 52-54).

2. Movsēs Khorenats'i, II 10. The text was edited by A. V. Charian, *Ewsebiosi Kesaras'woy Patmut'iwn Ekeghets'woy* (Venice, 1877). For the Syriac original see W. Wright and N. McLean, *The Ecclesiastical History of Eusebius Pamphili, with a Collation of the Ancient Armenian Version by A. Merx* (Cambridge, 1898); cf. P. Vetter, "Über die armenische Übersetzung der Kirchengeschichte des Eusebius," *Theologische Quartalschrift* 63 (1881), 250-276.

3. H. Tēr-Petrosyan, "Barsegh Kesarats'u 'Vets'oreayk'i' hayeren t'argmanut'yan nakhōrinakě," *Patma-Banasirakan Handes*, Part 2-3 (1983), 264-278. Cf. also L. Leloir, "Divergences entre l'original syriaque et la version arménienne du commentaire d'Ephrem sur le Diatessaron," *Mélanges Eugène Tisserant*, Volume II, Studi e Testi 232 (Vatican 1964), pp. 303-331.

4. For the text see J. Aucher, *Eusebii Pamphili Caesariensis Episcopi, Chronicon Bipartitum*, 2 vols. (Venice, 1818). The date of the rendering and its origin are discussed in the Introduction to J. Karst, *Die Chronik des Eusebius aus dem armenischen übersetzt*. Die Griechischen Christlichen Schriftsteller 20 (Leipzig, 1911).

5. R. W. Thomson, *Movses Khorenats'i, History of the Armenians* (Cambridge, MA, 1978), pp. 32-36.

6. Though long out of date the survey by G. Zarbhanalian, *Matenadaran haykakan t'argmanut'eants' nakhneats', dar 4-13* (Venice, 1889), gives a good idea of the range of authors translated.

7. *Sokratay Sk'olastikosi "Ekeghets'akan Patmut'iwn" ew Patmut'iwn Varuts' srboyn Seghbestrosi Episkoposin Hŕovmay*, M. Tēr Movsēsian, ed., (Vagharshapat, 1897). P. Peeters, "A propos de la version arménienne de l'historien Socrate," *Mélanges Bidez* (= *Annuaire de l'Institut de Philologie et d'histoire orientales*, 2 [1934]), pp. 647-675; repr. *Recherches d'histoire et de philologie orientales par. P. Peeters*, Vol. I, Subsidia Hagiographica 27 (Brussels, 1951), pp. 310-336.

8. K. Maksoudian, *Yovhannes Drasxanakertc'i, History of Armenia* (Atlanta, 1987), p. 244.

9. For example, the Pseudo-Dionysian corpus translated by Stephen of Siwnik', for which see R. W. Thomson, *The Armenian Version of the works attributed to Dionysius the Areopagite*, Corpus Scriptorum Christianorum Orientalium 488 (Louvain, 1987), p. xiii.

10. See Asoghik, *Patmut'iwn tiezerakan*, S. Malkhaseants', ed., (St. Petersburg, 1885), I 1 (p. 6).
11. R. W. Thomson, "The Maccabees in Early Armenian Historiography," *Journal of Theological Studies* 26 (1975), 329-341.
12. Thomson, *Moses Khorenats'i*, 25-29.
13. R. W. Thomson, "The Armenian Version of Ps.-Dionysius Areopagite," *Acta Jutlandica* 57 (1982), 115-123, esp. p. 115.
14. E.g., the "Anonymous Chronicle" based in Hippolytus: *Ananun Zhamanakagrut'iwn*, B. Sargisian, ed., (Venice, 1904), studied by Markwart and Bauer in A. Bauer and R. Helm, *Hippolytus Werke*, Vol. IV, *Die Chronik*, Die Griechischen Christlichen Schriftseller 36 (Leipzig, 1929), pp. 393-558.
15. There is as yet no critical edition of this text, which exists in more than one recension. The text, *Mikhayēli Patriark'i Asorwoy Zhamanakagrut'iwn*, has been published in 1870 and again in 1871 in Jerusalem; the translation, V. Langlois, *Chronique de Michel le grand, patriarche des syriens jacobites, traduite pour la première fois sur la version arménienne du prêtre Ischôk* (Venice, 1868), is from a different recension.
16. The first edition of the Armenian was published as *Hamaŕōt Patmut'iwn Vrats' ēntsayeal Juanshēri Patmch'i* (Venice, 1884). This is the edition cited in this article. The more recent edition by I. Abuladze (Tbilisi, 1953) was not available in the United States. The original Georgian comprises most of the first volume of S. Qaukhch'ishvili, *K'art'lis Ts'khovreba*, 2 vols. (Tbilisi, 1955, 1959). The brief study by N. Akinian, "Patmut'iwn Vrats'," in *Simēon Pghndzahanets'i ew ir t'argmanut'iwnnerē vratserēnē* (Vienna, 1951), is cited often below. For a general description of the Georgian Chronicles see C. Toumanoff, "Medieval Historical Georgian Literature," *Traditio* 1 (1943), 139-182, esp. pp. 161-176.
17. See F. Haase, "Die armenische Rezension der Syrischen Chronik Michaels des Grossen," *Oriens Christianus*, 5 (1915), 60-82, 271-284.
18. Akinian (as n. 16), p. 172.
19. For what survives see H. G. Margaryan, *Mkhit'ar Anets'i, Matean ashkharhavēp handisaranats'* (Erevan, 1983).
20. *Hawak'umn Patmut'ean Vardanay Vardapeti* (Venice, 1862), pp. 11-12. For Vardan's sources see R. W. Thomson, "The Historical Compilation of Vardan Arewelc'i," *Dumbarton Oaks Papers* 43 (1989), 125-226.
21. Akinian, pp. 172-173.
22. Qaukhch'ishvili (as n. 16), p. 014. C. Toumanoff, "The Oldest Manuscript of the Georgian Annals: The Queen Anne Codex (QA), 1479-1495," *Traditio* 5 (1947), 310-344.
23. Armenian text (as n. 16), p. 20; Georgian, p. 19.
24. Armenian, p. 89; Georgian, p. 195.
25. Armenian, p. 98; Georgian, p. 230.
26. Armenian, p. 118; Georgian, p. 336.
28. Vardan (as n. 20), p. 1.
29. E.g., Anania Shirakats'i, *Matenagrut'yunē*, A. G. Abrahamyan, ed., (Erevan, 1944), p. 325. Eghishē, *Matenagrut'iwnk'* (Venice, 1859), p. 322.
30. R. W. Thomson, *The Teaching of Saint Gregory* (Cambridge, MA, 1970), §§ 577-586, 620-631.
31. See R. W. Thomson, "Muhammad and the Origin of Islam in Armenian Literary Tradition," *Armenian Studies in Memoriam Haig Berbérian*, D. Kouymjian, ed., (Lisbon 1986), pp. 829-858.
32. An elaborate description of Heraclius's encounter with the princess of Siwnik' is found in the "Pseudo-Shapuh." See R. W. Thomson, "The Anonymous Story-Teller (also known as Pseudo-Šapuh)," *Revue des études arméniennes* 21 (1988-1989), 171-232, esp. 187-190.

34. See, e.g., R. W. Thomson, "The Armenian Version of David's *Definitions of Philosophy*," in *David Anhaght, the 'Invincible' Philosopher*, A. K. Sanjian, ed., (Atlanta, GA, 1986), pp. 37-46.

35. This article contains the results of a preliminary investigation. The final publication will include facing English versions of the Armenian and Georgian texts with accompanying commentary.

XVII

SOME PHILOSOPHICAL TERMS IN THE *TEACHING* OF GREGORY

Extensive theological treatises by early Armenian writers are few in number, so it is unfortunate that one of the most elaborate should be almost completely unknown to Western scholars. This is the *Teaching* of Gregory, the longest of the various documents included in the history attributed to Agathangelus. It is inserted into a sermon supposedly preached by Gregory to the court of Tiridates, but is marked as a separate section in the manuscripts and is only found in the Armenian text of the history (of the various versions only the Arabic shows any knowledge of the *Teaching* [1]). Despite its length, most scholars have passed over it with a mere mention, or at best the remark that its Christology dates from the period before the council of Ephesus, and the fullest account of this work is primarily designed to defend the author from charges of docetism [2]. Its content and vocabulary are of great interest for the history of early Armenian theology, and it is with the latter that the following pages are concerned. In recent years two publications have drawn attention to the fluid state of correspondence between Greek and Armenian technical theological terms [3], so an examination of the terminology of the *Teaching* may provide a stepping-stone for further study of the development of Armenian theological vocabulary.

The author of the *Teaching* did not intend to give a complete exposition of the Christian faith; rather he took a few basic ideas and developed them in detail. His prime concern was to show the continuity

[1] For the various recensions and versions of the history, cf. G. Garitte, *Documents pour l'Étude du Livre d'Agathange*, Studi e Testi 127, Vatican 1946.

[2] S. Weber, *Die katholische Kirche in Armenien*, Freiburg 1903. Cf. also, V. Inglisian, *Chalkedon und die armenische Kirche*, in *Das Konzil von Chalkedon*, ed. A. Grillmeier und H. Bacht, vol. II, Würzburg 1953. The present writer could not obtain the two following works : G. Toumayan, *Agathangelos et la Doctrine de l'Église arménienne au Vème siècle*, Lausanne 1879; J. M. Schmid, *Reden und Lehren des heiligen Grigorius des Erleuchters*, Regensburg 1872.

[3] P. Tekeyan, *Controverses Christologiques en Arméno-Cilicie*, Orientalia Christiana Analecta 124, Rome 1939; M. Tallon, *Livre des Lettres*, Mélanges de l'Université S. Joseph, XXXII, Fasc. I, Beyrouth, 1955.

of the Old and New Testaments, to present the redemption of mankind by Jesus Christ as the fulfillment of the eternal will of God which was revealed by the prophets. Hence his arguments centre in the proper interpretation of the Scriptures and his exegesis is amply supported by extensive quotations from the Bible. The doctrine of the Trinity is expounded at various points in the treatise, but there is no attempt to develop a theory of the union in Christ of God and man. The author was unaware of the Christological debates of the mid-fifth century and consequently his philosophical vocabulary is neither extensive nor subtle. But in the main his terms are employed in a consistent manner, and by a consideration of the various passages in which they occur, a basis for comparison with other works can be laid. All Christian philosophical thought starts from concepts originally expressed in Greek, so the four terms οὐσία, ὑπόστασις, φύσις and πρόσωπον, have been chosen as being the most essential for which the Armenian language had to find suitable equivalents.

The *Teaching* was composed before theological debate had crystallised philosophical terminology in Armenian, but its author was acquainted with several terms not found in the Bible which formed the frame for his exposition. It may, therefore, be interesting briefly to consider the renderings in the New Testament of these four terms, before examining their equivalents in the *Teaching*.

The first, οὐσία, does not occur (except in Luke 15. 12, meaning « property, possessions ») in the New Testament, nor do the Armenian equivalents զոյութիւն, իսկութիւն. The term էութիւն which is the usual translation of οὐσία, and an exact parallel to the Syriac rendering ܐܝܬܘܬܐ [4], occurs only once (Hebrews 1, 3), and there for ὑπόστασις. Ὑπόστασις was sometimes expressed in Armenian by հաստատութիւն, which in the New Testament usually retains its basic meaning of « making firm ». This term also seems modelled on the Syriac rendering, where only the second part of the Greek compound is expressed. As an equivalent for ὑπόστασις it occurs twice (Hebrews 3, 14; 11, 1), but frequently elsewhere to render : πληροφορία, βεβαίωσις, τὸ ἀμετάθετον, καταρτισμός, κατάρτισις, εἰλικρινεία, ἁδρότης, στερέωμα, ἑδραίωμα, where the Syriac has a similarly wide range of words. The narrower philosophical sense of ὑπόστασις

---

[4] The formation of էութիւն (an abstract noun based on the 3rd. person sing. of a verb) is a rare one in Armenian and may be a calque on ܐܝܬܘܬܐ, itself so formed.

PHILOSOPHICAL TERMS IN THE *TEACHING* OF GREGORY

was later rendered in Armenian by զօրութիւն, not an unequivocal term itself, meaning « power » and closer to the Greek ἐνέργεια. Φύσις in the New Testament is always translated by բնութիւն or its cognates (with a sole exception in Ephesians 2, 3) [5]. Πρόσωπον, in cases where the meaning « person » is intended, has no regular equivalent, either երեսք or դէմ being used.

There is no consistent employment of philosophical terms in the Greek New Testament nor, consequently, in the Armenian version. But Armenian writers developed their own usage and in the *Teaching* a few of the above mentioned words are not used at all, while others are given a more precise definition.

In the *Teaching*, էութիւն is the term applied to the existence of the Deity, never to any lesser creature. It refers to the only eternally existent Being; only the Son and the Holy Ghost share the էութիւն of the Father (259) [6]. In § 362 this expression is coupled with Աստուածութիւն and իսկութիւն: the three Persons of the Trinity are equal in these respects. The unity of the Trinity is frequently described as հակակ and in § 458 the word հակականութիւն is coined.

The term իսկութիւն (essence) is found in conjunction with էութիւն and the adjective իսկական is frequently applied to the Deity. The Trinity is defined as : « One Lord, three Persons, one hypostasis ... one in consubstantial glory ... one only in essence » (383) or « three perfect Persons, one perfect will ... one essence, one existence, one Deity » (382). But the author of the *Teaching* does not elaborate the difference between « essence » and « existence » or explain how he understood the exact connotation of these two terms.

The basic difference between the eternal existence of God and the transitory life of man is reflected in the antithesis between էութիւն and լինելութիւն. The latter word refers to created beings (262). This contrast between the two planes of existence is stressed by the author of the *Teaching* who changes a quotation from Philippians 2, 6 (οὐχ ἁρπαγὸν ἡγήσατο τὸ εἶναι ἴσα θεῷ), where the Armenian New Testament has լինել for εἶναι, into հաւալ (711). Here the emphasis is on being like God, so the appropriate verb to describe this truer existence is substituted.

---

[5] ἤμεθα τέκνα φύσει ὀργῆς : էաք արդարեւ որդիք բարկութեան.
[6] The numbers refer to the chapters of the critical edition by Ter-Mkrtčʿean and Kanayeançʿ, Tiflis 1909.

XVII

44

The verb գոյ is also used of the existence of God. The Word is described as having a գոյացութիւն without any beginning (391) and the Trinity has a common գոյութիւն for the three Persons (705). The equation of գոյութիւն with οὐσία and էութիւն with ὑπόστασις is found in the Armenian version of the anathemas [7] added to the Nicene creed, where the Syriac has ܐܝܬܘܬܐ and ܩܢܘܡܐ respectively. In the *Teaching* God's nature is referred to indifferently as էական or գոյական and God is described as never having been seen by anyone գոյիւ (382). Creation was made from what did not exist before; Adam was made and given life from the «non-existent» չգոյէն (275), more usually յոչընչէ (439, 620 etc.).

So what does not partake of the էութիւն of God was created from nothing and exists (լինել) on a lower plane. There is, however, some uncertainly in § 272 whether created beings are made from absolute non-existence or from some undifferentiated substance, like Anaximander's ἄπειρον. The Armenian reads: ամենայն արարածոց առեալ հրաման լինել յաննիւթոյ, ի չքաւոր յանկերպարան նիւթոյ, where the exact connotation of նիւթ is confused. Elsewhere in the *Teaching* նիւթ is defined as տարրական «material», but this is not very helpful as տարրական is only used in contrast to the «immaterial» Godhead or the souls of the angels. But since the writer refers frequently to the biblical doctrine of creation *ex nihilo*, it is unlikely that the one phrase «from formless matter» (յանկերպարան նիւթոյ) should be pressed in a Platonic sense; the author's habit of placing synonyms in juxtaposition to emphasise a point (a common feature of Armenian style) frequently leads to obscurities and inconsistencies.

---

[7] A similar phrase occurs in the anathemas of Abd-Isho (Book of Letters, p. 68). In the *Teaching* there is no clear distinction between οὐσία and φύσις nor between φύσις and ὑπόστασις. Although their Armenian equivalents may be used consistently on the surface, further inquiry into their precise connotation reveals an inadequate grasp of Greek philosophical ideas. Christ took a human nature, yet his own nature is unchanging (588). Here «nature» is the same as «hypostasis». Such ideas are in accord with Cyril's μία φύσις τοῦ Θεοῦ Λόγου σεσαρκωμένη. But the Armenians claimed to base their faith on Nicea, interpreted anachronistically by John Mandakuni who could write : « the Fathers at Nicea did not distinguish two or several natures... but they said one nature (բնութիւն, whereas the Nicene creed has էութիւն) ... the nature of the Word is the same as that of the Father... the nature of the Word is the divinity (Book of Letters, p. 33) ».

PHILOSOPHICAL TERMS IN THE *TEACHING* OF GREGORY

The equivalent of ὑπόστασις in the *Teaching* is not հաստատութիւն (which here retains its basic meaning of «firmament» or «confirmation»), but զորութիւն which sometimes keeps the meaning of «power», especially in compounds. The phrases «consubstantial hypostasis of the Trinity», «one hypostasis, three Persons» occur frequently, and in § 493 it is stated that the hypostasis of Christ was the same before, during and after the passion and resurrection. The «essential hypostasis» (ինքնաբուն զորութիւն) of God is opposed to the material created nature of man (263), whose creation in God's image is described in respect of rationality, not in respect of the մատուածաբուն զորութիւն.

«Nature» (բնութիւն) is a term of wider application than those so far discussed, in that all beings, created or eternal, have their own individual nature which has to be further defined before the differences between objects are apparent. The «nature» of God is described as եական, գոյական, uncreated, invisible etc. In § 362 occurs the curious phrase մի է ութիւն բնութեան which seems to be a forceful way of saying that the Deity can be defined as one existence. Christ humbled Himself, but «remained in his own nature» (378). He «put on human flesh and came down into our likeness, but remained in the glory of his Father's divine nature» (381). Those who were scandalised at his flesh, denied Christ's nature, for He was united to the flesh բնութեամբ (369).

Created substances have each their own nature. Water was made «from nothing into the nature of water» (453) and was turned into the «nature of fire» in the times of the sacrifices (544). Varieties of fruit have the same nature, while being different colours (i.e. genus and species, 643), whereas all plants are fixed in their own nature and cannot change (646). Among the material creatures, man has his own nature which Christ took upon Himself, thus becoming a complete man; whereas He Himself is by nature the only-begotten Son (588). But the mode of union of the two natures is not discussed. The Trinity is one consubstantial nature of three perfect Persons (703). Thus «nature» is a term of differing meaning to the context; its definition is not elaborated, nor is it clear what essential characteristics are necessary for an object to be «of the nature» of any given genus.

The expression used in the *Teaching* for «Person» is always անձն, with the sole exception of § 623 where the number of the Persons (երեսաց) in the Trinity is mentioned. Անձն means « self » or « soul », in which latter sense it is employed both of the angels (who have immaterial souls 324) and of men (576, in the Christian sense of « soul »). But generally this term is reserved for each of the three Persons of the Trinity, distinct as Persons, yet who are one hypostasis, one will and of consubstantial nature.

The author of the *Teaching* was thus not unaware of the niceties of philosophical terminology in theological argument. He never defines his terms, but does avoid ambiguities which were to cause such confusion later. Tekeyan has shown how գոյութիւն, բնութիւն, էութիւն and անձն varied in exact significance and degrees of correspondence at different periods [8]. The *Teaching* already employs these terms, which were to remain the key expressions of later Christological debate. Perhaps the simplicity of the author's thought prevented him from becoming immeshed in verbal obscurities, for whereas much of his exegesis of scriptural quotations is idiosyncratic in the extreme, yet the basis of his exposition is firmly rooted in the Bible.

An examination of the use of the above mentioned terms and their exact significance in each succeeding stage of theological thinking is the first step in any history of Armenian Christology. It is therefore of some interest to consider the connotation of these words in earlier treatises written before controversy became primarily concerned with Christology and the meaning of these terms underwent significant change and development.

Although the *Teaching* must antedate the sixth century when knowledge of the council of Chalcedon was brought to Armenia, yet the ideas implicit in this work are often in harmony with the subsequent dogmatic position of the Armenian church. There is scope for further research in the earliest expressions of Armenian Christian thought and the extent to which they moulded later ideas, for the Armenians remained firmly attached to traditional concepts and refused to accept the « innovations » of Chalcedon.

---

[8] Op. cit. esp. pp. 75 ff.

ADDITIONAL NOTES

A full translation of the *Teaching* with Introduction and commentary has been published: R.W. Thomson, *The Teaching of Saint Gregory: An Early Armenian Catechism*, Harvard Armenian Texts and Studies 3, Cambridge, Mass., 1970. The full Armenian text of Agathangelos has been reprinted from the 1909 critical edition: Agathangelos, *Pat'mowt'iwn Hayots',* Delmar, New York, 1980, with Introduction and brief Bibliography by R.W. Thomson.

For recent studies of the *Teaching* see now M. van Esbroeck, 'Le "De Fide" géorgien attribué à Hippolyte et ses rapports avec la "Didascalie" de Grégoire l'Illuminateur dans l'Agathange (BHO 330)', *Analecta Bollandiana* 102 [1984], 321–328; and for parallels in Syriac L. Ter-Petrosyan, 'Grigor Lusavorč'i Vardapetut'yan Asorakan Ałbyurnerě', *Banber Matenadarani* 15 [1986], 95–109.

XVIII

GREGORY OF NAREK'S *COMMENTARY ON THE SONG OF SONGS*

No person in the long course of Armenian Christianity is more beloved to the Armenian people than the poet Gregory of Narek (Grigor Narekatsi). Born in the middle of the tenth century, he was entrusted at an early age to the monastery of Narek (which is close to the southern edge of Lake Van) where his great-uncle Anania was abbot. Here he spent his whole life as monk and priest; he died in 1010 or a little earlier. Gregory's great fame lies in a collection of ninety-five mystical prayers (known in Armenian as the *Matean olbergut'ean*, 'book of lamentations'), each of which is entitled 'conversation with God from the depths of the heart'. Indeed, this book is often known simply as 'Narek', and it traditionally held a place in the Armenian household hardly less honourable than that of the Bible.[1] The *Book of Lamentations* was the product of his mature years, being finished in 1002, and was the culmination of a lifetime of literary activity. For Gregory is also noted for his hymns, his poems on religious festivals, his homilies, and his panegyrics on various holy figures. However, his earliest work, a *Commentary on the Song of Songs* written in 977,[2] has been surprisingly neglected. But perhaps this is not so odd, for Gregory of Narek's appeal derives from his poetry and mystical fervour, which are not the main features of this commentary. And Armenian biblical commentaries in general have been almost entirely ignored by recent scholars. So it may be a small service to the cause of classical Armenian literature if the contents of Gregory's commentary are summarized and some indication given of his sources—or at least of parallels in earlier Armenian texts and in Greek commentaries. For the monastery at Narek was an important centre of learning, and Gregory's own enthusiasm for Greek texts aroused suspicion in some of his Armenian contemporaries.

The *Commentary on the Song of Songs* was first published by the Mechitarist Congregation in Venice in 1789, and was reproduced in Gregory's *Collected Works* published there in 1827 and 1840. The text used for the following study is that in *Srboy Hawrn meroy Grigori Narekay Vanits vanakani Matenagrut'iwnk'*, (Venice,

---

[1] For a good translation with an informative introduction see I. Kéchichian, *Grégoire de Narek, Le Livre des Prières* (Sources chrétiennes 78) (Paris, 1961). A reproduction of the Armenian text published in 1948 at Buenos Aires, with an English introduction by James R. Russell, is issued by Caravan Books, Delmar, New York (1981).

[2] For the date and occasion of the composition of this commentary see the colophon at the end of the printed text, translated below, pp. 495–6.

1840), pp. 269-367. The biblical text given by Gregory as the basis for his commentary has been included in Oskean's collations for his edition of the Armenian version of the Song of Songs.³ But since that biblical text may be of interest to those unfamiliar with classical Armenian, and since Gregory's interpretations depend on his Armenian biblical text (which is often at variance with the Greek), I have translated each verse in full before giving a résumé of Gregory's commentary thereto.

Gregory of Narek (hereafter Narekatsi, to distinguish him from various other Armenian and Greek Gregories) explicitly states that he is following the *Commentary on the Song of Songs* by Gregory of Nyssa. But there is a great deal of material not found in Gregory of Nyssa (whose commentary ends at chapter 6, verse 9), and sometimes Narekatsi offers interpretations quite different from those in Gregory but which may on occasion be paralleled in other writers. But some of the contents naturally reflect Narekatsi's own concerns in the Armenia of his own time. The Armenian version of Gregory of Nyssa's *Commentary* has never been published. But it is clear from a comparison with the Greek text that Narekatsi does not follow Gregory word for word; rather he uses Gregory's interpretations and rephrases them. Likewise, when Narekatsi explicitly quotes other Greek writers such as John Chrysostom or Gregory Nazianzenus (the 'Theologian'), his quotations are only approximations. His quotations from earlier Armenian texts, however, are usually verbally close.⁴

The following texts are cited below merely by page number:

Cyril of Alexandria, *Fragmenta in Canticum*, Migne, *Patrologia Graeca*, vol. lxix, cols. 1277-93. Quotations from Cyril frequently appear in Armenian biblical commentaries that take the form of catenae.

Eusebius of Caesarea (ps.-), fragments published in J. B. Pitra, *Analecta Sacra*, v. 3 (Paris, 1883), pp. 529-37).

Gregory of Nyssa, *Homiliae in Canticum*, *P.G.* xliv. The references to Migne's columns are for ease of comparison; the patristic

---

³ H. Oskean, *Erg Ergotsi aṙajin ew erkrord T'argmanut'iwnē* (Vienna, 1924). This first appeared as a series of articles in *Handēs Amsorya*, xxxviii (1924), cols. 215-33, 297-311, 409-18. On the Armenian text of the Song see also S. Euringer, 'Ein unkanonischer Text des Hohenliedes (Cnt. 8. 15-20) in der armenischen Bibel', *Zeitschrift für alttestamentliche Wissenschaft*, xxxiii (1913), pp. 272-94.

Note that the numbering of the verses of the Song and of all books of the Bible is that of the 1805 Venice Bible, ed Y. Zōhrapean.

⁴ Identified quotations and allusions are elucidated in the notes to the text below.

GREGORY OF NAREK'S *COMMENTARY* 455

parallels adduced in the critical edition by H. Langerbeck (Leiden, 1960) are very valuable.
Hippolytus, Fragments in *Hippolytus Werke*, i, ed. N. Bonwetsch and H. Achelis (Leipzig, 1897). In addition to these and other fragments still unpublished, the text of a commentary on the Song appears in the MSS. 1138 (dated to A.D. 1347), 3215 (of the seventeenth century), and 4066 (dated to A.D. 1283) of the Matenadaran in Erevan. But the authors of the catalogue of that collection give no indication of its length.[5]
Origen, *Commentaria in Cant. Canticorum*, in *Werke*, viii, ed. W. A. Baehrens (Leipzig, 1925). Numerous Armenian manuscripts contain what is described as 'Origen's Commentary on the Song of Songs', the earliest extant being Matenadaran 2602 (of the thirteenth century) and 4066 (dated to A.D. 1283). But to judge from the length of these manuscripts and their other contents, this cannot be the full text of Origen's commentary.
Philo Carpasianos, *Enarratio in Canticum*, P.G. xl, cols. 28-153.
Procopius of Gaza, *Epitome in Canticum*, P.G. lxxxvii, cols. 1545-780.
Theodoret, *Explanatio in Canticum*, P.G. lxxxi, cols. 28-213.

After Narekatsi other Armenian scholars also composed commentaries on the Song of Songs: Nerses of Lambron (1153-98), unpublished; Vardan Areweltsi (1200-71), unpublished (but a translation of the fragments of *Hippolytus* found in Vardan appears in G. N. Bonwetsch, *Hippolytus Kommentar zum Hohelied* [*Texte und Untersuchungen*, xxiii, no. 2] (Leipzig, 1902), pp. 90-108; Gregory of Tat'ew (1340-1411), unpublished. There are very many Armenian manuscripts that contain excerpts from various commentaries on the Song. The most popular combinations are: Origen, Narekatsi, Vardan;[6] Origen, Gregory of Tat'ew.[7] Despite the large number of manuscripts of the Armenian version of Gregory of Nyssa's commentary, only once (Matenadaran 1138, dated to A.D. 1347) is this found with another commentary on the Song, in this case with Hippolytus. On the other hand, Gregory of Nyssa does figure prominently in the catenae.

Title: 'Song of Songs, which is of Solomon.'
Solomon means 'peace', indicating Christ who is our peace, as

[5] Ō. Eganyan, A. Zeyt'unyan, P'. Ant'abyan, *Tsutsak Dzeṙagrats Masht'otsi Anvan Matenadarani*, 2 vols. (Erevan, 1965, 1970).
[6] Matenadaran 1156, 1158, 6720, 9698, 9993.
[7] Matenadaran 1158 (with Narekatsi and Vardan), Jerusalem 49 (with Narekatsi), 479 (with Vardan), 766, 2177.

the apostle says (cf. Eph. ii. 14). Narekatsi here follows Gregory of Nyssa (791A).

i. 1: 'May he kiss me from the kisses of his mouth, for thy breasts are better than wine.'

The kiss from the mouth refers to Christ's saying: 'Whoever is thirsty let him come to me and drink' (John vii. 37). Here Narekatsi follows Gregory of Nyssa (779A). The breasts refer to the scriptures; the milk from the breasts (which means the words of scripture) is the cause of life. Here Narekatsi does not follow Gregory of Nyssa. But cf. Agathangelos (*Teaching*), sect. 441: the two breasts are the testaments of God which give the spiritual milk of knowledge.[8] For the two breasts as the two testaments see also Hippolytus (pp. 344, 346) and Philo Carpasianos (35B). Origen interprets them as 'dogmata et doctrinae' (p. 94).

i. 2: 'And the odour of thy oils than all sweet-smelling incense. Oil poured out is thy name. Therefore the maidens loved thee.'

The odour of oil refers to virtuous deeds. Here Narekatsi follows Gregory of Nyssa (781B-C). The oil poured out: what is poured from a vessel is imperceptible, just as the nature of God is imperceptible but is recognized from the sweet odour of the righteous. Here Narekatsi follows Gregory of Nyssa (784A).

The maidens are those made young again, being freed from sin. Cf. Philo Carpasianos: the maidens are those renewed by faith (41A).

i. 3: 'Let us run after thee to the odour of thy oils. The bride tells the maidens about the groom—what he granted her. The king led me into his chamber. The bride tells the maidens; and they say: Let us rejoice and be glad in thee. And we shall love thy breasts more than wine. The maidens mention to the groom the name of the bride. Rectitude loved thee.'

Running after your odour refers to those worthy of tasting the Word of God who pursue it without hesitating. Here Narekatsi follows Gregory of Nyssa (785A). The bride speaking is the Church (as Gregory of Nyssa, 785C); the maidens are the angels and saints.

The king led me to his chamber: i.e. he brought me from the garden, our natural habitat, to his kingdom. For the chamber as the kingdom see Procopius of Gaza, quoting Cyril of Alexandria

---

[8] The *Teaching of Saint Gregory* is a long catechism inserted into the *History* of Agathangelos (sects. 259-715). For a translation and commentary see. R. W. Thomson, *The Teaching of Saint Gregory* (Cambridge, Mass., 1970). The text of the *History* has been reproduced with a translation and commentary in R. W. Thomson, *Agathangelos: History of the Armenians* (Albany, 1976).

(1552C). For Hippolytus (p. 344) the king is Christ and the chamber is the Church.

The rejoicing is that of the just in the salvation of the Gentiles, and together they will be glad in Christ. The breasts here are God's commandments. The maidens are the friends of Christ the groom. Rectitude is the Lord, who is upright, as David says (Ps. xci. 16). Here Narekatsi follows Gregory of Nyssa (785D).

i. 4: 'The bride says: Black am I and beautiful, daughters of Jerusalem, like the tent of Kedar and like the pavilion of Solomon.'

Here Narekatsi refers to John (Chrysostom) to the effect that a translation into Greek cannot render the totality of the meaning in Hebrew.[9] He adds that the difficulty is even greater when translating into Armenian from Greek or Syriac, and he refers to Gregory of Nyssa (cf. 796A-B).

The bride means those among the Gentiles who believe. The daughters of Jerusalem are the just, also frequently called the daughters of the angels by the prophets, since they have modesty like women. For women are more bashful than men. For the daughters of Jerusalem as the just, cf. Philo Carpasianos (45B); Origen interprets them as souls (p. 113), and Hippolytus (p. 359) as the angels and pure ones.

Kedar means darkness, therefore the tent is that of Satan. Solomon's pavilion is the temple, the house of God, meaning the Church of the Gentiles. Here Narekatsi is following Gregory of Nyssa (792A). Cf. also Origen (pp. 113-16): Kedar means 'obscuritas'. But Hippolytus (p. 359) interprets it as 'wandering'. For Origen the reference to Solomon is to the Church of the Gentiles. Philo Carpasianos (45C) interprets the tents of Kedar and the skins of Solomon as those who came from the Jews and the Gentiles.

i. 5: 'Do not look at me, for I am blackened; because the sun looks askance at me. The sons of my mother fought against me; and they made me keeper of the vineyard, because I did not keep my vine.'

The blackness is blackness from sin, an interpretation found also in Hippolytus (p. 359), Philo Carpasianos (48A), and Procopius of Gaza, quoting Theodoret (1553D). The son of my mother is Satan. The keeper of the vineyard refers to Adam's being put in charge of paradise to work it. For this verse Narekatsi follows Gregory of Nyssa (797D); cf. also Hippolytus (pp. 359-60).

---

[9] The editor of the Armenian text of Narekatsi notes that John's *Commentary on Genesis* was intended. So the reference may be to *P.G.* liii, cols. 42-3.

i. 6: 'The bride says to the groom: Tell me, whom my soul loved, where dost thou pasture, where dost thou provide rest at midday? Perhaps I shall be as the one fallen into the flocks of thy companions.'

This verse refers to possible straying from the way; as Christ said: 'I am the good shepherd' (John x. 14), and 'If anyone enters through me, he shall live' (John x. 9). Cf. Gregory of Nyssa (801A).

i. 7: 'The groom says to the bride: If thou wilt not recognise thyself, (most) beautiful among women, follow the heels of the flocks and graze your kids among shepherds' tents.'[10]

This verse bids the bride remember the first gifts—paradise and glory—lost by sin but which she found through the groom. For the Lord requites you for your sins, as the Prophet says. The reference to kids is a warning about the contrast between sheep and goats. In this verse Narekatsi follows Gregory of Nyssa (804C).

i. 8: 'To my horse among the chariots of Pharaoh I shall liken thee, my near one.'

The horse of God is human nature, which was the dwelling-place of divinity; but through sin its driver became Satan—a parable for Pharaoh—with whom Christ fought with the cross; the type of the cross is Moses' rod with which he divided the sea and drowned Pharaoh. Cyril of Alexandria (1280C) explains the chariots as those τοῦ νοητοῦ φαραώ, as does Origen with an additional reference to his demons (p. 151). Philo Carpasianos (52A) links the chariots of Pharaoh to idolatry. Gregory of Nyssa (813B) refers rather to the mystical water whereby subjection to evil is overcome; for Gregory on the theme of the horse see 820A.

i. 9: 'The maidens say to the bride: Because thy cheeks became beautiful like (those) of a turtle-dove.'

(There is no direct quotation of the rest of this verse or of v. 10.)

The maidens are the apostles, prophets, and teachers who continually advise us to contemplate our supernal creation. The turtle-dove is a lover of purity, who will die for her consort if necessary, and will never be linked to another until her death. The reference to cheeks is a token of the fact that the face is the image of God. The bride is thus adorned with purity and with fear of the commandments like a collar, being pure from sin like silver and gold. For Origen (p. 156) the collar is *oboedientia*.

---

[10] In the absence of a critical text of Narekatsi's commentary I follow the text as printed in the 1840 edition. Its editor occasionally notes a variant reading (without indicating what manuscript he is using). Here 'lilies of valleys' is a variant found for 'tents of shepherds'.

GREGORY OF NAREK'S *COMMENTARY* 459

i. 11: 'Until (the) king receive thee in his bosom. The bride says to her own self and to the groom: my nard exhaled odour.'

The first part of this verse picks up the theme of the horse in v. 8. For the defeat of Satan involves a reversal of roles: instead of the groom being the rider, he will then take up the bride into his bosom and onto his shoulders (as Luke xv. 5).

i. 12: (As?) bunches of myrrh my nephew[11] will repose between my breasts.'

The references to spices and odours (in vv. 11 and 12) are supported by quotations from the N.T. that indicate such are those who believe in Christ: John iii. 33; 2 Cor. ii. 15. (Cf. Gregory of Nyssa, 824C, 825B). For Procopius of Gaza (1564C) the sweet-smelling oil refers to virtue, for Origen (p. 166) it is 'teaching', while he explains the bunches of myrrh as the one who holds doctrines in purity (p. 169). The sweet odour for Origen (p. 44) is good works.

It is the teaching of the sweet-smelling scriptures that lies between the breasts; cf. Gregory of Nyssa, 825B. Other commentators again explain the breasts as the two testaments (Cyril of Alexandria, 1281A; Philo Carpasianos, 56A). Hippolytus explains that it is Christ who lies between the breasts, since he mediated between the law and the gospel (p. 346).

i. 13: 'A flowering cluster of grapes (is) my nephew for me amidst the vineyards of Engad.'

The groom is called nephew, for the Word of God was incarnate among the Jews. And the Jews and Gentiles are brothers, since they are both from Adam. Here Narekatsi follows Gregory of Nyssa (836B–C).[12]

i. 14: 'The groom says to the bride: Behold thou art my near one; behold thou art my beautiful one; thine eyes (are) doves.'

'Near one' refers to the bride's being removed from sin and acquiring the pristine beauty of paradise; cf. Gregory of Nyssa (833A), and Hippolytus (p. 346). The dove is the Holy Spirit—as Origen (p. 173), Hippolytus (p. 362), Gregory of Nyssa (836B).

---

[11] The Armenian version of the Song consistently uses the term *ełbawrordi* (brother's son, nephew) to render ἀδελφιδός. Since Narekatsi on occasion interprets the 'brother' or 'son' of this compound (e.g. at i. 13), I have kept its literal meaning and not rendered as 'beloved'.

[12] Here Narekatsi adds a reference to the *Martyrdom of St. Ignatius*, though there is no exact verbal parallel with the Armenian text (in *Sop'erk'*, xxii (Venice, 1861), pp. 141–85).

i. 15: 'The bride says to the groom: Behold my nephew, but also beautiful. By our seat (are) shades.'

Now that the bride's eyes have been cleared of sin she can see what she could not see before. Although the groom took the body of our ugly (human) nature, yet he is beautiful because he joined his divinity to it; Narekatsi here quotes Ps. xliv. 3. Hippolytus explains the nephew as Christ (p. 362). Origen (p. 175) and Gregory of Nyssa (836B) add references to the incarnation, as does Narekatsi. For Narekatsi the shade is Christ.

i. 16: 'The beams of our houses (are) cedars, our ceiling cypresses.'

Cedars are sweet-smelling, suitable for building. Likewise the body of our Lord is fitting for building this house (the Church), to dwell in which we must purify ourselves. Narekatsi here quotes Heb. iii. 6. Cf. Gregory of Nyssa, 840A. The house is also explained as the Church by Origen (p. 175) and Hippolytus (p. 362). [Hippolytus adds that the beams refer to the Word of God who took flesh, and the ceiling (rafters) to the preaching of the apostles (p. 363).]

ii. 1: 'The groom says to himself and the bride: I (am) a flower of plains, a lily of valleys.'

This verse demonstrates the adornment of the earth on receiving Christ. Here the closest parallel to Narekatsi is the interpretation of Cyril of Alexandria (1281B) who notes that the verse refers to the ἐπιδημία of Christ.

ii. 2: 'As a lily among thorns, so (is) my near one among daughters.'

The daughters are those wedded to Satan—i.e. sinners. (For Origen, p. 179, they are those who do not believe.) The thorns need no explanation, says Narekatsi, since the Lord taught parables about them. The Song indicates the greater glory of the lives of the just than of the unworthy, and also the hope that the latter, the thorns, may turn back into lilies.

ii. 3: 'The bride says to the groom: As an apple in trees of (the) forest, so is my nephew among daughters. Under his shade I desired to sit, and I sat; and his fruit was sweet to my throat.'

The comparison with the apple increases the praise given the groom, since flowers only please the eye but an apple has also smell and strength as food. Here Narekatsi follows Gregory of Nyssa (844B); cf. also Philo Carpasianos (62A), who notes that apples provide both food and drink as well as a sweet smell. The forest is the forest of sin; while the fruit is the fruit from the tree of life, the

GREGORY OF NAREK'S *COMMENTARY*

apple of knowledge. Here Narekatsi quotes Ps. cxviii. 103, as does Gregory of Nyssa (844C).

ii. 4: 'The bride says to the maidens: Lead me to (the) house of wine. Set upon me love.'

This refers to insatiable desire for the words of God. As wine is the cause of joy and enables one to forget sadness in this life, therefore the free gifts of God are called wine, and the house of wine is the house of Christ. The love in this verse is God. Cf. Gregory of Nyssa (845B).

ii. 5: 'And strengthen me with oils. Pile up for me apples. Because I am sick with love.'

Oil here is mercy, as Hippolytus (p. 364); Gregory of Nyssa (848C) calls it ἀρετή. The apples refer to the beauty of good works, as Origen (p. 193); cf. Gregory of Nyssa, 849C-D. But for Cyril of Alexandria (1281C), Christ being the apple, those who are σύσσωμοι and συμμέτοχοι with him are apples.

The love is that of the saints for Christ's love according to Narekatsi; but it is love for the holy martyrs in Philo Carpasianos (64A). The saints were not distracted from joy in this love by tribulations. To this regard Narekatsi quotes Agathangelos: Trdat asks Gregory in his torments: 'Is this happiness?' and Gregory replies: 'Yes.'[13]

ii. 6: 'His left hand (is) on my head, and his right hand will embrace me.'

Here Narekatsi quotes Solomon at Prov. iii. 16: The right hand is longevity, the left hand glory and grandeur. This echoes Gregory of Nyssa (853A), Origen (pp. 55, 195), and Cyril of Alexandria (1281C). But Cyril adds that the left hand is the law, the right hand the gospel.

ii. 7: 'The bride says to the maidens: I shall adjure you, daughters of Jerusalem, by the powers and vigours of (the) field that you arise, awaken (his) love until he pleases.'

The maidens are angels and men who have become angelic, as Hippolytus (p. 364). For Philo Carpasianos the maidens are the souls of the holy prophets and apostles (64C). The field is the world and heaven; Gregory of Nyssa (856A) and Philo (64C) refer only to the world. The adjuration is that Christ's will may be fulfilled in us. The daughters of Jerusalem are the angels and saints.

---

[13] The reference is to sect. 105 of the *History* (see n. 8 above).

ii. 8: 'The bride, hearing the voice of the groom, says: The voice of my nephew. Behold he comes running over mountains, leaping over hills.'

The bride is the Church (addressing) the maidens from among the Gentiles. Here Narekatsi is following Gregory of Nyssa (864D); cf. also Origen (p. 201). The voice is that of the prophets. Here Narekatsi quotes Heb. i. 1, as Gregory of Nyssa (861A). The mountains and hills are the tyrannies of Satan trampled at Christ's coming; and the same power has been given to the apostles. Again Narekatsi follows Gregory of Nyssa (861D-864A).

ii. 9: 'My nephew resembles a roe or fawn on the mountains of Bethel. The bride gives a sign concerning the groom to the maidens: Behold he stood behind our wall, gazing through the window, looking through the lattice.'

The roe has the keenest sight of all animals, so to this Christ is likened. The fawn destroys the snake, as Christ did the invisible snake. Here Narekatsi follows Gregory of Nyssa (862B-864A), Origen (pp. 56, 201). Bethel means 'heaven', which separates the saved from the snake; cf. Gregory of Nyssa (864B), Origen (pp. 56, 216).

The wall is the body Christ took from the virgin; the window is the prophets; the lattice is the law. Through these shone previously the divine light which was fully revealed at Christ's coming. On this see Gregory of Nyssa (864C), Hippolytus (p. 365), Cyril of Alexandria (1285A-B); Origen (p. 220) notes that there are also many other interpretations at different levels. For Philo Carpasianos (65C) the wall is the law, the window the prophets, the lattice the apostles. Procopius of Gaza (1600B) quotes Nilus to the effect that the wall is the incarnate body hiding the Word, the window is the prophets, the lattice the apostolic preaching; or, the wall is the law, the window the senses kept pure, the lattice temptations.

ii. 10: 'My nephew replied to me and said: Arise, come (s.), my near one, my beautiful one, my dove.'

This is explained by Christ's saying: 'Come to me all who labour' (Matt. xi. 28). The dove refers to the putting on of the Holy Spirit, as Gregory of Nyssa (869A). 'Beautiful' refers to the washing of the font, and 'near one' indicates that we have become sharers of Christ's flesh (*marmnakits*, as Eph. iii. 6).

ii. 11: 'Because behold winter has passed; the rains have passed, gone and departed.'

The winter is idolatry that has passed at the coming of Christ.

Here Narekatsi follows Gregory of Nyssa (865c), Hippolytus (p. 365), Origen (p. 221). The rains refer to the deceit of Satan. But rain can also be destructive in a good sense, as when the demons were swept away at the time of the Flood.

ii. 12: 'Flowers have appeared in our land, the time of pruning has arrived. The voice of the turtle-dove has been heard in our land.'

The beauty of spring is caused by Christ's expelling winter. 'Flowers' refer to the just being adorned with virtues and piety; 'the time of pruning' refers to the separation of the impure from the holy. The 'voice of the turtle-dove' indicates that just as in springtime birds spread across the land, so at the coming of the spiritual springtime the saints rejoice—especially the apostles, prophets, and teachers (*vardapet*)[14] who bless God day and night by their preaching and angelic songs.

Hippolytus (p. 365) interprets the appearance of flowers as the prophets' preaching about Christ. Cyril of Alexandria (1285B) and Philo Carpasianos (69B) interpret the time of pruning as a spiritual harvest (cf. Matt. ix. 37). But Narekatsi's imagery is particularly reminiscent of the *Teaching of Saint Gregory* (in Agathangelos, esp. sect. 655), where the imagery of birds as examples of the resurrection is elaborated.

ii. 13: 'The vines have flowered, they have given their odour. Arise, come, my near one, my beautiful one, my dove, my perfect one.'

The vines refer to the faithful who have flowered in various ways with various odours: some by martyrdom, some by different virtues, some by good works. 'Arise' indicates that the journey to the kingdom does not end while we are in the body, according to the Lord's saying (at Mark xiv. 42; John xiv. 31).

ii. 14: 'And come, my dove, under the shade of the rock near to the rampart of the wall. Show to me thy face and make me hear thy voice. Because thy voice is sweet and thy face beautiful.'

The rock is Christ (here Narekatsi quotes 1 Cor. x. 4) and the wall is the commandments in scripture. So the verse commands us to live by the gospel and not the law, though by keeping the gospel one is not far from the law—of which Christ is the fulfilment. Gregory of Nyssa (877B–D) draws a sharper contrast between the two, and interprets the rock as the gospel. Narekatsi is close to Hippolytus' interpretation of the wall as the commandments (p. 366), and Origen's as the *dogmata* of Christ (p. 230). For Cyril of Alexandria

---

[14] On the Armenian office of *vardapet* see R. W. Thomson, '*Vardapet* in the early Armenian Church', *Le Muséon*, lxxv (1962), pp. 367–84.

XVIII

(1285B) Christ is rock, wall, and rampart; for Philo Carpasianos (72B) the rampart is the law.

'Show me thy face ... beautiful.' Here Narekatsi explicitly states that Gregory of Nyssa interprets this as said by the bride, not the groom as the text of the Song indicates. He agrees with Gregory, and interprets it as a request to Christ to show his face—i.e. no longer to speak through the prophets and the law, but to become visible to earthly creatures so they may see his glory. Cf. Gregory of Nyssa (880A-B).

ii. 15: 'The groom says to the maidens: Take (hold?) us little foxes, destroyers of vines. For our vines have flowered.'

This is said to the angels who are sent to minister to mankind, and to the apostles who were hunters for the whole world. Here Narekatsi follows Gregory of Nyssa (881A-B). The fox is Satan; the vines the Church—that is, the believers whom the apostles snatched from the teeth of the fox, from death to life. Hippolytus (p. 366) also interprets the fox as the Devil. But for Philo Carpasianos (73C) the foxes are heretics; he interprets the vines as the peoples who have faith.

ii. 16: 'The bride says something (like) this: My nephew (is) mine and I his; who pastures among lilies.'

The bride says this, seeing herself freed from being chased by the fox; she joyfully gives herself to the husbandman who broke down the partition, no longer being divided from the beloved by the wall of the law. Here Narekatsi follows Gregory of Nyssa (882D).

'I am his' means that henceforth no earthly desire or passion can separate the bride from the beloved—as we may see with regard to martyrs and ascetics. Here Narekatsi quotes Rom. viii. 35. Pasturing among lilies (and v. 17) until the shadows are dispelled refers to the fact that (Christ) no longer provides herbs, the food of brutish men, but heavenly food eaten by the saints who despised vain desires and remained in hope for the last day and will not be moved (= dispelled in v. 17) in their desire for the groom.

ii. 17: 'Until the day becomes light and the shadows are dispelled. Again,[15] my nephew resembles a roe or fawn on incense-bearing mountains.'

This repeats the theme of the keen-eyed roe and the fawn whose nature it is to trample serpents. Again Narekatsi follows Gregory of Nyssa (884C).

[15] 'Again': *dardzeal*. Narekatsi uses the participle of the verb *darnal* ('*to turn*') which also functions as the adverb 'again', in place of the singular imperative *dardzir* ('turn') of the standard Armenian biblical text.

GREGORY OF NAREK'S *COMMENTARY*

iii. 1: 'On my bed at night I sought whom my soul loved. I sought him and did not find. I called him and he did not give me voice.'

Narekatsi states that this verse needs a lengthy explanation, but he will merely give a brief account basing it on Gregory of Nyssa. The bride has passed beyond the knowledge imparted through parables and attained perfect knowledge of Christ. Like a weary man resting on his bed, so she, in the emotion of such illuminating knowledge that she had desired, rests as on a bed. Here Narekatsi quotes 1 Cor. xiii. 9 and 12 to indicate that we cannot attain such knowledge in this life—which is the 'night', the soul being hidden by the body as in a prison. Here Narekatsi quotes Ps. cxli. 8. On this passage cf. Gregory of Nyssa, 892. Philo is quite different (76c); he interprets the sleeping on the bed as sin.

The seeking and not finding emphasize the impossibility of a mortal tongue expounding the perfect truth; one must beware of taking the knowledge that comes from the prophets, apostles, and the gospels as the complete, perfect knowledge. Here Narekatsi quotes 2 Cor. xii. 4. Cf. Gregory of Nyssa (893B-C).

iii. 2: 'I arose and went around this city[16] in squares and streets. And I sought him and did not find. I called him and he did not give me voice.'

The city, streets, and squares are heaven and the angels therein, from whom she could not gain an understanding of the supernal mysteries. For Philo Carpasianos (77A), the streets and squares are the business of this world that leads to destruction.

iii. 3: 'The watchmen found me, who were going about in the city. I asked: Did you see whom my soul loved?'

They did not answer, realizing that they too did not have knowledge. For as much as a man attains knowledge, it is a basis for even higher knowledge. For Hippolytus (pp. 351, 367) the watchmen are the angels of the heavenly Jerusalem; cf. Narekatsi to v. 2 above. (For Hippolytus [p. 351] and Cyril of Alexandria [1285c] these verses describe the search of the women at the tomb of Christ.)

iii. 4: '(It was) as (but) a little (that) I passed among them, (that) I found whom my soul loved. Having found the groom, she says, I held him and did not let him go until I had brought him into the house of my mother and into the room of her who conceived me.'

'Whom my soul loved' is wisdom. 'When I had passed a little among them' means that I took refuge in faith and in the Holy

---

[16] *This city*: *k'ałak's*. The Armenian could also be interpreted as the acc.pl. without the demonstrative suffix *-s*.

Spirit. Here Narekatsi quotes 1 Cor. i. 21. The 'holding' is grasping by faith. The mother, house, and room of her that conceived us refer to paradise and heaven. For Philo (80A) the house is the house of wisdom.

iii. 5: 'The bride adjures the maidens this second time: I adjure you, daughters of Jerusalem, by the powers and vigours of the field, that you arise, awaken (his) love until he pleases.'

Narekatsi says that he has already explained this; see ii. 7. The verse illustrates how the great love of Christ makes men insatiable. The bride has attained greater grace and knowledge; but as if that were incomprehension, she adjures that love be awoken.

iii. 6: 'The groom says concerning the bride: Who is this who comes from the desert like a pillar of smoke, perfumed with myrrh and frankincense from all powders of sweet oils?'

The groom indicates the beauty of the bride—that is, of the believers—to the angels, who are the maidens of the parable. The desert indicates those who have fallen by wicked deeds. Cf. Gregory of Nyssa (897B). For Hippolytus (p. 356) the desert refers to the heathen, formerly deprived of Christ; while Philo (80c) interprets the desert as idolatry from which the Church ascended.

'Like a pillar of smoke' means enclosed in virtue and good works. Myrrh is the sign of mortality, frankincense that of a sweet-smelling way of life. First one must put to death the body of sin and join Christ in death, then by sweet-smelling conduct share the purity of Christ. Here Narekatsi follows Gregory of Nyssa (897C-D). Cyril of Alexandria (1285D) has the same exegesis, while Hippolytus (pp. 356, 368) notes that myrrh is for burial and frankincense is for the honour of God. Thus, adds Narekatsi, one can become the bride of Christ and rise up to Christ the groom.

iii. 7: 'The maidens say something (like) this: Behold the bed of Solomon. Sixty warriors (are) around it from among the warriors of Israel.'

They call the bride Solomon, wishing to indicate even more her beauty. For Solomon means 'peace', which is Christ, who reconciled God with men. Cf. Gregory of Nyssa (897D).

The number sixty refers to the twelve tribes of Israel (multiplied by) the five senses in man. As in the law there are twelve tribes and each purified by the five senses, and Israel was the bed (*gahoyk'*) of Solomon's kingdom, so now for this Solomon (= bride-church) the whole world is the bed where the will of God reposes. Cf. Gregory of Nyssa (901B-905A). The number sixty is interpreted differently in Hippolytus: at pp. 358-9 it is the sixty fathers from

Adam to Christ in Matthew; at p. 368 it is 10 × the six sense-organs (eyes, ears, nostrils). Philo Carpasianos (81A) says that the sixty mean those from circumcision and the law. Nilus, quoted in Procopius (1628D) merely speculates on the mathematical properties of the number sixty.

Narekatsi adds that the warriors in the new Israel are all the believing saints.

iii. 8: 'They all have a sword and (are) expert at war. [Now each sword at (the) thigh]¹⁷ from terrors of the night.'

This refers to the sword of the Spirit, i.e. the Word of God with which they became expert at battling the invisible enemy. The sword must not be put down but kept firmly attached. The terrors of the night are the dark (powers) that fell from heaven. For his interpretation of the sword Narekatsi follows Hippolytus (p. 368). But for Philo Carpasianos (81B) the sword is the law and modest thoughts that cut away carnal passions. Gregory of Nyssa elaborates on the theme of the weapon as obedience to the divine commandments (804B).

iii. 9: 'King Solomon made himself a palanquin from the wood of Lebanon.'

Solomon means Christ, from the seed of David, peacemaker and builder of the temple. Here Narekatsi follows Gregory of Nyssa (908A). Throughout the whole world the temple of God has been established by Christ, changing the type¹⁸ into truth, that is the Church. Cf. Gregory of Nyssa, and explicitly Philo Carpasianos (84B).

The wood of Lebanon means the Gentiles. Here Narekatsi quotes Ps. xxviii. 5 and refers to Moses' grinding the calf (Exod. xxxii. 20)—that is, Satan and his accomplices. Narekatsi is following Gregory of Nyssa (912D). But Philo interprets the trees of Lebanon as the holy men of old (84C).

iii. 10: 'He made its columns of silver, and its vault (*konkʻ*) of gold, and its canopy of purple, and its centre spread out adorned with precious stones, love from the daughters of Jerusalem.'

The gold, silver, and purple are indicative of the different groups in the Church: apostles, prophets, teachers, virgins, saints. Narekatsi quotes 1 Cor. xii. 28, following Gregory of Nyssa

---

[17] Narekatsi does not quote 'now . . . thigh' in giving the text for his commentary, but the commentary implies that version of the biblical text.

[18] *Type: awrinak.* Narekatsi does not often use this expression but rather refers to 'parable, *aṙak*'. For *awrinak* see Thomson, *Teaching*, pp. 15–16, and cf. at n. 36 below.

(913B–C). Philo (84C–D) is more explicit in associating the different groups with the parts of the palanquin; while Cyril of Alexandria (1288A) brings in a reference to the incarnation in his explanation of the gold.

The daughters of Jerusalem are the angels. Lebanon, forested with sins, was transformed into the palanquin of Christ adorned with the crown of thorns, which King Solomon put on its head, that is Christ, who took on his own head the curse of Gen. iii. 18. Here Narekatsi notes that he is following the interpretation of St. (Gregory) the Illuminator against Gregory of Nyssa.[19]

iii. 11: 'Go out and behold, daughters of Jerusalem, king Solomon (adorned) with the crown wherewith his mother crowned him on the day of his marriage and on the day of his joy.'

It is the Lord of the supernal Jerusalem who bears the crown which he took upon himself for the sake of the Church. The mother is Sion—which means 'mother', as Procopius of Gaza (1636D), quoting Nilus. But it is not Gregory of Nyssa's interpretation (916C); he follows the usual patristic exegesis that interprets Sion as 'look-out'. Hippolytus (p. 369) interprets the mother as God, who has neither masculine nor feminine gender (cf. Gregory of Nyssa, 916B).

The day of marriage and joy is the day of the passion, which the Lord called 'glory'. Here Narekatsi quotes John xii. 23. This follows Cyril of Alexandria (1288B) and Procopius of Gaza (1636D) quoting Nilus. We too rejoiced at that day, having been in sadness for 5,000 years because of the loss of paradise and having fallen from the glory which we possessed when robed in light.[20]

iv. 1: 'The groom says: Behold thou art my near one, my beautiful one. Thy eyes (are) doves, save for thy silence. Thy hair (is) as flocks of goats who appear from Galaad.'

The beauty involved is that purity from the font of the new creation which is superior to the old. Here Narekatsi mentions Gregory the theologian.[21]

---

[19] Narekatsi is referring to Agathangelos: in the *Teaching*, sect. 348, Christ's removing the curse is expounded; cf. also the *History*, sect. 85.

[20] The theme of the seven ages of a thousand years each is stressed in the *Teaching of Saint Gregory*. In the sixth age renewal from the evils and travail of the world was effected by Christ's coming. The seventh age will give rest. See sects. 668–71, and the *History* of Agathangelos, sect. 72.

[21] The editor of the Armenian notes that the reference is to 'On the Baptism of Christ'. Narekatsi seems to have in mind the end of *Oratio* 39 rather than *Oratio* 40. For the Armenian text of the *Orationes* of Gregory Nazianzenus see G. Lafontaine, 'La tradition manuscrite de la version arménienne des Discours de Grégoire de Nazianze. Prolégomènes à l'édition', *Le Muséon*, xc (1977), pp. 281–340.

GREGORY OF NAREK'S *COMMENTARY*

'Doves' indicate purity and sincerity. But one is enclosed in silence, for the ear lobes (?) are made of brick and are unable to comprehend the ineffable. [Narekatsi does not comment on the 'silence', which Cyril of Alexandria interprets as total obedience (1288B).] Hair is without sensation, therefore it is as if dead to the world. Likewise one should be unaffected by all passions. Here Narekatsi follows Gregory of Nyssa (921C). Philo Carpasianos (88C) identifies the hair with the multitude of the Church.

iv. 2: 'Thy teeth (are) as flocks of shorn (sheep) who come up from the baths. They are all bearers of twins, and none is childless.'

Narekatsi notes the purity and pleasing quality of washed wool; cf. Gregory of Nyssa (925B). Hippolytus (p. 370) and Philo (89B) explicitly relate this to baptism. The second part of the verse refers to instruction and the explanation of scripture.

iv. 3: 'Thy lips are as a red line; and thy speech (is) beautiful. Thy cheeks (are) as the rind of a pomegranate, save for thy silence.'

Red refers to blood; while the line (or 'thread') refers to the snare that entraps men and brings them to God. Hippolytus (p. 370) notes that the red is the blood of the lamb; cf. Gregory of Nyssa (928C).

The pomegranate has two natures: its visible nature is rough, while its invisible nature is pleasing and a cause of health. Likewise, the bride of Christ—i.e. the Church—is outwardly veiled but inwardly provisioned with faith, hope, and love. As the inside of a pomegranate is desirable food, so also are virtuous lives that are performed with sweat and labour. Here Narekatsi follows Gregory of Nyssa (929B–C). Hippolytus (p. 370) notes that the skin of the pomegranate hides the inner fruit; and Procopius of Gaza, quoting Nilus, indicates that the outside of a pomegranate has a repellent taste but preserves the fruit inside safely (1645C). Philo (89C) associates the pomegranate with the red colour of Christ's blood.

The 'silence' refers to the fact that (the invisible Church?) is not now apparent, being surrounded by the weakness of the flesh. Here Narekatsi quotes 1 Cor. ii. 9.

iv. 4: 'As the tower of David (is) thy neck, which is built in T'alpiot'. A thousand shield are hanging around it, and all arrows of fully-armed (men).'

The number 1,000 is explained by reference to Ps. lxvii. 18, as Gregory of Nyssa (936A); while the shield is the shield of faith (as Eph. vi. 16) which hangs around the neck and beautifies it.

Hippolytus explicitly interprets the tower as the Church (p. 370); for him the armed men are the angels, and the shield that of the Holy Spirit. Philo interprets the neck as revealing the human nature of Christ (92A).

iv. 5: 'Thy two breasts (are) as two twin kids who pasture in the lilies.'

The two breasts are the two natures in man—body and soul; here Narekatsi follows Gregory of Nyssa (937B–C) and Hippolytus (p. 371). Cyril of Alexandria interprets them as ethical and dogmatic instruction (1288C); while for Philo (92C) they are the two testaments—as at i. 1. Narekatsi adds that the body has two eyes—the soul and the mind; cf. vii. 3 below.

The pasturing among lilies refers to the abandonment of thorns for spiritual food; cf. Gregory of Nyssa (937D), Hippolytus (p. 371), and Philo (92D) for similar interpretations.

iv. 6: 'Until the day becomes bright and the shadows are removed. I went alone to the mountain of myrrh and to the hill of frankincense.'

The day and light are the Holy Spirit and Christ who dispels shadows from the mind. Here Narekatsi quotes Ps. xxxv. 10. Thereby the mind and heart are illumined; these lie between the breasts (as Gregory of Nyssa, 936C–D) from which comes milk for spiritual nourishment. For Hippolytus also (p. 371) the coming of the day is the Spirit bringing grace.

Here Narekatsi adds a 'brief' explanation from 'the apostle' of the whole person, which is the Church: the various graces therein are like the senses and limbs in the body. The eye is the prophets who foresaw this grace. The neck supports the head with its senses, which is likened to David's tower (as in iv. 4) built for the warriors, who are Paul and those like him, whence life is distributed to the Church. The stomach refers to St. Gregory the Illuminator, John (Chrysostom) and their like, of whom the Lord bears witness: 'Rivers of living water will flow from his stomach (John vii. 38)'—that is, the grace of the Spirit. The teeth with red lips ruminate on the words of scripture, making the unclear clear and illuminating the lesser members in the body—i.e. in the Church—whereby the man is made complete and becomes the bride of Christ.

According to Narekatsi the second half of the verse is likened by the blessed John (Chrysostom) to Isa. lxiii. 3.[22] The mountain of myrrh is death, against which Christ fought in single combat for us.

---

[22] I have not found the precise passage.

The hill of incense means that, united with his divinity, he trampled the winepress (as Isa. lxiii. 3 just quoted) on the cross. Cf. Gregory of Nyssa (944C).

iv. 7: 'Altogether beautiful art thou my near one; and there is no spot in thee.'

The beauty and spotlessness were brought about by the crucifixion and death and through the blood of the lamb. Those who draw near to him share in his death and receive the sweet odour, in the image of incense. Cf. Gregory of Nyssa (940B). But Philo (93B) explains the beauty as caused by the bath of regeneration. (See also the next verse.)

iv. 8: 'Come bride from Lebanon; come from Lebanon; thou wilt come and pass from the beginning of faith, from the top of Sanir and Hermon, from dens of lions and from mountains of leopards.'

This refers to coming from the mountain forested with sin to faith, born again from the font of Jordan which flows between these mountains. Washed therein the bride becomes beautiful. The regions of lions and leopards refer to idolatry. Here Narekatsi follows Gregory of Nyssa (944D-945A). Hippolytus (p. 371), Cyril (1288C), Eusebius (534), and Procopius (quoting Nilus, 1656B) all echo the theme of idolatry. But Philo (63B) interprets Lebanon as λευκασμός—a patristic etymology for 'Lebanon'[23]—which refers to baptism, a theme he had stressed for the previous verse.

It is worth noting that although Narekatsi is following a common patristic exegesis of this verse (though, as usual, he quotes no source), he adds at the end of the paragraph: 'as it seems to me.'

iv. 9: 'Thou hast affected our heart, our sister bride. Thou hast affected our heart with one of thy eyes and with one necklace of thy neck.'

This is said by the friends of the groom, i.e. the angels. Here Narekatsi follows Gregory of Nyssa (948A) and Hippolytus (p. 372). 'Affected our heart' (*srtatsutser* could also mean 'heartened') means that you have given us spirit and heart to see what we did not know, i.e. (Christ's) providential love; this follows Gregory of Nyssa (948B).

The sister is the Church, which with only one eye surpasses us who have two. We are strong in two natures—in sight and neck (!) —yet through you have learned the ineffable mystery. These two eyes are interpreted by Cyril of Alexandria (1288D) as one to see truth, one vanity; so the single eye refers to single-mindedness.

---

[23] See *A Patristic Greek Lexicon*, ed. G. W. H. Lampe (Oxford, 1961-8), s.v. λευκασμός.

472

Philo (96A) explains that we have two bodily eyes, but one in the heart. And Procopius (1657B) quotes Nilus to the effect that two eyes are for bodily and for spiritual things. The necklace round the neck refers to the yoke of Christ, as Gregory of Nyssa (952C), Hippolytus (p. 372), and Cyril of Alexandria (1289A).

Narekatsi goes on to affirm that the coming of the bride from Lebanon does not refer to one occasion but to a continual progress in the life of virtue; he refers explicitly here to Gregory the theologian.[24]

iv. 10: 'For thy breasts have become beautiful, my sister bride; for thy breasts have become beautiful from wine. And the odour of thy garments (is better) than all incenses.'

As breasts give nourishment to those born on earth, so in the Church purity of heart is nourishment to the saints, for the heart lies between the breasts. The change from milk (as 1 Cor. iii. 2) to wine refers to the solid food and drink of the perfect. Here Narekatsi follows Gregory of Nyssa (956A). Philo (96B) interprets the breasts as the two testaments (as iv. 5, etc.) which are beautified by spiritual wine—i.e. Christ's blood. Procopius (1660A) contrasts the milk with spiritual wine—which is the mystical blood. Narekatsi adds that as wine gives joy, so the words of the Holy Spirit flowing from the hearts of the saints (i.e. from the breasts) arouse the audience and give nourishment. For Hippolytus (p. 372) the joy is internal, when one thinks of God's love in one's heart.

The odour of garments like incense refers to the sweet smell of virtue and good works; here Narekatsi follows Gregory of Nyssa (957C) and Procopius (1660B, quoting Nilus). Philo (96B) refers here to the εὐωδία of the commands of the gospel; while Hippolytus (p. 372) interprets the odour of garments as a right heart and right faith. Narekatsi adds that good works not only provide salvation for the doers thereof, they also give help to those near to them and those who see them, both during their lifetime and even more so after death—even if much time has elapsed between.[25]

iv. 11: 'Thy lips drip honey, my sister bride. Honey and milk (are) beneath thy tongue. And the odour of thy garments (is) as the odour of frankincense.'

Honey is sweet and pleasing teaching with which those affianced

[24] The editor of the Armenian text notes that the reference is to 'On the New Sunday', i.e. *Oratio* 44. The general thought is similar to the exhortatory second half of this oration.

[25] The historian Łazar P'arpetsi refers to this verse in the sermon given by John Mandakuni that concludes his *History* (Tiflis, 1904, p. 181). He contrasts in general terms the wine of the old dispensation with that of the new.

to Christ feed men. As milk is for children, so is honey for the perfect. Cf. Gregory of Nyssa (960c). For Hippolytus (372) the honey refers to holy prayer; while Philo (96c) interprets the lips as teachers, the honey as fine words preaching repentance, and milk as the catechism of the law. The tongue refers to such teachers as the blessed John (Chrysostom) or the theologian (Gregory of Nazianzen).

The odour of garments refers to the sweet-savoured sacrifice of those who offer their wills, minds, and bodies to God. Cf. Gregory of Nyssa (957A). Hippolytus (p. 372) sees a reference to the baptismal robe here; while Philo (96c) says that the observance of the commandments is a sweet odour to Christ.

iv. 12: 'A garden enclosed (is) my sister bride, a garden enclosed and a sealed fountain.'

It is sealed lest it provide food and drink to foreign sheep; one should not throw pearls before swine. Narekatsi follows the general line of Gregory of Nyssa (964) here, though Gregory does not have the allusion to Matt. vii. 6. Philo Carpasianos (96c) interprets the sealing as being closed to the Devil, but open to the spiritual groom, Christ. Cyril of Alexandria, however (1289A-B), interprets the garden as the world and the spring as unction after baptism.

iv. 13-14: 'Thy sending forth (is) a paradise of pomegranates with fruit of trees, a flower with nard. Nard and saffron and aromatic reed and cinnamon with all woods of Lebanon; myrrh and aloes with all prime oils.'

For these two verses Narekatsi says he will abbreviate the detailed explanation of 'other' teachers. He quotes Gal. v. 22 and Col. iii. 12 with various additional virtues that are fruits of the Spirit. Some are bitter from their use, like myrrh; some sweet, like oils; some pleasant to behold, like flowers. (Adorned) with these the bride is god's garden. For Hippolytus (p. 372) the various flowers of these two verses are multifarious good deeds; myrrh and aloes refer to death, as also noted by Philo (97B).

Narekatsi then discusses these flowers in greater detail. The oil which smoked on the altar of Moses was a type of the myriad virtues of the saints—which please God more than incense and sacrifices. The pomegranate-tree, before the fruit ripens, does not please its eaters, being surrounded by thorns; likewise with God's garden in this world. First one must live in tribulations and endure temptations from friends and from Satan; if one endures, one becomes a fruit pleasing to God. Cf. Gregory of Nyssa (969B ff.).

474

Whoever is wedded to Christ and becomes his garden, at first lives among thorns—i.e. virtues—and then is food for Christ the groom.

Nard and saffron: one is warm, the other sweet-smelling. So one must be fired with love for Christ and give off the sweet odour of virtue and good works. 'They say' of saffron that it is intermediate (*mijasahman*), not too cool and not too hot. This teaches us to flee the immoderate and to live moderately. Cf. Gregory of Nyssa (972A). Likewise in matters of faith we should not comprehend more than what is written or examine the inscrutable, but believe in the omnipotent power of God. Nor in mourning for sins committed should we be excessive and despair of salvation, acting like Judas.[26] The lesson of saffron is that we should not diverge to right or left.

The aromatic reed (calamus) is the sweetest-smelling of all types of incense and was therefore used on the altar for sacrifices. Cf. Gregory of Nyssa (972D). As for cinnamon, 'they say' that if it is introduced into a boiling kettle it extinguishes the heat of the water; if thrown into a hot bath, it cools the house. Other such 'unbelievable' things are said of it. If a man is asleep and there is cinnamon beside him, one can ask him a question and he replies if the cinnamon is put in his mouth. This teaches that a man who gives himself to God seems to be a man, but is not a man. For if thoughts of fornication or anger or other passions assail him he does not receive them, but is like the angels who are awake and passionless. On all this, cf. Gregory of Nyssa (973A–C).

Myrrh is a token of Christ's death and burial, as for Gregory of Nyssa (976C). Aloes and precious oils refer to the divinity united with the body in which (Christ) endured death. The wood from Lebanon is man coming from the forest of sin (cf. iv. 8), putting sin to death by sharing in Christ's passion and death, and becoming Christ's bride, united with him by purity of life. Here Narekatsi quotes Rom. vi. 3–5; cf. Gregory of Nyssa (976C).

iv. 15: 'A fountain of gardens, a well of living water and flowing from Lebanon.'

Here the bride's beauty is further elaborated, being called a source of gardens. Even God was called a well. Here Narekatsi quotes Jer. xvii. 13, John iv. 10, 14; following Gregory of Nyssa (977C). Just as those who share Christ's death and are wedded to him participate in the sweet-odour of (his) divinity, so he who becomes the bride becomes a well of living water, even if he came from Lebanon—the forest of sin.

---

[26] Excessive grief and un-Christian behaviour at funerals are features of pagan Armenian practice frequently attacked by early Armenian historians and theologians.

iv. 16: 'Awake north (wind), and come south (wind). Blow (s.) on my garden, and my spices will smell.'

The north (wind) is Satan and all his works, far from the warmth of the sun and therefore frozen—just as those far from the sun of righteousness are full of satanic thoughts and frozen by sin. Cf. Gregory of Nyssa (984C).[27] The south wind melts the ice of unrepentance. Here Narekatsi also follows the exegesis of Hippolytus (p. 372).

The blowing of the Holy Spirit into the garden of Christ causes various graces to blossom among men. (Here Narekatsi quotes 1 Cor. xii. 8-10.) This is the interpretation of Philo (97D), who explicitly equates the garden with the Church. Procopius (1669A), quoting Nilus, notes the blowing into the garden causes virtues to flourish. The spices refer to Paul, Peter, and their ten companions, to 'our' saint (Gregory) the Illuminator, John Chrysostom, and innumerable others like them. Cf. Gregory of Nyssa (985A-B).

v. 1: 'The bride begs that her groom may descend: May my nephew descend to his garden and eat the fruits of his trees. I entered my garden, my sister and bride; I gathered my myrrh with spices; I ate my bread with my honey; I drank my wine with my milk. Eat, my near ones; drink and become drunk, my brothers.'

The bride's entreaty indicates the entreating of God by the pious. The eating is explained in terms of John. iv. 34—as also by Gregory of Nyssa (985C)—and Matt. xxv. 35—as in Gregory (989A).

She is called sister and bride because whoever does God's will is wedded to him. The reference to myrrh indicates Christ's death. Procopius (1672B), quoting Nilus, interprets the myrrh and spices as indicative not only of Christ's death but also of his resurrection. Bread with honey means that (God?) did not only feed me with the bread of virtue but was also as sweet to me as the honeycomb—just as the blessed teachers, (Gregory Nazianzenus) the theologian and John (Chrysostom), who speak from God's mouth. He ordered Peter to eat the same food in the figure of the linen (sheet—as Acts x. 11), indicating that God gives nourishment to both Gentiles and Jews without distinction. Cf. Gregory of Nyssa (992A).

The wine refers to Christ's blood and the cup of death (Matt. xx. 22 and parallels), while the milk refers to becoming like children—as Matt. xviii. 3. 'Eat, my near ones, and drink' refers to communion. The drink that Christ drank he gave to the apostles, to the Church and bride, in remembrance of his death. This sacrifice we offer on the altar. Cf. Gregory of Nyssa (989B-C) and Procopius (1672D),

---

[27] Cf. also the *Teaching of Saint Gregory*, sect. 635, for the theme of sin and ice.

quoting Nilus. Here Narekatsi refers to John Chrysostom and Gregory Nazianzenus.[28]

v. 2: 'I sleep, and my heart is awake. The bride is aware of the groom knocking at the door. Open to me, my sister, my near one, my dove, my perfect one. Because my head has been filled with dew and my hair with light rain(drops) of the night.'

Sleeping and awake Narekatsi explains thus: 'As by the divinity I was awake in the tomb and asleep by the death of the body, so they who drink this drink are awake with me by the immortality of the Lord. Although, having human nature, they sleep yet they are awake, bearing in themselves the grace of the Spirit.' This explains the endurance of the apostles and martyrs, and especially of St. Gregory the Illuminator, who recited long prayers for seven days while suspended upside down and being beaten by ten men.[29] Cyril of Alexandria (1289B) and Philo (100B) interpret the sleeping as Christ's death on the cross, and the being awake as his despoiling of hell.

The groom knocking at the door is Christ summoning us to the kingdom of heaven. Narekatsi here quotes Luke xii. 35-7, as Gregory of Nyssa (996C, 997B). The 'opening' refers to the illumination of the bride by baptism; through the birth of the Spirit and by drinking the mystical blood she became 'sister' and 'near'; justified by the Spirit she took on the nature of a 'dove' and became 'perfect', since sons of God are perfect. Unless we preserve the grace and glory given us, we resemble our ancestor who lost immortality and paradise.

The references to 'head' and 'hair' indicate the wounds he received for our sake that will be revealed at the second coming and also our ingratitude. Here Narekatsi quotes Luke xxii. 44 to stress the afflictions borne by Christ so that the bride might attain the purity of a dove.

[Narekatsi does not explain the dew or raindrops to which Gregory of Nyssa devotes attention (1004).]

v. 3: 'The bride says something (like) this: I have stripped off my robe. How shall I put it on? I have washed my feet. How shall I dirty them?'

The robe is the garment of punishment for my sins which with labour and sweat Christ stripped off; so I cannot put it on again. Here Narekatsi follows Gregory of Nyssa (1004D). The washing is

---

[28] The reference to Chrysostom is to *In Matthaeum*, lxxxii, sect. 1; that to Gregory Nazianzenus is an adaptation of the introduction to *Oratio* 21.

[29] The reference is to Agathangelos, *History*, sects. 74 ff.

baptism, just as Christ washed the apostles' feet; cf. Gregory of Nyssa (1008B). How can I sully myself through sins like fornication and murder, being now robed in light and having the power to reach heaven and dance (*parel*) with the angels? Philo (101B) interprets the putting off of the robe as Christ's resurrection.

v. 4: 'My nephew put his hand through the opening, and my stomach was agitated at him.'

The 'hand' and 'opening' indicate the partial nature of our ability to comprehend the mystery of Christ. Narekatsi here quotes 1 Cor. xiii. 12; cf. Gregory of Nyssa (1012A). He adds that in this world only a hint of the ineffable blessings of the future life is given—like a drop of water compared to the sea, a lamp to the sun, or a child in its mothers' womb to an old man. The second half of the verse has the same meaning, as indicated by Dan. x. 16 or 2 Cor. xii. 4; cf. also Gregory of Nyssa (1012B).

The 'hand' can refer to the Son, who is the right hand of God, and the 'opening' to the body which he united to the divinity.[30] For as an opening is insignificant with regard to a palace (*tachar*, or 'temple'), so is our nature with regard to the divinity. But, says Narekatsi, the first explanation is more 'pleasing to me'.

v. 5: 'I arose to open to my nephew. My hands dripped myrrh; and my fingers filled with myrrh (were) on the handles of the bolt.'

When God revealed his mysteries through narrow windows, the eyes of my soul were opened, my soul awoke from the stupor of sin, I put off earthly passions and put my sins to death. Therefore we must mortify the limbs of the body before God and the divine mysteries can enter. Narekatsi follows Gregory of Nyssa (1016C).

Myrrh is a sign of death, and hands are the doers of works. The hand of Christ reaches the hand of the bride—that is, of the faithful—who approach the groom by purity. Here Narekatsi quotes Luke xiv. 26 and Matt. vii. 14; cf. Gregory of Nyssa (1024C–D). Narekatsi adds a disquisition on repentance (which is too late if made on the last day of one's life) and on the rewards and joy provided to the just at the final judgement. Christ the groom loved all men, Jews and Gentiles. Union with the groom is attained by baptism, communion, and separation from the sins of the world.

v. 6: 'I opened to my nephew. My nephew passed by. My soul went out at his word. I sought him and did not find. I called him and he did not give me voice.'

On studying scripture I raised the eyes of my mind to see the

[30] For the 'opening' as referring to the Incarnation see Origen, quoted in Lampe, *Lexicon*, s.v. ὀπή.

inscrutable depths of his grace and opened my heart to comprehend his knowledge, but he eluded me. 'My soul went out' indicates that when I thought I had attained knowledge, I realized how far I was from understanding. Here Narekatsi quotes Eccles. i. 18, and indicates that the more one desires to know by studying scripture, the greater one's pain at realizing the incompleteness of one's knowledge. Narekatsi follows the general line of Gregory of Nyssa (1028A-B).

v. 7: 'The guards who go about in the city found me. They struck (and) wounded me. The guards of the walls took from me my clothes.'

The guards are the guardian angels. Narekatsi quotes Heb. i. 14 and Deut. xxxii. 8 (the latter according to the Septuagint, not the standard Armenian). Cf. Gregory of Nyssa (1033B). Narekatsi notes that angels watch over the various provinces and cities of the unbelievers; amongst the believers each person has his own angel; but the saints have several, in accordance with Ps. xxxiii. 8—also quoted by Gregory of Nyssa (1033B). But the striking and wounding was the work of thieves and demons.

From the saints or angels I had hoped to learn about God's mysteries. But they disappointed me and so the robe of my expectation was stripped away. None the less, I shall persist— which leads to the next verse. Cf. Gregory of Nyssa (1037B). Philo (105C) takes the opposite line and explains the robe (or veil) as ignorance.

v. 8: 'I adjured you, daughters of Jerusalem, by the powers and vigours of the field: if you find my nephew, tell him that I am sick of love for thee.'

Such is the love of the Church for God, of which the martyrs are evidence. As examples, Narekatsi adduces Gregory (the Illuminator),[31] and the address of Hadrian to the martyrs whom he then joined.[32] The 'field' is the world, as in Gregory of Nyssa (1041C). The force that holds the world firmly is Christ. The love is illustrated by a conflate of Rom. viii. 35 and 38. For Philo (108B) the adjuration is the declaration of the Church's desire for God.

v. 9: 'The daughters of Jerusalem and the guards of the walls ask the bride: What is thy nephew from (other) nephews, most beautiful of women? What is thy nephew that thou hast thus adjured us?'

Narekatsi refers to what he wrote previously—at ii. 7 (?).

[31] The reference is to Agathangelos, *History*, sects. 96 ff.
[32] The reference is to the *Martydom of Adrianos*, but the parallel is not verbally close to the Armenian text in *Vkayk' ew Vkayabanut'iwnk'*, i (Venice, 1874), p. 29.

v. 10: 'The bride gives a sign concerning the nephew. My nephew is white and red, choice among myriads.'

The white and red refer to the human body and blood which Christ took from the virgin. The conception, however, was not from a man's seed; the virgin remained a perpetual virgin even after the birth. The 'choice among myriads' refers to this unique birth without labour or pain, one full of joy. Narekatsi is following Gregory of Nyssa (1052C–1053C).

v. 11: 'His head is of finest gold. His hair (is) curly, black like a raven.'

As finest gold (*oski kepʻazeay*) is purer and more precious than other gold, so is our head Christ superior to all in heaven and earth. He not only did no sin (as Isa. liii. 9) but purified us from it (as Heb. iv. 15). Narekatsi follows Gregory of Nyssa (1056 A–B). The dark hair is a mark of beauty in young people. One should not be surprised at the imagery of gold, gems, and things prized in this world; here Narekatsi quotes Rom. i. 20, as Gregory of Nyssa (1049B).

v. 12: 'His eyes (are) doves amidst abundant waters; washed with milks, sitting on abundant waters.'

The eyes are 'doves' because he is sincere and guileless, not looking crookedly like men but straight and penetrating. Cf. Gregory of Nyssa (1057D). 'Washed with milk', for milk reveals only its own nature—unlike water which reflects the nature of other things. Narekatsi follows Gregory of Nyssa (1060B).

The sitting on abundant waters means that as water is a mirror to the sun, so is he revealed in those who purify themselves from sin. Narekatsi here alludes to Ps. i. 3, as Gregory of Nyssa (1061A). For Philo (109A), the waters are the bath of regeneration.

v. 13: 'His cheeks, like plains of spices, exhale the sweet odour of perfumers. His lips (are) a lily; they drip abundant myrrh.'

The cheeks refer to the detailed instruction of teachers, leaders of the Church, who with a perpetual motion of their cheeks sweeten the minds of mankind. Cf. Gregory of Nyssa (1065B). 'Plains' refer to the spreading out of this teaching—not so difficult as to be unintelligible and cause despair, not so easy as to invite ridicule, but the middle way, as they bring the illumination of scripture from their mouths to men's minds by tireless mastication. The myrrh is an indication of death and teaches us to mortify our limbs and senses. Cf. Gregory of Nyssa (1065D), and Cyril of Alexandria (1289B).

480

v. 14: 'His hands are gold (pl.) worked on a lathe, filled with gems of Tarsis. His stomach (is) a plate of ivory adorned with sapphire.'

As pots are turned on a lathe and thus purified and embellished, so is the nephew's hand pure from sin like gold. Narekatsi follows Gregory of Nyssa (1069A-B). But Philo (109C) interprets the hands as those of Christ on the cross.

'Gems': *akambk'* is ambiguous in Armenian, referring to precious stones or to eyes. Narekatsi takes the latter interpretation and quotes Ezek. x. 12.[33] This is applied to Christ: although he took our nature from the virgin, yet being united with the divine nature all his members were sight and vision—unlike the separate function of individual parts of a human body. Here Narekatsi alludes to 'our Illuminator Gregory'.[34] His stomach is not a mere receptacle of food and drink but a container of the divine scriptures. From this stomach flow living waters; being a source of divine wisdom, so incorruptible, it is undecaying ivory. Cf. Gregory of Nyssa (1073A-1076B).

v. 15: 'His legs (are) pillars of marble set on golden bases. His stature (is) like Lebanon, choice like cedars.'

The first part of this verse indicates the dispensation (*tnawrēnut'iwn*) of Christ, of the perfect mingling of humanity and divinity. So the impious Nestorius should be ashamed, the companion of the Jews and colleague of the Muslims (*mahmetakanats*)[35] who confused the divinity. The marble and gold bases of pillars refer to the immaculate hypostasis, the divinity united with the body. Cyril of Alexandria (1289C) interprets the columns as Peter and John, made of marble for their strength; the column and base of the Church are the two commandments—love of God and of one's neighbour. For this cf. Gregory of Nyssa (1077D).

How can the single person (the incarnate Christ) be likened to a multiplicity of cedars? Although he was enclosed in the flesh, yet his stature was superior to the cedars of Lebanon. This is a 'parable,

---

[33] F. Müller, 'Bemerkung über Grigor Narekatshi', *Wiener Zeitschrift für die Kunde des Morgenlandes*, viii (1894), pp. 208-10, takes this as proof that Narekatsi did not use a Greek text of Gregory of Nyssa's commentary, but used the Armenian version. However, Narekatsi frequently differs from Gregory, and the ambiguity is there in the Armenian biblical text.

[34] The reference is to Agathangelos; see especially sect. 367 of the *Teaching*.

[35] For Armenian attitudes to Islam at this period see R. W. Thomson, 'Muhammad and the Origin of Islam in Armenian Literary Tradition', *Memorial Volume to H. Berbérian* (in press); idem, 'Armenian Variations on the Baḥira Legend', *Eucharisterion, Essays presented to Omeljan Pritsak* (Harvard Ukrainian Studies, 3-4) (1979-80), pp. 884-95.

example' (ařak, awrinak),³⁶ just as 'house of Jacob' (in Luke i. 33) means in fact the whole earth.

v. 16: 'His throat is full of sweetness; and (he is) altogether desirable. That is my nephew, and that my near one, daughters of Jerusalem.'

The sweetness refers to the words spoken by the divine throat, of which Narekatsi quotes numerous examples. Here he has the same explanation as Philo Carpasianos (112B).

v. 17: 'The daughters of Jerusalem ask where her nephew went. Where went thy nephew, most beautiful among women? Where went thy nephew? and we shall seek with thee.'

The daughters of Jerusalem are the angels, inhabitants of the heavenly Jerusalem, who learned about the incarnate Christ from men (to this effect, Narekatsi quotes Eph. iii. 10) and joined with them in praise. The bride is called 'most beautiful' because of the beautiful way of life acquired by the Church through Christ's coming. 'Among women' is added, because being a bride refers to women.

vi. 1: 'My nephew descended to his gardens, to plains of spices, to pasture in the flower-garden and to gather among the lilies.'

The garden refers to the believers who have wedded Christ who said: 'I am the vine and you the branch' (John xv. 5). The garden and flower-garden are the same, just as nephew and shepherd are the same. Narekatsi then contrasts the comments in Ezek. ch. xxxiv concerning bad shepherds with the good shepherd (John x. 11, 14) who nourishes us with virtue and righteousness among the lilies—i.e. the flowers of faith and purity. Here he follows Gregory of Nyssa (1093A–B).

(Narekatsi has no reference to the 'descent' as Christ's descent to hell, as Philo, 112D.)

vi. 2: 'I am my nephew's, and my nephew is mine, who pastures amidst lilies.'

Narekatsi here quotes John x. 5 and 27 to illustrate the unbreakable love of the bride for the beloved. The flock follows the shepherd who gives as nourishment first his own body and blood, and then ineffable blessings—here the sweetness of the understanding of scripture, and there (in the future world?) the knowledge which is beyond understanding. Narekatsi here alludes to (Gregory

---

³⁶ Cf. n. 18 above.

of Nazianzen) the theologian.[37] Cyril of Alexandria (1289D) takes this verse to refer to the purity of scripture and the teaching of the saints.

vi. 3: 'The groom says to the bride: Thou art beautiful, my near one, as a sweet odour; thou art beautiful as Jerusalem, as a wonder drawn up.'

This indicates the desirable beauty of the incarnate Word who appeared like us but whose beauty is beyond our corruptible nature. Cf. Gregory of Nyssa (1097B). The groom blesses the beauty of the bride, transformed by baptism. Here Narekatsi again alludes to Gregory of Nazianzen.[38] Those who look at God and draw near to him acquire his beauty, just as a wick when put to a lamp takes on the same light.[39] Likewise, as he who approaches a 'sweet odour' takes on that sweet odour, so he who approaches God becomes divine. Jerusalem refers to heaven, the groom's dwelling-place. The wonder refers to the change from blackness of sin (before the bride drew near to the groom) to wonderful purity. (Here Eusebius, 536, stresses the unity of the law and the gospels.)

vi. 4: 'Turn thine eyes from me, because they startled me. Thy hair (is) as flocks of shorn (sheep) which appeared from Gaḷaad.'

Just as staring at the sun blinds the eyes, so excessive gazing at the depths of the knowledge of God dazzles the eyes of the mind. The same comparison is found in Theodoret (168C). For not even the angels can understand God, let alone men. Thus Moses averted his face (Exod. iii. 6), as did Elijah (3 Kgs. xviv. 113).

The hair of the groom became black because he took our sins upon himself. We were justified and made white by baptism and the washing of the font. The flocks from Gaḷaad are the multitude of believers.

vi. 5: 'Thy teeth (are) as flocks of shorn (sheep) which come up from the baths. They are all bearers of twins, and there is none barren among them.

The teeth grind on the word of life, like flocks of sheep passing from the bath of spiritual water which makes them purer than washed sheep.

---

[37] The editor of the Armenian text notes that the reference is to the 'Second Homily on the Pascha', i.e. *Oratio* 45.

[38] The editor of the Armenian text notes that the reference is to 'On the Birth of Christ,' i.e. *Oratio* 38.

[39] This figure is also used by Narekatsi in his *Prayer* 93, sect. 17 (p. 260 of the 1840 edition). It has a parallel in the Armenian version of Basil of Caesarea's *Hexaemeron*, iii. 7 (Venice, 1830, p. 57), a version strikingly divergent from the Greek original.

GREGORY OF NAREK'S COMMENTARY

For the second half of the verse Narekatsi adduces Isa. liv. 1, which illustrates the multitude of believing Gentiles and their fruitfulness in the life of virtue, and Isa. lx. 8.

vi. 6: 'As a red line are thy lips; and thy speech (is) beautiful. As the rind of a pomegranate (are) thy cheeks, except for thy silence.'

The redness refers to the blood of Christ, as Gregory of Nyssa (1105D) and Philo (116D). The rind of a pomegranate is also red; whereas the inside is sweet, providing health for the sick but offering it in silence—as the elect of God show outwardly but little of their good work, hiding their virtue and piety inwardly in silence. Cf. Gregory of Nyssa (1108A-B). However, at the last judgement the hidden will become visible and the silent become heard. Then will be revealed the multitude of saints who endured suffering in this period of 6,000 years, to become queens, concubines, and maidens for Christ the groom (see next verse).

vi. 7: 'They are sixty queens and eighty concubines, and maidens without number.'

This refers to the multitude who will rejoice with Christ at rest in the eighth (millennium), having laboured in the six ages, as St (Gregory) the Illuminator says.[40] The number sixty has two interpretations: being either 6 × 10 or 5 × 12. The five twelves refer to the twelve tribes of Israel and the five senses, as also Procopius (1721A) quoting Philo. The tribes of Israel were called queens, as being senior to the Gentiles. Here Narekatsi alludes to Rev. vii. 5 ff. Cf. Procopius (1720C) who quotes Nilus to the effect that the 60 queens are those in Judaism. The concubines and maidens refer to the Gentiles, who exceeded the Jews in number. Sixty also refers to the six ages of toil; those who laboured therein gained the title of queen for their great love of God—notably the Mother of God, John the Baptist, the protomartyr, the apostles, our Illuminator Gregory, John the teacher of the world (Chrysostom), the theologian who expounded the Trinity (Gregory Nazianzenus). Here Theodoret (172D) merely refers to the six days of creation.

The eighty concubines laboured less than the queens but more than the maidens, so they will be crowned; these are the martyrs. Those who will attain the kingdom by their way of life and

---

[40] This is a reference to the theme of the ages elaborated in Agathangelos; see n. 20 above. But Narekatsi refers to the age of rest as the *eighth*, not the *seventh* as in Agathangelos. Gregory of Nyssa (1113D) refers to the ὀγδόη, but his general interpretation of this verse is different from that of Narekatsi. The theme of eight ages is echoed in Anania of Shirak; see further, R. W. Thomson, 'Number Symbolism and Patristic Exegesis in some Early Armenian Writers', *Handēs Amsorya*, xc (1976), cols. 117-38.

repentance are without number; these are the ascetics, those who were impoverished in the body, and who departed this life in repentance. In similar fashion the Illuminator enumerates the repentant, the confessors, martyrs, and teachers.[41]

vi. 8: 'One is my dove, my perfect one; one is she of her mother, choice of her parent. The daughters saw her and praised; queens (saw) and blessed her.'

Although there are many named in the previous verse, yet they are one by baptism, being doves of the mother Church and sons of the Holy Spirit their parent. The Spirit gives birth through baptism, and the Church gives nourishment through the body and blood of Christ. Cf. Philo (117B), who interprets 'one' as referring to the Church. Here Narekatsi alludes to Basil,[42] and expands on the theme of the Church as mother who should be loved more than a physical parent. Those who separate themselves from the Church—from her breasts which are scripture—perish eternally. Here Narekatsi quotes Ps. lvii. 4. Such people have been false to their oath (*ukht*) at baptism to love their father, God, and mother, the Church. Satan has taken them from their mother like slavers (*mardavačaṙ*) who steal children from their parents. Nor will mercy be given those who dishonour the Church by worshipping in streets and public places instead of before the altar where the Holy Trinity dwells.

The daughters and queens are the angels. That angels, who are close to God, should praise mankind is a sign of the glory man has attained. Narekatsi applied to the angels the comments of the prodigal son's elder brother (Luke xv. 29–30), for the angels are the elder brothers (*andranik*) of the Church in heaven.

vi. 9: 'Who is this who has appeared as the morning, beautiful as the moon, choice as the sun, as a wonder drawn up?'

This indicates the wonder of the angels at earthly nature attaining such glory, which is similar to the exposition in Procopius (1724C, quoting Nilus). The just are those who shine like the sun, as the Lord said (Matt. xiii. 43). Philo (117D), however, interprets the sun as the sun of righteousness.

vi. 10: 'The groom says to the bride: To gardens of walnut-trees I went down to look at the fruit of streams, to see if the cypress was

---

[41] This is a reference to the homilies known as *Yačakhapatum*, attributed to Gregory the Illuminator; in no. 16 the various kinds of saints are enumerated.

[42] The editor of the Armenian text notes that Narekatsi is referring to the 'Eulogy on Saint Stephen'. This would be *Oratio* 41 by Basil of Seleucia, *P.G.* lxxxv, cols. 461–73. But the quotation in Narekatsi does not appear in the Greek text.

flowering, if the vine was flowering, if the pomegranates were flowering.'

The garden of walnut-trees is the world; man who inhabits it is the walnut. This has two natures: the outer shell, of wooden nature, and the rich interior—just as the soul is wrapped in the body. Eusebius (536) also interprets the nuts as being rough on the outside and having a spiritual interior. If men drink from the streams of the Spirit, says Narekatsi, they will become flowering cypresses and fruitful vines. For the walnut will be squeezed into the cup of the heavenly groom and become food for the heavenly king, as the pomegranate is for (earthly) kings. Procopius (1757A) notes, as at iv. 3, that the pomegranate has a hard and bitter exterior, but inside is sweet fruit.

The going down refers to the descent in the body of God the Word to give the perfect fruits of salvation to the earth that had been 'ploughed' by the law and prophets. Eusebius interprets in similar fashion the garden as scripture. Philo (120A) merely notes that the descent is that of the Only-begotten.

vi. 11: 'The bride says to the groom: There I shall give my breasts to you. My soul did not know. (He?) set me as the chariots of Aminadab.'

When the bride hears of the groom's descent she says that she nourished him, as the Godhead demands of mankind, with purity and holy love. The ignorance is interpreted that God seeks nothing from men save a pure heart. In such people he rests. Narekatsi here quotes Isa. lxvi. 2, but reading 'rest' (*hangeayts*) for 'look' (*hayetsayts*). The 'rest' is interpreted as being 'like chariots' as the groom rises up in glory.

vi. 12: 'The daughters and queens say to the bride: Turn, turn, *somnatsi*. Turn, turn, and let us look at you.'

Again these are angels amazed at the transformation of mankind from evil to good. Now we have surpassed the angels; for their nature is impassible, but despite our weak nature we have overcome passions.

[For *somnatsi* see vii. 1.]

vii. 1: 'The groom says to the daughters and queens: What do you see in the *somnatsi*, who has come as troops of armies? For thy steps with shoes have become beautiful, daughter of Nadab. The harmony of thy hips (is) the likeness of woven necklaces, works of the hands of a craftsman.'

Somnatsi in the Armenian O.T. renders 'Shunammite', as 3 Kgs.

i. 3 of Abishag (Σωμανιτης in LXX). The Armenian text of the Song in Zohrab has *ogolomatsi* at vi. 12 and *odolomatsi* at vii. 1,[43] but the apparatus notes the reading *somnatsi* (which is found in later editions, e.g. Constantinople 1895). But Narekatsi glosses *somnatsi* as *sidonatsi*—i.e. of Sidon. The bride was so called because of her great wickedness, for they were assiduous in idolatry and all impiety.

'Daughter of Nadab' indicates that the offspring of impure ancestors became the daughter and bride of Christ. (A reference to Num. xxvi. 61?) The reference to shoes means that they no longer have bare feet susceptible to the stings of the serpent, but fortified with shoes of righteousness are immune to the serpent's bites. As the Saviour washed the apostle's feet, so are they cleansed from sin and received the power to tread on serpents and scorpions; here Narekatsi quotes Eph. vi. 15.

As the feet were protected from the serpent, so was the head raised up away from the destroyer who fell from the heights of paradise. Narekatsi interprets *bardz* (hip) as *bardzr* (high). *Bardz* can also mean 'pillow'. So Narekatsi continues: as a pillow raises and supports the head, so knowledge of the scriptures provides support and repose for all those afflicted and storm-tossed in their minds.

Just as a necklace is woven from various pearls, so knowledge of the scriptures is woven from the prophets, the law, the apostles, teachers, martyrs, ascetics, the gospels—like a cushion holding up the brains not letting them fall to the ground. In this simile the ground is the false teaching of heretics who divide the dispensation of Christ into two natures and interpet scripture in different ways—such as Arius, Macedonius, Nestorius (the impious destroyer of the world), and a myriad other heretics, who have wrong views on life, food, the nature of created things, heaven, earth, angels, men, the future coming, the fearsome tribunal, and everlasting hell.

There are still now many who teach such errors, for two reasons: (1) because they do not study scripture but reckon their own understanding to be sufficient, just as the first philosophers could not escape idolatry; (2) through sin men are far from the wings of the Spirit, an impure spirit having entered them. However, the heads of the saints do not rest on such but on the (support) woven by the hands of the true craftsman—the Holy Spirit.

[For Cyril of Alexandria (1292A) the craftsman is Christ.]

---

[43] On this term see S. Euringer, 'Das Nomen gentilicum der Braut im armenischen Hoheliede', *Handēs Amsorya*, xli (1927), cols. 617-24.

vii. 2: 'Thy navel (is) a well-turned bowl, not lacking mixed wine. Thy stomach (is) as a stack of wheat enclosed by a lily.'

Just as well-turned bowls are attractive in themselves and promote the enthusiasm of servers to pour the wine, so the bowl free of sin receives the grace of the Spirit, the sweetness of pure wine, the drink mixed from the old and new scriptures. For Cyril of Alexandria (1292A) the mixture is Christ's blood.

The meaning of stomach is interpreted by our St (Gregory) the Illuminator[44] and 2 Cor. iv. 7. This demonstrates the power of God in that a weak vessel holds the heavy and intolerable. As may be seen in creation: heaven and earth are placed over a weak (support) but it holds everything without tottering. In like fashion the weak nature of the Mother of God held the incomprehensible nature of the Word of God mingled with the flesh (taken) from her. Likewise weak mankind received the grace of the Spirit in their stomachs; piled up like stacks of wheat, ground by the teeth of instruction, it became bread for those hungering and thirsting for spiritual food.

The wonderful colours as of lilies invite the angels to look, as in vi. 12.

vii. 3: 'Thy two breasts (are) as two twin fawns of a roe.'

These refer to the two aspects of man—soul and mind, as the theologian (Gregory Nazianzenus) says.[45] These both have a relation to the heart, where the breasts lie, and therefore he calls these two aspects breasts. Like breasts that are a vessel of milk for children, so minds and souls are lively and sharp-sighted like roes (cf. ii. 9); they show the unerring path to those who follow, keeping them from snares.

vii. 4: 'Thy eyes (are) as the lake of Esebon at the gates of many daughters. Thy nostrils (are) as the tower of Lebanon which looks towards Damascus.'

With reference to the first half of this verse Narekatsi says that that land is very distant, but he understands it to be high up, having at its base the great lake. Likewise the eyes of the bride—the Church— made large by the Spirit look up inflexibly to the gates of heaven, where the daughters of the hosts of angels dwell, serving the king of heaven.

As the tower has a splendid outlook, so the nose desires the splendid sweet odour of oil from the heavenly Damascus—the city of heaven. Narekatsi here refers to Paul's conversion as he

---

[44] The reference is to the homilies called *Yačakhapatum*, where in no. 20 the 'erring stomach of inebriates' is castigated.

[45] Cf. iv. 5 above.

XVIII

488

approached Damascus and the opening of his eyes by Ananias. That sweet odour he provided to the Gentiles. Philo (125C) makes the same reference to Paul.

vii. 5: 'The braids of thy head (are) as purple (pl.); as a king, crown on head, in the courses of arenas.'

Those heads which are adorned with the glory of the heavenly groom are splendid in purity as if with purple robes and like a crown on kings' heads. The crown refers to martyrs especially the forty (of Sebaste) and the Łevondeans.[46] A crown is put on a head, since that is the most honourable part of the body where the brains are lodged—the source of wisdom and the origin of life—as well as the eyes, nose, taste, ears, and mouth. The brain teaches the various virtues, and this is proclaimed by the crown, as Solomon says; Narekatsi here quotes Prov. i. 9.

vii. 6: 'Because thou become beautiful and delightful, love in thy voluptuousness.'

Here the groom resumes under 'beautiful and delightful' the individual praises of the bride. This refers to the beauty of a man who subjects all his senses to God and deifies them, thus becoming worthy of hearing these words from Christ. For this all the saints abandoned the present world for a life of virtue. Their 'love' was as intense as that of earthly grooms with physical bodies for their brides.

vii. 7: 'Thy stature resembled a palm-tree, and thy breasts bunches of grapes.'

Narekatsi merely notes that the parallel of the bunches of grapes has been made before (cf. i. 13).

vii. 8: 'I said: I shall mount the palm-tree, I shall grasp its stature. And thy breasts will be as a bunch of grapes of the vine, and the odour of thy nostrils as an apple.'

Narekatsi draws attention to the unbounded love of God for the saints. He refers to God's appearance to Jacob (Gen. xxviii. 11-16), and again quotes Isa. lxvi. 2 in the version noted at vi. 11. In contrast to the height of the palm-tree, God humbled heaven, descended and grasped our nature because of his ineffable love for us. As bunches of grapes arouse one's eyes by their sight before being eaten, so the words of grace that flow from the breasts of the heart first fructify the ears and then delight the heart. Cyril of

---

[46] The Łevondeans are St. Łevond and his companions whose martyrdom in Iran is described by the historians Ełishē and Łazar.

Alexandria (1292B) also notes that the breasts are compared to vines since they give spiritual delight.

The odour of nostrils refers to the sweet smell of a pure life, like that of apples, which the heavenly groom appreciates more than the sacrifices of darkness. It is not the smell of roasting that is sweet to God, but that of those who offer purity. Narekatsi refers to God's pleasure at the 'sweet odour' (*hot anush* at Gen. viii. 21) but associates it with Abel.

vii. 9: 'And thy throat as noble wine; going with my nephew to rectitude, being sufficient with my lips and teeth.'

As wine gives joy to those who drink it, so do the songs of the saints and of the pure and the words of their throats delight the heavenly groom more than the songs of angels. This is not surprising, for man has overcome the passions of his earthly nature, whereas the angels are impassible. Narekatsi refers back to vi. 12 and vii. 1.

'Going with my nephew' means that freed from this sinful world and its snares the bride followed her beloved in the way of righteousness taught by him. Narekatsi here quotes Acts i. 1; Matt. xi. 29; John viii. 49, xviii. 23; Luke xxiii. 34. He gives a long description of aspects of Christ's earthly activity, which we should imitate. The power to do so comes from communion in the body and blood of Christ which are consumed with 'lips and teeth'. We become 'sufficient' (*bawakan*, or 'capable') to do this, unlike the angels, yet are not consumed by the inconceivable—just as the Theotokos was not consumed when she received him in her womb, or the bramble bush.

vii. 10: 'I (am) my nephew's, and towards me (is) his turning.'

By this food (cf. vii. 9) the bride and groom are united, as illustrated by John vi. 56, xvii. 21. For Cyril of Alexandria (1292B–C) the turning refers either to the second coming or to the people of the Jews.

vii. 11–12: 'Come, my nephew; let us go out to the field, let us rest in villages. Let us be early to the vineyards; let us see if the vine is flowering, the cypress is flowering, the pomegranates are flowering.'

Narekatsi refers back to vi. 10 which concerns the coming of Christ to earth to seek the seeds sown by the prophets and to see if they were flowering. For Philo (135B), the 'field' is the world, as at ii. 4. The groom loves to go around with the bride as Christ 'went about' (*shrjēr*, frequent in the N.T.) with the apostles, not only in

Judaea but among the Gentiles. So after the ascension he went around through the apostles, their disciples, teachers, and martyrs, to preach and see the fruit of the word of faith. The apostles did not reach the end of the world (Narekatsi quotes Matt. xxviii. 20), though now one can see flowers among all the believers. But one must still go around seeking those gone astray and the lost. An example is our Illuminator; here Narekatsi refers to Gregory's prayers.[47]

Of those who turned to the faith, some bore fruit but not knowingly—like the centurion, Cornelius or even Paul who was pure according to the righteousness of the law. Some were fruitless, like Onesimos[48]—which is the cypress. The bunch of grapes and pomegranate refer to those who did not attain full knowledge of God.

vii. 13: 'The mandrakes gave their smell at the gates with all fruit-bearing (trees?); new by old, which my mother gave me I have kept for thee, my nephew.'

This indicates the various fruits of the faithful, their virtues, and the ways in which they bore witness: some by blood, some by asceticism, some by virginity, some by responsibility as prelates and priests, some by poverty and sickness, some who gave of their riches to the general good. All are united in their love of God, fear of hell, and desire for the kingdom. New and old refer to the peoples; mother is the Church and Holy Spirit who gave birth through the font and nourished by Christ's blood.

viii. 1: 'Who will give (allow?) thee, my brother, to suck my breasts? Having found thee outside, I shall kiss (thee), and thou shalt not mock me.'

The first part of the verse refers to the insatiable desire of the saints to apprehend God's glory. Here Narekatsi quotes Philem. iii. 13. Sucking the breasts means receiving Christ's love. For Cyril of Alexandria (1292C) it refers to the Church praying for the Saviour's ἐπιδημία, to be suckled by the virgin. Eusebius (533) also refers this verse to the incarnation, as does Procopius (1737D).

The second part of this verse means that those who tasted such love, despised wives, children, possessions, and glory, were perfected by poverty, blood, and death, kissed Christ and were kissed by him. For Cyril of Alexandria (1292C) the finding refers to Christ's crucifixion outside Jerusalem. But for Philo Carpasianos (140A) this refers to the abandonment of earthly considerations.

---

[47] See Agathangelos, *History, passim.*
[48] But in Philem. xi he is described as *anpitan* ('useless') rather than Narekatsi's *anptul* ('fruitless').

viii. 2: 'I shall take and lead thee to the house of my mother and to the room of the one who conceived me. I shall give thee drink from the wine of perfumers, from the syrup of pomegranate-trees.'

'House' is explained by Heb. iii. 6, the house of the Holy Spirit and of our mother father (see viii. 5). Here Narekatsi quotes Basil.[49] The room refers to the dwelling-place of the Trinity. The joy of wine and syrup of pomegranates are the knowledge of the heart with regard to God's good intentions. But for Cyril of Alexandria (1292C) the pomegranates are the saints.

viii. 3: 'His left hand around my head, and his right hand will embrace me.'

This refers to the groom's protection and oversight for the bride, who is the Church.

viii. 4: I adjured you, daughters of Jerusalem, by the powers and vigours of the field, that you arise, awake (his) love until he wishes.'

This has been explained before (i.e. ii. 7, iii. 5, v. 8); it refers to the manifold gifts of grace bestowed on us. The daughters of Jerusalem are the angels, who are urged to join in praising God as the bride does not regard herself adequate. Here Narekatsi quotes the example of the one grateful and nine ungrateful lepers (Luke xvii. 12-19) as explaining the phrase 'awake (his) love'.

viii. 5: 'The daughters and queens say: Who is this who comes up, rendered white, leaning upon her (his) nephew? The groom says to the bride: Under the apple I aroused thee. There my mother delivered thee; there she who bore thee travailed.'

The angels are amazed at the purity of our sullied nature that was given such grace and united to Christ; leading them by the hand he brings men to where the hosts of angels dwell.

The apple is healthy food for the sick, suitable for kings, sweet to the smell—as our St. Gregory the Illuminator says.[50] To an apple are likened the words of the law and prophets. But to Philo (144A) the apple, which is both food and drink, refers to communion. Just as hens, sitting on eggs, hatch them over a long time by their warmth; so our human nature was placed for a long time under the law and prophets, was travailled by God the Father and Son and begotten by our common Mother. Since he (Solomon, author of the Song) said 'travail'—which is a characteristic of a mother— therefore he called the father of Christ 'mother' (cf. viii. 2). So the Father travailed through the law and prophets, begat by water and

---

[49] Cf. n. 42 above. Again the quotation is not in the Greek text.
[50] This may be a reference to Agathangelos, *Teaching*, sect. 643.

the Spirit his sons—the brothers of Christ. Here Narekatsi quotes 'the blessed teacher John (Chrysostom)'.[51]

viii. 6: 'Set me as a seal over thy heart, and as a ring over thy arm. Because love is (as) strong as death, and jealousy (as) firm as hell. Its wings (are) wings of a furnace of fire.'

The sealing is lest one fall and forget the blessings of Christ's dispensation. Do not give your heart or arm to Satan.

Love as strong as death refers to those who give up love of God for love of this world; for such God's wrath will be like death. Those wives who exchange their husbands for paramours will also endure wrath like death—to which effect Narekatsi quotes Prov. vi. 34. So one must beware of Satan who steals away our love for Christ like a paramour—for which we would indeed suffer death and hell. (For fire, see the next verse.)

viii. 7: 'And many waters will not be able to quench love, and rivers will not restrain it. If a man were to give all his life for his love, with scorn they would mock him.'

This kind of love is illustrated even by worldly love. For the love of a parent or spouse cannot be extinguished by rivers, sword, fire, or death. All the more with love for God, which overcomes fire, waters, bonds, torture, prison, wife, and children. Cyril of Alexandria (1292D) interprets the fire as the walls of the Church.

The second part of the verse indicates that God's love is not like that of men—the greater it is the more it is despised by men. But warmed by this love, the saints conquered the world and its temptations.

viii. 8: 'Our sister is small and has no breasts. What shall we do for our sister on the day on which she will be bespoken?'

This is said by the angelic powers concerning the bride, who is the new Church from among the Gentiles. She is called 'sister' because she was created by the same single Creator. 'Small' refers to the lowly earthly nature, for although it is yoked in the body to the soul, it is still inferior to the angels. Here Narekatsi quotes Heb. ii. 7.

The breasts refer to the storehouses of heart and mind. But for Philo Carpasianos (148B, as elsewhere) the breasts refer to the two testaments. The angels are in doubt since they know our nature cannot endure the immaterial. The second part of the verse thus refers to the mystery of the incarnation, the sufferings of Christ,

---

[51] The editor of the Armenian text notes that this is a reference to the 'Second Homily on Matthew'; cf. *P.G.* lvii, col. 21, but the parallel is not verbally close.

and the inability of all men to believe, since they had no place for the Holy Spirit who would show them that the impossible is possible for God.

viii. 9: 'If she be a wall, we shall build over her silver towers. And if she be a door we shall provide for her cedar boards.'

Narekatsi remarks: 'I said at the beginning (see i. 4) that the prophetic statements do not tally because there has been transformation: from Hebrew to Hellene, from Hellene to Greek,[52] from Greek to Syriac and then to Armenian.' He does not attempt any figurative interpretation.

viii. 10: 'The bride is emboldened. I (am) a wall and my breasts (are) as a tower. I was in his eyes as (one who) found peace.'

This means: Do not worry about my weak nature, for by the power of the Almighty my weak nature is stronger than a wall and my breasts are like towers. For what you (i.e. the angels) could not endure, my weak nature endured and believed. I who was lost like a sheep and was waging war with heavenly and earthly (beings) because of our rebellion, have now found peace through the cross of the groom. Procopius interprets (1748B): though I seem small to you (the angels), I am perfect in the eyes of the groom.

viii. 11: 'Solomon had a vineyard in Beḷmawon. He gave his vineyard to guardians. Each man would bring from his fruit thousands of silver.'

Beḷmawon is a rich land in Judaea, whereby he allegorizes the land and its inhabitants. Procopius (1748C) interprets the name as 'multitudes', but for Cyril of Alexandria (1292D) it means 'among the believers'. Solomon is Christ, our peace, and the vineyard means the believers; Philo (149C) more explicitly refers it to the Church. The bringing of fruit means that everyone, great or small, must give account at the coming of the heavenly king Solomon: spiritual and temporal leaders, kings, princes, and other ministers. Those who have not fulfilled zealously their duties will be punished by Christ. Narekatsi expiates at some length on piety, accountability, repentance, and Christian responsibilities. As examples he refers to Trdat's edicts while he was still an idolatrous king[53] and to the Persian king's solicitude.[54] If non-Christians were concerned

---

[52] Narekatsi's distinction between Hellene (*hellenatsi*) and Greek (*yoyn*, the usual Armenian term) with regard to language is most curious. It does not appear in the text at n. 9 above where Narekatsi is adapting John Chrysostom. In his discussion of the properties of various languages, Vardan (*Hawak'umn Patmut'ean* (Venice, 1862), p. 12) refers to the language of the 'Hellenes' but clearly means 'Greek'.

[53] The reference is to Agathangelos, *History*, sects. 130, 136.

[54] The reference is to the letter of Mihrnerseh in the *History* of Eḷishē (p. 26 of the Erevan, 1957 edn.).

for their duty to those under their charge, how much the more should Christians. The 'keepers' are all those with responsibility, but also every individual, for we all shall have to give account of our thoughts, words, and deeds at the coming of Christ. The thousands refer to the perfect fruit of the just, which is likened to silver because of its purity, refined by fire seven times.

viii. 12: 'I have my vineyard before me. Thousands to Solomon and two hundreds to those who guard its fruit.'

The first phrase means that there is no longer any veil dividing the heavenly and earthly, as indicated by 1 Cor. xiii. 12. For the second part of the verse Narekatsi refers to the theologian (Gregory of Nazianzen).[55]

The thousands refer to the greater joy of God at finding men upright and fruitful, than that of men themselves. The two hundreds refer to the two natures, soul, and body. (Philo, 152B, again refers to the two testaments in order to explain two hundred.) Just as 10, 100, and 1,000 are perfect numbers, so is Christ perfect in divinity and humanity.

Those who guard the fruit are those who guard themselves as well as all those in authority (as the previous verse). All will receive rewards from Christ.

viii. 13: 'The bride says: Thou who sittest in gardens, others obey thee, make thy voice audible to me.'

The groom had called the bride 'vineyard', and others previously 'garden'. Here she calls herself the groom's garden that preserves the fruit of the vine. Quite different is Cyril of Alexandria, for whom sitting in gardens refers to the oversight of the churches (1292D).

'Make thy voice audible' may be explained by Matt. xi. 29. The bride asks that only the groom's voice be audible to her so she may unerringly follow him, as John x. 5, 27. The 'others' are all in heaven and earth who look to you. Cyril interprets this part of the verse as the desire of the bride that the groom expel evil and come to the saints (1293A).

viii. 14: 'Flee, my nephew, and resemble the roe or fawns on incense-bearing mountains.'

The bride's request resembles those of the prophets for God's aid; for the roe and fawns are sharp-sighted and swift. This also refers to the suddenness of the second coming.

[55] The editor of the Armenian text notes that the quotation is from 'On the Epiphany of Christ'. It has no parallel in *Oratio* 38, but is a rendering of the last paragraph of *Oratio* 39 (*In Sancta Lumina*).

As the roe and hind live on high mountains, here the reference to incense-bearing mountains means that men should live in virtue and sweet-smelling piety and then fly up to the groom, to the mountain which is heaven—as the theologian (Gregory of Nazianzen) says.[56] Here Narekatsi expands on the parable of the wise and foolish virgins. He again refers to Nazianzenus with reference to the second coming.[57] One should not say that there is no hell for Christians and that God is merciful—for this is to deceive oneself with false hopes.

Narekatsi concludes by indicating that whatever scripture, the prophets, gospels, apostles, and teachers tell us is but a parable of the future, truly perfect knowledge. Thus the Song of Songs teaches us about Christ's coming, his death, resurrection, and second coming, the Church, the diversity of manifestations of the Spirit and the various Christian virtues. He ends with two more references to Gregory Nazianzenus.[58]

Colophon

In 426 of the Armenian era (A.D. 977), I Gregory, priest from Narek, son of Bishop Khosrov Andzevatsi, was asked by Gurgēn, the pious ruler crowned by Christ, son of King Abusahl Hamazasp,[59] to expound the awesome words of Solomon and to explain the deep secrets contained therein, which are sweet to hear. For he speaks about the groom and bride, about the beauty of the breasts, red lips and cheeks, the desirable eyes, the sister, nephew, and maidens, and all other such words of passion and of the delight of hearts for the union of love. Hearing which, men interpreted them in various ways with uncomprehending minds.

So the king, being concerned with such a matter, sent to me once and then again. I was unable to oppose him, for I realized that the

---

[56] The editor of the Armenian text notes that the reference is to 'On the Baptism of Christ' (cf. n. 21 above), but the quotation does not tally with the Greek.

[57] This, according to the editor of the Armenian, is also from 'On the Baptism of Christ', but it is not found in the Greek.

[58] These are identified by the editor of the Armenian text as to the 'Second Homily on the Pascha' (cf. n. 37 above), and 'On the Baptism of Christ', but they do not tally with the Greek.

[59] Abusahl Hamazasp was king of Vaspurakan 953-72. He was succeeded by his first son Ashot (972-83) and then by his second son Gurgēn (983-1003); see the list in *The Cambridge Medieval History. IV: The Byzantine Empire*, ed. J. M. Hussey, pt. i (Cambridge, 1966), p. 784. Narekatsi distinguishes 'ruler (*ark'ay*)' from 'king (*t'agawor*).'

command was pleasing to God, and I interpreted the Song of Songs at his order. Although the task was beyond me I undertook it for fear of disobedience, lest the royal command remain unfulfilled. Yet this was very foolhardy of me, worthy of reproof from many and likely to draw punishment from God. But in placing the royal command before these two considerations, of divine and mortal (reproof), I think I am justified. For it is the command of Christ himself that one should obey kings as God; the one who is obedient God reckons as his, and the one who is found disobedient he reckons also as his. So I beg you readers not to blame me again for undertaking what was beyond my merit, for I could not fail my exacting summons. Trusting in the Holy Spirit, I decided not to disregard this request, and began my enquiry with prayers and tears. And he, looking on my unworthiness, and at the fervent wish of the one who solicited (the commentary), opened my mouth to expound and abbreviate it to the glory of Christ. Amen.[60]

---

[60] K. K'iparean, 'S. Grigor Narekatsi ew "Erg-Ergots"-i Meknut'iwně', *Bazmavēp*, cxix (1961), pp. 1-10, points out that the colophons of works ascribed to Gregory of Narek are not entirely consistent. Following N. Akinean, he regards the Gregory who composed this commentary as a priest from the village of Narek. But my purpose here was simply to examine patristic sources used in the commentary. The study of its relationship to other works by Narekatsi must await another occasion.

Additional Note: The text of the Commentary has been translated by V. Mistrih, 'Commentario sul cantico dei cantici di Gregorio di Narek', *Studia Orientalia Christiana Collectanea* 12 [1967], 465–534; 13 [1968/69], 199–261.

XIX

VARDAN'S *HISTORICAL COMPILATION* AND ITS SOURCES

The *Historical Compilation* or *Chronicle* [*Hawak'umn Patmut'ean*] of Vardan Arewelcʻi is a synopsis of several thousand years of Armenian history. It includes personal reminiscences of the author, but is primarily an abbreviation of previously written sources: the excerpts deal with various aspects of Armenian life, political and ecclesiastical concerns predominating, arranged in chronological order. Since Vardan compresses the long history of Armenia from the creation of the world down to A.D. 1267 into just 164 pages of text[1], such brevity necessarily entails a rather radical selection from the abundant material available in the thirteenth century. The *Chronicle* is therefore interesting as a guide to what a medieval Armenian scholar considered important and significant. It has further value, in that Vardan quotes from some sources now lost and offers his own recollections of persons and events of his time.

This *Chronicle* has not escaped the attention of modern scholars. But generally excerpts have been studied rather than the work as a whole, and less emphasis has been placed on the way in which Vardan adapts his sources than on identifying the earlier historians he quotes[2]. Since Vardan often combines his sources to create a new version of events, his book has to be used with some care. The following, however, is not intended as an essay addressing directly the reliability of Vardan as a historian, but rather as an attempt to identify his sources, which are mostly unacknowledged, and to indicate how he put together his own narrative.

---

[1] The Armenian text has been published twice: J.-B. EMIN, *Hawak'umn Patmut'ean, Vseobschaja Istorija Vardana Velikogo*, Moscow, 1861; Ł. ALIŠAN, *Hawak'umn Patmut'ean Vardanay Vardapeti*, Venice, 1862. The text cited in this article is that of Venice 1862. For a discussion of the MSS see J. MUYLDERMANS, *La domination arabe en Arménie, extrait de l'Histoire Universelle de Vardan*, Louvain, 1927, p. 9-29.

[2] The only general study is that of M. BROSSET, *Analyse critique de l'Histoire de Vardan*, in *Mémoires de l'Académie des Sciences de St. Pétersbourg*, 7ᵉ série, 4, no. 9 (1862), p. 1-30. Brosset was primarily interested in Vardan as a source for dating. Since the study of Muyldermans (see n. 1) Vardan's work has been extensively quoted in G. GARITTE, *La Narratio de Rebus Armeniae* (*CSCO* 132, Subsidia, 4), Louvain, 1952; V. MINORSKY, *Studies in Caucasian History* (Cambridge Oriental Series, 6), London, 1953; J. LAURENT, *L'Arménie entre Byzance et l'Islam depuis la conquête arabe jusqu'en 886*, nouvelle édition revue et mise à jour par M. CANARD, Lisbon, 1980. For the section on early Seljuq history see D. KOUYMJIAN, *Mxit'ar of Ani on the rise of the Seljuqs*, in *REArm*, 6 (1969), p. 331-353, and IDEM, *Problems of medieval and Muslim Historiography: the Mxit'ar of Ani fragment*, in *IJMES*, 4 (1973), p. 465-475.

Vardan places himself in the established tradition of Armenian historians. His direct teacher was the notable Yovhannes Vanakan, who had himself written about the Mongols and whose pupils included the historian Kirakos of Gandzak³. Vardan acknowledges by name a number of other, earlier historians to whom he was indebted. The curious thing is that the extent of his debt is never admitted, nor the fact that many writers who are not mentioned by name also were prime sources.

One may set out schematically the ways in which Vardan uses his sources:

1. a source is named and quoted directly.
2. a source is named but quoted at second-hand.
3. a source is indicated but not named — e.g. «some say», «others say».
4. no source is indicated.

The first two are sometimes difficult to distinguish. Thus, on p. 20, Eusebius of Caesarea is quoted as the source for the number of 3730 years covered by the Pentateuch. Yet in this passage Vardan is following the Armenian version of the *Chronicle* of the Syrian Patriarch Michael, who gives identical information⁴.

1. Vardan quotes few non-Armenian sources directly. He notes that the historian Socrates (whose work was available in Armenian translation) praises the emperor Jovian⁵; this is immediately followed by a different view, introduced by the phrase «some say», to the effect that Jovian was an Arian. Aristotle is mentioned by name when Vardan is discussing the nature of the physical world; the Armenian version of the Pseudo-Aristotelian *De Mundo* is probably intended⁶.

Of native Armenian authors a good number are mentioned by name. Moses Xorenacʻi — the most significant of all Armenian historians — is

---

³ For Vanakan and his pupils see H. OSKEAN, *Yovhannēs Vanakan ew iwr dprocʻē*, Vienna, 1922. Vanakan's history is lost; that of Kirakos has been edited by K. MELIKʻ-ŌHANJANYAN, *Kirakos Ganjakecʻi. Patmutʻiwn Hayocʻ*, Erevan, 1961.

⁴ The following references to Michael are to the French translation by V. LANGLOIS, *Chronique de Michel le grand*, Venice, 1868, which offers a longer text than the Armenian, *Žamanakagrutʻiwn Tearṅ Mixayēli Asorwocʻ Patriarkʻin*, Jerusalem, 1871.

⁵ Vardan, p. 44; Socrates, III 22, IV 24 (*Sokratay skʻolastikosi Ekełecʻakan Patmutʻiwn ew Patmutʻiwn varucʻ srboyn Siłbestrosi episkoposin Hṙovmay*, ed. M. TER-MOVSESEAN, Ejmiacin, 1897.

⁶ Vardan, p. 4. The *De Mundo* is printed in the collection of works attributed to David the «Invincible» Philosopher, *Dawtʻi Anyałtʻ pʻilisopʻayi Matenagrutʻiwnkʻ*, Venice, 1932, p. 517-542.

quoted for the chronology of the early fifth century[7]. Vardan also knows of traditions concerning the career of Moses and his fight for «orthodoxy» against the faith of Chalcedon[8]. But he never alludes to the real importance of Moses' *History* as a source of information and a model of historical writing. There is a passing reference to «the holy Ełišē» who had discussed the language of the angels. But Vardan does not indicate in what work that topic is discussed, or whether the author is the same as the Ełišē who wrote the *History of Vardan and the Armenian War*[9].

Referring to events of the early tenth century Vardan notes that «the holy patriarch John saw with his own eyes that gloomy time and wrote [his *History*] as a memorial for future generations»[10]. But Vardan does not make it clear when he is actually quoting directly from the *History* of John Catholicos rather than from another source for the same period such as Asołik. This latter is quoted (but not verbatim) only once, though his *History* was continually before Vardan's eyes[11].

Uxtanēs is mentioned as establishing a festival in honour of the forty martyrs of Sebaste[12]. The account of their passion is abbreviated from that in the *History* of Uxtanēs, but Vardan does not indicate either that the former actually wrote a history or that he (Vardan) used it here and elsewhere. When discussing the history of the Turks in Khorasan Vardan specifically mentions the otherwise unknown «Vahram, son of Tigran», as a source, and more importantly the priest Mxitʻar Anecʻi[13]. Mxitʻar's *History* has survived only in fragmentary form, without the section used here by Vardan. But that the latter admired the work of Mxitʻar is clear from his later description of Mxitʻar's translation of a Persian work on astronomy, to which he had also added diagrams[14].

---

[7] Vardan, p. 52; Moses, III 55-6. But in this passage Vardan also adds information from John Catholicos and Asołik.

[8] Vardan, p. 54-5. For these traditions see further B. KENDALL and R. W. THOMSON, *Definitions and Divisions of Philosophy by David the Invincible Philosopher* (*University of Pennsylvania Armenian Texts and Studies*, 5), Chico [California], 1983, p. xv-xvii.

[9] Vardan, p. 12. On p. 51 Vardan refers to Ełišē as a pupil of Sahak and companion of Moses and David. Vardan's account of the Armenian War is quite at variance with that of Ełišē (*Ełišē vasn Vardanay ew Hayocʻ Paterazmin*, ed. E. TER-MINASYAN, Erevan, 1957), being closer to that in John Catholicos and Asołik.

[10] Vardan, p. 87; cf. John Catholicos (*Yovhannēs Drasxanakertcʻi. Patmutʻiwn Hayocʻ*, ed. M. EMIN, Tiflis, 1912, and Delmar [N.Y.] 1980), p. 366.

[11] Vardan, p. 54; cf. Asołik, *Stepʻanos Tarōnecʻwoy Patmutʻiwn tiezerakan*, ed. S. MALXASEAN, St. Petersburg, 1885, II 2.

[12] Vardan, p. 42; cf. Uxtanēs, *Patmutʻiwn Hayocʻ*, Vałaršapat, 1971, I 61.

[13] Vardan, p. 94.

[14] Vardan, p. 137. The surviving part of Mxitʻar's work has recently been republished, *Mxitʻar Anecʻi. Matean ašxarhavēp handisaranacʻ*, ed. H. G. MARGARYAN, Erevan, 1983.

Vardan's own teacher had been Yovhannēs Vanakan. Only once is he mentioned by name, when Vardan refers to the histories of the Mongols written by Vanakan and «our brother the *Vardapet* Kirakos». Vanakan's work has not survived, but that of Kirakos is a most important and detailed history, concentrating on the thirteenth century. Vardan notes that he has summarised the information given by these two historians concerning the Mongols[15].

There are also several historical works with which Vardan was familiar and whose existence he acknowledges without specifically attributing any given information to them. Koriun, the biographer of Maštocʻ, and the historian Łazar of Pʻarpi are mentioned as scholars who were sent abroad in order to bring back to Armenia copies of books worthy of translation[16]. Nearer his own time Vardan refers to the works of Yovhannēs Sarkawag (which included a *History* now lost) and to the *Chronicle* of Samuēl Anecʻi[17]. He gives no overt clue as to his use of these sources, but a reference to the relationship between king David II of Georgia and Sarkawag in the first person indicates that Sarkawag's *History* is being quoted[18]. For the latter knew king David well, whereas Vardan was not born until nearly a century later.

2. In Vardan's *Historical Compilation* there also appear a few authors whose works were not known directly to our author, but whose names he knew at second-hand. Thus the «John» quoted for information concerning the judges of the Old Testament is not John Catholicos, but John of Antioch; for here Vardan is relying on Michael the Syrian, who had clearly identified his sources[19]. The reference to Africanus immediately following is taken from the same passage in Michael, whose *Chronicle* also provided the allusion to «Apolimos the Hebrew Philosopher» and to the «Sybil»[20].

3. On occasion Vardan notes that he is quoting from some source but he does not indicate which one. For example, in the Introduction where he describes the nature of the physical universe, he refers to «philoso-

---

Vardan was particularly indebted to it for his account of the career of Muhammad; see R. W. THOMSON, *Muhammad and the Origin of Islam in Armenian Literary Tradition*, in *In Memoriam Haïg Berbérian*, Lisbon, 1986, p. 829-858.

[15] Vardan, p. 146-7.
[16] P. 51, 53.
[17] P. 121.
[18] P. 120.
[19] Vardan, p. 22; Michael, p. 54.
[20] Apolimos: Vardan, p. 20; Michael, p. 49. Sybil: Vardan, p. 21; Michael, p. 52.

phers»[21]. The *De Mundo* attributed to Aristotle was an important source here, but Vardan follows traditional Armenian ideas, and his views can be paralleled in several earlier writers such as Eznik, Ełišē, or Anania of Širak[22]. «Learned men» in the same section refers to a discussion of various metals and substances, such as that in the short work *On Nature* by Išox[23]. (The latter had rendered Michael's Syriac *Chronicle* into Armenian, which in turn Vardan had himself revised)[24]. The reference to «doctors» describing the painful birth of Cain is curious, though the direct source (the *Death of Adam*) does indicate that Cain's birth was marked by affliction[25].

Vardan also refers to «the more elaborate histories»[26] and to the «detailed writers»[27]. By the first he means Michael and Kirakos, by the second Vanakan and Kirakos. On one occasion he merely says «as we have heard and seen in writing». Here Vardan is describing the organisation of the Armenian kingdom in Parthian times; he is following the elaborate account in Moses Xorenacʻi (without so stating explicitly), but wishes to acknowledge a variant opinion — in this case one based on the «Primary History»[28]. Vardan is also familiar with Georgian sources. He refers to «their books», having in mind the *Georgian Chronicles* or their Armenian adaptation attributed to Juanšēr[29].

Not all of Vardan's information came from written sources. He quotes at length the experiences of his earlier contemporary Yovhannēs Tuecʻi, who had visited the holy land. Vardan explains that Yovhannēs had personally narrated some of his stories, and that others he had heard from a monk who accompanied Tuecʻi[30].

But by far the most usual way for Vardan to hint that he is following a previous account is by stating «as they (or some, or others) say», or by using a similar phrase such as «it is said». In such cases no further

---

[21] Vardan, p. 3.
[22] Eznik, *De Deo*, ed. L. Mariès and C. Mercier (*P.O.*, XXVIII, 3, 4), Paris, 1959, # 2, 32; Ełišē, p. 33; Anania, *Yałags erkri*, in *Anania Širakacʻu Matenagrutʻyunē*, ed. A. Abrahamyan, Erevan, 1944.
[23] Išox, *Girkʻi veray bnutʻean*, ed. S. Vardanyan, Erevan, 1979.
[24] Michael, p. 375.
[25] Vardan, p. 5; cf. *Ankanon Girkʻ*, I, ed. S. Yovsepʻeancʻ, Venice, 1896, p. 24.
[26] Vardan, p. 128.
[27] P. 151.
[28] P. 31. Cf. Moses Xorenacʻi, I 8, and Sebēos, *Patmutʻiwn* (ed. G. Abgaryan, Erevan, 1979), p. 53.
[29] For the Armenian adaptation (*Hamaŕōt Patmutʻiwn Vracʻ ēncayeal Juanšēri patmičʻi*, ed. A. Tiroyan, Venice, 1884) see I. Abulaje, *Kʻartʻlis Cxovrebayi kam Vracʻ Patmutʻyan hin hayeren tʻargmanutʻiwnē*, in *Banber Matenadarani*, 1 (1941), p. 31-40; reprinted in I. Abulaje, *Sromebi*, IV, Tbilisi, 1985, p. 153-162.
[30] Vardan, p. 154-5.

clue is provided; when several writers or texts contain parallel information it is not always easy to determine Vardan's immediate source. The following authors seem to provide the source for passages introduced by such a general comment. They are listed in order of appearance, not including the bible which is quoted on nearly every page.

Apocryphal texts dealing with biblical themes: p. 6.
The *Chronicle* of Michael: p. 6, 7, 9, 11, 14, 15, 17, 20, 21, 22, 25, 26, 44, 110.
The *Chronicle* of Eusebius (which is also quoted via Michael): p. 19, 23.
Moses Xorenacʻi: p. 29 (also in Michael), 30, 31, 36 (also followed by Asołik), 52.
Zenob: p. 37 (with addition from Uxtanes), 39.
Dašancʻ Tʻułtʻ (or earlier tradition?): p. 40.
A source on the relics of St. Gregory: p. 41.
Pʻawstos: p. 46.
John Catholicos: p. 47, 75.
Asołik: p. 52, 85.
A source on Moses Xorenacʻi and David the Philosopher at Chalcedon: p. 55.
Moses Dasxurancʻi: p. 68.
Samuēl Anecʻi: p. 89 (or Kirakos?).
Source(s) on the history of Ani: e.g. p. 108 (cf. p. 97, where Mxitʻar Anecʻi is quoted. But it is not clear if he is the source for all the information about Ani in Vardan's work).
Matthew of Edessa: p. 110, 118.
Kirakos: p. 143, 144, 150.

There are other passages introduced by «some say», etc., the sources for which have not been identified.

4. In general, however, Vardan does not identify his sources or hint that he is following a previous author. Such passages are too numerous to be listed here, since it requires a full commentary to elucidate them[31]. But a brief summary of Vardan's main themes will indicate that sources other than those already identified were also grist to his mill.

The *Chronicle* opens with a discussion of the nature of God and of the physical universe. In addition to echoes of the Pseudo-Aristotelian *De Mundo* there are reminiscences here of the *Teaching of Saint Gregory* (from the *History* of Agathangelos) and David the Philosopher's *Defini-*

---

[31] An English translation of Vardan's *Chronicle* with a commentary on the sources has been prepared by the present author.

tions of Philosophy. Vardan does give details of David's legendary exploits [32], but he has no reference to the philosophical texts ascribed to him. His only reference to Agathangelos is as author of the inscription at Mcbin (the «Primary History»)[33]; the omission of all reference to the classic account of Armenia's conversion to Christianity is astonishing.

Like Moses Xorenacʻi and the Patriarch Michael (ultimately themselves dependent on Eusebius's *Chronicle*), Vardan correlates the biblical narrative of Genesis with the earliest histories of other nations. Here it is interesting to note that Vardan shows interest in Georgian traditions, referring to «their books»[34]. For the early history of Armenia Vardan does not follow Moses Xorenacʻi consistently. He was acquainted with the *Primary History* (which Moses himself attacked), and often abbreviates other Armenian authors such as Pʻawstos, John Catholicos, Asołik, or the Armenian rendering of Michael, thus providing a resume at second or third hand. His reliance on Zenob has already been noted[35]; the sequel attributed to John Mamikonean he also used for the life of Saint Gregory the Illuminator. For the life of Maštocʻ and the activities of the first translators patronised by the Catholicos Sahak Vardan does not follow directly the biography of Maštocʻ by Koriun, but generally uses the later accounts in Moses Xorenacʻi and Asołik. Likewise, with regard to the famous revolt of 450/1 described in detail by Ełišē and Łazar, it is the versions in John Catholicos or Tʻovmay Arcruni that provide the information. Ełišē is named as a companion of Koriun, while Łazar is entitled «historian»[36]. But it is surprising that although the latter is used for the period following 451, the classic account of the revolt by Ełišē is ignored.

Vardan's reference to Uxtanēs has already been noted[37]; that he was the source for information about the rupture of the Armenian and Georgian churches is passed over in silence. The name of Sebēos does not appear once in the pages of Vardan's *Chronicle*, yet he was the prime source for the Armenian involvement in the Byzantine-Persian wars that marked the same period, and for the Muslim conquest of the Eastern Mediterranean in the third decade of the seventh century. For his long account of Muhammad and the origin of Islam Vardan follows a source first used by Mxitʻar of Ani, but as usual does not give any

---

[32] See above at n. 8.
[33] Vardan, p. 31; cf. Sebēos, p. 47.
[34] See above at n. 29.
[35] See above, p. 348.
[36] Vardan, p. 51.
[37] See above at n. 7.

indication concerning the origin of his information[38]. Likewise, for the period of Muslim domination in the seventh to eighth centuries Vardan uses Łewond (whose *History* he never names), but more often relies on the later John Catholicos or Asołik. It is noteworthy that Vardan is the first to quote verbatim from the letters attributed to the emperor Leo III and the caliph Umar II which appear in the *History* of Łewond; though the tenth century historian Tʿovmay Arcruni and Vardan's contemporary Kirakos refer to the correspondence without quoting it[39]. Vardan is also the first to quote from the correspondence between the Byzantine Patriarch Photius and the Armenians. This is first mentioned by Asołik, but like the Leo-Umar letters, in its present form is of Armenian origin[40].

For the history of the ninth century Vardan combines or abbreviates the information in John Catholicos and Asołik. John had noted that his prime source was the work of Šapuh Bagratuni[41]. This being now lost, it is impossible to be certain whether or not Vardan was directly acquainted with it, since he never refers to Šapuh by name or even indirectly. However, when Vardan describes the origin of Bagratid kings of Armenia and Georgia with details unattested elsewhere, the suspicion that he knew Šapuh Bagratuni at first hand is not unreasonable[42].

In the tenth and early eleventh centuries the Byzantine empire expanded eastwards, gradually bringing most of Armenia within its borders and dispossessing the rulers of the small kingdoms of Vaspurakan, Ani, and Kars. Asołik, Matthew of Edessa, and Michael were important sources for the period, and Vardan's debt to these writers has already been noted. But the classic Armenian account of the incorporation of Armenia into the empire and the ensuing rapid loss of Byzantine territory to the Turks is that of Aristakēs Lastivertʿci. Vardan makes no mention of this important source, to which he was much indebted.

---

[38] See above at n. 14.
[39] Vardan, p. 73; ŁEWOND, *Patmutʿiwn* (ed. K. EZEAN, St. Petersburg, 1887), p. 42-98; Tʿovmay Arcruni, *Patmutʿiwn Tann Arcʿruneacʿ* (ed. K. PATKANEAN, St. Petersburg, 1887), p. 105; Kirakos, p. 66. The text of the letters betrays Armenian inspiration; these (at least in their present form) are probably a later interpolation into Łewond's *History*. See S. GERO, *Byzantine Iconoclasm during the Reign of Leo III* (*CSCO, Subsidia*, 41), Louvain, 1973, p. 153-171.
[40] Vardan, p. 82-5. On the authenticity of the Armenian version see GARITTE (as n. 2), p. 372-5, and LAURENT (as n. 2), p. 344-354.
[41] John Catholicos, p. 7, 111, 131, 141.
[42] Vardan, p. 81-2.

For his description of events in Southern Armenia and of the Crusades Vardan continues to follow Matthew (or his Continuator) and Michael. For events in Northern Armenia and Georgian controlled Ani, however, his sources are not so clear. An oblique reference to king David II suggests that John Sarkawag (mentioned only as an eminent *vardapet*, not specifically as a historian) was a direct source. The existence of a *Chronicle* by Samuēl of Ani is also explicitly noted by Vardan, but this is a very cursory work and was not the source for much of Vardan's detailed knowledge of events in Ani[43].

As he comes closer to his own time Vardan is more explicit about other writers. The *Histories* of his teacher Vanakan and fellow-pupil Kirakos are acknowledged[44], and for events of the thirteenth century Vardan could draw on personal reminiscences or information passed on directly by eye-witnesses such as Tuecʿi. Nonetheless, where he is the first witness to events described in more detail by later writers such as Mxitʿar Ayrivanecʿi or Stepʿanos Orbelean, some unidentified or lost written source must be behind Vardan's resume. He may have known the *Chronicle* of Smbat Sparapet and that of Grigor of Akancʿ, but the last part of his own work follows the narrative in Kirakos or the continuation to Michael.

The foregoing review of Vardan's sources for his *Chronicle* does not give us a full picture of the historical texts available to him. No doubt he was familiar with works he did not have the occasion to use directly or which were not suitable for his immediate purpose. Nor were historical works the only ones of interest to Vardan, since he wrote on grammar, on geography, and most especially on theology[45]. The purpose of this brief study is rather to point out that Vardan does not always use the source closest to the period he is describing, and that he often combines versions of the same episode found in different books to produce a new variant. His *Chronicle* is valuable as a witness to books now lost and to oral traditions and reminiscences of his acquaintances. But it is especially valuable as a personal document — not merely for the description of Vardan's meeting with Hulagu, but in general as evidence for what educated men of his day thought worthwhile to record for posterity.

---

[43] See above at n. 17, 18.
[44] See above at n. 3.
[45] Grammar: *Vardan Arewelcʿi. Meknutʿiwn Kʿerakani*, ed. L. G. XACʿERYAN, Erevan, 1972. Geography: *Ašxarhacʿoycʿ Vardanay Vardapeti*, ed. H. PĒRPĒREAN, Paris, 1960. Theology: see Oskean (as n. 3) for bibliography, and more recently Pʿ. ANTʿABYAN, *Vardan Arevelcʿu Žllankʿē*, in *Banber Matenadarani*, 8 (1967), p. 157-181.

Vardan was widely read, if not very original in approach. His *Chronicle* is not a great work of literature, but its author is not unworthy of inclusion in the canon of Armenian historians.

ADDITIONAL NOTES

The Venice edition of the Chronicle has been reprinted with Introduction by R.W. Thomson, *Vardan Areveltsi: Chronicle*, Delmar, New York, 1991. For a translation and commentary see R.W. Thomson, 'The Historical Compilation of Vardan Arewelc'i', *Dumbarton Oaks Papers* 43 [1989], 125–226. Two corrections to the commentary should be made:

Page 77, note 1: Not 'Kamax' but 'Kalmax' for which see C. Toumanoff, *Studies in Christian Caucasian History*, Georgetown 1963, p. 454, n. 64.
Page 101, para. 57: Alp'aslan was Tughril's nephew, not cousin.

INDEX

Since there is no common transliteration system for all the articles printed in this volume, I have added some cross-references between Armenian names transliterated according to the system used in the *Revue des études arméniennes* and the commonly accepted English forms. In general Armenian names have been indexed under Armenian spellings, e.g. 'John' Chrysostom, but 'Yovhannēs' Sarkawag. But foreign names cited only once have usually been left in the form as originally printed. Purists may deplore inconsistency, but ordinary readers are unlikely to be confused. Entries are in alphabetical order, regardless of diacritical marks.

Abas, Catholicos of Ałuank': V 83
Abasgia: I 37
Abdisho: XIII 57; XVII 44
Abgar: I 27; IV 142, 143; V 79, 86; XIV 121; XVI 83
Abraham [in OT]: IV 137; VIII 118; 124, 129, 138; IX 113; X 830, 840, 845
Abraham Catholicos: I 35; V 84
Abu-Bakr: X 857
Abusahl Hamazasp: XVIII 495
Acacius of Melitene: I 31; III 40; XII 459
Achilles Tatius: IV 145
Acilesene [Ekełeac']: II 16
Acts of Peter and Paul: VII 337
Adam: II 25; VI 191–3; VIII 121, 130, 133, 136, 138
Adamantius: XII 467
Addai [*see* also Thaddaeus]: I 27; IV 142; V 79, 85, 86; VII 340
Afrahat: IV 147; VIII 119, 120; XV 43
Africanus: XIX 346
Agat'angełos [cf. *Teaching of St Gregory*]: I 27; II 16; III 30–6, 41; IV 141, 142; V 79, 85, 86, 88; VI 191, 193; VII 331–4, 336, 337; VIII 121–3, 125, 126, 129, 132, 136; IX 104, 106–9, 114; XII 466, 468, 469; XVI 87; XVII 41; XVIII 461; XIX 349
Aghtamar: II 19; V 79, 85; IX 102
Ahikar: I 41
Alans [language of]: II 25
Alarodians: II 10
Albanians: *see* Ałuank'
Alcibiades: IV 146; XV 40
Alexander: I 34; IV 143; VII 333; XV 43
Alexander Romance: IV 141, 146; XV 43
Alexandria: I 29, 31, II 15; IV 145; XV 39

Ali: X 837, 856
Aloros: VI 202
Ałuank': I 32, 33, 35; III 40, 44; V 78, 80, 83
Ambrose: XII 461
Amiran-Darejaniani: I 41
Ammianus Marcellinus: II 13, 15
Anahit: II 16, 17; VII 334
Anania [of the fiery furnace]: VII 340
Anania of Hałbat: V 82
Anania of Narek: XIII 64, 65; XVIII 453
Anania of Širak: IV 144, 145; V 82; VI 193, 194, 199, 201–3; VIII *passim*; IX 105; XII 467; XV 39, 44; XIX 347
Anastas: V 78
Anatolius: XII 461
Andrew: I 28; V 78
Ani [on the Axurean]: I 37, 40; IX 108; XIX 350, 351
Ani [Kamax]: II 19; XVI 87
Antioch: I 31; IV 139, 144; VII 335; XII 458; XV 39; XVI 86
Antiochus: IV 137; VII 333, 338
Antony: II 13; 14
Anushirvan: VII 336
Aphraates: *see* Afrahat
Aphthonius: IV 146
Apollinarius: IV 144; XII 467
Apostolic Canons: XI 311
Apostles: IX 109
Ara: XV 41
Arabia: X 845
Arabic: I 30, 38, 40
Arabs: X 831
Aragvi: I 28
Aramaic: III 33
Aramazd: I 28; XVI 87

INDEX

Ararat [region]: II 18
Ararat [mountain]: II 18; V 88
Aratus: IV 145
Araxes [river]: I 37; II 12; V 79
Aretas: V 86
Argina: IX 108
Argives: XV 40
Arian heresy: I 30
Arians: V 82
Aristakēs [son of Gregory]: III 141; IV 39
Aristakēs Lastivertc'i: IX 103; XVI 87; XIX 350
Aristides: XII 467
Aristotle: I 40; VI 203; VII 329; XV 38; XIX 344
Aristotelian logic: I 30; IV 145
Arius: IV 144; X 841; XVIII 486
Armavir: XI 307
Armenia Prima: VII 339
Armenos: II 10, 15
Arminiya: I 35
Arsacids: III 32; VII 339, 340
Arshak I: VII 338
Arshak II: II 15
Arshak III: II 19
Artashat: VII 335
Artashes: II 10, 11; VII 338; XVI 85
Artavazd: I 29; II 12, 14; IV 138, 139; VII 338; XII 470
Artaxata: II 12
Artaxias: *see* Artashes
Artsruni [family]: I 36; V 86
Ashkenaz: II 18; IV 142
Ashot I: II 22
Ashtishat: I 26; III 32, 35; IX 106
Asia: IV 143
  Central Asia: I 29
Asia Minor: I 29
Asołik: *see* Step'annos of Taron
Assyria: IV 143
Ašxarhac'oyc': II 19; IV 143; VI 203
Athanasius [of Alexandria]: IV 135; V 80; XII 460, 461, 463, 466, 468; XIII *passim*; XIV 116, 121; XV 45
Athanasius [of Mt. Athos]: I 38
Athenogenes: V 79; IX 18
Athens: I 29; IV 139, 145; XIV 116; XV 38
Athos: I 38, 39
Atticus: XII 461
Augustine: II 17
Avarayr: III 42; IV 136, 137
Ayrarat: I 34; II 19, 20
Azat [river]: I 35; II 24; III 41; XIV 121
Azerbaijan: I 36; X 840

Babel [Tower of]: VI 200, 204; VIII 122, 137; XVI 85
Babgen: XII 461
Babylon: IV 143
  [= Baghdad]: X 857
Babylonians: XI 308
Bacchides: VII 333
Bacurius: I 27, 28
Baghdad: I 36; X 857, 858
Bagrat III: I 37
Bagratids: *see* Bagratuni
Bagratuni [family]: I 36, 37; IV 137, 138, 143; V 86; VII 338, 340; XIX 350
Bahira: *see* Sargis Bahira
Balavariani: I 38
Bartholomew [apostle]: I 28; III 29; V 84, 88; IX 109; XIV 121
Bartholomew of Edessa: X 837
Basil II: XVI 87
Basil of Caesarea: IV 139, 144; V 80; VI 194, 195, 197, 201, 202, 204; XI 312; XII 460, 461, 463, 466–8; XIII 47; XV 42, 45; XVI 82; XVIII 484, 491
Behemoth: VI 204, 205
Beirut: IV 140; XV 39
Bel: IV 143; IX 113; XVI 85
Bethlehem: VIII 138
Bible: XVII 42, 43; *see also* s.v. authors of biblical books and persons mentioned. Allusions to biblical passages are not noted.
Biwrasp Aždahak: XI 307
Black Mountain: I 38, 39; XII 466
Black Sea: I 27
Boeotians: XV 40
Book of Letters: V 82–4; XII 461; XIV 121
Bolnisi Sion: I 33
Byzantium, Byzantines: *passim*; *see also* Constantinople

Caesarea [in Cappadocia]: I 26, 32; III 31, 32, 39; XII 457
Callimachus: IV 146
Cappadocia: I 26, 37; II 13; III 30, 32; VII 338
Caspian Sea: II 13; III 44
Caucasus [languages of]: II 25
Cerinthus: X 841, 856
Chalcedon [council]: I 32–4; III 40, 41, 45; V 78, 81, 83; XII 461; XIII 57; XVII 46; XIX 345
Chaldaeans: VI 203; XI 306–8
Cherson: XII 461

INDEX

Christ [only theologically significant references are noted]: I 31; VIII *passim*; IX 107; XIV 121; XVII *passim*
Chorukh [river]: I 36
Christmas [date of]: V 80, 84
Cilicia: I 31, 37; III 39; VII 338
Claudius: V 86
Clement of Alexandria: II 16
Clement of Rome: XIV 119
Cleopatra: II 15
Colchis: I 27
Constans II: XIV 119
Constantine I: I 28, 30; III 39; IV 145; V 78; VII 337, 339
Constantine II: VII 337
Constantinople: I 27, 30, 31, 35, 36, 39, 40; II 24; III 37, 38, 41; IV 140, 141, 144, 145, 147, 148; V 80, 83, 84, 88; XI 305, 306; XII 458, 459; XIV 116, 119; XV 39; XVI 82
Constantinople [council]: V 82
Constantius: I 28
Corbulo: II 14
Cosmas Indicopleustes: VI 198
Crimea: I 27
Cross [of Christ]: V 78, 79; VIII 121, 122
Crusades: XIX 351
Ctesiphon: XII 465
Cyril of Alexandria: I 31, 32; XII 460, 461, 463, 468; XIII 47, 55–7, 63; XIV 116, 121; XVII 44; XVIII *passim*
Cyril of Jerusalem: V 81; VIII 119, 130; XI 309; XII 460, 463, 468; XV 38
Cyril of Scythopolis: V 78, 81
Cyrus: VIII 138

Damasus: VII 337
Daniel [OT]: VIII 119
Daniel [Syrian bishop]: I 27; III 33; XII 459
Darius: II 15; VIII 125
Dašanc' T'ułt': XIX 348
David [consul]: XIV 116
David ['Invincible' philosopher]: IV 146, 147; VI 193, 203; XI 308; XV *passim*; XIX 348, 349
David [OT king]: VII 339; VIII 124, 126, 129; XVI 85
David II [the 'Builder']: XVI 83, 87; XIX 346
David Curopalates of Tayk': I 38
David of Ganjak: XI 309, 310
David of Sasun: *see Sasnadzrer*
David and Jacob [commentators]: XIV 121

Death of Adam: XIX 347
De Mundo: VI 193–5, 197, 200, 203; XIX 344, 347, 348
Demetrius [king]: VII 334
Dio Cassius: II 14, 15
Diocletian: V 79; IX 114
Diodore of Tarsus: XII 461, 467
Dionysius of Alexandria: III 30; XII 457
Dionysius the Areopagite: I 39; IV 145; V 81, 84; VI 199; VIII 130; XII 463, 464; XIV *passim*; XV 39, 45
Dionysius Thrax: IV 138, 146; XV 44
Dvin: I 40; X 830
Dvin [councils] in 505: I 34; III 40; XII 461; XIII 57
  in 555: I 34; III 41; V 83; XII 461, 462
  in 608: I 35
Dzirav: VII 338

Edessa: I 29, 31; II 19; III 30, 37; IV 140, 142, 143; V 79, 80, 85; VII 340; IX 111; XII 459; XVI 81
Egypt: I 32, 35; II 14; VII 333; X 837; XIV 116
Egyptian [language]: II 25
Ejmiacin: II 18; III 31, 32, 38; XII 460
Ejmiatsin: *see* Ejmiacin
Eleazar Maccabaeus: VII 338, 340
Elias: *see* Elijah
Elijah: VIII 132, 134, 135
Ełišē: I 33, 41; II 23, 24; III 41–4; IV 131, 137, 139, 142, 146–8; V 87, 88; VI 191, 196, 198, 201–3; VII 332, 335–7, 341; VIII *passim*; IX 104, 110; XI 307, 309, 310; XII 460, 467, 469; XV 38; XVI 86, 87; XIX 345, 347, 349
Ephesus [council]: I 31; III 40; IV 140; V 80; XII 459, 461; XVII 41
Ephrem Mcire: I 39
Ephrem the Syrian: IV 147; VI 199, 201, 204; XI 308; XII 462, 467; XV 43
Epictetus [letter to]: XIII *passim*
Epicureans: XV 40
Epiphanius: XI 312; XII 464, 467; XIV 116
Epiphany [feast]: V 80
Er: II 15, 16
Erez: II 16; VII 334
Esayi Nč'ec'i: XIV 116–18, 121
Esther [book of]: VIII 338
Ethiopia: X 845
Ethiopian army: IV 138
Euphrates: II 17; VIII 121
Euripides: IV 146, 147
Europe: IV 143

Eusebius of Caesarea: II 17, 18; III 30;
  IV 138, 139, 141, 143, 147; VI 191;
  VII 339, 341; XII 457, 460, 469;
  XIV 121; XVI 81–3; XVIII 454, 471;
  XIX 344, 348
Eusebius of Emesa: XII 465
Euthalian prologues: VII 331
Euthymius [of Mt. Athos]: I 38, 39
Euthymius Zigabenus: X 838
Eutyches: IV 144; XIII 47, 68
Eve: VI 191, 192; VIII 130
Ezekiel: IX 109
Eznik: I 31, 41; IV 140, 141, 145–7;
  VI 194–8, 200–3; VII 334; X 858;
  XI 307–10; XII 459, 467, 468; XV 39,
  41; XVI 85; XIX 347

Faustos: *see* P'awstos
Franks: IX 109

Gabriel [archangel]: X 837
Gagik: II 23; V 79, 84, 85; IX 102
Gahnamak: IV 143
Gaianē: II 18
Galerius: III 31, 32
Ganja: I 40
Garizim: VII 333
Gayl [river]: V 77
Gazara: VII 335
Gehon [river]: VIII 121
Gelati: I 40
George [saint]: V 78
George Hamartolus: X 836, 837, 840
George of Pisidia: VI 196, 198, 203
Georgia: I *passim*; III 37, 38, 41;
  XVI *passim*
Georgian Chronicles: VI 201; XVI *passim*;
  XIX 347
Georgians: III 40, 41, 44; IV 148; V 81–4;
  XII 461, 465, 466
Germanos [of Constantinople]: XIV 116,
  119
God: XVII *passim*; *see also* Christ,
  Trinity
Gogarene: I 33
Golden Fleece: II 10
Goths [king of]: VII 333
  language of: II 25
Greece, Greeks: *passim*
Gregory: *see* s.v. Grigor for Armenians of
  this name
Gregory of Nazianzus: I 39; IV 139, 141,
  144, 146; V 82; VII 329, 341; XII 460,
  461, 464, 466, 468; XIII 47; XV 38;
  XVIII 454, 468, 472–95

Gregory of Nyssa: V 82; XII 461, 464, 466,
  468; XIII 47, 63; XIV 116; XV 38;
  XVIII *passim*
Gregory Thaumaturgus: XII 464, 466
Grigor Aršaruni: VI 205; IX 113
Grigor the Illuminator: I 16, 17, 30;
  II 16; III 29–35; IV 136, 137, 141;
  V 78, 79, 85, 88; VI 193; VII 333,
  334; IX 106, 109, 114; XII 457, 458,
  465, 468; XVII 41; XVIII 461, 470,
  475, 476, 478, 483, 487, 489;
  XIX 349
  as author of homilies: IX 102; *see also*
    Yačaxapatum Čaṙk'
  'Canons' of Grigor: XI 311
  'Questionnaire' of Grigor: XI 308
Grigor Magistros: I 39; IX 105, 109, 110,
  112, 113; X 841; XV 38
Grigor of Narek: VI 196, 197, 205; IX 102,
  104, 105, 109, 112, 113; XI 309–11;
  XIV 116; XVIII *passim*
Grigor, bishop of Ṙštunik': V 77
Grigor of Tat'ev: X 829, 858; XIV 120;
  XVIII 455
Grigor Tłay: IX 109
Grigor Vkayasēr: I 39
Grigoris: I 27; III 44
Gurgēn Arcruni: V 84

Haciwn: V 79
Hadrian [martyr]: XVIII 478
Hagar: X 830
Halbat: XIV 117
Ham: IV 143
Hamam: XIV 121
Hamazasp Arcruni: X 832
Hannibal: II 11
Hatsiwn: *see* Haciwn
Hayk: II 18; IV 143
Hebrew [language]: XVI 86; XVIII 493
Hector: VI 146; XV 40
Helen [mother of Constantine]: V 79
Helen of Adiabene: V 86
Helen of Troy: XV 40
'Hellenistic School': IV 146; XV 45
Henotikon: I 32; III 40, 41; XII 461
Heraclius: V 77–9; X 830, 838;
  XVI 87
Hermes Trismegistus: VI 200, 203
Herod: IV 138; V 86
Herodotus: II 10, 12, 15, 16
Hesiod: IV 146
Hesychius: V 80
Hippolytus: IV 142; XII 467;
  XVIII 455–75

Homer: IV 138, 146; XV 40
  As error for Hermes Trismegistus:
    IV 146
Horeb [mount]: VI 192
Hrač'eay: VII 340
Hŕip'simē: I 28; II 18; V 79, 87; VII 333;
    IX 114
  Church of: IX 111
Hulagu: XIX 351
Huns: XI 309
  language of: II 25
Hyrcanus: VII 338

Ibas: XII 461
Iberia: I passim; see also Georgia
Ibn Ishaq: X 837, 838
Ignatius: XII 461
Ilium: see Troy
India: II 17; VI 203
  Indian language: II 25
Infancy Gospel: VIII 138
Iran: II 19, 24; IV 136; see also Sasanian
    Iran
Irenaeus: VIII 126; XII 462, 464; XIII 55
Isaac: see Sahak
Isaiah: VIII 136
Isaias: see Esayi
Ismael, Ismaelites: X passim
Israel: II 24; IV 137; VII 339; VIII 134;
    XVI 86
  New Israel: VII 339; IX 109
Išox: VI 197, 198, 200, 202–5
Italy: IV 145
Iviron [monastery]: I 39; V 84

Jacob [OT]: VIII 132
Jacob of Nisibis: I 27; II 18; III 32;
    VIII 119
James [brother of the Lord]: V 81
Japheth: II 18; IV 137, 142, 143; VI 191
Jason: II 10
Jerome: II 17
Jerusalem: I 30; IV 144; V passim;
    VIII 131; X 854
  Heavenly Jerusalem: IV 136; V 84;
    IX 111
Jews: III 42; IV 137; V 87; VII 333, 338,
    339; VIII 135; X 831, 837, 841
  Jewish colonies: III 33; IV 138, 148
John: see s.v. Yovhannēs for Armenians
    of this name
John [evangelist]: VIII 121, 130
John of Antioch: XIX 346
John the Athonite: I 38
John the Baptist: V 79, 86; IX 106

John Chrysostom: II 17; IV 141; V 80;
    VII 329, 341; VIII 130; XI 309, 310;
    XII 460, 461, 464, 464–8; XIII 47, 63;
    XVIII passim
John of Damascus: X 836, 837, 840–3
John Italos: I 40
John of Jerusalem: V 83; XII 465
John Petritsi: I 39, 40
Jordan [river]: VIII 131; IX 109
Josephus: IV 138, 139; V 87; VII 337, 341;
    XVI 82, 83
Jovian: XIX 344
J̌uanšēr: X 842, 843, 857; XV 44;
    XVI passim; XIX 347
J̌uari: I 28
Judaea: II 17
Judas Maccabaeus: VII 333–5
Julfa: I 37
  New Julfa: I 37
Julian of Halicarnassus: XIII 59, 60
Julius [pope]: XII 461; XIII 63
Justin [historian]: II 13
Justin I: I 33
Justinian: I 31, 34; II 13

Kakheti: I 37
Kałert': X 845, 854, 856; XVI 86
Kanonagirk': V 82
Kars: I 37; IX 108; XIX 350
Kirakos Ganjakec'i: IX 108, 109; X 841,
    842, 856; XIV 116, 120; XVI 87;
    XIX 344, 346–8, 350, 351
Khachik: see Xač'ik
Khazar [language]: XVI 86
Khorasan: XIX 345
Khosran: see Xosran
Khosrov: see Xosrov
Khosrovik: see Xosrovik
Khuran: see Xuran
al-Kindi: X 840
Kiwrion: I 34; V 83
Knik' Hawatoy [Seal of Faith]: XII 462,
    465, 466; XIII 48, 558, 59, 63–5;
    XIV 115, 120
Komitas: V 78; XII 462; XIV 115
Korduk': I 27; II 18
Koriwn: I 27, 28; II 23; III 36–8; IV 140–2,
    147; V 80; VI 191; VII 331–3, 336,
    337; XII 459; XIX 346
Kushans: XVI 84
Kyrion: see Kiwrion

Labubna: XI 309; XIV 121
Laodicaea [council]: VII 330
  Canons of: XI 311, 312

6 INDEX

Latin [language]: II 25
Latins [Catholic monks]: I 39
Lavra [on Mt. Athos]: I 38
Łazar P'arpec'i: I 33; II 19, 21; III 36, 42, 43; IV 136, 137, 144, 148; V 79, 81, 87; VI 191, 205; VII 332, 335–7, 339; XI 307; XII 460, 467, 469; XVI 86; XIX 346, 349
Lazica: I 28, 34
Leo I [emperor]: VII 339
Leo III [emperor]: X 831, 839; XIX 350
Leo I [pope]: XIV 121
  Leo's 'Tome': XII 461
Leviathan: VI 204, 205
Łewond [historian]: X 831, 838, 839, 844
Łewond [priest]: IV 136, 137; XVIII 488
Łewond [pupil of Mastoc']: IV 140, 141
Libanius: IV 139; XII 458
Libya: IV 143
Louis the Pious: XIV 117
Lucullus: II 11
Luke [evangelist]: VIII 121
Lysias: VII 335

Macarius I of Jerusalem: V 82, 83
Macarius II of Jerusalem: V 82, 83
Maccabees: II 23; III 42; IV 136, 137, 148; V 87; VII *passim*; XII 460; XVI 82
Macedonius: XVIII 486
Magi: II 15
Mamikonean family: I 36
Man in the Panther's Skin:
  see *Vep'xis-Tqaosani*
Manazkert [synod]: XIII 60
Maniton: XI 309
Manuel [architect]: IX 102
Manuel Mamikonean: VII 335; XI 306, 307
Mar Abas Catina: IV 143
Marcian [emperor]: I 32; III 42
Marcion: XII 467; XIII 68
Marcionites: XI 307
Mari: VII 335
Mark [evangelist]: VIII 121
Mary [BVM]: I 38; IX 114
Masis [mount]: VII 333
Massagetae: III 44; VII 335
Maštoc': I 26, 28, 29, 31, 33; III 33–40, 45; IV 139–41, 144–8; V 80, 89; VII 329, 331–3; IX 109; XII 457–9, 461, 467; XIV 121; XV 38, 39, 43; XVI 81; XIX 346, 349
Mas'udi: X 845
Mattathias Maccabee: IV 137; VII 335, 336, 338

Matthew [evangelist]: VIII 121
Matthew of Edessa: XIX 348, 350, 351
Maurice: I 35, 37; III 41, 44; V 77
Maxentius: VII 339
Maximian: II 17; III 30
Maximos [the Confessor]: XIV 118
Mazdaean [religion]: VII 336
Mazdaeans: V 87; X 831
Mecca: X 840, 845
Medes: II 16
Medina: X 837
Melchior: VIII 138
Melchisedek: VIII 138
Meletius of Antioch: V 82
Melitene: III 37; IV 140; V 80; XIV 120
Merhujan Arcruni [8th cent. martyr]: X 832
Merujan Arcruni [apostate]: VII 335; XI 306
Meruzanes: II 17; III 30; XII 457
Mesopotamia: I 35; II 18; VI 204
Methodius: XII 467
Michael II [emperor]: XIV 117
Michael Psellus: I 40
Michael the Syrian: VI 201, 202; X 837, 843; XV 44; XVI 83; XIX 344, 346–51
Mihran: see Mirian
Milan [edict of]: III 31
Milvian Bridge: VII 339
Mirian: I 27, 28; XVI 86
Mithra: II 15
Mithridates: II 11
Modestus: V 78
Mongols: XIX 344, 346
Moses [OT]: IV 137, 140; VI 192, 193; VII 339; VIII 124, 134, 135; IX 113; X 830; XVI 85
Moses II [Catholicos]: I 34, 35; II 24; III 41; V 82; XIV 121
Moses, bishop of Tsurtavi: V 85
Movsēs Dasxuranc'i: IV 145, 146; V 78, 80; X 840; XI 309, 311; XIV 115; XIX 348
Movsēs Xorenac'i: I 41; II 18, 19, 21, 22; III 37, 38; IV 137–9, 142, 143, 145–7; V 79, 82, 86–8; VI 191, 202; VII 332, 336–41; XI 307, 309–11; XII 467, 469; XIV 116, 121; XV 37–9, 41, 42; XVI 81–3, 85–7; XIX *passim*
Mtskheta [Mcxet'a]: I 28
Mu'awiyah: I 36; X 830
Muhammad: V 77; X *passim*; XVI 86; XIX 349
Mushel: VII 335
Muslims: I 35–7; II 24; X *passim*; XIX 350

INDEX

Mxit'ar of Ani: X 836, 841–54, 856; XVI 83; XIX 345, 348, 349
Mxit'ar of Ayrivank': VI 192, 198, 201, 204; IX 106; XVI 84; XIX 351
Mxit'ar Goš: XI 312; XIV 120

Narek [monastery]: XVIII 453
Narratio de Rebus Armeniae: V 83
Narses [shah]: III 31
Nebuchadnezzar: IV 137; VII 340
Nemesius: VI 202, 204
Neoplatonism: I 30, 40; IV 145
Nero: II 12, 14, 15
Nersēs I: III 35, 36, 39; V 81, 82; XII 458; XV 38, 42
  'Canons' of: V 87; XI 311
Nersēs II: I 33
Nersēs III: XIV 119
Nersēs of Lambron: VI 193, 205; XIII 64; XIV 120; XVIII 455
Nersēs Šnorhali: VI 198, 202; IX 105, 112; XI 312; XIV 120
Nestorius: I 32; IV 144; XIII 47, 56; XVIII 480, 486
Nestorians: I 33; III 41, 45; XIII 69
Nicaea [council]: I 32; III 39, 41; IV 140, 141; V 80; VIII 124; XIII 58, 68; XVII 44
Nicene Creed: XVII 44
Nicanor: VII 335
Nicephoras Phocas: I 38
Nilus: XVIII 462, 467–84
Nineveh: IV 143
Nino: I 28
Noah: II 18; IV 137; VI 191; VIII 129, 138
  Noah's Ark: I 27; III 32; V 84; VIII 119, 123; IX 110, 112
Nor Getik: IX 108
Nonnus: IV 146; XI 308, 309

Old Persian Empire: II 10
Olympiodorus: XV 38, 39
Olympus [mount]: I 38
Origen: VII 339; XVIII 455–63
Orpheus: XV 43
Ovid: IV 144

Pahlavuni family: III 31, 34
Palestine: I 30, 33, 37, 38; V 83; VII 340; X 837, 841
Pamphylia: II 15
Pap: II 13
Papag: XI 307
Paradise: VIII 121, 123, 130; IX 110

Parthia: II 13; III 43; IV 138; V 87
Patronice: V 79
Paul of Alexandria: VI 202; XI 305, 312
Paul of Samosata: XIII 47
Paulicians: X 831
P'awstos Buzand: I 27, 28; II 18, 23; III 32, 34–6; IV 138, 147; V 82, 86, 87; VI 191, 202; VII 331, 332, 334–6, 338; XI 306, 309–11; XII 458; XV 41, 42; XIX 348, 349
Persian [language]: II 25; literature: I 40, 41
Persians: *passim*
Peter: *see* s.v. Petros for Armenians of this name
Peter [apostle]: VIII 130, 137
Peter of Alexandria [Mongus]: XII 465
Peter the Iberian: I 34
Petritsos [monastery]: I 40
Petros Getadarj [Catholicos]: XVI 87
Pharaoh: VII 339
Philo [Jewish philosopher]: I 30; IV 136; VI 191, 194; VII 329, 341; VIII 118; XII 467; XV 44
Philo Carpasianos: XVIII *passim*
Philo of Tirak: XVI 82
Philoxenus: XII 462
Phison [river]: VIII 121
Phoenicia: VII 333
Phrygia: II 10, 18
Physiologus: VI 198; XV 42
Pinehas: IV 137
Plato: II 15, 16; VI 193; VII 329; XV 38, 40, 41
Pliny [the Elder]: II 19
Plotinus: XV 41
Plutarch: II 10, 12, 13, 22; IV 139, 147
Pompeius Trogus: II 13
Pontus: III 30
Porphyry: XV 38
Priam: IV 138
Primary History: II 18; IV 143; XIX 347, 349
Proclus [patriarch of Constantinople]: I 31; III 40; XII 459, 461, 465
Proclus [philosopher]: I 40
Procopius [historian]: II 13; XVI 82
Procopius of Gaza: XVIII 455–93
Prohaeresius: IV 139
Proverbs [translation of]: IV 140; XII 459
Psellus: XVI 82
Pseudo-Callisthenes: IV 145; *see* also *Alexander Romance*
Pseudo-Šapuh Bagratuni: V 77–9; X 840, 856, 857

Ptolemy Philopator: VII 332, 33
Pythagoreans: XV 40

al-Qadisiyah: X 830
Qipchaqs: XVI 85
Qur'an: X 839, 841, 845, 854

Raman: X 845
Rayy: X 857
Red Sea: VII 339; XVI 85
Rhipsime; *see* Hrip'sime
Rome [in Italy]: II 12; IV 144–6; V 79; VII 339
  In the sense of 'Roman empire' or 'Byzantium': *passim*
Root of Faith: XIII 64, 65, 69
Ṙštunik': V 77
Rufinus: I 27; IV 140

Sabas: V 81, 83
Sahak I: I 26, 29, 31; III 39; IV 140; V 80; VII 331; IX 103, 109, 113; XII 458, 459; XIV 121; XIX 349
  Canons of: IX 113
Sahak III: XIII 61, 63, 64, 69; XIV 121
Sahak Arcruni: X 832
Šahapivan [council]: IV 142; XI 311, 312
Saint Catherine's Monastery: V 78
Salman: X 838, 839
Samosata: IV 140
Samuel of Ani: X 841–5, 854, 856; XVI 86; XIX 346, 348, 351
Sanatruk: V 86
Šapuh Bagratuni: XIX 350; *see also* Pseudo-Šapuh
Saracen [etymology of]: X 843, 844; XVI 84
Sarah: X 843, 844
Sargis Bhira: X 837, 841, 857
Sarmatians: VI 204
Sasanian Iran: I 35, 37; III *passim*; IV 137, 148; VII 335, 336; XVI 86
Sasna-dzrer: I 41
Sasunc'i Davit': X 857; *see also* *Sasna-dzrer*
Satan: VIII 137
Scythians: VII 333
Seal of Faith: see *Knik' Hawatoy*
Sebēos: I 36; II 24; V 78, 83; VII 336; IX 108; X 830–2, 838, 854; XII 465, 466; XIV 119; XIX 349
Seleucids: III 42; VII 336
Seljuks: I 37, 40

Sem: IV 143; VIII 138
Semiramis: II 19; XV 41
Serapion [Letters to]: XIII 53
Seth: VIII 138
Severian of Gabala: XII 465
Severus: IV 140; XIII 59
Shah Abbas: I 37
Shahapivan; *see* Šahapivan
Shambat: VII 340
Shapuh III [shah]: I 26
Shapuh Bagratuni: *see* Šapuh
Shushanik: *see* Šušanik
Simeon [hermit]: V 77
Simeon of Beit-Arsham: III 40
Simeon of Julfa: IV 146
Simon [apostle]: I 28; XIV 119
Sinai [mount]: I 38, 39; IV 140; V 78; VIII 113
Siwnik': V 79; VII 333
Smbat [tutor of Artašēs]: VII 338
Smbat I [king]: II 23
Smbat Bagratuni: II 24; III 44
Smbat Sparapet: VI 199; XIV 120; XIX 351
Socrates: XV 40
Socrates Scholasticus: XVI 82, 83; XIX 344
Sodom: VIII 124
Solomon: VII 339; VIII 125, 129, 132; IX 110
Spain: I 36
Statius: IV 144
Stephen: *see* s.v. Step'annos for Armenians of this name
Stephen [protomartyr]: V 77, 78
Step'annos Imastaser: XII 464
Step'annos Orbelean: IX 108; XIV 116; XVI 83; XIX 351
Step'annos of Poland: XIV 115, 119; XVI 83
Step'annos of Siwnik': II 25; IV 145, 146; V 81, 84; XII 465; XIII 60, 63, 64; XIV *passim*; XV 45
Step'annos of Taron: IX 108; XIII 64, 69; XIV 120; XV 37, 38; XIX 345, 348–50
Strabo: II 10, 12, 13, 16, 19
Studion [monastery]: I 38
Suetonius: II 15
Suida [lexicon]: II 15
Šušanik: I 33
  Life of: I 41
Svaneti: I 39
Syria, Syrians: I 26, 28, 29, 32–5, 39; II 17; III 39; IV *passim*; VII 333, 338

INDEX

Syriac: I 26, 29, 31, 38; II 25; III 33, 37, 38, 45; IV *passim*; V 80; VI 191; VII 329, 330, 334, 337; X 829; XI 306; XII 458, 467, 470; XV 43; XVI 81, 82, 86; XVIII 457, 493
Syrian Martyrs [*Vkayk' Arewelic'*]: IV 147

Tabari: X 845
Tabor [mount]: V 78
Tacitus: II 12, 14
Tat'ev: IX 108
Taurus: V 78
Teaching of Addai: IV 142; VII 340; see also Labubna
Teaching of Saint Gregory: V 81; VI 191, 194, 196–8, 200, 204; IX 104, 114; XIII 57; XVI 86; XVIII 456, 463, 468; XIX 348; see also Agat'angelos
T'ēodoros K'rt'enawor: IX 114
T'ēodoros Řštuni: I 36; X 830
Tertullian: II 17; III 29
Thaddaeus: I 28; III 29, 30, 41; V 88; VII 340; IX 109
 'Canons' of: XI 311; see also Addai
Theodore: see s.v. T'eodoros for Armenians of this name
Theodore [brother of Heraclius]: X 837
Theodore of Mopsuestia: I 31, 32; III 39, 40; XII 459, 461
Theodoret: VII 337; XII 461; XIII 56; XIV 121; XVIII 455, 457, 482, 483
Theodosiopolis [Karin, Erzerum]: IV 144
Theodosius I: I 26; V 82
Theognis: XV 40
Theon: IV 145
Theophanes: X 836, 837, 840; XVI 82
Theophilus of Alexandria: XII 461
Thessaly: II 10, 18
Thomas: see T'ovma
Thucydides: IV 146
Tiberius I: V 86
Tiberius II: IV 144
Tiflis: I 40
Tigran the Great: II 10, 11, 22; IV 138, 139, 146, 147; VII 337, 338, 340; XV 40; XVI 86
Tigranocerta: II 11
Tigris: VIII 121
Timothy Aelurus: XII 461, 462, 464, 465; XIII 49, 63
Timothy of Ephesus: XIV 119
Tiridates I: II 12, 14, 15; for Tiridates III/IV [first Christian king of Armenia] see s.v. Trdat
Tobias: V 86; VII 340

Torgom: II 18; IV 142; V 87; VI 191; XVI 86
T'ovma Arcruni: II 19, 22, 24; IV 148; V 79, 84–6; IX 102; X 832–40, 850; XIX 349, 350
Trdat [III/IV]: I 26, 28, 30; II 16; III 31–4, 45; IV 141, 143; V 78, 79, 85; VI 193; VII 333, 334; IX 106, 107; XII 469; XVIII 461, 493
Trebizond: I 27; IV 144; XVI 87
Trinity: VI 205, 206; VIII 118; IX 111; XVII *passim*; see also Christ, God
Tripoli: VII 334
Troy [Ilium]: IV 138, 146
 Trojan War: IV 138, 145
Tsałats'-kar: IX 108
Turks: I 40; XIX 345
Tychikos: IV 144, 145

Umar II: X 831, 839; XIX 350
Uxtanēs: XIII 64; XIX 345, 349

Vahagn: VII 333, 334; IX 106
Vahan of Golt'n: X 831
Vahan Mamikonean [in P'awstos]: VII 335
Vahan Mamikonean [in Łazar]: III 42; IV 136; VII 339; XI 308; XII 460
Vahram, son of Tigran: XIX 345
Vałaršak: II 21
Vałaršapat: III 32, 38; IX 107
Valens: III 39
Valentinus: XII 68
Van [lake]: I 36; II 18, 19; IX 102
Vanakan vardapet: X 844; XIV 120; XIX 344, 346, 347, 351
Vanatur: VII 333, 334
Varag [mount]: V 79, 84, 85
Vard: V 77–9, 84
Vardan Arewelc'i: VI *passim*; IX 106, 109; X 841, 844, 854–6; XI 309; XV 42; XVI 84, 87; XVIII 455; XIX *passim*
Vardan Mamikonean I: I 33; III 41, 43; IV 136, 137; VII 335
Vardan Mamikonean II: I 34
Varsken: I 33
Vasak of Siwnik': III 43; XII 469
Vaspurakan: I 37; XIX 350
Vaxt'ang: XVI 85
Venus: X 836
Vep'xis-Tqaosani: I 40, 41
Vis-Raminiani: I 41
Vŕam-Šapuh: I 26
Vrkan: III 44

Vrt'anēs [son of Gregory]: V 82, 83; VII 335
Vrt'anēs, bishop of Siwnik': V 82

Xač'ik: XIII 63, 69; XIV 120
Xenophon: II 12
Xerxes I: II 10
Xosran Arcruni: V 86
Xosrov [Armenian king]: VII 333
Xosrov [shah]: XII 465
Xosrov ['translator']: V 80
Xosrov Anjewac'i: VI 193; IX 102; XVIII 495
Xosrovik T'argmanic': V 80
Xuran Arcruni: V 86

Yačaxapatum Čaṙk': VI 195, 197, 202, 205; VIII 117; see also Grigor the Illuminator
Yazkert III: X 830
Yovhannēs ['doctor']: V 84
Yovhannēs II [Catholicos]: V 81, 83
Yovhannēs Awjnec'i [John of Odzun]: V 82; VI 196; VIII passim; IX 103, 106, 108–12; X 831; XIII 60, 61

Yovhannēs Drasxanakertc'i [John Catholicos]: I 36; II 22; VIII 108; X 840; XIX 345, 348–50
Yovhannēs Mandakuni: VI 195, 202; VIII 120, 128, 135; XI 308–12; XII 466; XIII 57; XVII 44
Yovhannēs Mamikonean: XIX 349
Yovhannēs Mayragomec'i: XI 308
Yovhannēs Sarkawag: IX 109; XVI 87; XIX 346, 351
Yovhannēs Tuec'i: XIX 347, 351
Yovsēp' [hermit]: V 78

Zacharias, patriarch of Jerusalem: V 83
Zacharias Rhetor: IV 140
Zarmayr: IV 138
Zayd: X 840
Zeno: I 32, 33; III 40; XII 461; see also Henoticon
Zenob: XIX 348, 349
Zerubabel: V 86; VIII 132; IX 110
Zeus: VII 333
Zoroaster: XI 308
Zoroastrian priest: II 15
Zoroastrianism: III 35, 38, 42, 43; XII 467
Zurvanites: XI 307; XII 467